PUBLIC VALUE MANAGEMENT, MEASUREMENT AND REPORTING

STUDIES IN PUBLIC AND NON-PROFIT GOVERNANCE

Series Editors: Luca Gnan, Alessandro Hinna, Fabio Monteduro

Recent Volumes:

STUDIES IN PUBLIC AND NON-PROFIT GOVERNANCE
VOLUME 3

PUBLIC VALUE MANAGEMENT, MEASUREMENT AND REPORTING

EDITED BY

JAMES GUTHRIE
*Department of Accounting and Corporate Governance,
Macquarie University, Sydney, Australia*

GIUSEPPE MARCON
*Department of Management, Ca' Foscari University of Venice,
Venice, Italy*

SALVATORE RUSSO
*Department of Management, Ca' Foscari University of Venice,
Venice, Italy*

FEDERICA FARNETI
*Department of Sociology and Business Law,
School of Economics, Management and Statistics,
University of Bologna — Forlì Campus, Forlì, Italy*

United Kingdom — North America — Japan
India — Malaysia — China

Emerald Group Publishing Limited
Howard House, Wagon Lane, Bingley BD16 1WA, UK

First edition 2014

Copyright © 2014 Emerald Group Publishing Limited

Reprints and permission service
Contact: permissions@emeraldinsight.com

British Library Cataloguing in Publication Data
A catalogue record for this book is available from the British Library

ISBN: 978-1-78441-011-7
ISSN: 2051-6630 (Series)

ISOQAR certified
Management System,
awarded to Emerald
for adherence to
Environmental
standard
ISO 14001:2004.

Certificate Number 1985
ISO 14001

INVESTOR IN PEOPLE

CONTENTS

v

LIST OF CONTRIBUTORS

Francesco Badia	Department of Economics and Management, University of Ferrara, Ferrara, Italy
Michele Bigoni	Queen's University of Belfast, Belfast, UK
Elena Borin	Department of Economics and Management, University of Ferrara, Ferrara, Italy
Enrico Bracci	Department of Economics and Management, University of Ferrara, Ferrara, Italy
Mikael Holmgren Caicedo	Stockholm Business School, Stockholm University, Stockholm, Sweden
Suresh Cuganesan	The University of Sydney Business School, University of Sydney, Sydney, Australia
Giulio Curiel	Department of Economics, Business, Mathematics and Statistics, University of Trieste, Trieste, Italy
Fabio Donato	Department of Economics and Management, University of Ferrara, Ferrara, Italy
James Downe	Cardiff Business School, Cardiff University, Cardiff, UK
John Dumay	Department of Accounting and Governance, Faculty of Business and Economics, Macquarie University, Sydney, Australia
Kim van Eijck	Wisselwerkers. Academic Entrepreneurs, Amsterdam, The Netherlands

Paolo Esposito   Department of Business Studies, Faculty of
                             Economics, University of Eastern
                             Piedmont "Amedeo Avogadro," Novara,
                             Italy

Federica Farneti   Department of Sociology and Business
                             Law, School of Economics, Management
                             and Statistics, University of Bologna –
                             Forlì Campus, Forlì, Italy

Enrico Deidda   Department of Economics and
   Gagliardo   Management, University of Ferrara,
                             Ferrara, Italy

Enrico Guarini   Department of Business Administration,
                             Finance, Management and Law, University
                             of Milano-Bicocca, Milan, Italy

James Guthrie   Department of Accounting and Corporate
                             Governance, Macquarie University,
                             Sydney, Australia

Kerry Jacobs   School of Business, UNSW Australia,
                             Canberra, Australia

David Lacey   University of the Sunshine Coast, Sunshine
                             Coast, Australia

Mariannunziata   Queen's University Management School,
   Liguori   Queen's University, Belfast, UK

Berit Lindemann   Wisselwerkers. Academic Entrepreneurs,
                             Amsterdam, The Netherlands

Giuseppe Marcon   Department of Management, Ca' Foscari
                             University of Venice, Venice, Italy

Maria Mårtensson   Stockholm Business School, Stockholm
                             University, Stockholm, Sweden

Steve Martin   Public Policy Institute for Wales, Cardiff
                             University, Cardiff, UK

Guido Modugno   Department of Economics, Business,
                             Mathematics and Statistics, University of
                             Trieste, Trieste, Italy

Patrizio Monfardini	Department of Economics and Business Science, University of Cagliari, Cagliari, Italy
Paolo Ricci	Department of Law, Economy, Management and Quantitative Methods (DEMM), University of Sannio, Benevento, Italy
Pasquale Ruggiero	Department of Business and Social Studies, University of Siena, Siena, Italy; Brighton Business School, University of Brighton, UK
Salvatore Russo	Department of Management, Ca' Foscari University of Venice, Venice, Italy
Mariafrancesca Sicilia	Department of Management, Economics and Quantitative Methods, University of Bergamo, Bergamo, Italy
Alessandro Spano	Department of Economics and Business Science, University of Cagliari, Cagliari, Italy
Ileana Steccolini	Department of Public Policy and Management, Bocconi University, Milan, Italy
Kerstin Thomson	Stockholm Business School, Stockholm University, Stockholm, Sweden
Giulia Ventin	University of Trieste – Staff of the Dean, Trieste, Italy
Zeger van der Wal	Lee Kuan Yew School of Public Policy, National University of Singapore, Singapore

PART I
INTRODUCTION

PUBLIC VALUE MANAGEMENT: CHALLENGE OF DEFINING, MEASURING AND REPORTING FOR PUBLIC SERVICES

James Guthrie and Salvatore Russo

INTRODUCTION

The concept of public value is widely discussed in the literature (see Alford & O'Flynn, 2009; Moore, 1994, 1995), as is its realization and measurement (see Moore, 2005, 2006, 2013; Talbot, 1999, 2005, 2008, 2010, 2011).

Since late last century, the debate on public sector reform has been marked by the emergence of theories, concepts and values around the paradigm of new public management (NPM) (see Broadbent & Guthrie, 1992; Guthrie, Olson, & Humphrey, 1999) and now network governance and public services (Broadbent & Guthrie, 2008). The concept of public value has been increasingly associated – usually within the expression 'public value management' – with the process of public administration modernization. The two movements (NPM and public value management) represent two different responses to two long-standing questions: what are the best ways to manage public services in order to optimize the relationship

Public Value Management, Measurement and Reporting
Studies in Public and Non-Profit Governance, Volume 3, 3–17
Copyright © 2014 by Emerald Group Publishing Limited
All rights of reproduction in any form reserved
ISSN: 2051-6630/doi:10.1108/S2051-663020140000003001

between resources, services and citizens? And how do we account for performance and such relationships appropriately (Cuganesan, Jacobs, & Lacey, 2014)?

However, how public value is conceptualized and practised is an important question. Therefore, the contemporary debate has shifted on how the public sector can meet community expectations in regard to issues of fiscal crisis, sustainability and providing public services. For instance, in the case of the European Commission's 'Value for Citizens' initiative in which public sector activities are expected to focus on public value creation and citizen empowerment.[1]

Understanding the gap between expectations of citizenship and resources available for public services is an important topic worthy of debate. However, an equally important topic is how public value is identified, managed, measured and reported.

There have been two important recent developments in the literature. First is Moore's (2013) book, which poses several basic questions (and answers many of these using North American case studies) about how, when and why public agencies can and should use public value performance measurement and management systems to enhance organizational performance, strengthen public accountability and create conditions that allow citizens, elected officials and public managers to align and pursue a vision of public value creation. We will label this the measurement and management turn in public value. Second is the number of calls for more studies of the application of public value in practice. There have been calls for research that is aimed at developing and evaluating new techniques, examining conditions for successful implementation and explicitly developing practical implications and guidelines for practice (van Helden & Northcott, 2010) and adopting action research (Cuganesan, Guthrie, & Vanic, 2014). We will label this the practice turn. The following articles contribute to both of these as many of the contributions explore aspects of public value management and measurement via case studies.

AIM OF THE BOOK

The aim of this book is to commence a dialogue about public value management and the measurement and the reporting of public services in relationship to theory and practice. In supporting this dialogue we have held a number of forums over several years to discuss these matters and our aim has been achieved insofar as the participants, including the authors represented below, have investigated contemporary challenges in this space.

What is unique about this book is that over 80% of the contributed articles are associated with public value and engagement with practice. These authors not only provide a continental European perspective, but also Australian, Swedish and English perspectives. That is, many of the contributions focus on explicit implications for practice in the public sector and public services. Recently, Jacobs and Cuganesan (2014) proposed that future public sector research should involve greater co-mingling of diverse researchers, policymakers and practitioners in the 'doing' of research that addresses significant problems confronting our society. Creating empathy with those charged with tackling multidimensional issues that are highly resistant to resolution can only benefit the research enterprise. While 'inviting the outside in' may pose threats of capture or demystification, we argue that this fades in comparison to the potential benefits of creating a mutual understanding of how public value research can contribute to a broader public sector context. Many of the articles selected for this volume illustrate the complexities, development and potential for the management, measurement and reporting of public value in particular contexts. Answering the challenge, we aim to extend and develop, working with colleagues and reaching audiences outside of our traditional boundaries of scholarly disciplines and across research–practice divides, perhaps striving towards a 'brave new world' where academics and practitioners increasingly engage in the doing of inter-disciplinary accounting public sector research programmes (Jacobs & Cuganesan, 2014).

THE ARTICLES IN THE BOOK

The articles are presented in three parts, with each part having a central theme. Part I comprises the introduction and overview. Part II comprises the majority of the book and consists of 11 articles, which are case studies and empirical investigations into aspects of public value management, measurement and reporting. The final Part III consists of several articles that are more theoretical in nature and contribute to the ongoing debates in the literature. Each of the articles is now discussed in detail.

In the next article, Cuganesan et al. (2014), from Australia, highlight that the recent literature talks about late or post-NPM trends, which place a greater emphasis on networks of joined-up government and public value. While public value theorists emphasize the central role of performance measurement, the function of performance measures within a networked context that characterizes inter-agency cooperation and coproduction in service delivery is insufficiently explored in the literature.

Cuganesan et al. (2014) focus on the role of accounting performance measurement in the creation of public value, using a case study that explores this question in the context of the network associated with the justice portfolio within the Australian Commonwealth. They use the concepts of bonding and bridging social capital to theorize the use of performance measurement in governmental networks.

Cuganesan et al. (2014) found that there was relatively little use of performance measures that reported network level performance and the primary emphasis was on building social capital with funders rather than across network partner agencies. They concluded that existing Australian public sector performance measurement practices are not supportive of intra-governmental networks and therefore the notion that improvement in performance measurement will deliver public value needs further reflection.

In the article titled 'Performance Measurement of Local Public Service Networks', Martin and Downe (2014) from Cardiff Business School, United Kingdom, provide an insightful analysis of the issues associated with measuring the performance of local public service networks in the United Kingdom. This important topic reflects two key features of recent public-management reforms in western countries: the implementation of performance management systems (under NPM) and the creation of public service partnerships.

Their article explores the interplay between two potentially contradictory developments in accountability research and practice: the desire to measure the performance of public services and the drive to improve them through partnership working. Comprehensive Area Assessment (CAA) represents an ambitious attempt to develop an area-based approach capable of reconciling these imperatives. It succeeded in encouraging improved partnership between local public services, but failed to engage the public in holding services to account. Because functionally organized government departments continued to operate sector-specific assessment frameworks alongside CAA, there was little impact on the bureaucratic burdens inspection placed on assessed bodies.

In the article titled 'Developing Strategy to Create a Public Value Chain', Dumay from Macquarie University, Australia, provides a timely case study of the application of how strategic management can be developed in a public sector organization to help visualize its public value. His action research case involves work with the Sydney Conservatorium of Music (the Conservatorium), a Faculty of the University of Sydney (Australia). This organization has a long history of developing fine musicians and is considered a world class music education institution.

Dumay (2014) builds upon Moore's (2013, p. 6) call that strategic management is 'a missing idea' that the public sector has not fully embraced. His paper presents an example of a public sector based 'value-chain' (see Moore, 2013, p. 14), which demonstrates how it is possible for public sector organizations to develop and articulate a public value creating strategy.

In the article titled 'Public Value as Performance: Politicians' and Managers' Perspectives on the Importance of Budgetary, Accruals and Non-Financial Information', Liguori, Sicilia, and Steccolini (2014), from Milan, Italy, contribute to the literature on public value by examining politicians' and managers' perspectives on financial and non-financial information (NFI), investigating the importance they attach to the different facets of performance information. They undertake this important examination by using the results of a survey of politicians and managers in Italian municipalities. Their contribution focuses on both financial (i.e. budgetary- and accruals-based) and NFI and the views of organizational actors.

In their conclusion, the authors state that public value and performance measurement are multifaceted concepts. Both can be captured by different types of information and evaluated according to different criteria, which will also depend on the category of stakeholders or users who assess information. So far, most literature has considered the financial and non-financial facets of performance as virtually separate, giving rise to two almost independent streams of studies. Similarly, in practice, financial management tends to be decoupled from non-financial performance management. However, this research shows that only by considering their joint interactions can we achieve an accurate representation of what public value really is.

However, Liguori et al. (2014) offer a final warning on NFI as a measure of public value. NFI, indeed, is not an alternative, but rather complementary, to financial information. The latter remains a fundamental element of performance measurement due to its role in resource allocation and control. The importance recognized by the users suggests that the financial and non-financial systems must be considered together, rather than separate, as two sides of the same coin.

In the article titled 'The Quest for Public Value in the Swedish Museum Transition', Thomson, Caicedo, and Mårtensson (2014) from Sweden argue that NPM was initially considered best applied to 'harder' sectors like utilities such as telecom and energy, but now includes central government policy areas such as welfare administration, universities and culture. The aim of their article is to focus on the issue of public value creation in a 'softer' public policy area, namely culture and specifically museums. Using a case study they explore the issue: what is public value in the context of public museum management and how is public value created?

They explore three key issues of convergence and divergence within the NPM and public value theoretical frameworks as a gateway to the empirical findings and ensuing discussion. Their study of museums indicates that NPM is incomplete and unable to encompass the plurality of, and dependencies between, conceptions of museum management and thus also the plurality of, and the dependencies between, conceptions of public value. For instance, focusing on customers might be an important part of museum management development, but it may need to be complemented by a stakeholder orientation, where citizens are among the stakeholders, and by a conservation orientation that acknowledges that in order to be exhibited collections need to be taken care of and preserved. Indeed, focusing only on a customer orientation may not serve museums well, insofar as it may promote short-termism and does not express the cultural contribution a museum makes to society, which in turn may endanger the sustainability of cultural heritage for future generations.

In the article titled 'Performance Management Systems and Public Value Strategy: A Case Study', we go back to Italy, but stay focused on cultural organizations. Bracci, Gagliardo, and Bigoni (2014), from Ferrara, Italy, use a case study to explore the role of performance management systems in a not-for-profit organization in pursuing a public value strategy. Drawing on the public value dynamic model, the article presents the results of a case study of implementation of a performance management model named the Value Pyramid, within a public-owned theatre organization from 2007 to 2012.

Their case study examines the Municipal Theatre, home of Maestro Claudio Abbado's Orchestra, one of the city of Ferrara's artistic and cultural highlights of international repute. Opened in 1798, the Theatre experienced two significant legal transformations (into a Municipal Institution in 1994 and a private foundation with the Municipality of Ferrara as the sole shareholder in 2009).

As shown in the case of the theatre, public value was applied as a performance management system over five years to ascertain what is valuable or otherwise, where to allocate resources and to focus on continuous improvement in public services. At the same time, the process of measuring public value needs to be integrated within a performance management system, in order to steer and influence behaviour, as well as for the purposes of resource allocation and the performance assessment of the public managers and employees. Overall, the authors found that a strategic orientation should be made on the decision- and policy-making processes that, in turn, shape the constraints on performance. Consequently, for these authors if public value is the strategy, public service organizations are called to measure, manage and account for public value in an integrated way.

In the article titled 'Strategic Practices of Creating Public Value: How Managers of Housing Associations Create Public Value', the authors focus on a Netherlands experiment with social housing and public value creation. van Eijck and Lindemann (2014) from the VU University Amsterdam provide insights into how theory and practice do not necessarily align. The issue they explore is what happens when the theories of public value and partnering are applied to a housing association context within the Netherlands. From a behavioural perspective, they learned that little is known about what managers – as they develop into social entrepreneurs – do when managing spaces for public value, and it is unclear what explains this expanded practice. From an institutional perspective, they learned that the influence of institutional pressures on the extended practice of managing space for public value is not being sufficiently taken into account. After all, it is not obvious that civil society managers are able to break free from and alter the existing traditional institutions that shape their everyday practice.

The central topic of this article was to explore and explain the (in)ability of public managers in Dutch social housing to create and demonstrate public value. Dutch housing associations can at best be characterized as private, not-for-profit organizations that provide 'social housing' for citizens with low incomes and groups with special needs. Due to decentralization in the mid-1990s housing associations have developed into autonomous organizations held accountable for identifying, prioritizing and meeting local public needs. Their main challenge has been to recognize and utilize this new (democratic) space and to reconsider the boundaries of their social responsibilities. Subsequently, the housing associations are challenged to revise and adapt the ways in which they authorize, manage and realize their public services in order to improve their ability to create and demonstrate their public value.

Their findings show that managers use different strategic practices in public value creation as they deal with conflicting factors, such as institutional pressures and organizational (self-)interests. In conclusion, they indicate that it is difficult for managers to demonstrate the public value created and there appears to be a complex process involved in its identification, measurement and reporting.

In the article titled 'Conceptual Framework and Empirical Evidence of Public Value: The Case of the Italian Higher Education Sector', we return to Italy for a case study focusing on higher education. Modugno, Ventin, and Curiel (2014), from the University of Trieste, provide a theoretical and case-based methods article to explore the issue of public value within the Italian higher education sector. The stated purpose of their analysis is to understand whether the public value approach will improve Italian universities' performance and also whether contemporary reforms introduced by the Italian government are proceeding in this direction. In the article three elements of public value are explored:

1. the way Italian universities conceive the delivery of public value and how they communicate it;
2. the relationship of the universities with their stakeholders, including policymakers; and
3. the internal governance and how this aspect influences the managers' capability to implement each university's strategy.

Moreover, the national funding for the Italian higher education sector is in decline: funding has been reduced in the last three years from €7,087 to €6,565 million. Consequently, Italian universities find themselves trying to attract funds from competitive research grants, student fees and the private sector. The authors argue that in facing these challenges, Italian universities must include the management and reporting of public value. The public value approach emphasizes the link between legitimacy and the capability to improve the financial and political support for public organizations. Hence, it could be the ideal perspective for redesigning processes and organizations, since it values not only outcomes, but also processes that may generate trust or fairness.

The case study involves four Italian universities and their representation of public value over the 2007–2009 period. The analysis focuses on the description and measurement of the public value delivered, and how public value is identified, measured and reported. In conclusion, this article highlights the case of the Italian higher education sector and the importance of the rules of governance for public value production. The analysis shows that the actual governance of the Italian universities does not favour the construction of a public value proposition by the universities' managers. This aspect raises the more general question of identifying the necessary conditions for realizing the public value proposition and determining its presence in all public administrations.

In the article titled 'Politics and Public Services: Looking Beyond Economic Rationality and Public Value', we stay in Italy, this time focusing on a state-owned corporation. Monfardini and Ruggiero (2014) aim to understand whether NPM and public value theory are sufficient to guide the strategic behaviours public sector organizations adopt for their service delivery companies. They explore two theoretical approaches (NPM and public value) to understand strategic decisions in the public sector. Results show that NPM provides decision makers with indications about what to do, while the adoption of public value, despite its explicit strategic purposes, appears to be more problematic for decision makers.

Their case of Aeroporto di Siena s.p.a. highlights poor financial performance over many years, due to the lack of interest in the airport by commercial carriers caused by a weak demand for air services. It is therefore difficult to argue that the NPM could support the decisions made by the shareholders to keep the corporation operating. A managerial approach would suggest winding up the corporation, due to its poor efficiency and dwindling market. Because of this contrast between theory and practice, the actual survival of the corporation means that criteria other than that suggested by NPM have been adopted in the strategic decision-making process. The case study explores the question: is public value more useful in explaining and justifying the survival of the Aeroporto di Siena s.p.a.?

In the article titled 'Harmony in Hierarchy? How Politicians and Public Managers Prioritize Crucial Public Values', we go back to the Netherlands and explore various interpretations of public value. van der Wal's (2014) article answers the following central research question: how do Dutch political elites and administrative elites differ in their interpretation and prioritization of public values? He uses a qualitative interview study to compare the public value prioritizations of ministers, members of parliament and senior public managers in The Netherlands. Based on 65 interviews he highlights how government elites interpret and assess four crucial public values: responsiveness, expertise, lawfulness and transparency.

The past decade produced a heated debate among academics and practitioners about the alleged erosion of the traditional 'social contract' between politicians and senior civil servants. It is clear that emphasizing and exaggerating mutual differences is not very conducive for fruitful collaboration between the political and administrative elite in their pursuit of public value.

van der Wal (2014) summarizes his findings by indicating that public managers see it as their responsibility to point out risks of particular decisions to their political bosses, and even their political adversaries, to provide critical 'counter-advice'. Public managers seem to be able to align their immense influence potential with democratic responsibilities. He concludes by stating that perhaps we worry too much about the erosion of mutual trust between government elites, and all that is needed is an increased mutual understanding of each other's position towards, and enactment of, public values.

In the article titled 'Co-governing Public Value in Local Authorities', we go back to Italy and this time the focus is on local government and the use of participatory governance tools and activities. Badia, Borin, and Donato (2014) are from the University of Ferrara, and their article analyses the potential contribution of co-governance and co-creation of public value, in the context of the financial crisis. In their article, co-governance has two elements: first, the relationship of the public body with another body (private, public, owned company) and second, the relationship and involvement of citizens through various management tools and activities. This article is both theoretical and empirical. Concerning the latter it reports an empirical survey on Italian municipalities, considered the closest public body to citizens.

The results of their survey indicate that more than 50% of the entities in the sample have introduced co-governance or participatory governance tools and activities (respectively, 59.18% and 61.22%). However, Italian local authorities still face problems in implementing co-governance and participatory tools, especially in relation to their high cost and the lack of knowledge needed for implementing these tools and activities. In general, local authorities consider citizens' participation in these co-governance and participatory governance processes insufficient.

The next article titled 'Public (Dis)value: A Case Study', by Esposito and Ricci (2014), discusses the concept of public (dis)value. This concept is designed to incorporate the destruction of public value and in their article, the focus is on a case study of the return of assets to the community, seized from the Mafia. The article's contribution is novel, taking a different approach to the concepts of public value discussed elsewhere in the book.

Finally, for Part II, we have an article titled 'Measuring Public Value in Bureaucratic Settings: Opportunities and Constraints' by Guarini (2014), which takes the same approach and method of measuring public value and tests it in two local governments. In doing so it aims to shed light on barriers to implementing the public value paradigm in practice.

Turning to Part III, three articles explore theoretical issues in more depth. The first is the article by Marcon, from the Ca' Foscari University of Venice, exploring theories associated with 'traditional public administration' (TPA), NPM, 'new public governance' (NPG) and 'public value management'. In his article, the theoretical frameworks within which public value have been operationalized are explored. The measurement of public value is illustrated via public value (in the singular) and public values (in the plural) and its multiple performance objectives for public sector organizations are addressed. This article highlights the promising potential of public value linked to performance measurement/management and is intended to provide a picture of the path along which public value management can conceivably be deployed.

The next article in Part III is that of Spano (2014), from the University of Cagliari, which explores several theoretical perspectives concerning the issue of public value measurement, a neglected area in public value literature. In his article, it is argued that public value can be produced by a single organization or be the joint action of different organizations. As a consequence, public value can be measured at both individual organization level and at a network level considering a group of organizations working jointly. Furthermore, public value can be measured in reference to a specific policy or programme or alternatively as a whole in order to understand how much public value a specific organization produces. Measuring public value related to a policy or a programme may also allow comparisons between different organizations implementing similar policies or programmes. He concludes that in order to measure public value, it is first necessary to set the reasons for the measurement.

The final article in Part III is that of Farneti and Dumay (2014). Their theoretical article uses a previous work (Dumay, Farneti, & Guthrie, 2010) to argue for sustainable public value. Their article critically reviews the latest Global Reporting Initiative (GRI) guidelines and argues for a normative approach by using Gray's (2006) ecological and eco-justice (EEJ) framework in order to produce public value inscriptions of sustainability to represent sustainable public value. What we do observe is that the GRI continues to develop while scant attention is paid to furthering the draft Supplement for Public Agencies, which remains in its pilot form since its inception in 2005.

The GRI is considered to be a global framework for metrics and reporting around social, environmental, policy impact, operational and governance issues. Recent changes to the GRI are somewhat enlightening because several of the changes begin to address a more comprehensive view of how any organization, including public agencies, can contribute to an EEJ approach to sustainability. As Dumay et al. (2010) previously argued, if guidelines continue to approach sustainability from a 'managerialistic' approach then there is little hope of public sector agencies adopting EEJ practices.

In conclusion, the editors are indebted to the many people who made the series possible, especially the presenters and authors whose work appears in this series. The authors of the articles have been generous in their time and attendance at various events, as well as expressing their insights in the articles in this collection.

The editors are also grateful for the number of colleagues who participated in contemporary debates at our workshop in Venice. All articles in this series were the subject of independent refereeing and editing, that is, a double-blind review process and considerable commentary and editing. We thank all the reviewers involved in this project.

Our thanks are due to Fiona Crawford and Sara Haddad from the Editorial Collective for their outstanding effort in editing and project management to bring this series to fruition. Finally, we are deeply indebted to Julz Stevens, Macquarie University and Knowledge Research, for her oversight and research support before, during and after the Venice event and this publication.

NOTE

1. http://ec.europa.eu/information_society/newsroom/cf/dae/itemdetail.cfm?type=372&typeName=Reports and studies&item_id=4821

REFERENCES

Alford, J., & O'Flynn, J. (2009). Making sense of public value: Concepts, critiques and emergent meanings. *International Journal of Public Administration, 32*(3–4), 171–191.

Badia, F., Borin, E., & Donato, F. (2014). Co-governing public value in local authorities. In J. Guthrie, G. Marcon, S. Russo, & F. Farneti (Eds.), *Public value management, measurement and reporting* (Vol. 3, pp. 269–289). Studies in Public and Non-Profit Governance. Bingley, UK: Emerald Group Publishing Limited.

Bracci, E., Gagliardo, E., & Bigoni, M. (2014). Performance management systems and public value strategy: A case study. In J. Guthrie, G. Marcon, S. Russo, & F. Farneti (Eds.), *Public value management, measurement and reporting* (Vol. 3, pp. 129–157). Studies in Public and Non-Profit Governance. Bingley, UK: Emerald Group Publishing Limited.

Broadbent, J., & Guthrie, J. (1992). Changes in the public sector: A review of recent alternative accounting research. *Accounting, Auditing and Accountability Journal, 5*(2), 3–31.

Broadbent, J., & Guthrie, J. (2008). Public sector to public services: 20 years of alternative accounting research. *Accounting, Auditing and Accountability Journal, 21*(2), 129–169.

Cuganesan, S., Guthrie, J., & Vranic, V. (2014). The riskiness of performance measurement in the public sector: A review of progress and research agenda. *Financial Accountability and Management, 30*(3), 279–302.

Cuganesan, S., Jacobs, K., & Lacey, D. (2014). Beyond new public management: Does performance measurement drive public value in networks? In J. Guthrie, G. Marcon, S. Russo, & F. Farneti (Eds.), *Public value management, measurement and reporting* (Vol. 3, pp. 21–42). Studies in Public and Non-Profit Governance. Bingley, UK: Emerald Group Publishing Limited.

Dumay, J. (2014). Developing strategy to create a public value chain. In J. Guthrie, G. Marcon, S. Russo, & F. Farneti (Eds.), *Public value management, measurement and reporting* (Vol. 3, pp. 65–83). Studies in Public and Non-Profit Governance. Bingley, UK: Emerald Group Publishing Limited.

Dumay, J., Farneti, F., & Guthrie, J. (2010). GRI sustainability reporting guidelines for public and third sector organizations: A critical review. *Public Management Review, 12*(4), 531–548.

Esposito, P., & Ricci, P. (2014). Public (dis)value: A case study. In J. Guthrie, G. Marcon, S. Russo, & F. Farneti (Eds.), *Public value management, measurement and reporting* (Vol. 3, pp. 291–300). Studies in Public and Non-Profit Governance. Bingley, UK: Emerald Group Publishing Limited.

Farneti, F., & Dumay, J. (2014). Sustainable public value inscriptions: A critical approach. In J. Guthrie, G. Marcon, S. Russo, & F. Farneti (Eds.), *Public value management, measurement and reporting* (Vol. 3, pp. 375–389). Studies in Public and Non-Profit Governance. Bingley, UK: Emerald Group Publishing Limited.

Gray, R. (2006). Social, environmental and sustainability reporting and organisational value creation? Whose value? Whose creation? *Accounting, Auditing and Accountability Journal, 19*(6), 793–819.

Guarini, E. (2014). Measuring public value in bureaucratic settings: Opportunities and constraints. In J. Guthrie, G. Marcon, S. Russo, & F. Farneti (Eds.), *Public value management, measurement and reporting* (Vol. 3, pp. 301–319). Studies in Public and Non-Profit Governance. Bingley, UK: Emerald Group Publishing Limited.

Guthrie, J., Olson, O., & Humphrey, C. (1999). Debating developments in new public financial management: The limits of global theorising and some new ways forward. *Financial Accountability and Management, 15*(3–4), 209–228.

Jacobs, K., & Cuganesan, S. (2014). Interdisciplinary accounting research in the public sector: Dissolving boundaries to tackle wicked problems. *Accounting, Auditing and Accountability Journal, 27*(8), 1412–1437.

Liguori, M., Sicilia, M., & Steccolini, I. (2014). Public value as performance: Politicians' and managers' perspectives on the importance of budgetary, accruals and non-financial information. In J. Guthrie, G. Marcon, S. Russo, & F. Farneti (Eds.), *Public value management, measurement and reporting* (Vol. 3). Studies in Public and Non-Profit Governance. Bingley, UK: Emerald Group Publishing Limited.

Marcon, G. (2014). Public value theory in the context of public sector modernization. In J. Guthrie, G. Marcon, S. Russo, & F. Farneti (Eds.), *Public value management, measurement and reporting* (Vol. 3, pp. 323–351). Studies in Public and Non-Profit Governance. Bingley, UK: Emerald Group Publishing Limited.

Martin, S., & Downe, J. (2014). Performance measurement of local public service networks. In J. Guthrie, G. Marcon, S. Russo, & F. Farneti (Eds.), *Public value management, measurement and reporting* (Vol. 3, pp. 43–64). Studies in Public and Non-Profit Governance. Bingley, UK: Emerald Group Publishing Limited.

Modugno, G., Ventin, G., & Curiel, G. (2014). Conceptual framework and empirical evidence of public value: The case of the Italian higher education sector. In J. Guthrie, G. Marcon, S. Russo, & F. Farneti (Eds.), *Public value management, measurement and reporting* (Vol. 3, pp. 189–224). Studies in Public and Non-Profit Governance. Bingley, UK: Emerald Group Publishing Limited.

Monfardini, P., & Ruggiero, P. (2014). Politics and public services: Looking beyond economic rationality and the public value. In J. Guthrie, G. Marcon, S. Russo, & F. Farneti (Eds.), *Public value management, measurement and reporting* (Vol. 3, pp. 225–241). Studies in Public and Non-Profit Governance. Bingley, UK: Emerald Group Publishing Limited.

Moore, M. (2005). *Creating public value: Strategic management in government*. Harvard, MA: Harvard University Press.

Moore, M. (2013). *Recognizing public value*. Harvard, MA: Harvard University Press.

Moore, M. H. (1994). Public value as the focus of strategy. *Australian Journal of Public Administration, 53*(3), 296–303.

Moore, M. H. (1995). *Creating public value: Strategic management in government*. Harvard, MA: Harvard University Press.

Moore, M. H. (2006). Recognising public value: The challenge of measuring performance in government. In J. Wanna (Ed.), *A passion for policy. Essays in public sector reform*. Canberra: ANU E Press.

Spano, A. (2014). How do we measure public value? From theory to practice. In J. Guthrie, G. Marcon, S. Russo, & F. Farneti (Eds.), *Public value management, measurement and reporting* (Vol. 3, pp. 353–373). Studies in Public and Non-Profit Governance. Bingley, UK: Emerald Group Publishing Limited.

Talbot, C. (1999). Public performance – Towards a new model? *Public Policy and Administration, 14*(3), 15–34.

Talbot, C. (2005). Performance management. In E. Ferlie, L. E. Lynn, Jr., & C. Pollitt (Eds.), *The Oxford handbook of public management*. Oxford: Oxford University Press.

Talbot, C. (2008). *Measuring public value*. London: The Work Foundation.

Talbot, C. (2010). *Theories of performance*. New York, NY: Oxford University Press.

Talbot, C. (2011). Paradoxes and prospects of public value. *Public Money and Management, 31*(1), 27–34.

Thomson, K., Caicedo, M., & Mårtensson, M. (2014). The quest for public value in the Swedish museum transition. In J. Guthrie, G. Marcon, S. Russo, & F. Farneti (Eds.), *Public value management, measurement and reporting* (Vol. 3, pp. 105–128). Studies in Public and Non-Profit Governance. Bingley, UK: Emerald Group Publishing Limited.

van der Wal, Z. (2014). Harmony in hierarchy? How politicians and public managers prioritize crucial public values. In J. Guthrie, G. Marcon, S. Russo, & F. Farneti (Eds.), *Public value management, measurement and reporting* (Vol. 3, pp. 243–268). Studies in Public and Non-Profit Governance. Bingley, UK: Emerald Group Publishing Limited.

van Eijck, K., & Lindemann, B. (2014). Strategic practices of creating public value: How managers of housing associations create public value. In J. Guthrie, G. Marcon, S. Russo, & F. Farneti (Eds.), *Public value management, measurement and reporting* (Vol. 3, pp. 159–187). Studies in Public and Non-Profit Governance. Bingley, UK: Emerald Group Publishing Limited.

van Helden, G. J., & Northcott, D. (2010). Examining the practical relevance of public sector management accounting research. *Financial Accountability and Management, 26*(2), 213–240.

PART II
CASE STUDIES ON PUBLIC VALUE MANAGEMENT, MEASUREMENT AND REPORTING

BEYOND NEW PUBLIC MANAGEMENT: DOES PERFORMANCE MEASUREMENT DRIVE PUBLIC VALUE IN NETWORKS?

Suresh Cuganesan, Kerry Jacobs and David Lacey

ABSTRACT

Purpose — *This article focuses on the role of accounting perfor-mance measurement in the creation of public value in the context of the network associated with the justice portfolio within the Australian Commonwealth.*

Design/methodology/approach — *We use concepts of bonding and brid-ging social capital to theorize the use of performance measurement in government networks.*

Findings — *We find that there is relatively little use of performance mea-sures that reported network level performance and the primary emphasis was on building social capital with funders rather than across network partner agencies. We therefore conclude that existing Australian public*

Public Value Management, Measurement and Reporting
Studies in Public and Non-Profit Governance, Volume 3, 21–42
Copyright © 2014 by Emerald Group Publishing Limited
All rights of reproduction in any form reserved
ISSN: 2051-6630/doi:10.1108/S2051-663020140000003000

sector performance measurement practices are not supportive of intra-governmental networks and therefore the notion that improvement in performance measurement will deliver public value needs further reflection.

Research limitations/implications − *The research scope is restricted to governmental network performance measures from a justice portfolio budget perspective. Despite the focused attention of the research, the application of the findings has relevance across all government portfolios and broader public management more generally.*

Practical implications − *Despite calls for accountability and governance innovation where public value is delivered across organizational boundaries through dependency and collaboration, the case environment offers little evidence that forms of performance measurement over the period examined recognize this practicality. The research primarily adds considerable weight to the argument that the delivery of public value by networks requires an evolution in accountability and performance reporting away from traditional institutional forms of performance representation.*

Originality/value − *The research is highly novel in its unveiling and examination of contemporary performance measurement reporting from a network perspective.*

Keywords: Public value; network; performance measures; accountability; social capital

The increasing emphasis on the whole of government delivery of services requires agencies to work together to develop budgeting and reporting arrangements that meet both the accountability obligations of individual agencies and also contribute to the collective achievement of and accountability for whole of government outcomes.

− Australian National Audit Office (2007, p. 16).

INTRODUCTION

While the term New Public Management (NPM) has been used to describe reform trends in many different countries, researchers now argue that rather than a clear set of doctrinal components as defined by some authors (see e.g. Hood, 1991, 1995), NPM reforms are actually a process of complexity with unexpected outcomes (Hood & Peters, 2004). Some authors have even argued that the NPM trend is dead and gone (Dunleavy, Margetts, Bastow, & Tinkler, 2006). One of the most interesting aspects of this late/post-NPM era is the notion of public value, which has been presented as a way to address the weaknesses inherent in an outcome focus of NPM and to return the focus to one on the importance of process (Moore, 1995; O'Flynn, 2007). However, Moore (2005, p. 116) acknowledges that the determination and the delivery of public value is particularly complex and challenging where managers are crucially dependent upon agencies and people outside their direct control to produce the results for which they are accountable. Therefore, further work is required to explore the provision of public value across multiple agencies and the whole of the government.

Literature, such as the work of Hood (1991, 1995), seemed to indicate that NPM reforms involved a process of decentralization and decoupling, however, more recent trends may be in the opposite direction, with a greater emphasis on networks, the whole of government, reintegration and the operation of complex systems (Dunleavy et al., 2006; Hood & Peters, 2004).[1] Recent trends towards 'joined-up' government (Ling, 2002; Wilkins, 2002) and 'whole-of-government' (Christensen & Lægreid, 2007) have added complexity to the public administration landscape, engendering more intricate linkages between agencies and requiring them to focus on achieving the outcome of an entire portfolio. While the notion of networks of public administration is not new, authors such as Hood and Peters (2004) and Dunleavy et al. (2006) suggest that there is a trend towards a greater focus on networks of public administration where different yet inter-related government agencies combine in joint or at least interdependent policy delivery activities in the creation of public value. Adding to this is the increasing recognition that the public policy landscape is characterized by complex and multidimensional problems, and that 'forms of [public] organization and governance that are designed around collaboration, partnership and network appear to be more suitable for the task' (Williams, 2002, p. 105). Therefore Moore (2013) argues that recognizing public value requires the development of better performance measurement systems. These enhanced performance measurement systems are particularly critical when managers are required to exercise the kind of 'political management' necessary when responsibility is shared, split or diffused across multiple agencies and actors (Moore, 1995, p. 189).

Existing research indicates that the delivery of public value across networks requires collaboration, and norms of partnership and reciprocity and this in turn requires new governance and accountability mechanisms

(Powell, 1990; Ring & van de Ven, 1992; Sako, 1992). Developing and maintaining lateral accountabilities (in the way described by Moore, 1995) that cut across organizational boundaries is important and accounting mechanisms can play a strong part through either enabling or constraining such efforts. However, most research has examined networking within the private sector and the extent to which public sector governance and accountability mechanisms are supportive or restrictive of network-building efforts, and therefore networks in the delivery of public value remain under-explored. This stands in marked contrast to the claimed importance of establishing inter-governmental networks (Dawes, Cresswell, & Pardo, 2009; Weber & Khademian, 2008) to deal with 'tangled' or 'complex' problems of public policy and service delivery.

Hence, this article examines how governance and accountability mechanisms in the public sector support intra-governmental networking efforts necessary to deliver public value, with intra-governmental networks comprising relationships between government agencies, other agencies as joint partners in policy delivery and central funding authorities. It explores one governance and accountability mechanism in particular, being the institutionalized framework of accounting performance measures that individual government agencies are required to report upon as part of explicating their strategies, programmes and budgets. Performance measurement's importance as a means of establishing accountability for performance and as a central plank of NPM reforms has been well established (Hood, 1991, 1995; Osborne & Gaebler, 1992). From this perspective, performance measures allow evaluations of individual agencies' performance by funding authorities and potentially inform discussions and decisions about future resource allocation (Brignall & Modell, 2000). Performance measures can also promote collaborative efforts and norms of partnership and inter-dependency amongst joint partners in policy delivery. Finally, performance measures are one means through which the creation of public value can be both supported and assessed (Moore, 2013). However, while the need for enhanced performance measurement is recognized, the public value literature (see e.g. Moore, 2013) is only beginning to struggle with the complexities of performance measurement in inter-agency settings. Therefore this article seeks to address this gap in the public value thinking by drawing on Putnam's (2000) notion of social capital and bridging strategies to examine the extent to which performance measurement practices support and enable *both* networking with funding authorities as well as with policy delivery partners. Understanding the relationship between performance measurement practices and the challenges of funding and policy delivery partners is critical if Moore's (2013, p. 416) challenge to develop 'reliable public value propositions' and operationalize these as a 'public value scorecard' is ever to be achieved.

The empirical domain of our investigation is the Australian federal government portfolio. Within this domain there are policy statements about the importance of networking and existing initiatives to encourage networking. This is supported by a report that concludes:

> Whole of government approaches have been implemented to address a wide range of issues, from crisis management and improving service delivery, to dealing with significant policy challenges ... The [Australian Public Sector] APS is learning how to work in this environment, and there have been positive results. At the same time, the implementation of whole of government approaches in these areas has also confirmed how difficult more connected approaches can be to implement. (Commonwealth of Australia Australian Public Services Commission, 2007)

The specific network chosen for investigation comprises the different yet inter-dependent Commonwealth agencies involved in administering criminal justice within the Commonwealth Attorney-General's Department portfolio. Within this portfolio, it has been claimed that:

> We are strengthening our capability on whole-of-government issues. For example, we are boosting our capacity to provide assistance across government on constitutional issues. We are also developing a national crisis coordination capability to improve whole-of-government responses in the times of crisis. We will continue to focus on improving the coordination and leadership of the portfolio by the [Attorney-General's] Department, building upon the work we have done to further strengthen our relationships with all portfolio agencies. (Attorney-General Department, 2009, p. 10)

More broadly, the need for agencies involved in intelligence and investigations to collaborate, share information and coordinate activities is widely recognized, with the relatively recent *9/11 Commission Report* (National Commission on Terrorist Attacks Upon the United States, 2004) being a highly publicized example in acknowledging and making recommendations to foster this imperative.

RELEVANT LITERATURE

Performance Measurement in the Public Sector

Decentralized government with a stronger focus on the achievement of outcomes has been a taken-for-granted doctrine by both policy makers and advocates of public sector reform. Osborne and Gaebler (1992), in what was arguably the most visible popularization of NPM reform, devoted an appendix to 'the art of performance measurement'. Central to their understanding was the notion that there needed to be a shift away from performance measures focused on 'inputs and processes' and towards performance measurements based on 'outputs and outcomes'. Therefore central to many reform initiatives was the notion that there needed to be a corresponding transformation in the practices of performance measurement along the line advocated by Osborne and Gaebler (1992).

The role and importance of performance measurement was also evident in the academic literature, with Hood (1991, 1995) presenting formal and measurable standards of performance and success as one of the seven doctrinal components of NPM. In addition, contemporary introductions to public management and governance tend to present public sector performance measurement in terms of the cybernetic ideas of input, process, output and outcome (Halligan, Bouckaert, & van Dooren, 2010). In that context there has been a suggestion that the public sector at large should move from input-based performance measurement towards performance output and outcome focused metrics grounded within a clear vision of agency efficiency and effectiveness. NPM advocates and government policy initiatives would suggest that there has been a shift away from input and process control towards output and outcome controls.

Yet despite (or perhaps because of) these normative predictions researchers who have conducted empirical research have identified the challenges in developing and implementing performance measurement systems in the public sector and deficiencies in current practice (see Carlin, 2005; Carnegie & West, 2005; Guthrie, 1994; Guthrie & Parker, 1998; Kloot & Martin, 2000; Lee, 2008; Modell, 2004; O'Faircheallaigh, Wanna, & Weller, 1999; Walker, 2001, 2002). These studies typically find: that agencies establish broad performance measures of little relevance to their objectives; a reliance on financial measures that are inappropriate to the public sector or that result in a pre-occupation with efficiency; and a high turnover of performance measures and the quantitative measurement of outcomes that only emerge over the long term and which cannot be linked back to specific agencies and their outputs.

The majority of studies of performance measurement in the public sector focus on individual agency accountability to the detriment of issues of network. Only a few studies have considered the role of performance measurement in supporting inter-governmental networks (Ryan & Walsh, 2004; Walker, 2001). These studies highlight the fact that many existing performance measurement frameworks fail to recognize the existence of inter-dependencies across different government agencies (Ryan & Walsh, 2004) and how collaboration and coordination is required in order that the outputs of many entities actually contribute to government portfolio objectives. Walker (2001) found that in relation to external performance reporting most measures were typically individualized to a particular agency and not reflective of wider dependencies. These small groups of studies focus on performance measures as contained in annual reports, overlooking the fact that Portfolio Budget Statements, which contain funding allocations for the forthcoming year, also contain performance indicators. Indeed, it would not be unreasonable to expect that the performance measures associated with the budgetary statements would be more 'network' focused because a given portfolio (such as justice) might cut across a number of departments while the reports of a particular department would be less network focused because they are orientated towards the activities of a single department.

In summary, research to date presents a view of performance measurement practice in the public sector as deficient. Of relevance to this article, there has been limited focus on how performance measurement practice might engender networking and particular networking strategies in the public sector. The few studies that have examined this issue have focused on annual reporting, eschewing other documents such as Portfolio Budget Statements, which contain performance measures and which have significance in terms of being documents that are linked to budgeting practices in government. Reports from practice support further work on examining performance measures and intra-government networking. In its review of the Government Performance and Results Act the United States Government Accountability Office (2007) found serious weaknesses in inter-agency coordination and the pursuit of common objectives, while the Australian Auditor-General has acknowledged that the issue of accurately reflecting individual and cross-agency performance in the public sector poses considerable challenges because of complex inter-relationships (McPhee, 2008). Given the limited research to date, this article examines how performance measurement practice supports intra-governmental networking efforts.

Moore (1995) reflects a positive if somewhat naive approach to performance measurement challenges. Moore (1995) suggests that more extensive use of performance measurement systems would underpin the recognition and creation of public value and aid in calling managers and employees to account for public value (see Moore, 2013, p. 1). However, Moore (1995) did acknowledge that contexts of decentralized co-production, which require high levels of inter-agency coordination, posed particular challenges to the delivery of public value and that they require highly developed 'political management' skills. Moore (2013) extended this idea to suggest that public value might be delivered in these kinds of complex operational settings through the use of strategic management and the presentation of public value 'balanced scorecards'. However, this proposition is dependent upon the nature of the relationship between performance measurement systems and the complex operational and institutional networks that increasingly characterize the operational environments found within the public sector.

Therefore the relationship between performance measurement and networks is both conceptually and operationally important and this is evident in public sector settings. In order to explore the relationship between performance measurement and networks it is necessary to develop a theoretical framework of the operational practices. In this article, we draw on notions of social capital to argue that governance across a network poses particular problems as there is a choice whether actors invest in measuring and reporting the performance of one part of the network or in measuring and reporting the performance of the network as a whole.

Inter-Organizational Networks and Social Capital

The proliferation of network forms of organization has attracted the attention of researchers across the fields of accounting, economics, organizational theory, sociology and technology over a number of years. This research has been concerned with investigating the rationale for these 'hybrid' forms, their characteristics and how they are to be governed. Network organizational forms typically have been situated between the ideal types of markets and hierarchies (Williamson, 1985, 1993), with the corollary notion that these forms require governance mechanisms other than market-based mechanisms or hierarchical norms of authority and are fast gaining widespread acceptance (Powell, 1990; Ring & van de Ven, 1992). Responding to calls for more research into controls and governance mechanisms in inter-organizational arrangements (e.g. Hopwood, 1996; Otley, 1994), an extensive literature has emerged. This literature has examined and identified a number of inter-organizational and intra-organizational influences over the governance mechanisms used, and how these might inter-relate to each other as part of a package (for recent reviews, see Caglio & Ditillo, 2008; Håkansson, Kraus, & Lind, 2010).

In contrast to the focus of much of the above research, this article considers how mechanisms of accountability between individual agencies and centralized government support their ability to network, and effectively communicate, coordinate and engage in joint activity. To help explicate this, the notion of 'social capital' is utilized. Increasingly, social capital is examined as part of understanding the ability of an organization to network. Both Lin (2001) and Field (2008) highlight the growing importance of notions of social capital and the links between social capital and networks. Lin (2001) argues that the middle-level structures of institutions and networks are the central locus of social capital. Yet the dynamics between networks and institutions are not clear and the role of social capital in that process is complex.

Bourdieu and Wacquant (1992) make the argument that the value of social capital is not found in itself but rather is dependent on a particular field or context. In addition, social capital can be understood both as a resource in the creation of networks and a resource in sustaining networks. Putnam (2000) distinguishes between these two roles with the terms 'bridging' and 'bonding'. In Putnam's terminology bridging is about connecting between people who are different and who may share different values. In effect, bridging is a structural dimension that involves the creation of networks across institutional boundaries. However, bonding is a relational dimension where the socialization is between people who share similar background and values and therefore is about reinforcing and sustaining values in a group. Therefore, bridging involves the creation of networks while bonding supports the maintenance of existing networks.

Given the above facts, this article focuses on the bridging strategies that are facilitated through performance measurement and reporting practices in a networked context. Bridging strategies are particularly relevant in NPM where formal control mechanisms such as performance measures may enhance bridging by 'demonstrating capabilities and reputation to funding agencies, government and potential alliance partners' (Chenhall, Hall, & Smith, 2010, p. 743). We build on work such as this by examining *different types of bridging strategies* that are made possible by contemporary performance measurement and reporting practice in government.

Specifically, government agencies may follow *bridging strategies to funding authorities as non-networked entities* as part of securing future resource allocations and economic resources. Actions as part of this would involve claiming individualized agency (rather than network) accountability for performance outcomes. Supporting this, Brignall and Modell (2000) argue that the concerns of funding authorities are central to the design of performance measurement systems in government while, more broadly, there is research that finds inter-organizational relationships are influenced significantly by the relationships that each partner has with influential parties (Chua & Mahama, 2007). Alternatively, agencies may pursue *bridging strategies to funding authorities and policy delivery partners as individualized entities providing services within a network*. This involves agencies claiming performance in terms of the value of their activities and outputs for others in the network with which they partner or to which they deliver services. In this regard, the performance is defined and evaluated and recognizes that other (recipient) agencies are dependent on an agency's services but eschews a shared identity in the form of the network. Finally, agencies may pursue *bridging strategies to policy delivery partners as a (joint) networked entity*. Here, performance is measured and reported about a network object with achievements and performance being represented in a manner that highlights shared inputs, activities, outputs and outcomes. Given this, our research question can be phrased as: how does the *object of analysis* of performance measurement practice facilitate: (a) bridging strategies oriented towards funding authorities; and (b) bridging strategies oriented towards other partners in policy delivery?

RESEARCH CONTEXT AND METHOD

Research Context

For the empirical investigation, we have selected government agencies that form part of the Department of Justice portfolio within Australia. Within Australia, law enforcement groups typically rely on intelligence agencies to support and execute investigative effort. Intelligence agencies are equally reliant on law enforcement agencies to act upon such intelligence as a performance measure. Investigative agencies depend on prosecution services that in turn depend on courts for hearing schedules and, to some extent, prosecutorial outcomes (Cox & Wade, 2001). Fig. 1 shows each of these dependence inter-relationships and the defined outcomes for each agency in the network.

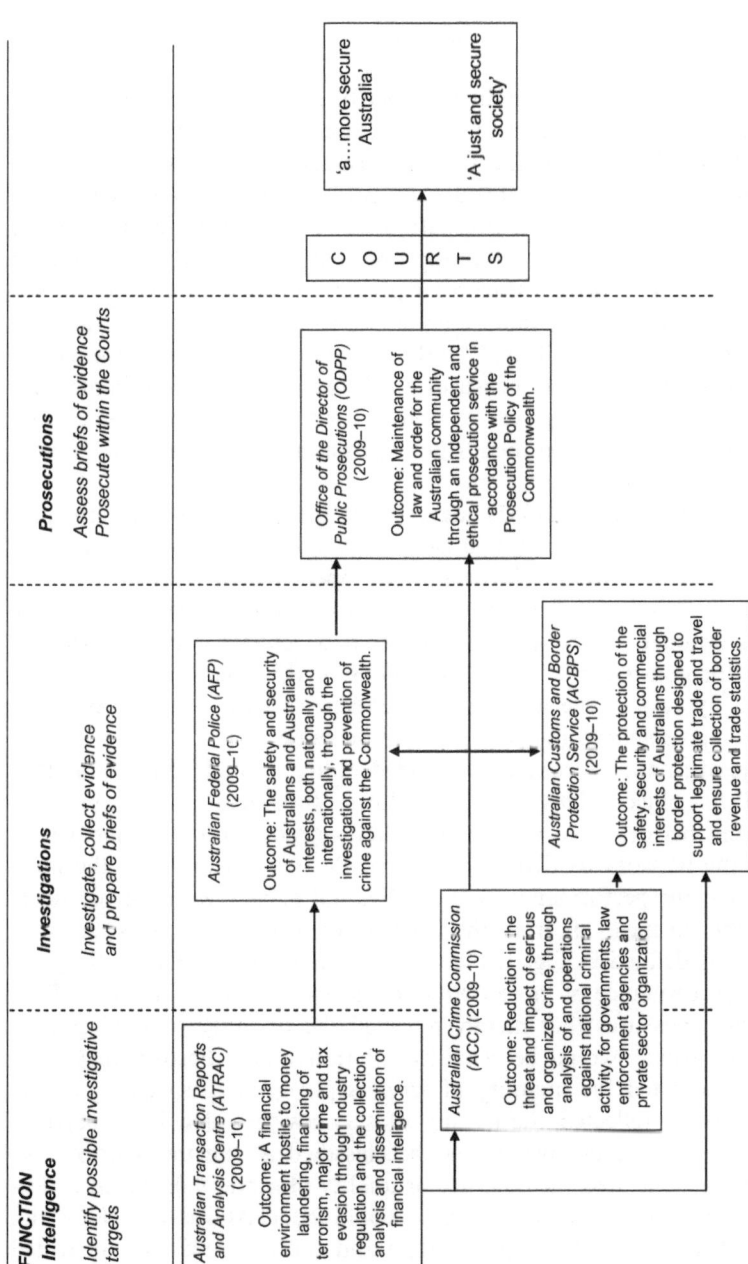

Fig. 1. Inter-Organizational Criminal Justice Network with 2009–2010 Outcomes Statements.

Method

The unit of analysis was the individual performance measure.[2] To identify
the public accountability performance measures of each of the government
agencies depicted in Fig. 1, the Portfolio Budget Statements across three
years comprising 2008–2009 through to 2010–2011 were obtained. These
documents typically contain information about the strategic direction of
the agency, a budget estimate and appropriated funds for the forthcoming
year as well as over a further three-year period, the outcome that comprised
the results or impacts that the agency is expected to achieve and the programmes that are to be delivered by the agency in order to achieve its stated outcomes. Performance measures are listed for each programme with
targets for the forthcoming year as well as for a further three-year period.
Each of these was identified for further analysis as they represented a measure coupled with targets.

Guthrie and Mathews (1985) suggest that the coding of data into pre-
defined categories requires certain protocols. They highlight the need for
categories of classification to be clearly and operationally defined such that
the membership of each item of analysis in a particular category can be
readily ascertained. They also indicate that a reliable coding process is
necessary for consistency. For the purposes of this study, all coding was
performed by two of the authors independent of each other to establish
and ensure agreement, robustness and completeness.

Each performance measure was coded along a single dimension that
evaluated its object. This was as follows: Individual – the measure
reflected the performance of the individual agency with no reference to
others in the network as defined in Fig. 1; Partner/Customer – the measure reflected the performance of the individual agency with specific reference to other agencies or from the perspective of other agencies receiving
its services as defined in Fig. 1; Network – the measure reflected the joint
or shared performance of more than one agency as defined in Fig. 1. Thus
performance measures that merely reflected the quantity of services provided by an agency would be classified as 'Individual'. Performance measures that indicated the quantity of services provided to specific partners
or customers or reflected the quality of services provided from partner/
customer agency perspectives would be classified as 'Partner/Customers'.
Measures that indicated the quantity or quality of services delivered collectively by multiple agencies in Fig. 1 would be classified as 'Network'.
Examples drawn from the empirical data and coding process are provided
in the next section.

RESULTS: PRACTICES OF PERFORMANCE MEASUREMENT

We examined the object of performance each measure was evaluating and report the results of this analysis in terms of the average number over the three years. This is presented in Table 1. While there was variety across the agencies, the majority of performance measures reflected the performance of the individual agency as a non-networked entity and in isolation to any other agency in Fig. 1. There is no perceived co-variation in objects of performance measurement practice and agency position in the network. Participants located early in the sequence of network activities (upstream) did not measurably deviate from participants located late (downstream) in network activities in terms of whether they chose to report the accomplishments of their agency as a non-networked entity, their achievements in relation to impact on a partner or customer agency as part of a network or their achievements as a collective of organizations.

In relation to partner/customer measures, an example drawn from AUSTRAC comprises a measurement of the 'value of AUSTRAC information and financial intelligence to partner agency and taskforce operations' (Australian Transaction Reports and Analysis Centre [AUSTRAC], 2009, Portfolio Budget Statement, 2009–10). Similarly, the ACC measured the impact of its intelligence in terms of whether 'Partner agencies agree or strongly agree that their understanding of the overall criminal environment has increased as a result of ACC intelligence' (Australian Crime Commission [ACC], 2009, Portfolio Budget Statement, 2009–10).

Moving beyond partner/customer to network-object performance measures, the AFP measured the 'estimated financial return' from its fraud cases that was contingent on not only intelligence it might have obtained from upstream entities but also the prosecution efforts of downstream

Table 1. Public Accountability Performance Measures by Object of Measurement (Average Over 3 Years).

Focus	Number of Performance Measures Reported by Agency					Performance Measures Reported by Agency (%)				
	AUSTRAC	ACC	AFP	ACBPS	CDPP	AUSTRAC	ACC	AFP	ACBPS	CDPP
Individual	15	3	20	76	4	83	43	69	99	100
Partner/Customer	3	4	5	0	0	17	57	17	0	0
Network	0	0	4	1	0	0	0	14	1	0
Total	18	7	29	77	4	100	100	100	100	100

agencies. In a similar fashion, other AFP measures of network performance assessed 'the number of high − very high impact cases reaching court' and 'Percentage of cases before court that result in conviction'. Both of these reflect the performance of the collective, with intelligence, investigations and prosecutions all working together to bring matters into the judicial process and securing conviction results. Similarly, the ACBPS measured 'Percentage of prosecution briefs completed, which resulted in a conviction'. For these few measures at least, inter-dependencies with other agencies involved in policy delivery were recognized and a network identity promoted.

We also examined the change in object of performance measures reported across the years investigated. This was to assess whether there were changing dynamics in the specific bridging strategies that are supported through performance measurement practice. This information is presented in Table 2. This shows an increasing trend of individual-object performance measures at the expense of reporting as a collective network or reporting impact on the partner or customer.

Table 2 shows that the majority (over 90%) of measures reported in 2010−2011 were individual-object focused, indicating that performance measures are being used as bridging strategies towards funding authorities in isolation from other network participants. Furthermore, there is a slight increase over time with the corresponding proportion of performance measures being 82% in 2008−2009. Hence bridging to funding authorities appears to be taking place at the expense of bridging to partner agencies in policy delivery, with this trend increasing over time.

In contrast there were few examples of bridging strategies to both funding authorities and policy delivery partners. Performance measures that reflected the achievements of individualized entities providing services to

Table 2. Public Accountability Performance Measures by Object of Measurement (Average Over 3 Years).

	2008−2009	2009−2010	2010−2011	2008−2009	2009−2010	2010−2011
	Number of KPIs			Percentage of Total (%)		
Individual	100	110	144	82	88	90
Partner/Customer	15	10	11	12	8	7
Network	7	5	5	6	4	3
Total	122	125	160	100	100	100

others within a network were only 7% in 2010–2011. Similarly, bridging strategies purely to policy delivery partners within the network was low at only 3% in 2010–2011. During the period of study (2008–2011) there was little evidence of a growing emphasis on network-focused performance measurements and if anything the proportion of performance measures that focused on the performances of individual agencies increased.

While both the literature and the policy statements would suggest that there is an increasing focus on notions of joined-up government and the importance of networks in the delivery of effective policy we would argue, based on this evidence, that there is little evidence of this focus in the details of the existing performance measurement system. The central focus is, and remains, on the relationship between the respective departments and the central authorities responsible for funding and there is little evidence of interest and active engagement with building and sustaining a cross-network performance perspective. Therefore the notion that performance measurement is sufficient to drive inter-agency co-operation and co-production across networks is not supported. Clearly agencies prefer to report and emphasize individual achievement above public-value-oriented collective action.

CONCLUSION

The public administration and management literature examining networks has expanded significantly over the past two decades. As McGuire (2006) observes in his review of the literature, prior research makes several points. First, collaboration and networks in the public sector are common, especially given that network structure has been shown to have a significant influence on policy outcomes (see also Berry et al., 2004). Second, there has been much focus on the characteristics and skills that are necessary for effective collaboration. Finally there is a focus on examining the effects of collaboration and networks on public sector outcomes. However, how public value outcomes can be achieved across these networks requires further reflection. While Moore (2005) presents this challenge as a task of 'political management' he also suggests (2005, 2013) that the enhancement of performance measurement systems could also assist in this area.

The findings of this article show that contemporary developments in performance measurement systems do not ideally support the creation of public value in the way articulated by Moore (2005, 2013). While practices of 'political management' described by Moore (2005, 2013) can be theoretically explained as the creation of inter-agency collaboration and co-production through fostering of social capital norms of trust and reciprocity, we find that it is primarily the institutional context that either engenders or limits lateral forms of accountability. From that perspective, structural and institutional arrangements (and therefore also practices of performance measurement) can both help and hinder the creation and the sustainment of public value.

In our analysis of existing performance measures within the Australian Commonwealth Justice portfolio we found that despite an environment where multiple agencies partnered and provided services to one another in delivering justice policy there was little evidence of forms of performance measurement that recognized the existence of a network and the importance of the co-production process to the creation of public value. Only a minority of measures reflected the role of agencies as service providers within a network, while even fewer focused on collective or portfolio performance. Our conclusion is that existing public sector governance and accountability mechanisms are not naturally supportive of the creation and sustaining of social capital necessary to deliver public value across inter-agency networks.

For researchers examining networks, there is a need to examine how 'macro' government accountability mechanisms influence and interact with 'network-object' accountability mechanisms and how this influences collaborative actions. For those interested in the relationship between network structure and the delivery of public policy outcomes through large-N research, the inclusion of macro-accountability mechanisms as an independent or moderating variable is suggested.

We also call for a shift in accountability mechanisms designed for hierarchical accountability between individual agencies and the 'government', or at least central funding agencies, to also encompass the lateral forms of accountability necessary for the creation of social capital. Despite the public administration and management literature indicating recognition of networks formed across agencies (Goldsmith & Eggers, 2004; Kickert, Klijn, & Koppenjan, 1997; O'Toole, 1997), we suggest that there are inherent barriers to the emergence and development of network-focused practice in the form of mechanisms designed to exercise performance scrutiny on single agencies that can 'crowd out' motivations to collaborate in ways that do deliver public value. Supporting this, many authors have noted a mismatch between the apparent benefits of collaboration and networking and inertia in practice (for a review of these studies, see McGuire, 2006).

While it would be wrong to dismiss the notions of joined-up government and whole-of-government on this basis, it is at least sufficient to raise questions about the nature and extent of the shift in structure as realized or practised, as suggested by some authors and to explore both the managerial and the performance measurement strategies necessary for the delivery of public value across complex inter-agency networks (and public-private partnerships). A plausible possibility is that performance measurement systems in government could be lagging other developments on intra-governmental networking that more meaningfully support the creation and sustainment of public value.

We would argue that the danger of the existing public administration literature is that it over-emphasizes the power of policy initiatives and underestimates the influence of administrative practices and structures such as performance measurement that are seen as critical to the recognition and delivery of public value. On this point, Ryan and Walsh (2004) argue that the vertical accounting information processes on which existing accountability frameworks are typically built are out of date, inflexible and in need of reform. Policy and formal guidance on lateral reporting mechanisms is one suggestion provided by Ryan and Walsh (2004) in overcoming existing limitations. Although their paper did not specifically address dependencies within inter-organizational networks, their concerns in relation to a wider policy framework support that can facilitate cross-agency performance reporting are supported by the findings of this study.

Finally, managers of policy delivery and administrators of networks need to consider how accountability mechanisms and performance measures support particular network behaviours in terms of where and how bridging occurs. Of the three bridging strategies examined, the vast majority (90%) of the performance measures reviewed were individual object-focused measures, which suggests bridging strategies towards funding authorities vis-à-vis other partners in policy delivery. Based on this we suggest that the primary social capital investment is on positively reflecting the activities of the department in a way that will secure additional funding and high levels of public/political recognition. In effect, existing performance measurement practices largely reinforce existing legally defined or structurally defined organizational boundaries. Therefore the delivery of public value and the role of 'political management' in the creation and sustainment of social capital arrangements within these complex settings needs further study and reflection.

This is important given the significant inter-dependencies that can occur between networks of public administration by virtue of operating within the same government portfolio for common or overlapping policy outcomes. While a necessary element of bridging and connecting to funding authorities is crucial as part of discharging financial accountability, attention must be devoted to other formal and informal mechanisms that are consistent with and support bridging to other network partners in enabling the creation of public value. While increased accountability and transparency of individual public sector agencies are laudable objectives, this is not sufficient to deliver the broader citizen orientated public value outcomes sought. This is because the network effects of departmental initiatives need to be increasingly scrutinized and investigated and possibly corrected for. For as Bardach (1998, p.13) observed:

> ... the same forces ... that have created relatively specialized agency structures ... also make collaboration difficult. From a narrow, constituency standpoint, collaboration is distinctly undesirable because it threatens to blur an agency's mission and the agency's political accountability for pursuing it.

In conclusion, it is our contention that, if networks of public administration are to flourish, public accountability mechanisms need to engender network identification (Huemer, Becerra, & Lunnan, 2004) such that possibilities for collaboration, co-operation and knowledge sharing across legally or structurally defined boundaries are enhanced. This is critical if the public value outcomes described by authors such as Moore (2005, 2013) are to be realized. In effect the objective of 'political management' is the creation of the forms of social capital that result in the alignment of agency's organizational and practical realities with the espoused policy directions and agency-specific institutional silos abandoned in favour of a network-based portfolio perspective. The danger is that without such a shift substantial resources will be wasted as the different elements within the network pull in their own direction rather than pulling together.

It is important to acknowledge the limitations of this study. We have outlined the potential of public accountability performance measurement mechanisms to support particular networking and bridging strategies based on the analysis of the reported performance measures across one Australian Commonwealth portfolio in a defined time period (2008–2011). Further work needs to investigate more fully the extent to which these effects manifest within agencies and across other areas and how they are moderated by other influences at the inter-organizational and intra-organizational levels. Therefore, the examples provided are limited to one national context and, within that, one portfolio, albeit an important one for network collaboration. As such, ongoing work will need to examine the extent to which the findings obtained here are generalizable to the support of public value creation initiatives in other settings of public administration. Overall, there is a challenge to engage with the effects of network accountability mechanisms for network strategizing and action.

NOTES

1. There is some debate about whether this is a new trend in practice or a shift in academic understanding of the complexity of the real world. For example, Bardach (1998) provides evidence of this network trend in 1984 where local government associations engaging in joint planning and policy development and 'working in the thicket of interjurisdictional networks' (p. 5). In effect the NPM doctrinal notion of public sector disaggregation and downsizing may be a major oversimplification.

2. Performance measures relating to outputs that were not part of the network being analyzed were excluded. Also, in some cases a single performance indicator was measured at a sub-category level. Where these situations were encountered the performance indicator was counted as single rather than multiple.

REFERENCES

Attorney-General Department. (2009). Annual report 2008–09. Commonwealth of Australia.
Australian Crime Commission. (2009, August 1). *Portfolio budget statement 2009–10.*
Australian National Audit Office. (2007). *Application of the outcomes and outputs framework.* Canberra: Commonwealth of Australia.
Australian Transaction Reports and Analysis Centre. (2009, 1 August). *Portfolio budget statement 2009–10.*
Bardach, E. (1998). *Getting agencies to work together: The practice and theory of managerial craftsmanship.* Washington, DC: Brookings Institution Press.
Berry, F. S., Brower, R. S., Choi, S. O., Goa, W. X., Jang, H., Kwon, M., & Word, J. (2004). Three traditions of network research: What the public management research agenda can learn from other research communities. *Public Administration Review, 64*(5), 539–552.
Bourdieu, P., & Wacquant, L. J. D. (1992). *An invitation to reflexive sociology.* Chicago, IL: University of Chicago Press.
Brignall, S., & Modell, S. (2000). An institutional perspective on performance measurement and management in the new public sector. *Management Accounting Research, 11,* 281–305.
Caglio, A., & Ditillo, A. (2008). A review and discussion of management control in inter-firm relationships: Achievements and future directions. *Accounting, Organizations and Society, 33,* 865–898.

Carlin, T. (2005). Debating the impact of accrual accounting and reporting in the public sector. *Financial Accountability and Management, 21*(3), 309–336.

Carnegie, G., & West, B. (2005). Making accounting accountable in the public sector. *Critical Perspectives on Accounting, 16*, 905–928.

Chenhall, R. H., Hall, M., & Smith, D. (2010). Social capital and management control systems: A study of a non-government organization. *Accounting, Organizations and Society, 35*, 737–756.

Christensen, T., & Lægreid, P. (2007). The whole-of-government approach to public sector reform. *Public Administration Review, 67*(6), 1059–1066.

Chua, W. F., & Mahama, H. (2007). The effect of network ties on accounting controls in a supply alliance: Field study evidence. *Contemporary Accounting Research, 24*, 47–86.

Commonwealth of Australia Australian Public Services Commission. (2007). *Tackling wicked problems: A public policy perspective*. Canberra: Commonwealth of Australia.

Cox, S. M., & Wade, J. E. (2001). *Criminal justice network — An introduction*. Dubuque, IA: William C Brown Company.

Dawes, S. S., Cresswell, A. M., & Pardo, T. A. (2009). From "need to know" to "need to share": Tangled problems, information boundaries, and the building of public sector knowledge networks. *Public Administration Review, 69*, 392–402.

Dunleavy, P., Margetts, H., Bastow, S., & Tinkler, J. (2006). New public management is dead — Long live digital-era governance. *Journal of Public Administration Research and Theory, 16*(3), 467–494.

Field, J. (2008). *Social capital* (2nd ed.). London: Routledge.

Goldsmith, S., & Eggers, W. D. (2004). *Governing by network: The new shape of the public sector*. Washington, DC: Brookings Institution Press.

Guthrie, J. (1994). Performance indicators in the Australian public sector. In E. Buschor & K. Schedler (Eds.), *Perspectives on performance measurement in public sector accounting*. Berne: Paul Haupt.

Guthrie, J., & Mathews, R. (1985). Corporate social accounting in Australasia. *Research in Corporate Social Performance and Policy, 7*, 251–277.

Guthrie, J., & Parker, L. (1998). Managerialism and marketisation in financial management change in Australia. In O. Olson, J. Guthrie, & C. Humphrey (Eds.), *Global warning! Debating international developments in new public financial management*. Oslo: Cappelen Akademisk Forlag.

Håkansson, H., Kraus, K., & Lind, J. (Eds.). (2010). *Accounting in networks*. London: Routledge.

Halligan, J., Bouckaert, G., & van Dooren, W. (2010). *Performance management in the public sector*. London: Routledge.

Hood, C. (1991). A public management for all seasons? *Public Administration, 69*(1), 3–19.

Hood, C. (1995). The new public management in the 1980s: Variations on a theme. *Accounting, Organizations and Society, 20*(2–3), 93–109.

Hood, C., & Peters, G. (2004). The middle aging of new public management: Into the age of paradox? *Journal of Public Administration Research and Theory, 14*(3), 267–282.

Hopwood, A. G. (1996). Looking across rather than up and down: On the need to explore the lateral processing of information. *Accounting, Organizations and Society, 21*(6), 589–590.

Huemer, L., Becerra, M., & Lunnan, R. (2004). Organizational identity and network identification: Relating within and beyond imaginary boundaries. *Scandinavian Journal of Management, 20*, 53–73.

Kickert, W. J. M., Klijn, E., & Koppenjan, J. F. M. (Eds.). (1997). *Managing complex networks: Strategies for the public sector*. London: Sage.

Kloot, L., & Martin, J. (2000). Strategic performance management: A balanced approach to performance management issues in local government. *Management Accounting Research, 11*(2), 231–251.

Lee, J. (2008). Preparing performance information in the public sector: An Australian perspective. *Financial Accountability and Management, 24*(2), 117–149.

Lin, N. (2001). *Social capital: A theory of social structure and action*. Cambridge: Cambridge University Press.

Ling, T. (2002). Delivering joined-up government in the UK: Dimensions, issues and problems. *Public Administration, 80*(4), 615–642.

McGuire, M. (2006). Collaborative public management: Assessing what we know and how we know it. *Public Administration Review, 66*, 33–43.

McPhee, I. (2008). Public sector governance – Showing the way. Public Sector Governance Forum, Australian Institute of Company Directors and the Institute of Internal Auditors – Australia, Canberra, 4th September.

Modell, S. (2004). Performance measurement myths in the public sector: A research note. *Financial Accountability and Management, 20*(1), 39–55.

Moore, M. (2005). *Creating public value: Strategic management in government*. Harvard, MA: Harvard University Press.

Moore, M. (2013). *Recognizing public value*. Harvard, MA: Harvard University Press.

Moore, M. H. (1995). *Creating public value: Strategic management in government*. Harvard, MA: Harvard University Press.

National Commission on Terrorist Attacks Upon the United States. (2004). *The 9/11 Commission Report*. Retrieved from http://govinfo.library.unt.edu/911/report/index.htm

O'Faircheallaigh, C., Wanna, J., & Weller, P. (1999). *Public sector management in Australia* (2nd ed.). Melbourne: Macmillan.

O'Flynn, J. (2007). From new public management to public value: Paradigmatic change and managerial implication. *The Australian Journal of Public Administration, 66*(3), 353–366.

Osborne, D., & Gaebler, T. (1992). *Reinventing government: How the entrepreneurial spirit is transforming the public sector*. York: Plume.

Otley, D. (1994). Management control in contemporary organizations: Towards a wider framework. *Management Accounting Research, 12*(3), 289–299.

O'Toole, L. J. (1997). Treating networks seriously: Practical and research-based agendas in public administration. *Public Administration Review, 57*(1), 45–52.

Powell, W. W. (1990). Neither market nor hierarchy: Network forms of organization. *Research in organizational behavior, 12*, 295–336.

Putnam, R. D. (2000). *Bowling along*. New York, NY: Simon & Schuster.

Ring, P. S., & van de Ven, A. H. (1992). Structuring cooperative relationships between organizations. *Strategic Management Journal, 13*, 483–498.

Ryan, C., & Walsh, P. (2004). Collaboration of public sector agencies: Reporting and accountability challenges. *The International Journal of Public Sector Management, 17*(6–7), 621–631.

Sako, M. (1992). *Prices, quality and trust: Inter-firm relations in Britain and Japan*. Cambridge: Cambridge University Press.

United States Government Accountability Office. (2007). *Managerial cost accounting practices: Implementation and use vary widely across 10 federal agencies*, GAO-07-679, United States: Government Accountability Office.

Walker, R. G. (2001). Reporting on service efforts and accomplishments on a 'whole of government' basis. *Australian Accounting Review, 11*(3), 4–16.

Walker, R. G. (2002). Are annual reports of government agencies really general purpose if they do not include performance indicators? *Australian Accounting Review, 12*(1), 43–45.

Weber, E. P., & Khademian, A. M. (2008). Wicked problems, knowledge challenges, and collaborative capacity builders in network settings. *Public Administration Review, 68*(2), 334–349.

Wilkins, P. (2002). Accountability and joined-up government. *Australian Journal of Public Administration, 61*(1), 114–119.

Williams, P. (2002). The competent boundary spanner. *Public Administration, 80*(1), 103–124.

Williamson, O. (1993). Calculativeness, trust and economic organization. *Journal of Law and Economics, 36*, 453–486.

Williamson, O. E. (1985). *The economic institutions of capitalism: Firms, markets, relational contracting*. New York, NY: The Free Press.

PERFORMANCE MEASUREMENT OF LOCAL PUBLIC SERVICE NETWORKS

Steve Martin and James Downe

ABSTRACT

Purpose — *The article considers the challenges involved in measuring the performance of local public service networks through an empirical analysis of Comprehensive Area Assessments (CAAs), a short-lived but pioneering attempt to gauge the effectiveness of local governments, health trusts, police and fire services in England.*

Design/methodology/approach — *Primary data about the implementation and impact of CAAs were gathered using a mixed method approach, including surveys of local public services, inspectorates and residents together with focus groups and semi-structured interviews in 12 case study areas.*

Findings — *CAAs encouraged agencies to strive to achieve better partnership working but did not provide sufficiently robust comparative data to enable managers to benchmark their performance against other areas or identify good practice elsewhere. Policy makers hoped that citizens*

Public Value Management, Measurement and Reporting
Studies in Public and Non-Profit Governance, Volume 3, 43–64
Copyright © 2014 by Emerald Group Publishing Limited
All rights of reproduction in any form reserved
ISSN: 2051-6630/doi:10.1108/S2051-663020140000003002

would use CAAs to hold services to account but the process failed to attract media or public interest.

Implications − *The logic of a more 'joined-up' approach to performance assessment of local partnerships is compelling. But in practice it is diffi- cult to achieve because institutional arrangements at a national level mean that different sectors work within very different budget systems, professional networks and performance frameworks. Assessing the out- comes achieved by local partnerships also presents new challenges for inspection agencies and requires them to use new kinds of evidence.*

Originality/value − *This is the only attempt to date to evaluate CAAs and adds to an understanding of the challenges of assessing the perfor- mance of local public service partnerships. It highlights new questions for researchers and policy makers about the types of evidence needed to measure partnership performance and the extent to which the public may use the results.*

Keywords: Public services; partnership working; performance assessment

INTRODUCTION

This article analyzes the challenges involved in measuring the performance of local public service networks. This important topic reflects two key fea- tures of recent public management reforms in western countries: the imple- mentation of performance management systems and the creation of public service partnerships. Performance measurement is widely seen as a core com- ponent of new public management (Lapsley, 2008), a transnational phenom- enon (Pollitt et al., 1999) which has led to the transformation of formal institutions of monitoring (Power, 2003) and become a focus for accounting and accountability research (Modell, 2009). Increasing interest in partnership working is also reflected in a rapidly growing literature, with some scholars arguing that collaboration is now a hegemonic discourse (Skelcher & Sullivan, 2008) and the instrument of choice when it comes to implementing public programmes (Turrini, Cristofoli, Frosini, & Nasi, 2010).

As Hodges (2012) notes, local public service partnerships require new approaches to performance measurement. Existing frameworks focus on individual and organizational performance and depend on vertical lines of accountability. Partnerships cut across organizational boundaries in ways that blur responsibilities for outcomes and challenge existing definitions of performance. Hodges argues that there is a need to 'move away from the traditional entity perspective of accounting and accountability towards the accounting and accountability linkages of networks or partnership organisations' (2012, p. 33).

This article explores whether public service partnerships can be held to account for their performance, and if so how and by whom, by analyzing the implementation and impact of Comprehensive Area Assessments (CAAs), a short-lived but pioneering attempt to measure the performance of local public service partnerships in England. The next section briefly examines the emergence of partnership working in local public services. We then explain the objectives of CAAs before describing our research methods. The subsequent section of the article analyzes the implementation and impact of CAA. The final section discusses the implications of our findings for research and practice.

LOCAL PUBLIC SERVICE PARTNERSHIPS

There is a large and rapidly growing literature on the role of networks in policy formulation and public service delivery, including significant contributions from the 'Dutch school' (Kickert, Klijn, & Koppenjan, 1997; Klijn, 2008; Klijn, & Koppenjan, 2000), the United States (Provan & Milward, 1995) and Australia (Keast, Brown, & Mandell, 2007; Keast, Mandell, Brown, & Woolcock, 2004). These studies point to a range of reasons for the proliferation of partnership working. It is argued that networks enable governments to co-operate with non-state actors that bring valuable additional resources (including private finance) to the task of addressing complex policy problems (Kooiman, 2003; van Bueren, Klijn, & Koppenjan, 2003). Advances in information and communications technology have facilitated new types of interactions between organizations and the public (Dunleavy, Margetts, Bastow, & Tinkler, 2006) and local networks offer a means of achieving co-ordination among public services that have been fragmented by contracting out and marketization (Rhodes, 1997). They facilitate the flow of knowledge across organizational and professional boundaries, which can act as a stimulus for innovation and wider adoption of good practice. By working together, organizations can improve efficiency (e.g. by sharing buildings) and provide more 'joined-up' services (e.g. by linking websites and integrating customer contact centres) (Pollitt, 2003). The literature also identifies as an impetus for collaboration the growing recognition that some of the most persistent and pressing policy problems (such as social exclusion, economic inactivity and environmental sustainability) cut across organizational boundaries and can only be addressed through 'joined-up' policies and programmes (Agranoff, 2007; Rhodes, 2000).

The modernization agenda embarked on by the New Labour government in the United Kingdom reflected all of these partnership rationales. Ministers put 'joined-up government' at the heart of their plans to 'modernize' the way in which central government worked (Cabinet Office, 1999; Ling, 2002; Rhodes, 2000) and actively encouraged the formation of local public service partnerships (Currie, Grubnic, & Hodges, 2011). The 'local government modernization agenda', for example, sought to transform the quality and responsiveness of public services by encouraging partnership working among local authorities, the police, health and other providers (Downe & Martin, 2006). The 1998 Local Government White Paper argued that there was a need to 'create the conditions under which there is likely to be greater interest from the private and voluntary sectors in working with local government' (Department of Environment, Transport and the Regions [DETR], 1998, p. 57) and the Prime Minister insisted that 'It is in partnership with others – public agencies, private companies, community groups and voluntary organizations – that local government's future lies' (Blair, 1998, p. 13). Local authorities were expected to act as 'community leaders' who steered collective action by other public services and representatives of the private and voluntary sectors (Stoker, 2004). The government required local organizations to form Local Strategic Partnerships (LSPs), which developed medium-term 'community strategies' and drew up formal contracts (known as Local Public Service Agreements (LPSAs) and Local Area Agreements (LAAs)) with central government departments and set out targets for improvement (Gillanders & Ahmad, 2007; Sullivan & Gillanders, 2005).

LSPs cut across existing professional networks, institutional arrangements and lines of accountability. The health service, police and local government are overseen by different government departments, each of which continues to implement its own funding regimes. Local agencies were permitted to pool some of their funding and received 'performance reward grants' if they achieved the targets they had agreed to. The funding involved, however, was modest compared to their mainstream budgets, and the health service, police, education, social care, the prison, probation and fire and rescue services continued to be overseen by different national inspectorates that employed different methodologies, worked to different timescales, reported to different ministers and had minimal contact with each other. The Audit Commission worked with the Social Services Inspectorate (SSI) to produce joint reviews of social services, but other inspectorates continued to plough their own service-based furrows. Strong vertical ties between local service managers, inspectors and civil servants who came from the same professional backgrounds and shared a common sense of purpose impeded the development of horizontal linkages between sectors (Rhodes, 1999). Partnership working was often regarded as an 'added extra' that was grafted on to core statutory roles rather than a means of delivering truly integrated public services.

COMPREHENSIVE AREA ASSESSMENTS

There is a long history of external assessment of the English local government. In the 1990s, the Audit Commission used Citizen's Charter performance indicators to make comparisons between authorities (Bowerman, Ball, & Graham, 2001). The introduction of the Best Value regime in England in April 2000 led to external inspection of all local government services (Martin, 2000) and Comprehensive Performance Assessments (CPAs) introduced in 2002 judged the overall performance of each local council on a five-point scale (later changed to a four-point scale) (Downe & Martin, 2007). The scale and intensity of inspection in other sectors also increased dramatically in the early years of the Blair government. Several new inspectorates of local services were created and many existing agencies found their remits expanding into new areas and new types of assessment. There was, however, a growing recognition that assessment processes were fragmented with the Audit Commission, Office for Standards in Education (Ofsted), Care Quality Commission (CQC) and others operating largely in isolation. This, it was argued, made it difficult for local public service providers to work in partnership with each other.

CAA was introduced by the central government to address the problem. It consisted of two components: 'Organizational Assessments' and an 'Area Assessment'. Organizational assessments were sector specific and modelled on CPA. Separate reports were prepared for the police, local authority, primary (health) care trust (PCT) and fire service in each locality. External auditors assessed how well each of these agencies managed their financial resources and inspectorates judged the quality of the services they provided. The performance of all organizations was rated on a four-point star scale. The Audit Commission undertook the assessments of local authorities and fire services; PCTs were evaluated by the CQC, and Her Majesty's Inspectorate of Constabulary (HMIC) assessed the police. Area assessments were the really innovative component of CAA. They involved a joint judgement made by all of the inspectorates about how well local public services in an area were working together to achieve the objectives identified in their community strategies and LAAs. The inspectorates described this as 'a fundamental change in our approach to the assessment of local public services' designed to reflect the way in which local public services 'are increasingly working together' (Audit Commission, 2009, p. 4). It would, they argued, respond to three key criticisms of existing sector-based approaches to assessment: the disjuncture between local partnership processes and national performance frameworks; the costs and bureaucratic burdens that inspections imposed on assessed bodies and the lack of public involvement in holding public services to account for their performance.

CAA sought to address the first criticism of assessment frameworks that promoted rather than impeded local partnership working by assessing the ability of LSPs to address 'cross-cutting issues' like economic regeneration community cohesion and environmental sustainability. Green flags were awarded to partnerships with exceptional performance or outstanding improvement producing better outcomes for local people that are sustainable and from which others could learn. Red flags were used to signify areas where the inspectorates had jointly judged that there were significant concerns about outcomes not being tackled adequately. As such, it is a useful test case of the feasibility of developing assessment frameworks that are capable of making the transition from entity to network-based perspectives on accountability, which Hodges (2012) argues is needed but Kurunmäki and Miller (2006) doubt is possible.

CAA responded to the second complaint about the costs and bureaucratic burdens imposed on assessed bodies by seeking to achieve better co-ordination between the inspectorates. The scale, scope and cost of 'regulation inside government' had expanded steadily during the 1970s, 1980s and 1990s (Hood, Scott, James, Jones, & Travers, 1999; Power, 1997) but spiralled rapidly upwards during the New Labour era (Office of Public Services Reform [OPSR], 2003; Scottish Government, 2007). In addition, assessed bodies incurred increasing costs in order to make themselves 'auditable' (preparing plans, collecting performance data, hosting site visits and responding to reports and so forth), and this distracted staff from the 'core' tasks of service delivery (Hood & Peters, 2004). The UK government and the inspectorates argued that CAA would help to reduce the burden of inspection because it was based entirely on existing evidence – plans, performance indicators, citizen surveys and inspection reports. There were no new site visits, interviews with service managers or focus groups with users. It would also reduce duplication by the different inspectorates because they would now be able to co-ordinate their activities and agree a joint report.

As well as reducing costs, CAA was intended to engage the public more directly in holding public services to account for their performance. The use of star ratings in both local government and health, which led to league tables, was designed to provide 'simple measures' that were 'easily understood by the public' (Commission for Health Improvement, 2004, p. 3). However, except perhaps in the case of school league tables, this did not produce any great increase in the public's appetite for performance information (Pidd, 2005). For the most part, 'ordinary' members of the public remained largely unaware of how public services were managed (Pallot, 2003; Palmer & Thompson, 2005) and sceptical about official accounts of performance (Clarke, 2008). CAAs sought to address this problem by providing reports that were explicitly intended for public consumption. Area assessments were short and written in 'plain English', and they were uploaded to a new website known as 'Oneplace', which inspectorates hoped would be widely used by citizens.

DATA AND METHODS

We examined the extent to which CAA has managed to hold public service partnerships to account for their performance by focusing upon whether it had encouraged better partnership working, reduced the burden on assessed bodies and engaged the general public. We gathered primary data using mixed methods including focus groups, surveys of assessed bodies, inspectorates and households and semi-structured interviews across a range of case studies.

To understand the origins, objectives and implementation of CAA, we first undertook an analysis of published documents relating to its introduction and design. We then conducted two focus groups with the Audit Commission staff in September and October 2009. The first involved 16 of the most senior Audit Commission staff (some of whom were responsible for leading joint inspectorates' work on CAA); the second was with 'CAA leads' who led the implementation of CAAs. Following this, we conducted one-to-one semi-structured interviews with 20 senior staff from the Audit

Commission and the three other inspectorates that were most closely involved in CAA – Ofsted, the CQC and HMIC. Interviews followed a topic guide and the data from them and the focus groups was recorded in detailed contemporaneous notes. The interviews and focus groups examined in detail these respondents' expectations of CAA and whether it had lived up to them. We explored what impacts they believed the process had on local services, outcomes, partnership working and public accountability; whether it had reduced the burden that inspection places on local services; its usefulness (or otherwise) to regulators and central government and any improvements they would like to see in the process.

An online survey was sent to all chief executives of assessed bodies – local authorities and PCTs, Chief Constables and Chief Fire Officers (hereafter referred to as 'local public service leaders'). The sample was 616 and the response rate 40% (n = 246). The survey was conducted between December 2009 and January 2010 immediately after the publication of organizational and area assessments. It included questions about the way in which CAA had been conducted (the extent to which inspectorates co-ordinated their activities, the rigour and fairness of the judgements they reached; the costs to assessed bodies); the way in which results were communicated and the impacts on partnership working, local services and outcomes. Most questions were closed and asked respondents to rate CAA on seven-point Likert scales, but there was also space for respondents to explain their answers and give examples.

The survey of inspectorate staff was also conducted online. It was sent to 187 staff and achieved a response rate of 80% ($n = 150$) with a range of 68% to 100% from the different inspectorates. It was completed in November 2009 just after assessments had been completed but before the reports had been published. It asked a range of questions about the delivery of CAA; the extent to which inspection activity had been co-ordinated and perceptions of its costs and benefits to assessed bodies.

A household survey was conducted to assess public awareness and use of CAA reports and attitudes to inspection of local services. A total of 849 face-to-face, in-home, interviews across England were conducted in January 2010 (one month after the publication of CAA reports) by a public opinion company. The survey asked questions about knowledge and use of performance information on public services and, in particular, their experience of CAA compared to previous reporting regimes. Results were weighted by factors that are known to influence attitudes to public services including age, gender, deprivation, employment status and ethnicity.

Finally, in-depth semi-structured interviews were conducted with members of LSPs (up to 10 respondents in each area including local authority leaders, chief executives of assessed bodies and representatives of business and third sector) in nine localities between December 2009 and January 2010. We selected one LSP from each region of England and ensured there was a good spread of different types of partnership in terms of demographic and socio-economic characteristics, political control, local government administrative arrangements (i.e. unitary and two-tier structures) and performance (as indicated by the numbers of green and red 'flags' awarded in CAA reports). In order to encourage interviewees to speak freely, case studies were given fictitious place names that ensured that they would not be identified by inspectorates or government departments. Interviews were conducted using a topic guide that covered the same issues as the survey of assessed bodies. They were recorded and data were coded using a matrix modelled on the topic guide that enabled findings to be compared and lessons to be drawn between areas.

FINDINGS

Our analysis showed that there was strong support for the principles on which CAA was based. Local public service leaders particularly welcomed the focus on outcomes as opposed to individual services and the pledge that assessments would be more 'joined-up' and place less of a burden on assessed bodies. A typical view from those we interviewed was:

> the idea of CAA is very strong and I would like to move much more towards that ... it's better than CPA. The principle is 100% right. (Borough)

Another told us:

> The regulatory framework has to follow the way policy is going   looking across organisations. (Cathedral)

However, it was clear that it had proved difficult for CAA to fulfil some of these expectations.

Improving Local Partnership Working

CAA aimed to improve the quality of partnership working. Almost two thirds (64%) of local public service leaders and 60% of staff from the inspectorates reported that CAA had delivered a stronger focus on outcomes than previous assessment frameworks. 62% of local public service leaders reported that CAA reports took account of local priorities and the challenges facing their area. As one interviewee put it:

> it was an adult conversation. They [the CAA inspectors] absolutely understood the context ... and the journey. (Borough)

Local public service leaders reported that area assessments had been fair but contained few surprises. Only 5% said that reports had identified strengths they had not been aware of and just 7% said that they had identified previously undiagnosed weaknesses. Most LSPs had prepared a self-assessment and local service leaders believed that one of the reasons that the CAA reports failed to add value was that inspectors relied too heavily on the materials supplied to them:

> cut and pasted from our reports. (Cathedral)

> you tell them, they tell you back. (Southernshire)

Many had hoped for practical advice on how to improve but only 21% believed that the area assessment had provided this. Most had found verbal feedback from CAA leads useful but that written reports lacked sufficient detail. One interviewee complained that:

> The area assessment is simplistic to the point of being facile. (Midshire)

Another explained:

> The tone of it was so flat ... it said things like 'the schools are performing at the expected level' ... There was more detail in our own evidence. (Borough)

The lack of detailed analysis and divergence in the areas where green flags were awarded meant that it was difficult for LSPs to identify good practice from which they could learn.

Some interviewees expressed concerns about the robustness of the evidence used in area assessments. Most local public services leaders were not clear how judgements had been made and some interviewees told us that the awarding of green and red 'flags' had seemed to be an arbitrary process. They told us:

> It's right to focus on outcomes but it's difficult because there are not the right indicators [to measure them]. (Cathedral)

> Different people within the same organisation come to different conclusions about the same information. (Northernshire)

Another said:

> It felt like a bargaining process. They were determined to plant a red flag on us somewhere. (Milltown)

Local public service leaders reported similar views about organizational assessments. Most believed that they were accurate although 35% thought that they had overlooked important issues. However, only 3% said that these had identified strengths and 7% that they had highlighted weaknesses that their organizations were not already aware of. This contributed to a feeling that the process was not adding much value:

> We don't need an inspection to tell us things we already know. (Midshire)

Many interviewees were sympathetic towards what the inspectorates were trying to achieve and recognized that assessing outcomes (as opposed to service performance) was very challenging, but believed that CAA had been:

> totally under resourced ... The Audit Commission had over reached itself. (Milltown)

In spite of these reservations about the process, 68% of local public service leaders believed that CAA would lead to improvements in local partnership working. This was particularly evident in areas that did not have a strong track record of effective partnership working. An LSP member in one such area explained:

> It cemented the partnership and focused attention and resources on the big issues. It is really helpful to cross-cutting services like community cohesion ... For the first time, partners are discussing how to deliver things together in the area. (Milltown)

An interviewee from another LSP which had struggled with partnership working in the past reported:

> We had already woken up to the need for partnership, but it was still an 'in principle' commitment ... [CAA] drove joint ownership of higher level outcomes. (Port)

The majority of survey respondents believed that CAA would lead to improvements. Two thirds of respondents expected it to encourage improvement in their own organizations (66%), local services (63%) and outcomes for local people (63%). Almost a fifth (19%) reported that their LSP had already taken action to make improvements in response to a 'red flag' and half (50%) expected that they would do so in future. Nevertheless, only 30% thought that CAA was more likely than previous frameworks to encourage improvement in services and outcomes. One local authority chief executive told us that CAA lacked the hard edge of CPA:

> The CAA just captured what was happening, as a picture of what the partnership is doing, but as a driver for partnership change, it's a bit fluffy, it hasn't got enough teeth. (Borough)

Reducing the Burden of Assessment

The second aim of CAA was to reduce the costs and bureaucratic burdens that inspection placed on assessed bodies. Our results show that only 10% of local public service leaders reported that CAA had reduced the burden of inspection on their organizations. More than half (57%) reported that their staff had spent more time working on CAA than they expected. Staff in inspectorates agreed with this assessment. Only 24% believed that CAA placed less burden on assessed bodies than previous assessments, and some of the interviewees reported that the combination of organizational plus area assessments had actually increased rather than decreased the burden placed on them. We can, perhaps, put some of this down to this being the first year of CAA as over a third of assessed bodies that were surveyed expected CAA to be less time consuming the second time around.

Staff involved in CAA, both nationally and locally, felt they had generally worked well together and developed a better understanding of the partner inspectorates' roles and responsibilities. But two thirds (66%) of local public service leaders and 63% of inspection staff reported that the inspectorates had not 'come across as a joined-up team'. Only 23% of inspectorate staff believed that CAA had 'reduced the duplication of contact from different inspectorates' and local public service leaders reported that the biggest administrative burdens had been duplicate requests for information from different inspectorates. One reported that:

> It was like a forced marriage. (Southernshire)

Particular inspectorates received some criticism about their approach to CAA. For example,

> Ofsted were doing their own thing – they provided their own text very late in the day so the AC [Audit Commission] didn't know what they would say and there was no discussion. (Cathedral)

> Ofsted come and go as they please. (Northernshire)

The CQC came in for similar criticism. They:

> seemed like consultees rather than partners in the process. (Milltown)
>
> doing their own thing. (Northernshire)

Whilst, according to a LSP member in one area, HMIC had:

> not even bought a ticket for the journey. (Southernshire)

Staff from inspectorates accepted that the process had not been fully integrated. Only 24% believed that the area assessment was a genuinely joint judgement. This was partly because the level of commitment to CAA varied between inspectorates. Only 15% of local public service leaders believed that all inspectorates had been fully committed to the process and fewer than half (44%) of the inspectorate staff we surveyed reported that all of the inspectorates had been equal partners in the process. CAA leads were employed by the Audit Commission and there was a perception among some LSPs that the Commission was far more engaged with CAA than other inspectorates. Feedback on the CAA leads was overwhelmingly positive as they played an important role in acting as a conduit for the various inspectorates, liaising with local partnerships, providing constructive challenge and advice on 'best practice'.

Interviews with senior staff in Ofsted and the CQC and officials in their 'parent' government departments confirmed that these agencies were less convinced about the merits of an area-based approach and more wedded to sector-specific frameworks which they continued to operate alongside CAA.

> Structuring reports around local priorities probably makes more sense to local authorities, but sometimes did not therefore give sufficient focus to children and young people. (Senior officer, CQC)
>
> The inspectorates can't go further than Whitehall lets them. CLG was trying to persuade other departments to take a cross-cutting approach, but other departments have our own performance frameworks. So CAA isn't mainstream for us. (Senior official, government department)

This feeling from inspectorates and their government departments was clearly felt by those in our case studies. Typical comments from interviewees were:

> In our view, CAA was going to be a multi-inspectorate approach to match the multi-agency LSP approach. We didn't get that – we got five inspections one after the other. We were disappointed when we found out what CAA meant. (Metropolitan)

It felt like another layer has been introduced. (Milltown)

We have a whole range of these inspections. It would be nice if they all joined up. (Borough)

The CQC was undergoing a major internal re-organization at the time that CAA was conducted and this added to the difficulties of working with other agencies. A large majority (86%) of inspection staff reported that the timescale for completing CAA had also made joint working difficult and almost three quarters (73%) said that differences in the ways in which they worked had presented major challenges. Differences in the assessment methods had not been problematic but sharing data had proved difficult. 73% said there was confusion about when and in what form performance information would be shared among inspectorates. Only 31% said that they had received all of the information that they needed from other inspectorates. Just 17% reported that they had found using information provided by other agencies straightforward.

Public Engagement

The third expected outcome of CAA was to improve communication with the public in providing information on the performance of public services. Just over half (52%) of local public service leaders believed that CAA could enable members of the public to hold public services to account for their performance. Most (86%) reported that, in practice, there had been little interest in the results. Only 18% believed that CAA was a more effective way to engage the public than previous assessment frameworks. Whilst most had disliked the CPA scoring system, some believed this had been more accessible to the public than the narrative approach used in area assessments. Some interviewees believed that CAA reports had been written in accessible language:

It is readable. It's not civil service language – an effort has been made and it's a big improvement. (Cathedral)

but others complained that they had:

fallen between two stools ... dumbed down to the point where it lacked the detail that professionals want, but still written in local government speak so the public won't want to read it. (Milltown)

The narrative style was also seen as being too bland to capture the attention of the media or the wider public:

> You need headline issues to generate public interest in the reports. (Midshire)

Local public service leaders felt that the Oneplace website did not contain sufficiently detailed information to allow them to benchmark their performance:

> it contains high-level stuff, it is harder to dig down into it. (Midshire)

but would not be used by many members of the public either. One chief executive told us:

> If you find one person in a 1,000 who have read the report, you'll be doing very well. (Midshire)

The results of our household survey bore out these perceptions. Consistent with previous research (e.g. IPSOS-MORI, 2010), three quarters of respondents said that they would like to be informed about the performance of public services, and 89% supported the idea that local public services should be subject to external assessment. Almost two thirds (63%) believed it would be good if inspectorates worked together to produce an overall assessment (like that provided by CAA). However, 79% of respondents admitted that they knew little or nothing about whether or how services were assessed. Just 5% claimed to know that joint assessments were conducted; only 3% said that they had read a CAA report. Of these, few could recall accurately what they claimed to have read. Only 27% correctly reported the star rating given by organizational assessments to their local services. Their recall of 'red' and 'green' flags was even less accurate. Only 7% of the very small number of respondents who claimed to have read a CAA report remembered the number of 'red' flags and just 12% recalled the number of 'green flags' correctly.

Just 1% (seven respondents) said that they had visited the Oneplace website. The inspectorates own monitoring of visits to the website site found that there were thousands of hits in the first three months following the publication of CAA reports. However, the vast majority of these were from local authorities and local voluntary organizations such as citizens' advice bureaus. Rather than being consumed directly by the public, the data were being used by professionals acting as 'intermediaries' on behalf of service users and the wider public.

Around half of all respondents to the survey of assessed bodies (53%) and over two thirds of those from local authorities believed that the CAA process did not engage local politicians, so they were not acting as intermediaries for the public. The involvement of councillors seemed to be limited due to the lack of clarity over their role in the area assessment, given that this focused on the local partnership rather than on issues over which they had direct control.

DISCUSSION

As Kurunmäki and Miller (2006) observed, there was a tension in the modernizing government programme pursued by the New Labour government in the United Kingdom between the desire to measure the performance of public services and the drive to reform them by encouraging collaboration. Sector-specific assessment frameworks focused on individual services or organizations and managers faced punitive sanctions for failing to achieve short-term targets. This discouraged collaboration among services to achieve 'cross-cutting' outcomes that required concerted action by local partnerships. CAA represents an ambitious attempt to develop a 'technology' that is capable of reconciling these two distinct and potentially contradictory pressures. These tensions are not of course unique to the United Kingdom, and CAA therefore offers a test of the feasibility of moving towards more holistic, cross-sector assessments of outcomes that take account of the value added by networks, which is relevant to theory and practice in many other countries.

The logic of a more 'joined-up' approach to performance assessment is compelling. The design of CAA was consistent with key features of new public governance, which emphasizes joined-up government, network-based approaches to public service delivery and citizen engagement (Osborne, 2006; Rhodes, 2000). Our evidence suggests that these principles attracted widespread support from local public service leaders, who also appreciated a process that gave more emphasis to local context and priorities. However, our analysis shows how difficult it is to deliver a more integrated approach to performance assessment within existing institutional settings. Some of the difficulties that were encountered might be considered to be 'teething problems'. Inspectorates were seeking to implement an entirely new approach to a very tight timescale. It is not surprising that they found it difficult to bring together data which each of them held for the first time. Some of the key complaints about the new system could have easily been rectified. For example, the burden of inspection could have been reduced by introducing a lighter touch, more proportionate risk-based approach which targeted areas of greatest need or concern. However, the causes of many of the problems encountered by the inspectorates and the LSPs they were assessing were more deep-seated.

Despite its emphasis on a joined-up government, central government continued to be functionally organized. The four national inspectorates charged with implementing CAA were sponsored by four different departments and proved unable, and in some cases unwilling, to develop a seamless approach. Their different cultures, traditions and reporting mechanisms meant that they had varying levels of commitment to CAA. The Audit Commission and local authorities emerged as the champions of the area-based approach represented by CAA. Ofsted and the CQC were more concerned with the performance of the particular services for which their government departments were responsible and so remained strongly committed to sector-specific assessment frameworks and operated these alongside CAA. As a result, CAA became another 'layer' of inspection that was placed on top of, rather than replacing, existing assessments and failed to deliver the anticipated reduction in the bureaucratic burden on assessed bodies.

The related process of negotiating 'cross-cutting' targets in LPSAs and LAAs against which CAA assessed performance highlighted similar problems. LSPs found it difficult to navigate their way through a 'maze' of government departments, each of which was primarily interested in agreements as a means of meeting its particular departmental objectives rather than as a way of addressing the local priorities identified by LSPs in their community strategies (Gillanders & Ahmad, 2007). The lack of joined-up working within central government remains a problem, which has resulted in different inspectorates continuing to work independently and using different approaches. For example, Ofsted has recently announced more rigorous unannounced two-week inspections of services for looked-after children while the CQC is currently consulting upon moving away from regular inspections of all organizations and back towards a more risk-based model.

Joined-up approaches to performance assessment also pose challenges for local services. In particular there are questions about whether and/or how members of local public service partnerships can be held to account collectively (Kurunmäki & Miller, 2006). In the case of CAAs, local authorities were treated as the lead organization for area assessments. Most welcomed this but they acknowledged that it took them into unchartered waters where they risked being held responsible for the performance of networks that depended on the actions of other services over which they had only limited influence and no formal control.

Assessing whether joining-up actually improves public service delivery is a significant challenge for researchers (Hodges, 2012). Our evidence provides some support that CAA has helped to focus attention and resources on big ticket items and cross-cutting outcomes such as economic regeneration, community cohesion and environmental sustainability, but these are difficult to measure as they are influenced by a host of factors many of which are beyond the control of local partnerships. Moreover, improvements to outcomes such as these take time. As a result, it is unrealistic for assessors to seek to establish causal links between changes in outcomes and the actions of partnerships in the short term and perhaps even in the medium and longer term.

Area assessments fell back on judgements about partnership processes and capacity, which drew heavily on existing reports including the self-assessments that LSPs had themselves prepared, and were reported in a narrative style that lacked the (appearance of) rigour provided by harder edged star-rating systems like CPA. Assessed bodies complained that CAA reports did not tell them much that they did not already know. They also suspected the processes by which assessors had reached their judgements had been somewhat arbitrary. Public service leaders were not confident that there had been a consistent approach to judging performance and so doubted that green and red 'flags' provided a robust basis for benchmarking performance or identifying good practice. They therefore found that CAAs were of less value and more time consuming than they had expected. As a result, just 20% of those who we surveyed believed that the benefits outweighed the costs and only just over a third (37%) favoured repeating the exercise in future years.

Apart from providing a more holistic framework and reducing the burdens on assessed bodies, CAAs were supposed to provide the public with 'user-friendly' evidence so they could hold local public services to account for their performance. However, our study showed that public awareness of CAA reports was very low and few of the citizens who claimed to have read reports could recall their contents accurately. The CAA reports were written in accessible language that avoided technical terms and managerial jargon and the Oneplace website provided a way of making these reports readily available to the public. However, supplying the data did not stimulate any great public demand for it.

CONCLUSIONS

In 2010 a newly elected UK government abolished CAA in order to cut costs, reduce the burden on local government and pass power from Whitehall to local people. It argued that this would 'free up' local services 'to enable them to be innovative in the delivery of services, rather than merely seeking to raise performance against centrally established criteria to achieve good inspection results' (Department for Communities and Local Government [DCLG], 2011, para. 22). This means that there is now no cross-sector 'technology' to assess whether partnerships are delivering, to examine what accountability processes are in place (both upwards to central government and downwards to the public) and, particularly important in the current financial environment, whether existing arrangements are providing value for money. In place of external assessments, ministers anticipate that local citizens will act as 'armchair auditors' who will hold services to account.

The experience of CAA casts doubt on this 'localist' strategy – on three counts. First, CAA was widely seen by local public service leaders as having encouraged improvements in partnership working. Without this external prompt to work in partnership, and facing significant budget cuts, local services may choose to focus on their core statutory duties to the detriment of attempts to address longer term and cross-cutting outcomes. Second, as the narrative approach to CAA illustrates, assessments that do not provide robust comparative data deprive managers of the information they need in order to benchmark the performance of their services and identify and learn from good practice. Third, in spite of a considerable investment of time and funding in providing citizens with independently verified, accessible performance information, CAA failed to spark any significant media or public interest. Evidence from other studies suggests that 'personal experiences, anecdotes heard and reports of critical incidents may be much more important' (Pidd & Hayes, 2005, p. 8) than inspections or performance measures in shaping public views (see also MORI, 2003, 2005). It is not clear that simply providing information to the public will be sufficient to ensure effective accountability.

In addition to raising questions about the decision to abolish CAA, the evidence presented in this article has wider relevance and suggests a number of avenues for future research on performance measurements that go well beyond the fate of this particular policy. It suggests that there is a need for research to assess whether existing approaches to performance measurement can, in fact, be adapted to the assessment of post-bureaucratic networked organizational forms? If so, what forms of evidence and evidence gathering are required in the context of partnership working? What are the implications for assessed bodies and existing assessment agencies? And what role can the public be expected and enabled to play in digesting performance information and holding public organizations to account?

REFERENCES

Agranoff, R. (2007). *Managing within networks: Adding value to public organizations.* Washington, DC: Georgetown University Press.

Audit Commission. (2009). *Comprehensive area assessment: Framework document.* London: Audit Commission.

Blair, T. (1998). *Leading the way: A new vision for local government.* London: IPPR.

Bowerman, M., Ball, A., & Graham, F. (2001). Benchmarking as a tool for the modernisation of local government. *Financial Accountability and Management, 17*(4), 321–329.

Cabinet Office. (1999). *Modernising government.* London: HMSO.

Clarke, J. (2008). Performance paradoxes: The politics of performance evaluation in public services. In H. Davis & S. J. Martin (Eds.), *Public services inspection in the UK.* London: Jessica Kingsley.

Commission for Health Improvement. (2004). *A commentary on star ratings 2002/2003.*

Currie, G., Grubnic, S., & Hodges, R. (2011). Leadership in public services networks: Antecedents, processes and outcome. *Public Administration, 89*(2), 242–264.

Department for Communities and Local Government (DCLG). (2011). *The audit and inspection of local authorities.* Memorandum from the Department for Communities and Local Government submitted to the CLG Commons Select Committee.

Department of Environment, Transport and the Regions (DETR). (1998). *Modern local government: In touch with the people.* London: The Stationary Office.

Downe, J., & Martin, S. J. (2006). Joined up policy in practice? The coherence and impacts of the local government modernisation agenda. *Local Government Studies, 32*(4), 465–488.

Downe, J., & Martin, S. J. (2007). Regulation inside government: Processes and impacts of inspection of local public services. *Policy & Politics, 35*(2), 215–232.

Dunleavy, P., Margetts, H., Bastow, S., & Tinkler, J. (2006). *Digital era governance.* Oxford: Oxford University Press.

Gillanders, G., & Ahmad, S. (2007). Win-win? Early experiences of local area agreements. *Local Government Studies, 33*(5), 743–760.

Hodges, R. (2012). Joined-up government and the challenges to accounting and accountability researchers. *Financial Accountability and Management, 28*(1), 26–51.

Hood, C., & Peters, G. (2004). The middle aging of new public management: Into the age of paradox. *Journal of Public Administration Research and Theory, 14*(3), 267–282.

Hood, C., Scott, C., James, O., Jones, G., & Travers, T. (1999). *Regulation inside government.* Oxford: Oxford University Press.

IPSOS-MORI. (2010). *What do people want, need and expect from public services?* London: IPSOS-MORI.

Keast, R., Brown, K., & Mandell, M. (2007). Getting the right mix: Unpacking integration meanings and strategies. *International Public Management Journal, 10*(1), 9–33.

Keast, R., Mandell, M., Brown, K., & Woolcock, G. (2004). Network structures: Working differently and changing expectations. *Public Administration Review, 64*(3), 363–371.

Kickert, W., Klijn, E. H., & Koppenjan, J. (1997). *Managing complex networks.* London: Sage.

Klijn, E. H. (2008). Governance and governance networks in Europe. An assessment of ten years of research on the theme. *Public Management Review, 10*(4), 505–525.

Klijn, E. H., & Koppenjan, J. (2000). Public management and policy networks: Foundations of a network approach to governance. *Public Management, 2*(2), 135–158.

Kooiman, J. (2003). *Governing as governance.* London: Sage.

Kurunmäki, L., & Miller, P. (2006). Modernising government: The calculating self, hybridisation and performance measurement. *Financial Accountability and Management, 22*(1), 87–106.

Lapsley, I. (2008). The NPM agenda: Back to the future. *Financial Accountability and Management, 24*(1), 77–96.

Ling, T. (2002). Delivering joined-up government in the UK: Dimensions, issues and problems. *Public Administration, 80*(4), 615–642.

Martin, S. J. (2000). Implementing best value: Local public services in transition. *Public Administration, 78*(1), 209–227.

Modell, S. (2009). Institutional research on performance measurement and management in the public sector accounting literature: A review and assessment. *Financial Accountability and Management, 25*(3), 277–303.

MORI. (2003). *Trust in public institutions. New findings: National quantitative survey.* London: MORI.

MORI. (2005). *What is the public audience for 'area profiles'? Qualitative research findings.* Unpublished study conducted for the Audit Commission.

OPSR (Office of Public Services Reform). (2003). *The government's policy on inspection of public services.* London: OPSR.

Osborne, S. P. (2006). Editorial: The new public governance? *Public Management Review, 8*(3), 377–387.

Pallot, J. A. (2003). A wider accountability? The audit office and New Zealand's bureaucratic revolution. *Critical Perspectives on Accounting, 14*(1–2), 133–155.

Palmer, A., & Thompson, M. (2005). *Public attitudes to taxation and public services.* London: GfK NOP Social Research.

Pidd, M. (2005). Perversity in public sector performance management. *International Journal of Productivity and Performance Management, 54*(5–6), 482–493.

Pidd, M., & Hayes, M. (2005). *Public announcement of performance ratings: Implications for trust relationships.* Lancaster University Management School Working Paper No. 2005/30.

Pollitt, C. (2003). Joined-up government: A survey. *Political Studies Review, 1*(1), 34–49.

Pollitt, C., Girre, X., Lonsdale, J., Mul, R., Summa, H., & Waerness, M. (1999). *Performance or compliance? Performance audit and public management in five countries.* Oxford: Oxford University Press.

Power, M. (1997). *The audit society. Rituals of verification.* Oxford: Oxford University Press.

Power, M. (2003). Evaluating the audit explosion. *Law and Policy, 25*(3), 185–202.

Provan, K. G., & Milward, H. B. (1995). A preliminary theory of interorganizational network effectiveness: A comparative study of four community mental health systems. *Administrative Science Quarterly*, *40*(1), 1–33.

Rhodes, R. A. W. (1997). From marketization to diplomacy: It's the mix that matters. *Public Policy and Administration*, *12*(2), 31–50.

Rhodes, R. A. W. (1999). *Understanding governance*. Buckingham: Open University Press.

Rhodes, R. A. W. (2000). New Labour's civil service: Summing-up joining-up. *Political Quarterly*, *71*(2), 151–166.

Scottish Government. (2007). *The Crerar review: The report of the independent review of regulation, audit, inspection and complaints handling of public services in Scotland*. Edinburgh: Scottish Government.

Skelcher, C., & Sullivan, H. (2008). Theory-driven approaches to analysing collaborative performance. *Public Management Review*, *10*(6), 751–771.

Stoker. (2004). *Transforming local governance: From Thatcherism to New Labour*. Basingstoke: Palgrave.

Sullivan, H., & Gillanders, G. (2005). Stretched to the limit? The impact of local public service agreements on service improvement and central–local relations. *Local Government Studies*, *31*(5), 355–374.

Turrini, A., Cristofoli, D., Frosini, F., & Nasi, G. (2010). Networking literature about determinants of network effectiveness. *Public Administration*, *88*(2), 528–550.

van Bueren, E. M., Klijn, E.-H., & Koppenjan, J. (2003). Dealing with wicked problems in networks: Analyzing an environmental debate from a network perspective. *Journal of Public Administration Research and Theory*, *13*(2), 193–212.

DEVELOPING STRATEGY TO CREATE A PUBLIC VALUE CHAIN

John Dumay

ABSTRACT

Purpose — *This article presents a hands-on example of how the Sydney Conservatorium of Music developed a new strategy to create public value in the lead up to its centenary celebrations in 2015.*

Design/methodology/approach — *Traditional research methods, such as semi-structured interviews (Qu & Dumay, 2011), alongside a strategic workshop incorporating a group discussion method called 'The future, backwards' are utilized to canvass the knowledge and divergent diverse views of employees, who would be impacted by the strategy, and to identify both the congruence and divergence of their views in order to help shape the value the strategic plan creates. The theoretical underpinning of the process is based on narrative (Weick & Browning, 1986) and the micro-sociological theory (Westley, 1990).*

Findings — *The process used here offers an insight into how strategic management can be developed in a public sector organization to help visualize its public value.*

Implications — *The process fills a gap in the academic literature and provides information for strategic practice by developing insights into*

Public Value Management, Measurement and Reporting
Studies in Public and Non-Profit Governance, Volume 3, 65–83
Copyright © 2014 by Emerald Group Publishing Limited
All rights of reproduction in any form reserved
ISSN: 2051-6630/doi:10.1108/S2051-663020140000003003

how strategic management can be successfully employed in a public sector organization.

Originality/value − *The process provides an example of a public sector based 'value chain' demonstrating how a public sector organization developed and articulated a public value creating strategy.*

Keywords: Public value; strategy; value chain

INTRODUCTION

In early 2008, I was hired as a consultant to assist the Sydney Conservatorium of Music to develop a new strategy in the lead up to its centenary celebrations in 2015. In developing the strategy, I approached the project from a bottom-up rather than a top-down perspective and involved the employees of the Conservatorium as much as possible. I did this because I wanted to use the knowledge of the employees, they being the people with knowledge of how the Conservatorium works on a day-to-day basis, to set out the detail of how the wider strategic objectives of the Conservatorium could be put into action to create public value.

To do this I used traditional research methods, such as semi-structured interviews (Qu & Dumay, 2011), alongside a strategic workshop incorporating a group discussion method called 'The future, backwards'. The main purpose of these methods was to utilize the knowledge and diverse views of employees, who would be impacted by the strategy, and to identify both the congruence and divergence of their views in order to help shape the value the strategic plan creates. The theoretical underpinning of the process is based on the micro-sociological theory, which takes an organizational perspective utilizing narratives and the micro-sociological theory to explain that when an organization's employees are left out of strategic development processes extensive dissatisfaction amongst staff can result (Westley, 1990). Being involved in the development of the strategy means that employees have both knowledge and ownership of the strategy and public value articulation, often lacking in many organizations.

The process used here offers an insight into how strategic management can be developed in a public sector organization to help visualize its public value. This is important because according to Moore (2013, p. 6) strategic management is 'a missing idea', which the public sector has not fully embraced despite it being a cornerstone 'to which much of the success of modern business had been attributed'. Thus, developing insights into how strategic management can be successfully employed in a public sector organization fills a gap in the academic literature and practice. As part of filling this gap this article presents an example of a public sector based 'value chain' (see Moore, 2013, p. 14) that demonstrates how it is possible for public sector organizations to develop and articulate a public value creating strategy.

THE SYDNEY CONSERVATORIUM OF MUSIC

The Sydney Conservatorium of Music (the Conservatorium) is a Faculty of The University of Sydney (Australia). It has a long history of developing fine musicians and is considered a world class music education institution, arguably amongst the best in the world (see Collins, 2001). Its primary goal is to continue to build on its success and to further cement its reputation on the world stage as it approaches its centenary of foundation in 2015.

In 2008, the Conservatorium had over 600 academic and support staff, servicing over 4,500 students in tertiary, secondary and community-based education programmes. In addition, in 2007, it conducted over 170 concerts and 290 student recitals, attended by more than 23,000 people. To service these activities it has a budget of about AUD$17M, the majority of which is related to expenditure on staff. In this operating environment, the Conservatorium is being challenged by a number of issues, including:

- securing the necessary financial resources to carry out the mission of the Conservatorium;
- acquiring the physical and human resources necessary to carry out the mission of the Conservatorium; and
- developing and communicating the Conservatorium's strategic intent, activities and public value to its diverse range of stakeholders.

To plan for these challenges the Dean initiated a project in July 2008 to develop a new strategic outlook towards the Conservatorium's centenary celebrations in 2015. This project involved the help of a representative from the Board of Advice to the Conservatorium, me as an external consultant, academic staff and professional support staff of the Conservatorium. The result of this project was the creation of a strategic plan, which was published as a formal public document.

For my part, I was engaged by the Conservatorium to drive the project and to be responsible for delivering the final document. I became involved with the project through my academic association, as a mature PhD student, with a member of the Board of Advice. Through that association the Board member became particularly interested in my PhD topic, which provided the potential to examine the Conservatorium's strategic issues from a different perspective. As a result I was asked to develop a project proposal and to submit it to the Dean for approval.

In this project, a total of 28 academic and support staff managers were interviewed or involved in the research process and the production of the strategy document (Dumay, Walker, Greenwood, & Wauchope, 2008),[1] which was also supported by other internal sources of information as outlined in Table 1. The participants were chosen because they represented a cross section of employees across the organization who would be impacted by, and involved in, changes in strategic direction. The initial focus was on developing an understanding of the circumstances of the Conservatorium, using interviews and historical documents. This was followed by an extended period of involvement with the Conservatorium's employees in the development of the strategy document, which culminated in the conduct of a strategic workshop called 'The future, backwards'.[2] From this, we jointly developed a strategic value chain for the Conservatorium, which is at the heart of developing and implementing strategy.

Table 1. Data Sources.

Data Source	Primary Format	Date Produced
Interviews with senior academics and support staff	Digital voice recordings and transcripts	July–August 2008
Strategic workshop with staff	Strategic map and handwritten feedback from participants	August 2008
Online survey	Excel spreadsheet	July–August 2008
Prior strategic plan	Printed document plus supporting soft copy computer files	September 2006
2008–2015 Budget working papers	Spreadsheet	July 2008 – work in progress
Various internal and external documents related to the Conservatorium	Hard copy and computer files	Various dates from 2000 to December 2008
Conservatorium website	HTML documents	As at August 2008

DEVELOPING STRATEGY THROUGH NARRATIVE

The initial challenging aspect of the project was developing the framework of the strategic document. A primary objective of the project was to develop knowledge sharing by grabbing the attention of the employees who would read the strategy document and act upon it. The issue of attention was central to the development of the new strategy document because the previous 'strategic business plan', which consisted of 159 pages of material including text, spread sheets, diagrams, graphs and pictures, did not receive the attention desired. The problem, as expressed by the Conservatorium's Dean, was that readership of the document was limited to the professional management and senior academics of the Conservatorium and the University – basically those whose job roles made it necessary to be concerned with the future strategy of the Conservatorium. However, readership did not extend to the remainder of employees, students and other interested stakeholders. The consensus among the Conservatorium's management and senior academics was that there was an abundance of information but little attention, beyond those required to pay attention, being paid to the Conservatorium's strategy.

The issue of information versus attention has long been problematic in the so-called 'information age'. As Simon (1981, p. 167) comments below, what is required in designing a strategy is not necessarily more information, but to have attention paid to the information the organization wishes to communicate:

> The first generation of management information systems installed in large American companies were largely judged to have failed because their designers aimed at providing more information to managers, instead of protecting managers from irrelevant distractions of their attention. A design representation suitable to a world in which the scarce factor is information may be exactly the wrong one for a world in which the scarce factor is attention.

Thus, the desired outcome of the strategy document was not just to provide information about the strategic intent of the Conservatorium, but to convey necessary information to the management and make possible the participation in the strategy process the community of staff, students and stakeholders.

One of the problems identified with the prior strategy was that it was produced for a particular audience, in this case the professional management and senior academics of the Conservatorium and the University.

Specifically, the numbers used in the development of budgets and to communicate financial aspects of the strategy required specialist understanding, which at times was not even understood by particular members of this group. It was important that this miscommunication and misunderstanding not be repeated in the new strategy.

As Weick and Browning (1986) advocate, there are two forms of communication affecting organizational structure: 'argument' and 'narration'. Argument emphasizes the need for a hierarchical system where qualified agents are required to judge the argument and other agents are meant to follow those who judge. By using numbers that only the experts in the University finance department and a few other qualified employees of the Conservatorium could understand, many employees were excluded not only from the development of strategy but also its implementation and control.

In deference to 'argument', Weick and Browning (1986) claim 'narration' opposes argument because it can involve all members of the organization. This is because humans are seen to have 'narrative capacity', which is the ability to judge the probability and fidelity of narratives (Weick & Browning, 1986, p. 249):

> ... because I am basically a storyteller, just like everyone else, and because I use stories to determine, justify, and guide the storyline that I call my life, whenever I judge any facts of any communication, I will ask, first, does it cohere, and second, does it ring true?

All employees can potentially become involved in the strategic narrative, rather than just the accountants, managers and stakeholders who understand the numbers. This emphasizes the relevance of 'narration', which is seen to give greater meaning to the organization as a whole. This is because argument only emphasizes the transmission of information from the sender to receiver, whereas narration represents interactions that create social reality (Dumay, 2008). Narration was beneficial to the Conservatorium because it directly addresses the challenge faced in communicating its strategy to all employees. Narratives are the way humans have communicated and shared knowledge since spoken language evolved, so unfolding a narrative about strategy is an effective form of communication to share their knowledge of the Conservatorium's strategy.

As Czarniawska (1998) outlines, stories (and narratives) must have a structure in order for them to communicate effectively; most importantly they must contain a 'plot'. Thus, the first step in developing a strategic narrative was to develop the 'plot' about how the Conservatorium creates value. The development of a plot to articulate a strategy to produce public value through music is a challenge that the organization had struggled with in the past because the value the organization generates is not monetary. Thus, in order to understand the value creation plot, a simple way of expressing the collective strategic imperative of the organization, as expressed by its people, was required. To do this I used semi-structured interviews with employees to elicit the strategic narrative about creating value.

When doing this I did not just simply ask the same questions of each employee. Here each interview built on one another and influenced the questions asked in subsequent interviews. This process allowed me to go inside the Conservatorium and gather strategic narratives by way of the employees' responses to my questions and then stand back to make sense of what they said. This approach is novel because the focus is not so much on the content of the data retrieved from the interviews, but rather on the situation at hand, which was to develop a public value creating strategy. Here, I was concerned with the subjective opinions and narratives of the interviewees as I sought to mobilize these to develop a cohesive outcome. The interviews were used to gather insights into how the interviewees viewed the future direction of the Conservatorium. Rather than disclosing a mirror of reality, the employees disclosed their vision of the future (see Qu & Dumay, 2011).

The development of the narrative surrounding the public value creation plot needs to reflect the desires and ambitions of the organization as articulated by its employees. This is important from an organizational perspective because when the organization's employees are left out of strategic development processes extensive dissatisfaction amongst employees can result (Westley, 1990). It is the involvement in what Westley (1990, p. 337), utilizing the micro-sociological theory, identifies as 'strategic conversations' that is important here as the interviews identified that employees were not satisfied with, or had no previous involvement in, strategy development in its present state. This was evidenced by the following comments from Conservatorium employees when asked about their knowledge of the current strategy:

> This suggests close familiarity with the strategy. Most people don't have this, including me. When I've looked at some of these documents, I've thought that the education role was somewhat sidelined — unfortunately.

> If you had provided a strategy document to read and then asked these questions it would make sense.

... but I can't answer ... until I have read the strategic document.

There was a lack of knowledge sharing about the previous strategic document because the strategy was created in a top-down fashion, with mainly senior management and senior academics involved in its creation. This approach is seen as being problematic from an organizational perspective because employees, especially 'middle-management', want to become involved in strategic conversations. As Westley (1990, p. 350) explains, there are two reasons for this:

> They want access to powerful coalitions within the organization and they want access to organizational sense-making. To the extent that the discussion of strategic generalities is not linked to membership in the top status group, and to the extent that there is a power balance between functional coalitions, the desire for admission to such conversations based on purely political motivations may diminish. The desire for inclusion in strategic conversations for purposes of sense-making is likely to persist. Sense cannot be injected in others in a unidirectional process of communication; it is apprehended only through discourse and response.

The concept of sense-making is important as it is considered a primary outcome of narrative (see Dervin, 1998; Kurtz & Snowden, 2003; Snowden, 2002; Weick, 2001). Thus, by planting the seeds of 'strategic conversations' in the Conservatorium and by involving employees, a strategic value creation narrative was allowed to evolve. It is important to note here that because the process utilized the 'voice' of the Conservatorium's people, the strategic narrative developed becomes a joint artefact of their 'voice' and the 'voice' of the Conservatorium (see Tull & Dumay, 2007).

To exemplify this joint creation of voice several excerpts from the interviews are presented, which form and contribute to the narrative. These excerpts exemplify the raw narrative obtained from the semi-structured interviews in relation to developing the 'Student profile' as part of a strategic plot:

> I also see a considerable growth in post graduate research and the research area, and that again we will have a more highly specialized and skilled faculty in a whole range of areas in music which involve research capacity, including performance and research orientation within performance, and I think that's already starting to happen.

> And when I went in 2004 to London and was told well we really don't want to send any students out there, the fact that students are now coming here and going back and forth that's one measure that shows that we've risen in international prestige.

> Funding constraints and increased requirements for international accreditation are forcing institutions to reduce UG [under graduate] numbers. For example ... our

undergraduate courses barely have the resources to cover the basic skills, let alone the secondary skills which provide depth in future leadership.

... students work in the profession for which they were trained, e.g., opera companies, teaching institutions ... [and] students can be prepared for research or research/performance careers and be employable in these areas. Students seek out this institution at a national and international level. Staff and students are able to spend their energies achieving these outcomes.

Thus, each interview contributed to revealing the plot of the strategic value creation narrative for the future of the Conservatorium. This collective vision is expressed in Fig. 1 as the Conservatorium's 'Strategic Value Chain'.

The elements expressed in the 'Strategic Value Chain' were derived from analyzing the responses to the interviews, supported by reviewing internal documentation. The purpose of the espoused 'Strategic Value Chain' is to provide a high level, simple, narrative articulation of the strategic factors that lead to the production of value by the Conservatorium. In this regard the first four factors ('Attract and Retain World Class Educators and Administrators', 'Attract and Retain World Class Students by Becoming an Institution of Choice', 'Develop World Class Research and Performances' and 'Develop Key Benefaction Support for the Conservatorium') represent the strategic inputs required to achieve organizational value represented by the last two links: 'Placement of Graduates in Leading Roles in Music Education and in the Music Industry' and 'Recognition as a Sydney Icon, Australia's Premier Music Education Institution and in the Top 10 in the World'. Thus, it is the elements of the 'Strategic Value Chain' that form the plot of the story to be told of how the Conservatorium plans to proceed strategically in the future based on the knowledge and desires of its employees.

It was from this perspective that 'The future, backwards' strategic workshop became an invaluable part of the development of the strategic plan. In essence the workshop permitted and developed a multi-directional, discourse and response, 'strategic conversation' that promoted and allowed knowledge sharing among the attendees. This then planted the seed for

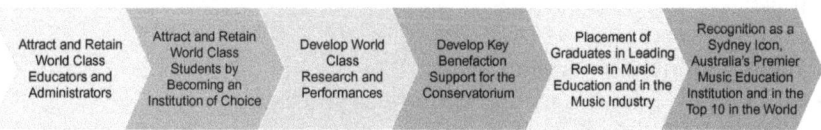

Fig. 1. The Conservatorium of Music's 'Strategic Value Chain'.

continued 'strategic conversations' over the ensuing time in which the strategy was being refined. It also served as a 'sense-making' mechanism for me as it enabled greater understanding and confirmation of the strategic plot that was identified earlier. Thus, 'The future, backwards' exercise was an invaluable tool in confirming the initial data collected from the semi-structured interviews and as a mechanism for involving staff in the strategy creation process. Additionally, it served to link individual opinions into a more cohesive 'voice' of the Conservatorium.

'The future, backwards' is a workshop method developed as an alternative to scenario planning and is designed to increase the number of perspectives a group can take on understanding their past and a range of possible futures.[3] Done properly it can help participants to discover entrained patterns of past perceptions about their workplace that are then used for determining its future. This allows participants to compare and contrast their different aspirations for the present and the future, which then becomes linked to strategy. The workshop I ran involved 12 of the 28 employees previously interviewed (intentionally without the Dean). The following text describes how I ran the workshop.

The first unique step in this process is the use of what is known as 'hexies', hexagon shaped post-it notes, custom made especially for this process. The hexies come in different colours and I used six colours to represent different aspects of the past, present and future as perceived by individual participants. The six-sides of the hexies allow them to connect better with each other when posted on a wall than traditional four-sided post-it notes. The post-it notes are also useful because participants can move them – and the ideas they contain – around on the wall during the workshop.

The workshop has five main phases. The first phase required participants to think about where the Conservatorium was at present and write whatever came to their minds on a hexie (yellow) and post (stick) it to the wall. When posting to the wall participants are encouraged to post each hexie next to another hexie with a related idea. Participants are also urged to move hexies around and rearrange them as new ideas are posted. During this initial phase I also explained the rules of the game, which are as follows:

- there is no right or wrong answer;
- be as creative, imaginary and extreme as you can;
- consider all behaviours, processes, characteristics, events, newspaper headlines, pictures – anything that helps describe the future state;

- do not channel all discussions/postings through one person – everyone contributes;
- discuss items and perspectives and experiences whilst posting – no silence!

In the second stage, I asked participants to look back in time to connect the series of events that led to the present and post these on the wall (blue hexies). There was no time limit and they were allowed to go as far back as they wanted. In the third stage, I asked participants to think of what heaven or hell as working at the Conservatorium would be like and post these ideas onto the wall (green hexies for heaven and pink hexies for hell). In the fourth stage, I asked participants to think about the series of events that would need to take place for either heaven or hell to occur and post these on the wall connecting from the past or present to the respective futures (light-green hexies for the path to heaven and light-pink hexies for the path to hell). The events that connect the past and present to the desired future (heaven) can be used to devise actions to be taken while the events leading to hell can be used to devise preventative actions (see Fig. 2).

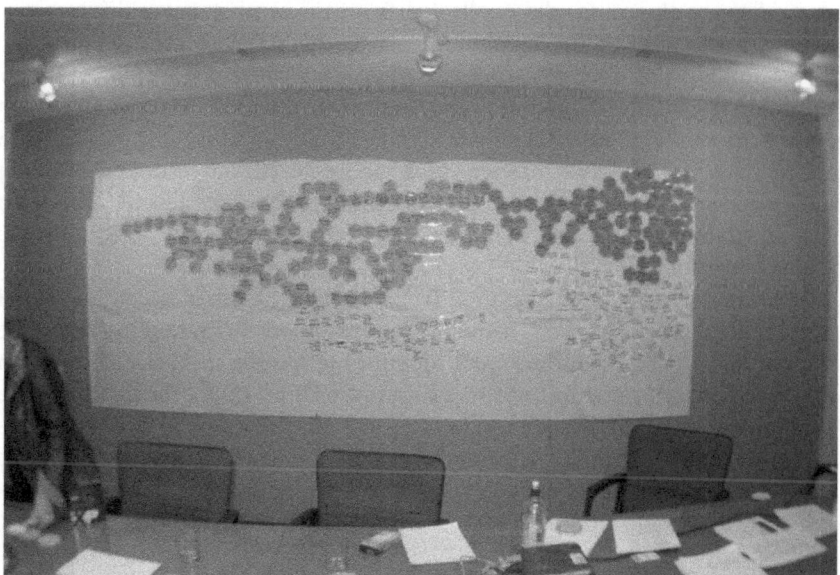

Fig. 2. The Completed 'The Future, Backwards' Wall.

'The future, backwards' strategic workshop permitted and developed a multi-directional, discourse and response, in which 'strategic conversation' enabled knowledge sharing among the attendees. This then planted the seed for continued 'strategic conversations' over the ensuing time the strategy was being finalized. It also served as a 'sense-making' mechanism for the attendees and for me as it enabled greater understanding and confirmation of the strategic plot that was identified earlier. This is evidenced in some of the feedback comments from the workshop participants:

> ... many complex ideas both positive and negative – good to give voice to both sides although much still based on effectively funding strategies.

> I have gained a better understanding of staff's concerns from different units and appreciate their honesty. Overall I also found that staff of the Conservatorium care about the place and the well-being of other staff members.

> It is interesting how much the comments engage with the Conservatorium's educational mission.

> Insightful experience is gained in terms of how people view the past and present and ... attitudes to outcomes.

Additionally, the 'The future, backwards' exercise was an invaluable tool in confirming the initial data collected from the semi-structured interviews and as a mechanism for involving staff in the strategy creation process. For example, the excerpts from the interviews presented earlier are now linked ideas, as developed in 'The future, backwards' workshop, which helped to make these ideas into a more cohesive story or plot. Fig. 3 shows how ideas from heaven such as research, government funding and increases in postgraduate student numbers become linked. This also served to link individual opinions into a more cohesive 'voice' of the Conservatorium.

The next excerpt is a narrative from the text of the strategic plan and exemplifies how ideas were brought together to contribute and formulate the strategic plot. Additionally, it identifies a specific initiative to develop postgraduate placements at the Conservatorium, thus transforming the plot into a desire for action.

Another core area for development is in our student profile. Over the past few years we have concentrated shifting the balance between undergraduate and postgraduate students towards greater postgraduate numbers. There are four reasons for this.

First, we are cognisant of the need for greater research output as the function of a University is for both the development of core skills and the

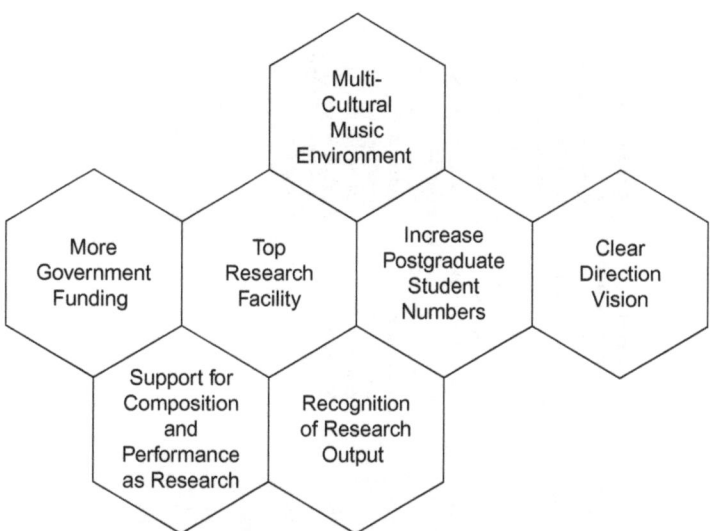

Fig. 3. Linkages between Strategic Concepts.

conduct of research. Thus, shifting the balance towards postgraduate places helps to increase our research outputs while at the same time maintaining core skill development.

Second, the manner in which Government funding is allocated to undergraduate degrees means we will continue to be challenged to meet the cost of delivering these programmes. By increasing the number of postgraduate positions the Conservatorium has the opportunity to diversify its revenue stream with income received from postgraduate student fees. These additional fees can then be utilized for improving resources for all students.

Third, the increase in postgraduate placements allows us to respond more quickly to the changing demands of students and the music profession.

Finally, this will afford the opportunity to increase the number of world class international postgraduate students at the Conservatorium. This is in keeping with the ever-increasing globalization and with the desire of the University to increase international student numbers through postgraduate studies. This in turn assists in raising the international status of the Conservatorium.

Within this narrative, the initiative of developing the student profile is identified as an important area of concern because of the need to develop increased postgraduate student numbers, which will in turn address

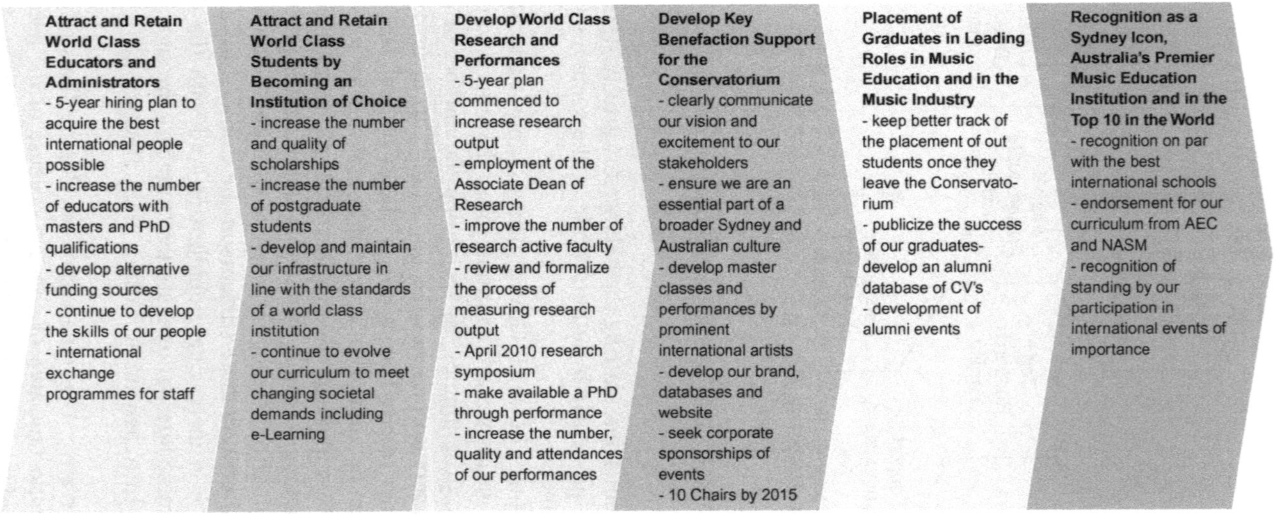

Fig. 4. Strategic Value Creation Plot and Initiatives.

Attract and Retain World Class Educators and Administrators
- 5-year hiring plan to acquire the best international people possible
- increase the number of educators with masters and PhD qualifications
- develop alternative funding sources
- continue to develop the skills of our people
- international exchange programmes for staff

Attract and Retain World Class Students by Becoming an Institution of Choice
- increase the number and quality of scholarships
- increase the number of postgraduate students
- develop and maintain our infrastructure in line with the standards of a world class institution
- continue to evolve our curriculum to meet changing societal demands including e-Learning

Develop World Class Research and Performances
- 5-year plan commenced to increase research output
- employment of the Associate Dean of Research
- improve the number of research active faculty
- review and formalize the process of measuring research output
- April 2010 research symposium
- make available a PhD through performance
- increase the number, quality and attendances of our performances

Develop Key Benefaction Support for the Conservatorium
- clearly communicate our vision and excitement to our stakeholders
- ensure we are an essential part of a broader Sydney and Australian culture
- develop master classes and performances by prominent international artists
- develop our brand, databases and website
- seek corporate sponsorships of events
- 10 Chairs by 2015

Placement of Graduates in Leading Roles in Music Education and in the Music Industry
- keep better track of the placement of out students once they leave the Conservatorium
- publicize the success of our graduates-
- develop an alumni database of CV's
- development of alumni events

Recognition as a Sydney Icon, Australia's Premier Music Education Institution and in the Top 10 in the World
- recognition on par with the best international schools
- endorsement for our curriculum from AEC and NASM
- recognition of standing by our participation in international events of importance

research, funding and student needs. This initiative will contribute to the desired value creation outcome of the strategy by raising the international profile and reputation of the Conservatorium.

The strategic value creation plot and related initiatives are summarized in Fig. 4, which shows how the planned activities of the Conservatorium can be articulated in a coherent and cohesive manner, devoid of argument (accounting numbers and concepts), so it can be understood by everyone, not just the experts. While it is important to have the narrative, the numbers can also be of use and should not be dismissed, provided that the narrative supports their inclusion (Mouritsen, Bukh, Larsen, & Johansen, 2002). In this case a set of numbers designed to measure the progress of the strategic initiative was advocated and its development is outlined next.

MEASURING THE PROGRESS OF STRATEGIC INITIATIVES

Developing the measures for the strategic initiatives was done by mapping the desired strategic outcomes as articulated in the narrative with available or desired measures. In developing indicators it was realized that there was a high likelihood that some of the desired measures would not be available as there may have been no need to collect these metrics in the past. The measures that were gathered are in response to, and correspond with, the value creation narrative. These are detailed in Table 2.

Table 2. Indicative Strategic Measures.

Measure	2005	2006	2007	2008	2009 (Forecast)	Desirable Trend to 2015
Number of undergraduate student enrolments	610	654	633	650	655	
Percentage of postgraduate students	15%	17%	19%	21%	23%	
Income from student fees ($,000)	775	1,036	1,045	1,354	1,770	
Percentage of international student load	6.2%	7.2%	7.1%	8.1%	8.9%	

Developing the indicators used in the strategic document is similar to the intent of measures developed for the Balanced Scorecard in that these measures are intended to provide a feedback mechanism for strategic initiatives in the future (Andriessen, 2004, p. 223; Kaplan & Norton, 2001). As shown in Table 2 the proposed measures are both financial (income from student fees) and intangible in nature. More notably these measures were developed as part of the overall 'strategic plot' without the need for specific frameworks to guide their development. This is important from a public sector perspective because as Moore (2013, p. 10) outlines it is important to:

> ... develop a concept of performance measurement that [is] strategic, not just technical ... the path to effective strategic management in government [runs] through the sustained, intelligent development of improved methods for recognizing public value creation.

Therefore, instead of using a predefined off-the-shelf performance management framework, we developed specific measures needed to monitor and communicate how public value is created and the strategy implemented.

This is considered important because there has been a raft of performance management frameworks developed, each advocating a specific issue to be addressed. This has been identified as problematic, as Andriessen (2004, p. 230) explains:

> In general, the field of ... performance measurement has paid little attention to organizational diagnosis and the 'why' question. It is often unclear what the organizational problem the methods intend to solve. Many methods ... can be characterized as 'solutions in search of a cause'.

Thus, the measures advocated in the strategy document are not 'solutions in search for a cause', but rather specifically targeted at understanding outcomes that can measure organizational performance in relation to the implementation of its strategy. Too often performance measurements seem irrelevant and lack meaning, even to the point of being misunderstood, especially if these measures are not tied to the strategic intent of the organization (see Ittner & Larcker, 2003); as has been outlined in the plot and subsequent public value creation narrative. Additionally, the strategy document does not contain the raft of measures that often accompany strategic documents. Here the intent was to keep the number of measures to a minimum so that they could be easily articulated and recalled. This is because there is a limit to how much information human beings can disseminate and transmit, which Miller (1956) postulates is generally limited to about seven simultaneous factors.

So while it is possible to include a plethora of measurements in strategy and performance management documents, there is the likelihood that there will also be a plethora of variances when comparing the results of measures against performance. In order to make the understanding of these variances meaningful people, as communication systems, transmit this information. Thus, the greater the plethora of measures, the more information about the variances must be processed and communicated. Too many measures and subsequent variances eventually leads to the what Miller (1956, p. 82) identifies as 'channel capacity' which is 'the upper limit on the extent to which the observer can match his responses to the stimuli we give him'. Thus, if a plethora of measures are created, the likely result is confusion as to which of the measures are important, which of the measures need to be prioritized when analyzing results and which need to be communicated and acted upon in order to guide the strategy.

CONCLUSION

In this article, I have outlined a novel bottom-up process used to develop a public value creation strategy using the knowledge of the employees of the Conservatorium. While the process is unique to this particular instance of strategy development it has implications for public sector managers in developing a public value creation strategy within their own organization.

First, it emphasizes the need to implement actions that promote two-way communications between employees rather than directives that merely present information or instructions to employees (see Shannon, 1948).

Second, it also highlights how a narrative, as opposed to numbers, allows the process of communication to develop, which in turn allows the public value creation strategy to be articulated and visualized. When managers outline a strategy in financial terms, most employees cannot make sense of the argument the numbers make because they are unlikely to have adequate expertise to judge what the numbers mean and take appropriate action (Weick & Browning, 1986). Additionally, it is difficult for the value created by public sector organizations to be quantified, especially in terms of dollars, because 'efforts to "monetize" the value being produced by public agencies and set it against costs incurred [is] particularly problematic' (Moore, 2013, p. 4). By allowing the public value creation narrative to unfold and be visualized, knowledge about how the strategy must be enacted becomes part of how the organization functions and is transferred to employees in a manner they can understand and act upon.

Third, the ability for employees to develop the strategic conversations further promotes a continuing discourse on the evolution of strategy (Westley, 1990). The development of strategy is, in fact, a continuous process that evolves over time and as the organization changes. Promoting a continuing strategic conversation in an organization thus has the ability to promote how public value is created because the conversations become ingrained into organizational life.

NOTES

1. A copy of the public version of the document can be downloaded from http://www.music.usyd.edu.au/docs/Conservatorium_LiteFINAL19Dec_2008.pdf
2. As the interviews were conducted during semester break some of the staff responded via an online survey and answered a similar set of questions as were asked in the semi-structured interviews.
3. For a more detailed explanation see http://cognitive-edge.com/library/methods/

REFERENCES

Andriessen, D. (2004). IC valuation and measurement: Classifying the state of the art. *Journal of Intellectual Capital*, 5(2), 230–242.

Collins, D. (2001). *Sounds from the stables: The story of Sydney's Conservatorium*. Crows Nest: Allen & Unwin.

Czarniawska, B. (1998). *A narrative approach to organisational studies*. Thousand Oaks, CA: Sage.

Dervin, B. (1998). Sense-making theory and practice: An overview of user interests in knowledge seeking and use. *Journal of Knowledge Management*, 2(2), 36–46.

Dumay, J. (2008). Narrative disclosure of intellectual capital: A structurational analysis. *Management Research News*, 31(7), 518–537.

Dumay, J. C., Walker, K., Greenwood, L., & Wauchope, B. (2008). *Strategic outlook 2008–2015*. Sydney: Sydney Conservatorium of Music.

Ittner, C. D., & Larcker, D. F. (2003). Coming up short on nonfinancial performance measurement. *Harvard Business Review*, 81(11), 88–95.

Kaplan, R. S., & Norton, D. P. (2001). *The strategy focused organisation*. Cambridge, MA: Harvard Business School Press.

Kurtz, C., & Snowden, D. (2003). The new dynamics of strategy: Sense-making in a complex and complicated world. *IBM Systems Journal*, 42(3), 462–483.

Miller, G. A. (1956). The magical number seven, plus or minus two: Some limits on the capacity for information processing. *The Psychological Review, 63*(2), 81−97.

Moore, M. H. (2013). *Recognizing public value*. Cambridge, MA: Harvard University Press.

Mouritsen, J., Bukh, P. N., Larsen, H. T., & Johansen, M. R. (2002). Developing and managing knowledge through intellectual capital statements. *Journal of Intellectual Capital, 3*(1), 10−29.

Qu, S. Q., & Dumay, J. (2011). The qualitative research interview. *Qualitative Research in Accounting & Management, 8*(3), 238−264.

Shannon, C. E. (1948). A mathematical theory of communication. *Bell System Technical Journal, 27*(July and October), 379−423, and 623−656.

Simon, H. A. (1981). *The sciences of the artificial*. Cambridge, MA: MIT Press.

Snowden, D. (2002). Complex acts of knowing: Paradox and descriptive self-awareness. *Journal of Knowledge Management, 6*(2), 100−111.

Tull, J., & Dumay, J. (2007). Does IC management make a difference? A critical case study application of structuration theory. *Electronic Journal of Knowledge Management, 5*(4), 515−526.

Weick, K. E. (2001). *Making sense of the organization*. Oxford: Blackwell.

Weick, K. E., & Browning, L. D. (1986). Argument and narration in organizational communication. *Journal of Management, 12*(2), 243−259.

Westley, F. R. (1990). Middle managers and strategy: Microdynamics of inclusion. *Strategic Management Journal, 11*(5), 337−351.

PUBLIC VALUE AS PERFORMANCE: POLITICIANS' AND MANAGERS' PERSPECTIVES ON THE IMPORTANCE OF BUDGETARY, ACCRUALS AND NON-FINANCIAL INFORMATION

Mariannunziata Liguori, Mariafrancesca Sicilia and Ileana Steccolini

ABSTRACT

Purpose — *The study contributes to the literature on public value and performance examining politicians' and managers' perspectives by investigating the importance they attach to the different facets of performance information (i.e. budgetary, accrual based- and non-financial information (NFI)).*

Design/methodology/approach — *We survey politicians and managers in all Italian municipalities of at least 80,000 inhabitants.*

Public Value Management, Measurement and Reporting
Studies in Public and Non-Profit Governance, Volume 3, 85–104
ISSN: 2051-6630/doi:10.1108/S2051-663020140000003004

Findings — *Overall, NFI is more appreciated than financial information (FI). Moreover, budgetary accounting is preferred to accrual accounting. Politicians' and managers' preferences are generally aligned.*

Research limitations/implications — *NFI as a measure of public value is not alternative, but rather complementary, to FI. The latter remains a fundamental element of public sector accounting due to its role in resource allocation and control.*

Practical implications — *The preference for NFI over FI and of budgetary over accruals accounting suggests that the current predominant emphasis on (accrual-based) financial reporting might be misplaced.*

Originality/value — *Public value and performance are multi-faceted concepts. They can be captured by different types of information and evaluated according to different criteria, which will also depend on the category of stakeholders or users who assesses public performance. So far, most literature has considered the financial and non-financial facets of performance as virtually separate. Similarly, in the practice, financial management tends to be decoupled from non-financial performance management. However, this research shows that only by considering their joint interactions we can achieve an accurate representation of what public value really is.*

Keywords: Performance measurement; non-financial performance; budgetary accounting; accrual accounting

INTRODUCTION

Public value is a multifaceted and elusive concept (Alford & O'Flynn, 2009; Bozeman, 2009; Williams & Shearer, 2011) that can be approached in different ways. Following Alford and O'Flynn (2009), it can be seen as: a *Paradigm*, responding to the challenge of balancing democracy and efficiency; a *Rhetoric*, designed to protect the sectional interests of bureaucrats and their organizations; a *Narrative*, a new lens for looking at public administration or as *Performance*, as a broader way of measuring government performance and guiding policy decisions. The latter definition of public value is the focus of this paper and is relevant for a number of reasons.

First, public value and performance are idiosyncratic in the public realm because of the absence of market mechanisms of control, the necessity of ensuring due transparency on political decision-making processes, the scant relevance of the profit measure and the importance of non-financial performance. Also, the ambiguity and complexity of performance, the presence of specific funding sources, the number and diversity of stakeholders (and, thus, information users) and the difficulty to match costs and revenues are some of the specificities of the public sector that require attention and consideration (e.g. Frumkin & Galaskiewicz, 2004; McKinley, Sanchez, Schick, & Higgs, 1995; Metcalfe, 1993).

Second, debates amongst academics and practitioners about performance measurement and management as a panacea in response to inefficiencies, ineffectiveness and lack of legitimacy of the public sector have increased (Lapsley, 1999, 2008; Pollitt & Bouckaert, 2004, 2011). Also performance measurement has become a controversial and critical issue, due to unexpected NPM implementation problems and effects (e.g. Hood & Peters, 2004; Lapsley, 1999, 2008, 2009; Panozzo, 1998). Public performance, indeed, cannot be merely assessed through the use of a single type of information, but requires the broader consideration of several aspects, data and criteria. These different facets of public performance are captured by different types of information. But which information is preferred by users?

The purpose of this study is to contribute to the literature on public value and performance measurement examining politicians' and managers' perspectives by investigating the importance they attach to the different facets of performance information. The extant literature has generally explored politicians' and managers' views and use of performance information separately, often focusing on one type of information at a time. In this contribution, we specifically consider both financial (i.e. budgetary- and accruals-based) and non-financial performance information and the views of organizational actors.

PUBLIC VALUE AND PERFORMANCE INFORMATION: DEFINITIONS, FACETS, USERS

Public Value as Performance

Value and performance concepts, definitions, measurement and management are affected by the specific features of the institutional and organizational contexts in which they are produced, perceived and interpreted.

According to the public administration and management literatures the differences between public and private entities (Boyne, 2002) will depend on ownership (Rainey, Backoff, & Levine, 1976, i.e. entrepreneurs or shareholders vs. political communities), funding (i.e. market prices vs. taxation/non-reciprocal revenues), and type of control (market vs. political forces) (Nutt & Backoff, 1993; Stewart & Ranson, 1988). From this, a series of consequences for the meaning and the measurement of public value as performance follow.

Public sector entities operate in a complex environment and must address the different needs of a multiplicity of stakeholders by performing a variety of activities and setting multiple goals (Ferlie, Pettigrew, Ashburner, & Fitzgerald, 1996; Metcalfe, 1993). This translates into the ambiguity, multiplicity and complexity of public organizations' goals and performances (Frumkin & Galaskiewicz, 2004; McKinley et al., 1995; Nutt & Backoff, 1993). Consequently, public performance has to be considered multifaceted and cannot be captured using narrow 'bottom line' financial information (FI) (Boyne, 2002; Farnham & Horton, 1996). More specifically, profit is not seen as a goal, but as a constraint for public sector entities (Farnham & Horton, 1996; Guthrie, 1998; Guthrie & Johnson, 1994), which should instead focus on non-financial performance. Public value cannot simply be captured by financial statements and, indeed, performance issues are wider than a mere evaluation of financial viability and encompass the long-term sustainability of political programmes and policies, and the capacity to pursue the public interest through the use of assets and the provision of services. As a consequence, performance and value measurement in the public sector has come to include both FI and non-financial information (NFI) and related tools and systems (van Dooren, Bouckaert, & Halligan, 2010).

The Financial and Non-Financial Facets of Public Value

Both FI and NFI are required to measure and evaluate public value performance. FI on public performance has traditionally been based on the budgetary model and intended primarily to ensure compliance with budget and limit spending. Under budgetary accounting, the adopted bases are obligation/commitment and/or cash (Jones & Pendlebury, 2000). Under the commitment basis of accounting, revenues are recognized when the right arises to a future cash inflow, and expenditures are recorded when the organization is committed to a future cash outflow. Under the cash basis, the accounting system records cash inflows and payments. Thus, the types of information available to users generally consist of expenditures (by nature and/or destination), revenues and funding sources, budgetary surplus/deficit and cash and attention is focused on budgetary compliance, the legitimacy of expenditure and the comparison between actual and estimated expenditure (Ter Bogt, 2003).

However, NPM reforms over the last few decades have recognized the increasingly important role of accrual accounting and NFI in providing relevant information and assessing the amount of public value created (Broadbent & Guthrie, 2008; Hood, 1991, 1995). The implementation of these processes has taken different paths in different countries and levels of government. In some cases, accrual accounting has replaced traditional budgetary accounting (especially in Anglo-Saxon countries), while elsewhere the latter has remained firmly in place. The literature generally views 'accrual accounting' as a defined and unequivocal concept. In reality, it is itself an umbrella term designating a wide range of solutions. A large variety of approaches can be found, ranging from the adoption of accruals reporting in conjunction with commitment-based budgeting, to the use of accrual-based data only for management control purposes, to the introduction of some sort of accrual-based management accounting for specific classes of inputs (e.g. supplies) within an otherwise traditional budgetary accounting system. Under the accrual basis, revenues are recognized when earned and expenses/costs are recognized when incurred; the final reports are the balance sheet and the operating statement (Anessi Pessina & Steccolini, 2007; Nasi & Steccolini, 2008). In the international literature, as well as in 'official' debates on public sector reforms, the accrual basis of accounting is claimed to have several advantages (Anessi Pessina & Steccolini, 2007), such as: (1) identification of costs of services and political programmes, emphasis on cost control, efficiency measurement and productivity, greater accountability on the use of resources; (2) easier definition of public-service tariffs; (3) greater attention to asset management; (4) more complete information on public organizations' liabilities; (5) possibility of measuring the impact of public policies on public organizations' financial position and long-term sustainability, focus on the long-term impact of decisions; (6) emphasis on intergenerational-equity measurement; (7) comprehensive evaluation of such choices as privatization, externalization, borrowing and so on and (8) possibility for constituents to better evaluate public organizations' performances.

Nevertheless, an increasing body of literature has criticized the adoption of accrual accounting by public organizations on both theoretical and practical grounds. From a theoretical viewpoint, Monsen and Nasi (1998, 1999) and Monsen (2002) argue that budgetary (or cash, or cameralistic) accounting is more consistent with the intrinsic nature of governments as discussed in the previous sections. From a practical viewpoint, the introduction of accrual accounting has raised significant implementation problems, and its actual results are still controversial (e.g. Anessi Pessina & Steccolini, 2007; Carlin & Guthrie, 2003; Guthrie, 1998; Hodges & Mellet, 2003; Liguori, Sicilia, & Steccolini, 2012; Nasi & Steccolini, 2008).

In addition to the emphasis on accrual accounting, NPM has also strengthened the role of NFI (ex-ante, ex-post, focusing on inputs, outputs, outcomes, etc.). The literature addresses the use of performance information to make decisions about service delivery as 'performance management'; on the contrary, 'performance budgeting' is referred to when performance information becomes part of the budgeting process during the development, implementation and evaluation phases (Rivenbark & Kelly, 2006).

As a consequence of the processes of modernization described above, three different types of performance information can be identified, which can coexist in the same organization and are available to internal users:[1] budgetary, accrual and NFI.

Politicians' and Managers' Views on Performance Information

Public value is potentially of interest to a number of stakeholders, and, thus, the number of potential users of public sector performance information is wide. Several studies have identified the actual users of public sector performance information and their preferences. For instance, they have shown that the number of actual users is generally small (Brusca Alijarde, 1997; Hodges, Macniven, & Mellett, 2002; Likierman & Vass, 1984; Nasi & Kohvakka, 2001; Priest, Ng, & Dolley, 1999) and that internal users appear to be more interested than external users (Atamian & Ganguli, 1991; Mack & Ryan, 2006, 2007; Steccolini, 2004). When considering the different facets of public value, and the various types of FI and NFI, several authors (e.g. Jones, Scott, Kimbro, & Ingram, 1985; Liguori et al., 2012; Mack & Ryan, 2006; Priest et al., 1999) have pointed out that users prefer performance information (i.e. information that goes beyond, but also includes, FI) to general purpose FI and budgetary (cash- and commitment-based) information to accrual information. Other authors have examined how managers use and see performance information (e.g. Lapsley, 1999; Moynihan & Pandey, 2010; Ter Bogt & van Helden, 2000), showing that accrual accounting is not always actually relevant in decision-making processes (Carlin & Guthrie, 2003; Hodges & Mellet, 2003; Jones & Puglisi, 1997; Newberry, 2002) and that performance measurement appears to be used more extensively (e.g. Mack & Ryan, 2006).

If in NPM reforms the role of managers as decision makers and direct users of accounting information has gained prominence, this has left the politicians' perspective in the background (Schedler, 2007). Indeed, only a narrow number of studies specifically take into consideration politicians' perceptions on the importance of information or compare them with managers' preferences. Several authors highlight a limited interest and use of performance information by political bodies (Brusca Alijarde, 1997; Ezzamel, Robson, Stapleton, & McLean, 2007; Paulsson, 2006), which rather prefer informal communication and NFI (Ter Bogt, 2001, 2003, 2004). According to Flury and Schedler (2006), managers are more interested in NFI and variable costs, whereas politicians focus their attention on full costs of services and benchmarking. Jansen (2008), taking into consideration the differences between politicians and managers, points out that the former focus on citizens and financial perspectives, whereas managers focus on internal (input/output) issues. Brusca Alijarde (1997) finds that politicians are among the least important users of financial reporting, due to insufficient training, whereas managers are the most important users. According to Ter Bogt and van Helden (2000), both politicians and managers prefer the old accounting tools and their related information. They tend to use mainly input-oriented information and hardly use the output-oriented information available. Paulsson (2006) finds that accrual accounting is used more in management than in politics and policy making. Finally, according to Liguori et al. (2012), politicians and managers' preferences tend to be more similar than expected, since they attach the same importance to performance information and are both very focused on external performance information rather than internal (similar results emerge in Saliterer & Korac, 2013).

The above literature review points out that the authors who have compared the information preferences of politicians and managers are still few, and that evidence is mixed. In the light of these gaps, the aim of our paper is to reflect, through the results of an empirical analysis, on the importance of the different information components that constitute public value for public sector managers and members of political bodies.

RESEARCH METHODS

To address our research aim we explore the perspective of the main two internal users: politicians and managers. In particular, we investigate politicians' and managers' views and the importance they attach to the different facets of performance information (namely, budgetary, accrual-based and non-financial). In order to carry out our research we conducted a survey on all Italian municipalities of at least 80,000 inhabitants (65 municipalities).[2]

Italian municipalities are an interesting representation of the continental European approach, characterized by the combination of the three types of information, where traditional budgetary accounting, kept under a commitment- and cash-basis, has been supplemented (but not replaced) by accrual-based reporting (balance sheet and operating statement) and non-financial performance indicators since 1995. The Italian 'flavour' of accrual accounting for municipalities is more precisely labelled as 'accrual-based reporting', since the budget is still structured according to the commitment basis of accounting, financial reports are similarly cash- and commitment-based, but they are also expected to include a balance sheet and an operating statement. Interestingly, double-entry bookkeeping is not mandatory. Alternatively, municipalities can derive their balance sheets and operating statements from their (cash- and commitment-based) budgetary-accounting statements through a complex system of year-end adjustments (Anessi Pessina, Nasi, & Steccolini, 2008). This long-term co-existence allows for an evaluation of the types of information and their use.

For each Municipality, three departments were selected in order to account for the heterogeneity of the activities (i.e. environment, public infrastructure and culture).[3] They can be placed along a continuum, where public infrastructures show the highest output measurability, followed by environment and culture. The top managers of the departments and elected politicians (i.e. those directly responsible for the services) were first contacted by phone (for a total population of 390 people) and subsequently administered an ad-hoc questionnaire by email. Respondents were asked to express their level of agreement on the overall importance attached to the different types of performance information as listed in Table 1, on the basis of a 1−5 Likert-scale[4] (where 1 = not important at all; 5 = very important). Also, public performance was considered as resulting from the assessment of elements within three different components: budgetary, accrual-based and NFI (see Table 2).

First, budgetary accounting items (i.e. revenues and funding sources, current expenditure by nature, current expenditure by destination, capital expenditure by nature, capital expenditure by destination, level of use of transfers from other levels of government, budgetary surplus/deficit, establishment of accounts receivable to be recovered and commitments to be paid) were adapted drawing on Pina and Torres (1996) and Anessi Pessina and Steccolini (2007).

Second, accrual accounting items (i.e. liability, liquidity, receivables, assets, cost of activities and services, depreciation) were named in a way to point out only the relevant pieces of information, which distinguish accrual- from cash-based accounting. They were selected on the basis of the relevant literature (Anthony, 2000; Funnel & Cooper, 1998; Kober, Lee, & Ng, 2010; Mellor, 1996), where, for instance, Anthony (2000) and Kober et al. (2010) point out the relevance of items such as costs, receivables, liability and assets; Anessi Pessina and Steccolini (2007) emphasize the role of depreciation.

Third, NFI was classified in terms of efficiency, activities and outputs, customer satisfaction, service quality and appropriateness and future activities (Pina & Torres, 1996). Respondents were asked to score the importance of all the above items, recognized to be the main pieces of information provided by each of the three considered accounting systems (e.g. depreciation can be retrieved only from accrual-based reporting). We investigated their overall perceived importance irrespective of the specific decision situation. This approach stems from the need to take into consideration the diversity of decision situations faced by our respondents and also reflects the methods adopted by previous studies (e.g. Brusca Alijarde, 1997; Jones et al., 1985; Moynihan & Pandey, 2010). Relying on respondents' personal opinion on the importance of the types of information, of course, does not provide an assessment of their actual use and influence on decision making. This could be the object of further research.

In order to investigate the importance of the types of information and their components, a statistical analysis was performed by comparing the significance of the difference in means between politicians' and managers' answers. In particular, a *t*-test for unpaired observations was conducted. As a further check on the validity of our results, we also performed a cluster analysis of the three types of information (budgetary, accrual-based and non-financial) including a set of personal variables accounting for the respondents' personal characteristics and background (i.e. age, gender, private sector experience, accounting education background, years of experience in the public sector, role (analysis available from authors)). The cluster analysis returned four groups with results similar to the *t*-test previously performed (i.e. the types of information still tend to cluster around the two performed roles (politicians vs. managers)) irrespective of the personal variables, which do not show particular patterns across the four emerging groups.[5] The importance attached to the different types of information, instead, still varies across the roles. The following sections report the results and the discussion focusing only on the *t*-test analysis.

FINDINGS

This section presents the views of politicians and managers on the different types of performance information. Table 1 presents the summary statistics. The overall response rate is 23% (104 respondents), where managers

Table 1. Politicians' and Managers' Information Preferences: Descriptive Statistics.

Performance Information	N	Minimum	Maximum	Mean	Std. Dev.	Variance
Future activities	101	2	5	4.22	.782	.612
Revenues and funding sources	100	2	5	4.19	.775	.600
Current expenditure by nature	99	1	5	3.76	.991	.981
Current expenditure by destination	99	2	5	3.89	.856	.732
Capital expenditure by nature	99	1	5	3.65	1.043	1.088
Cost of activities and services	101	1	5	3.81	.902	.814
Level of use of transfers from other levels of government	101	1	5	3.57	1.080	1.167
Budgetary surplus/deficit	100	1	5	3.61	1.081	1.170
Establishments of account receivables to be recovered and commitments to be paid	99	1	5	3.75	1.034	1.068
Compliance with growth and stability pact requirements	101	1	5	3.69	1.084	1.175
Liquidity	100	1	5	3.14	1.287	1.657
Debts	101	1	5	3.20	1.158	1.340
Receivables	101	1	5	3.08	1.181	1.394
Assets	100	1	5	3.16	1.061	1.126
Depreciation	99	1	5	2.76	1.221	1.492
Efficiency	101	1	5	3.81	.987	.974
Activities and outputs	97	1	5	3.74	.960	.922
Customer satisfaction	100	1	5	4.22	.836	.699
Service quality and appropriateness	101	1	5	4.28	.873	.762
Capital expenditure by destination	99	2.00	5.00	3.7677	.99825	.996
Valid N (listwise)	90					

represent 54% and politicians 46%. A preliminary ANOVA analysis showed that the type of department does not seem statistically significant in affecting the responses (all *p*-values are greater than 5%). The response rate across the different items is also quite consistent (the lowest rate is related to activities and outputs with 96% of responses).

Table 2 summarizes the results by distinguishing the information items into the three components defining public value: budgetary accounting, accrual accounting and non-financial performance. Politicians attach more importance to virtually every type of information, since their average perception of importance is higher than managers' (3.80 and 3.56, respectively).

We found that in no case did the type of department affect the preferences at a statistically significant level. This may appear counter-intuitive if we consider the body of literature that points out the relevance of task features (such as measurability, programmability, uncertainty) in influencing the focus of the information system (Chenhall, 2003; Merchant, 1982). Such a result suggests that, rather than being influenced by the type of activity performed, the perceptions on the importance of information reflect shared ideas, which tend to be similar within the same organization. The role played (e.g. politician vs. manager) thus seems to affect performance information preferences more than the actors' organizational position.

The results obtained show that non-financial performance is the most important type of information according to both managers and politicians (respectively 4.02 and 4.09), followed by budgetary accounting information (respectively 3.64 and 3.92). Accruals-based information appears to be the least appreciated by both categories of users (3.04 for managers and 3.72 for politicians).

NFI is ranked as the most important for both users. Looking at the individual rankings, managers attach the highest importance to future activities, followed by service quality and appropriateness, customer satisfaction, activities and outputs and efficiency. Politicians attribute predominant importance to service quality and appropriateness, followed by customer satisfaction, future activities, efficiency and, finally, activities and outputs.

Among budgetary accounting items, for all users the central issue appears to be funding sources (average scores 4.32 for politicians and 4.09 for managers). This is consistent with the traditional view of budgetary accounting in the public sector, where appropriations represent a constraint for expenditures and are, thus, the most important item to be considered in order to plan activities. As far as the expenditure information is concerned,

Table 2. Politicians' and Managers' Perceived Importance of Performance
Information: Differences and Overlappings.

Departments Information		Total	
		Politician	Manager
Budgetary accounting			
Revenues and funding sources	Means	4.32	4.09
	Std. Dev.	0.67	0.84
Current expenditure by nature	Means	3.77	3.75
	Std. Dev.	1.00	0.98
Current expenditure by destination	Means	3.89	3.89
	Std. Dev.	0.81	0.89
Capital expenditure by nature	Means	3.75	3.56
	Std. Dev.	0.99	1.08
Capital expenditure by destination	Means	3.84	3.71
	Std. Dev.	0.80	1.13
Level of use of transfers from other levels of	Means	3.82[a]	3.39[a]
government	Std. Dev.	0.87	1.19
Budgetary surplus/deficit	Means	4.02[a]	3.29[a]
	Std. Dev.	0.79	1.17
Establishments of account receivables to be	Means	4.07[a]	3.49[a]
recovered and commitments to be paid	Std. Dev.	0.90	1.07
Compliance with growth and stability pact	Means	3.82	3.60
requirements	Std. Dev.	1.10	1.07
Overall Mean		3.92	3.64
Accrual accounting			
Liquidity	Means	3.25	3.05
	Std. Dev.	1.29	1.28
Debts	Means	3.45[a]	3[a]
	Std. Dev.	0.99	1.24
Receivables	Means	3.23	2.96
	Std. Dev.	1.12	1.22
Assets	Means	3.41[a]	2.96[a]
	Std. Dev.	0.97	1.09
Cost of activities and services	Means	3.84	3.79
	Std. Dev.	0.78	0.99
Depreciation	Means	3.11[a]	2.47[a]
	Std. Dev.	1.22	1.15
Overall Mean		3.72	3.04
Non-financial performance			
Efficiency	Means	3.98	3.68
	Std. Dev.	0.90	1.04
Activities and outputs	Means	3.80	3.70
	Std. Dev.	1.00	0.93
Customer satisfaction	Means	4.28	4.18
	Std. Dev.	0.88	0.80
Service quality and appropriateness	Means	4.30	4.26
	Std. Dev.	0.90	0.86
Future activities	Means	4.11	4.30
	Std. Dev.	0.81	0.75
Overall mean		4.09	4.02

[a]Significant at 5%.

current data are overall ranked as more relevant than capital data by both politicians and managers.

Managers show a significantly lower consideration of the surplus/deficit, which is municipalities' 'bottom line'. The higher importance politicians attach to this item can be explained in two ways: on the one hand, the impact that the news about a surplus/deficit can have on the media and on the electorate; on the other hand, its impact on the future availability of resources (positive in case of surplus, negative otherwise).

Also the more 'technical' information on commitments to be paid and establishments of account receivables to be recovered[6] seems to attract the attention of politicians significantly more than managers. As these items are part of the surplus/deficit, this further strengthens the second explanation proposed above and casts some doubts on managers' attention towards efficiency, consistent with the findings concerning non-financial performance.

Finally, the information on the transfers by other levels of government is significantly more important for politicians than managers. The politicians' preference, moreover, can be explained by their higher sensitivity towards the actual amount of available resources, which is usually considered the main means for increasing political consensus.

Accrual-based information appears to be overall the least important. More specifically, accrual accounting seems to be valued especially for its importance in highlighting the cost of services and activities; whereas its role in representing consumption is surprisingly under-rated. Depreciation shows by far the lowest score across all the investigated items, although it is significantly more important for politicians.

Among accrual items, after costs, the 'best' relative rankings pertain to debts (significantly more important for politicians) and liquidity. These items recall the information traditionally provided by budgetary accounting. Moreover, both users appear to be more worried about debts than receivables. Such results can be explained by their necessity to control debt in order to comply with the Growth and Stability Pact.[7] This is supported by the relatively high score they give to the related item within the budgetary accounting group.

DISCUSSION

In this section the results are discussed in the light of the literature previously discussed, pointing at possible explanations.

Concerning public value, the most important information component for both politicians and managers is NFI. This makes sense because stakeholders are more likely to evaluate public value drawing on actual results rather than mere accounting figures. Moreover, NFI can capture the dimension of public value and performance that FI cannot represent: the external impacts of organization's activities.

Both politicians and managers place emphasis on the external dimension of performance. Our results indicate that managers feel responsible for service quality, customer satisfaction and the overall public value generated as much as politicians and is further confirmed by their emphasis on future activities.

The second type of information of relevance is budgetary accounting information, followed by accrual-based. All users appear to focus on liquidity, whereas politicians are more interested in information about financial resource availability, and final aggregate budgetary results (since they reflect the potential to satisfy their constituents and raise consensus). This information is mainly gathered from budgetary accounting documents. Even when considering accrual-based information, respondents tend to put the accent on those aspects that most resemble budgetary items. For example, managers do not rate as important information about solidity and assets, which should be, instead, acknowledged as the real 'value added' provided by accrual accounting. These differences may reflect the Italian strong traditional bureaucratic culture, which emphasizes conformity to predefined rules over the achievement of results themselves (Cristofoli, Ditillo, Liguori, Sicilia, & Steccolini, 2010; Hyndman et al., 2014).

The different importance attached to information leads to a further question: why does accrual accounting play the least important role in the assessment of the generated performance and value? There are different possible explanations for our findings. The first relates to culture and inertia (Cristofoli et al., 2010; Hyndman et al., 2014). Budgetary accounting, having being used for a long time, could be better known and understood by internal users. The second is linked to the context under analysis. In Italian municipalities, as in other continental European governmental entities, accrual-based documents have only supplemented budgetary documents, and can be simply derived from the latter through a series of year-end adjustments. As a consequence, accrual-based information is often seen as a mere formality due to the specific design of the system (Anessi Pessina & Steccolini, 2007). However, after more than ten years from the introduction of the new accrual-based tools, their perceived importance is still scant. In light of our results, one might also argue that the shift towards accrual accounting at the international level does not seem to answer users' actual needs for the evaluation of the value created. On the contrary, this tends to rely more on non-financial or traditional budget information.

CONCLUSION

Public value and performance are multifaceted concepts. They can be captured by different types of information and evaluated according to different criteria, which will also depend on the category of stakeholders or users who assess public performance. So far, most literature has considered the financial and non-financial facets of performance as virtually separate, giving rise to two almost independent streams of studies. Similarly, in practice, financial management tends to be decoupled from non-financial performance management. However, this research shows that only by considering their joint interactions we can achieve an accurate representation of what public value really is.

In this paper we propose a reflection on the importance internal users (i.e. politicians and managers) attach to different components and aspects of public value: NFI and FI (cash- and accrual-based). Through a survey of Italian municipalities, we found that overall, NFI was more appreciated than FI. Moreover, budgetary accounting is preferred to accrual accounting.

Overall, contrary to previous studies (Flury & Schedler, 2006; Schedler, 2007), there are few differences between the two categories of internal users. Preferences are generally aligned. Consequently, politicians and managers, although bringing different rationalities, represent two interconnected, rather than separate, worlds, giving the impression that they feel they are 'in the same boat'. This might be explained in part by the fact that the tools available for use by politicians and managers have been traditionally the same. As a consequence, they tend to focus on the same type of information, as they are not provided with any forms of differential reporting.

The preference for NFI over FI and of budgetary over accrual accounting suggests that the current predominant emphasis on (accrual-based) financial reporting might be misplaced. It could be worthwhile for both policy makers and practitioners to pay more attention to the peculiar relevance that budgeting, budgetary principles and budgetary reporting, as well as non-financial information, have in the governmental sector.

A final warning has to be expressed on NFI as a measure of public value. NFI, indeed, is not alternative, but rather complementary, to FI. The latter remains a fundamental element of public sector accounting due to its role in resource allocation and control. That their relative importance is recognized by users suggests that the financial and non-financial systems must be considered together, rather than separate, as two sides of the same coin.

NOTES

1. We adopt here the definition of internal users as actors who operate within the organization and are directly involved in decision-making processes.

2. From the total number of municipalities (68) we selected those where the elected political bodies are temporarily replaced by a central government delegate (3).

3. The selection criterion drew on Brown and Potoski's (2003) classification of output measurability of service provided. Measurability of output, in fact, affects both managers' ability to identify indicators for monitoring activities and politicians' ability to understand them. Moreover, it influences the contents of accounting tools.

4. Previous studies show that an intrinsically ordinal variable with more than four categories can be treated as continuous (Bentler & Chou, 1987; Ter Bogt, 2004).

5. The results of this further test are available from the authors.

6. These definitions are taken from the Council regulation (EC, Euratom) No. 1605/2002 of 25 June 2002 on the Financial Regulation applicable to the general budget of the European Communities.

7. The Stability and Growth Pact (SGP) is an agreement by European Union member states related to their conduct of fiscal policy, to facilitate and maintain Economic and Monetary Union of the European Union. Member states adopting the euro have to meet the Maastricht convergence criteria (an annual budget deficit no higher than 3% of GDP and a national debt lower than 60% of GDP or approaching that value) or try to adopt measures to gradually satisfy them.

REFERENCES

Alford, J., & O'Flynn, J. (2009). Making sense of public value: Concepts, critiques and emergent meanings. *International Journal of Public Administration, 32*(3–4), 171–191.
Anessi Pessina, E., Nasi, G., & Steccolini, I. (2008). Accounting reforms: Determinants of local governments' choices. *Financial Accountability and Management, 24*(3), 321–342.

Anessi Pessina, E., & Steccolini, I. (2007). Effects of budgetary and accruals accounting coexistence: Evidence from Italian local governments. *Financial Accountability and Management, 23*(2), 113–131.

Anthony, R. N. (2000). The fatal defect in the federal accounting system. *Public Budgeting and Finance, 20*(4), 1–10.

Atamian, R., & Ganguli, G. (1991). The recipients of municipal annual financial reports: A nationwide survey. *The Government Accountants Journal, 40*(3), 3–21.

Bentler, P. M., & Chou, C. P. (1987). Practical issues in structural modeling. *Sociological Methods and Research, 16*(7), 8–117.

Boyne, G. A. (2002). Public and private management: What's the difference? *Journal of Management Studies, 39*(1), 97–122.

Bozeman, B. (2009). Public values theory: Three big questions. *International Journal of Public Policy, 4*(5), 369–375.

Broadbent, J., & Guthrie, J. (2008). Public sector to public services: 20 years of alternative accounting research. *Accounting, Auditing and Accountability Journal, 21*(2), 129–169.

Brown, T. L., & Potoski, M. (2003). Transaction costs and institutional explanations for government service production decisions. *Journal of Public Administration Research and Theory, 13*(4), 441–468.

Brusca Alijarde, M. I. (1997). The usefulness of financial reporting in Spanish local governments. *Financial Accountability and Management, 13*(1), 17–34.

Carlin, T. M., & Guthrie, J. (2003). Accrual output based budgeting systems in Australia. *Public Management Review, 5*(2), 145–162.

Chenhall, R. H. (2003). Management control systems design within its organizational context: Findings from contingency-based research and directions for the future. *Accounting, Organizations and Society, 28*(2–3), 127–168.

Cristofoli, D., Ditillo, A., Liguori, M., Sicilia, M., & Steccolini, I. (2010). Do environmental and task characteristics matter in the control of externalized local public services? Unveiling the relevance of party characteristics and citizens offstage voice. *Accounting, Audit and Accountability Journal, 23*(3), 350–372.

Ezzamel, M., Robson, K., Stapleton, P., & McLean, C. (2007). Discourse and institutional change: Giving accounts and accountability. *Management Accounting Research, 18*(2), 150–171.

Farnham, D., & Horton, S. (1996). Managing public and private organizations. In D. Farnham & S. Horton (Eds.), *Managing the new public services*. London: Macmillan.

Ferlie, E., Pettigrew, A., Ashburner, L., & Fitzgerald, L. (1996). *The new public management in action*. Oxford: Oxford University Press.

Flury, R., & Schedler, K. (2006). Political versus managerial use of cost and performance accounting. *Public Money and Management, 26*(4), 229–234.

Frumkin, P., & Galaskiewicz, J. (2004). Institutional isomorphism and public sector organizations. *Journal of Public Administration Research and Theory, 14*(3), 283–307.

Funnel, W., & Cooper, K. (1998). *Public sector accounting and accountability in Australia*. Sydney: University of New South Wales Press.

Guthrie, J. (1998). Application of accrual accounting in the Australian public sector: Rhetoric or reality? *Financial Accountability and Management, 14*(1), 1–19.

Guthrie, J., & Johnson, M. (1994). Commercialisation of the public sector: Why, how and for what? A prospective view? In K. Wiltshire (Ed.), *Governance and economic efficiency* (pp. 87–108). Sydney: CEDA.

Hodges, R., Macniven, L., & Mellett, H. (2002). Annual reporting mechanisms of national health care service trusts. *Public Money and Management, 22*(3), 49–54.

Hodges, R., & Mellet, H. (2003). Reporting public sector financial results. *Public Management Review, 5*(1), 99–113.

Hood, C. (1991). A public management for all seasons. *Public Administration, 69*(Spring), 3–19.

Hood, C. (1995). The new public management in the 1980s: Variations on a theme. *Accounting, Organizations and Society, 20*(2–3), 93–109.

Hood, C., & Peters, G. (2004). The middle aging of new public management: Into the age of paradox? *Journal of Public Administration Research and Theory, 14*(3), 267–282.

Hyndman, N., Liguori, M., Meyer, R. E., Polzer, T., Rota, S., & Seiwald, J. (2014). The translation and sedimentation of accounting reforms. A comparison of the UK, Austrian and Italian experiences. *Critical Perspective on Accounting, 25*(4/5), 388–408.

Jansen, E. P. (2008). New public management: Perspectives on performance and the use of performance information. *Financial Accountability and Management, 24*(2), 169–191.

Jones, D. B., Scott, R. B., Kimbro, L., & Ingram, R. (1985). *The needs of users of governmental financial reports*. Stamford: Government Accounting Standards Board.

Jones, R., & Pendlebury, M. (2000). *Public sector accounting*. Harlow: Pearson.

Jones, S., & Puglisi, N. (1997). The relevance of AAS 29 to the Australian public sector: A case for doubt? *Abacus, 33*(1), 115–133.

Kober, R., Lee, J., & Ng, J. (2010). Mind your accruals: Perceived usefulness of financial information in the Australian public sector under different accounting systems. *Financial Accountability and Management, 26*(3), 267–298.

Lapsley, I. (1999). Accounting and the new public management: Instruments of substantive efficiency or a rationalizing modernity? *Financial Accountability and Management, 15*(3–4), 201–208.

Lapsley, I. (2008). The NPM agenda: Back to the future. *Financial Accountability and Management, 24*(7), 7–96.

Lapsley, I. (2009). New public management: The cruellest invention of the human spirit? *Abacus, 45*(1), 1–21.

Liguori, M., Sicilia, M., & Steccolini, I. (2012). Some like it non-financial … Politicians and managers views on the importance of performance information. *Public Management Review, 14*(7), 903–922.

Likierman, A., & Vass, P. (1984). *Structure and form of government expenditure reports: Proposals for reform*. London: Chartered Association of Certified Accountants.

Mack, J., & Ryan, C. (2006). Reflections on the theoretical underpinnings of the general-purpose financial reports of Australian government departments. *Accounting, Auditing and Accountability Journal, 19*(4), 592–612.

Mack, J., & Ryan, C. (2007). Is there an audience for public sector annual reports: Australian evidence? *International Journal of Public Sector Management, 20*(2), 134–146.

McKinley, W., Sanchez, C. M., Schick, A. G., & Higgs, A. C. (1995). Organizational downsizing: Constraining, cloning, learning. *Academy of Management Executive, 9*(3), 32–44.

Mellor, T. (1996). Why governments should produce balance sheets. *Australian Journal of Public Administration, 55*(1), 78–81.

Merchant, K. (1982). The control function of management. *Sloan Management Review, 23*(4), (Summer), 43–55.

Metcalfe, L. (1993). Public management: From imitation to innovation. In J. Kooiman (Ed.), *Modern governance*. London: Sage.

Monsen, N. (2002). The case for cameral accounting. *Financial Accountability and Management, 18*(1), 39–72.

Monsen, N., & Nasi, S. (1998). The contingency model of governmental accounting innovations: A discussion. *The European Accounting Review, 7*(2), 75−288.

Monsen, N., & Nasi, S. (1999). Comparing cameral and accrual accounting in local governments. In A. D. Bac (Ed.), *International comparative issues in government accounting*. Boston, MA: Kluwer.

Moynihan, D. P., & Pandey, S. K. (2010). The big question for performance management: Why do managers use performance information? *Journal of Public Administration Research and Theory, 20*(4), 849−866.

Nasi, G., & Steccolini, I. (2008). Implementation of accounting reforms. An empirical investigation into Italian local governments. *Public Management Review, 10*(2), 173−194.

Nasi, S., & Kohvakka, J. (2001). Perceived usefulness of accrual accounting information in central government agencies in Finland − A survey study. Presented at the Annual Congress, European Accounting Association.

Newberry, S. M. (2002). The conceptual framework sham. *Australian Accounting Review, 12*(3), 47−49.

Nutt, P., & Backoff, R. (1993). Organizational publicness and its implications for strategic management. *Journal of Public Administration Research and Theory, 3*, 209−231.

Panozzo, F. (1998). Management by decree. Paradoxes in the reform of the Italian public sector. *Scandinavian Journal of Management, 16*(4), 357−373.

Paulsson, J. (2006). Accrual accounting in the public sector: Experiences from the central government in Sweden. *Financial Accountability and Management, 22*(1), 47−62.

Pina, V., & Torres, L. (1996). Methodological aspects in efficiency evaluation of public hospitals. *Financial Accountability and Management, 12*(1), 21−36.

Pollitt, C., & Bouckaert, G. (2004). *Public sector reform. A comparative analysis*. Oxford: Oxford University Press.

Pollitt, C., & Bouckaert, G. (2011). *Public sector reform. A comparative analysis: New public management, governance, and the neo-Weberian state* (3rd ed.). Oxford: Oxford University Press.

Priest, A., Ng, J., & Dolley, C. (1999). Users of local government annual reports: Information preferences. *Accounting, Accountability and Performance, 5*(3), 49−62.

Rainey, H., Backoff, R., & Levine, C. (1976). Comparing public and private organizations. *Public Administration Review, 36*(2), 33−44.

Rivenbark, W. C., & Kelly, J. M. (2006). Performance budgeting in municipal government. *Public Performance and Management Review, 30*(1), 5−46.

Saliterer, I., & Korac, S. (2013). Performance information use by politicians and public managers for internal control and external accountability purposes. *Critical Perspectives on Accounting, 24*(7−8), 502−517.

Schedler, K. (2007). Unleashing change. A study of organizational renewal in government. *Public Administration, 85*(1), 246−248.

Steccolini, I. (2004). Is the annual report an accountability medium? An empirical investigation into Italian local governments. *Financial Accountability and Management, 20*(3), 327−350.

Stewart, J., & Ranson, S. (1988). Management in the public domain. *Public Money and Management, 8*(2), 13−19.

Ter Bogt, H. (2001). Politicians and output-oriented performance evaluation in municipalities. *European Accounting Review, 10*(3), 621−643.

Ter Bogt, H. (2003). Performance evaluation styles in governmental organizations: How do professional managers facilitate politicians work? *Management Accounting Research, 14*(4), 311−332.

Ter Bogt, H. (2004). Politicians in search of performance information. *Financial Accountability and Management, 20*(3), 221–252.

Ter Bogt, H., & van Helden, G. J. (2000). Accounting change in Dutch government: Exploring the gap between expectations and realizations. *Management Accounting Research, 11*(2), 263–279.

van Dooren, W., Bouckaert, G., & Halligan, J. (2010). *Performance management in the public sector*. London, New York: Routledge.

Williams, I., & Shearer, H. (2011). Appraising public value: Past, present and futures. *Public Administration, 89*(4), 1367–1384.

THE QUEST FOR PUBLIC VALUE IN THE SWEDISH MUSEUM TRANSITION

Kerstin Thomson, Mikael Holmgren Caicedo and Maria Mårtensson

ABSTRACT

Purpose — *The aim of this paper is to investigate the nature of public value in the context of Swedish public museum management and how it is created.*

Design/methodology/approach — *The museum context is introduced, and assumptions and principles underpinning new public management (NPM) and public value management, along with examples of applicability and implementation in museums, are presented. Three key issues of convergence and divergence within the theoretical framework — strategic orientation, accountability and performance — are identified and introduced as a gateway to the empirical findings and the ensuing discussion.*

Findings — *NPM-oriented values have become part of the strategic orientation of the museum sector. The results of this study show that there exist at least three conceptions of museum management that are*

Public Value Management, Measurement and Reporting
Studies in Public and Non-Profit Governance, Volume 3, 105–128
ISSN: 2051-6630/doi:10.1108/S2051-663020140000003005

based on two different strategic orientations, that is, accessibility and conservation, which also point to different conceptions of value.

Social implications – *Museum management can be seen as the management of tensions between conservation and accessibility and between customer orientation and stakeholder orientation towards the creation of museum value.*

Originality/value – *The findings will assist museum management determine not only what value is but also for whom it is valuable, taking into account both present and future generations.*

Keywords: Museum; Sweden; public value management; new public management

INTRODUCTION

By the early 1980s a new discourse had begun, first in academia and later amongst the political elite, which paved the way for a new design and delivery regime in public organizations (Osborne, 2011). It was termed 'new public management' (NPM). NPM was articulated as a label for the shift in public management style (Hood, 1991, 1995) from traditional public administration, which was firmly linked to the welfare state and where the role of managers was to ensure that rules and appropriate procedures were followed (Stoker, 2006), to models and clusters of ideas from the conceptual framework of private sector practice. As a consequence, traditional public administration practices were conceptualized into management and accountability issues, and the citizen became a customer or consumer.

Albeit to varying degrees, NPM has touched every branch of the public sector. However, NPM was considered to be applied to 'harder' sectors like regulation of utilities such as telecommunications and energy, but the distinction between 'harder' and 'softer' policy areas has come into question (Christensen & Laegreid, 2011). Now NPM practices also include policy areas such as welfare administration, universities and culture. In this paper we aim to focus on the issue of public value creation in a 'softer' public policy area, namely culture, and specifically, in museums.

As argued by Painter (2011), many of the prevailing features of managerialism are the product of lessons learnt from the failings of NPM, rather than being one more private sector import. Moreover, there are lessons that have been learned within the public sector that, contrary to the emphasis on management as a generic and purely instrumental activity (Saint-Martin, 2000), point to the issue of public value and its creation as the distinctive feature of public management (Moore, 1995). In other words, the creation of public value is conceptualized as the central activity of public managers, just as the creation of private value would be the central activity of private sector managers. But the issue of value creation in the public sector poses several questions: for whom and how is value created? How can it be evaluated and sustained? If researchers can advance, even incrementally, the study of public value beyond its current ambiguous and unbounded status, then those advances could serve many different theory developments and practical purposes (Joergensen & Bozeman, 2007).

NPM features in museums include not only the much-debated effects of the emphasis on commercialism and misguided accounting practices (e.g. Carnegie & Wolnizer, 1996; Hooper, Kearins, & Green, 2005; Thompson, 2001), but also the value-enhancing effects of audience focus and increased professionalization (e.g. Foley & McPherson, 2000; Gilmore & Rentschler, 2002; Kotler & Kotler, 2000). For instance, Griffin and Abraham (2001) argue that, in assessing a museum's merits, the focus must be on how to develop the critical values that distinguish museums from other public institutions, and how they contribute to the community and to society, even to the uplifting of the human spirit. Accordingly, they argue, it is these roles that many governments have forgotten in the pursuit of just financial resources.

We now pose a further question: what is public value in the context of public museum management and how is it created?

In what follows, we briefly introduce the museum context, and the transition from having a primarily custodial role to being an institution in the service of society. As the museums in this study are public museums, subject to policies influenced by concepts of public value, we present assumptions and principles underpinning NPM and public value management (PVM), along with examples reported on applicability and implementation in museums. Finally, three key issues of convergence and divergence within the theoretical framework are identified and introduced as a gateway to the empirical findings and the ensuing discussion.

THE MUSEUM CONTEXT

Museums are part of our cultural heritage and have traditionally and predominately been custodial institutions with a prime interest in collecting and preserving (Gilmore & Rentschler, 2002). Based on an educational ideal that valued the delivery of information, the objectivity of facts and the transferability of knowledge, museums fulfilled their purpose by producing authoritative, didactic displays, which were arranged to illustrate conventional hierarchies and classifications. However, the focus has gradually changed, and museums are no longer seen as sites that passively preserve and exhibit received cultural capital. This change is reflected, for instance, in the statutes of the International Council of Museums (ICOM), and the changes in the aims and definitions of museums that have taken place therein. Whereas museums were described in 1946 as 'collections open to the public' (ICOM, 2007), in contemporary times they reflect a changing societal environment:

> A museum is a non-profit, permanent institution in the service of society and its development, open to the public, which acquires, conserves, researches, communicates and exhibits the tangible and intangible heritage of humanity and its environment for the purposes of education, study and enjoyment. (ICOM, 2007)

For museums to be outstanding depends on their purpose, the value of their collections and the quality of their programmes. Management is only one of several dimensions of a museum's operations, but it is arguably one of the critical prerequisites to successful operation and therefore requires attention.

The museums in the empirical study below are Swedish state agencies, subject to changes in the governmental framework, as well as changes in the focus of museum operations.

NEW PUBLIC MANAGEMENT IN MUSEUMS

NPM brought together assumptions and principles, articulated as doctrines by Hood (1991, 1995), in what has been described by Pollitt and Bouckaert (2000) as a 'shopping basket', multi-facetted and adjustable to suit intentions to change. Adapted by Boston (2011) and complemented with references to other public sector researchers, the following illustrates how NPM draws on agency theory and managerialism.

First, there is a stress on private sector styles, that is, a belief that differences between public and private sector organizations are not generally significant; they can − and should − be managed on more or less the same basis (see also Benington & Moore, 2011; Christensen & Laegreid, 2011; Lapsley, 2008). Also, there is an emphasis on management rather than policy, in particular a stress on management as a generic, purely instrumental activity. Second, there is an emphasis on visible hands-on management; a preference for straight-line accountability, with single rather than multiple principals, vertical rather than horizontal accountability and unitary rather than collective leadership. Third, there is a stress on cost cutting and efficiency, and a dis-aggregation of public services to their most basic units with a focus on cost management (Osborne, 2011). There is an emphasis on inputs and outputs control, evaluation, performance management and audit (Osborne, 2011), a shift from process accountability to accountability for results.

NPM advanced the introduction of 'economic rationality' to the public sector. Policy prescriptions shaped by neo-liberalism provided a strong foundation as lower economic growth and large fiscal deficits called for expenditure savings, inevitably affecting the resources available to public agencies (Boston, 2011). Verhoest, Roness, Verschuere, Rubecksen, and MacCarthaigh (2010) highlight the specific feature of the 'policy– operations' split, dividing public sector tasks into policy preparation and policy operations. Policy preparation is to be performed by those who are democratically legitimated. Policy operations are to be performed by agencies, mainly as implementers, with either no role or a small one in policy. Thus accountability was redefined from political accountability to managerial accountability (Broadbent & Laughlin, 2003). In New Zealand, an early adopter of NPM, a call was made for using more measurable standards and financial data for managerial accountability. Such a governmental requirement to report service performance by way of performance indicators was, however, criticized by museums for being based on crude indicators and stressing accounting-based measures (Thompson, 2001), as well as being a one-size-fits-all application of an accounting standard to entities differentiated in their purpose (Carnegie & Wolnizer, 1996; Hooper et al., 2005).

Nonetheless, NPM practices found their way into domains not traditionally governed by rationales of economic logic and accounting such as healthcare, education and, in this particular case, public museums (Cooper & Hopper, 2007). Indeed, increased economic strain, squeezed budgets and the need to make public funding a priority caused tighter regulation for public sector accounting (Thompson, 2001) and accountability (Carnegie & Wolnizer, 1996; Rentschler & Potter, 1996), which subsequently have affected publicly financed museums and other domains.

The focus on consumer orientation and customer service is an example of a common denominator of NPM in public services and service management in the private sector. Thus, it was not surprising that service management ideas diffused to government service activities, given the extent to which service management ideas swept through the private sector (Fountain, 2001). In a market-oriented approach in line with NPM, experience became accepted as the outcome, or 'product' of the museum (Kotler & Kotler, 2000), with the museum as a provider and the visitors as customers that consume the museums' services as a part of their leisure experience. As Kesner (2006) argues, such views marginalize the aesthetic encounter and make it equal to a commodity, which museums are expected to package and deliver. According to Zan, Bonini, and Gordon (2007), the wholesale adoption of marketing practice might well lead to the detriment of activities rooted in research and preservation of cultural heritage as a public good.

Introducing NPM practices in the museum setting has also raised a discussion about managerial experience. Managers from business backgrounds were introduced in response to pressure from government, sponsors and citizens, causing a shift from curatorial to managerial values (Foley & McPherson, 2000). For example, three-year business plans including goals, outcomes and performance measures were introduced as requirements for cultural and historical organizations by the Canadian government. This promoted a vision of the organization as a business subject to instrumental reasoning that can be seen as an integral part of the influence of NPM. Oakes, Townley, and Cooper (1998) made a longitudinal study of the implementation of such a plan and its effects as plans and performance measures were reported through standardized accountability reports and showed that evaluation was increasingly built on how the museums were able to produce and market their 'product' to their 'customers'. Replacing meanings within the cultural field with those defined in reference to the external market led to a shift in what was valued. Economic capital became more important whilst cultural capital was valued but only to the extent that it could be transformed into economic capital (Oakes et al., 1998). As argued by Diefenbach (2009), that even though NPM has led to quite a few improvements, its unintended consequences may outnumber the positive outcomes insofar as the whole idea of financial measurement devalues any qualitative values and narratives that may be used to understand public value.

PUBLIC VALUE AND THE EMERGING PUBLIC VALUE MANAGEMENT

Moore (1995) realized the need for public managers to envision public value and made an effort to build a conceptual framework. Managers should not simply deploy resources to accomplish mandated purposes; they must interact with the political system through continuous dialogue. There are three key questions to be answered to test the adequacy of their vision of the organizational purpose: is it publicly valuable? Will it be politically and legally supported? Is it administratively and operationally feasible? This will focus their managerial attention outward, to the value of the organization's production; upward, to the political definition of value and downward and inward, to the current performance.

According to Moore (1995), political management is a key function that public sector managers must perform on behalf of a broader society. Political management focuses on designing, developing and operating the ongoing decision-making process to produce high-quality decisions. The decisions could be either within the scope of authority of the individual manager, or in cooperation with others (e.g. government-wide, on single issues). Moore (1995, p. 189) states: 'What makes political management necessary is that public managers share the responsibility with other officials, and with citizens, for deciding what would be valuable to produce with public resources and for actually producing what they agreed would be valuable to produce'.

What is publicly valuable, according to Moore (1995), must be judged against citizens' expectations of justice and fairness as well as efficiency and effectiveness. The organization must therefore be available to the political overseers through the development of appropriate accounting systems that measure the performance and costs of the organization's operations, preferably, as Moore (1995) advocates, through analytic techniques such as programme evaluation and cost-effectiveness analysis. Public value, then, in terms of collectively defined objectives emerges from a process of collective decision-making. Cost–benefit analysis on the other hand defines value in terms of what individuals as 'customers' desire.

Compared with the writings of NPM, Moore's work was originally produced primarily for practitioners, supporting the public manager's crucial role in public strategy definition and legitimacy building (Saz-Carranza, 2012). From its launch as a conceptual framework for the public sector in 1995, public value has now been defined in theoretical terms and academic interest in it is mushrooming (Benington & Moore, 2011). It has started to gain significant interest in some policy-making circles as well (Talbot, 2009), and Stoker (2006) and O'Flynn (2007) speak of a new paradigm, with the achievement of public value as its core objective. Recognizing the legitimacy of a wide range of stakeholders, it points towards a more collaborative, consultative approach. In effect, politics, seen as broader than party politics, is central in the public value paradigm and 'breathes life into the whole process' (Stoker, 2006, p. 46).

Nevertheless, the debate around public value and its relation to politics has at times been contested. For instance, Rhodes and Wanna (2007) point to the limits of public value and set out to rescue government from 'platonic guardians'. The challenge of public managers is, according to Stoker (2006), to engage in a dialogue about preferences and to ensure that activity fits a valued purpose (for efficiency), that goal setting and oversight is negotiated and established (for accountability), and that individual capacity to obtain rights and assume responsibilities is developed (for equity). Other theoretical contributions in the field of public value include its categorization of public values (Joergensen & Bozeman, 2007; Meynhardt, 2009) and widening the issue to focus on what adds value to the public sphere, not just short-term outputs but in the sustainable long run (Benington, 2009).

Empirical evidence from studies on museums and public value in a managerial context is comparatively scarce. In a case study on a New Zealand museum, Legget (2009) argues that understanding stakeholder perspectives is a key task for museum managers. Assessment priorities were rated, and although difficult to develop into readily assessable performance indicators (PIs), they served to focus attention on activities and responsibilities for which PIs might be practicable. Scott (2010) introduces a typology based on a study of museum professionals and a visiting and non-visiting public in Australia. Value tended to be measured on a limited number of PIs such as number of visitors, willingness to pay, media comments and rankings although there is a widely held perception within the profession that these measures are insufficient to capture benefits and impacts arising from engagement with arts and cultural heritage. What Scott (2010) found to be lacking was formal processes by which public value could be recognized to inform government policy and planning. In other words, there is a lack of knowledge and understanding of public needs and value. According to Scott (2010), a joint effort on the part of museums, the public and stakeholders, including the government, is called for to develop a set of shared indicators, founded in a values topology, and future evaluation models will need to be aligned with a values-based paradigm.

IDENTIFYING KEY ISSUES OF CONVERGENCE AND DIVERGENCE

Hood (1991, 1995) points out that accountability and various principles aligned with performance seem to be fundamental. Stoker (2006) and

Table 1. New Public Management versus Public Value Management.

	New Public Management	Public Value Management
Accountability	Politicians set public goals and targets, and hold managers to account for delivery. Upward accountability via performance contracts, outwards to customers via market mechanisms	Goal setting is negotiated. Multiple accountability towards political and other stakeholders, as well as towards citizens as overseers of government, as customers and as funders/taxpayers
Performance	Managers aim to meet agreed performance targets. Managing inputs and outputs to ensure economy, efficiency and customer satisfaction. Focus on results and responsiveness based on consumer surveys. Focus on the creation of value emerging from individual desires	Managers aim to meet collectively defined objectives. Managing for multiple objectives, respond to citizen/user preferences, renew mandate and maintain trust. Focus on the creation of value emerging from collective desires

Source: Adapted from Stoker (2006), O'Flynn (2007) and Horner and Hutton (2011).

O'Flynn (2007) also focus on these two key issues when highlighting convergence and divergence between NPM and PVM in their findings (Table 1).

The differences in accountability and performance between NPM and PVM also bring forth differences in strategic orientation. The focus of NPM on creating value based on individual desires marks an orientation toward the customer, and in extension toward the market (Diefenbach, 2009), while PVM is orientated toward value in terms of a desire that is agreed upon collectively in discussion with stakeholders (Horner & Hutton, 2011).

Thus, the three key issues identified within the theoretical framework and selected as a gateway to the empirical findings presented in this paper and the ensuing discussion are as follows: strategic orientation, accountability and performance.

A STUDY OF SWEDISH NATIONAL MUSEUMS

The national museums in this study are Swedish state agencies. Apart from legislation and ordinances, the framework is set by the mandate or statutory instruction for each individual agency or museum, stating its purpose, and the details of its funding. Appropriation directions and feedback requirements are coupled with annual budget decisions and separate assignments. The statutory instruction is formulated in activities, such as exhibitions, conservation, supporting other museums, etc., and the feedback requirements include reporting back on special assignments and delivering statistics.

The source of the empirical findings is an ongoing study of the creation of public value in cultural heritage and public museums. Respondents were selected for having two roles, as a director general of a state agency and the head of one or several museums. For example, the 'National Maritime Museums' runs three public museums. These are the Vasa Museum and the Maritime Museum in the city of Stockholm and the Naval Museum in the city of Karlskrona. Out of a total population of 10, eight directors general participated, representing 20 national museums. All but two are located in Stockholm or its vicinity. The upward accountability of the national museums is to the principal, the Ministry of Culture.

In the interviews, open-ended questions aligning strategic orientation, accountability, organization and performance were answered with long narrative responses. The interviews were recorded and transcribed *ad verbatim*. Data were coded or organized into coherent categories, and connections and patterns between the clusters of statements were identified. The mapping of qualitative data was guided by the inner coherence and meaning in the material that had been collected. The mapping was carried out in two steps: first, focusing on the impact of NPM, and second, on indications of relevance and applicability of PVM.

The empirical findings are structured under the following headings in accordance with the key issues identified.

(a) Strategic orientation – presenting and analyzing how the museum directors interpret the mandate.
(b) Accountability – presenting and analyzing how and in what ways the museums are made accountable.
(c) Performance – presenting and analyzing how museum directors look upon performance management and measure alignment with orientation and accountability.

Strategic Orientation

The mandate given by the principal, the Ministry of Culture, is interpreted by the directors, manifested in the strategic orientation and integrated into the operational planning and activities of museums. Regarding strategy for the modernization of museums the respondents describe a move from predominately collection management towards increased focus on how to attract and satisfy visitors. In other words, the focus and strategic orientation of museums seems to be shifting from being closely tied to aspects of conservation to a more 'contemporary' focus on accessibility. One respondent remarked:

> Lately, museums have chosen to prioritize the customer perspective more and more ... and we talk about how to find new ways to reach those who don't visit us.

Thus visitors are increasingly labelled as 'customers'. One respondent, however, dislikes the word customer because it is associated with the running of a business, that is, it is seen as a private sector-oriented label. In contrast to a private business, museums not only have a mandate to welcome customers as individuals but they also have a more general mandate that includes fostering contact with the public in a more general sense. Instead of customers some interviewees argue that 'visitors' – physical or virtual, existing or potential – is a more common and neutral label. However, other respondents argue that there are a number of different concepts in use among employees, for example, 'users', 'visitors', 'guests', 'consumers' or 'customers', and they all have their strengths and weaknesses:

> Some employees react negatively when we speak of customers, perhaps because of the associations to the business world. I think it is mainly the older workforce who prefer to use the more neutral term visitor. Also when we had free entrance it didn't feel right to use the word customer. But an important part of my work as a leader was to introduce a sort of customer thinking in the organization, or citizen-orientation as the government calls it.

In addition to a change in label toward a more customer-oriented approach, other activities have also been initiated. For example, opening hours have been extended in order to accommodate after-work visits. Moreover, museums offer additional services such as restaurants and museum shops to a greater extent, while also targeting a wider group of visitors though special programmes and offers – some of them commissioned by the government – to target groups such as children and people with disabilities, who traditionally do not visit museums.

However, the introduction of the above-mentioned activities and offerings at museums is not the only example of a stronger focus on accessibility. Changes are also taking place in the way external communication is conducted; branding has become a tool to communicate with different target groups about the museum, what it offers and what it stands for. The importance of having a strong museum brand was mentioned by several interviewees in connection with sponsoring. The success of a museum's brand is thus key to securing sponsorships, because sponsors want their own brand to be connected with successful exhibitions. Thus public museums are dependent on sponsorship, without which many exhibitions would not take place. Sponsors view the museum's collections differently than from the traditional museum perspective. As one respondent pointed out, they are not so interested in conservation or collection care. Rather, they are interested in exposing the museum's collections to visitors.

Several respondents explained that there has been a change in focus from collection management, where objects are stored in storehouses to preserve them for future generations, towards a greater focus on presenting museum objects as a tool for 'winning' the daily competition for visitors' free time. According to the interviewees, this transition calls for new managerial skills (i.e. what in NPM terms has been labelled 'new managerialism') where traditional museum professions such as curators and conservators have been complemented with professions found outside the museums. One such example is the growing number of communications managers within the museum sector with experience of dealing with media and the business world. Another example is managers with financial skills. This latter group has been recruited to take care of planning and financing, for instance, large and special exhibitions. The interviewees described those in this profession, who are skilled in accounting, as important, as those large and special exhibitions involve considerable risk-taking. Further, these exhibitions are financed partly or fully by fees or sponsors, not by government appropriations, which makes this profession much sought after.

Besides the demand for new skills and experience from the private sector, the empirical findings indicate a shift in leadership profile. Earlier focus was on professional competence, manifested in an academic degree (e.g. PhD or professor). Being director general calls for managerial skills, time and effort in running a state agency in addition to museum-specific skills.

In summary, the respondents mostly described the move towards visitor-driven operations in positive terms. However, much concern was also expressed over the declining interest in conservation:

> I think it is very important for the museum sector. To maintain trustworthiness you must be able to handle the conservation. With such big focus on accessibility there is a risk that it will lag behind. I think this is a key issue really, to keep a high quality in conservation.

One of the respondents was concerned about the old generation leaving and the loss of knowledge that would ensue. It was very difficult, almost impossible, to recruit personnel with such a knowledge of the collection objects. Exposing versus collecting objects is also a much discussed topic in the museum community:

> Still there will always remain a classic conflict, that between displaying the objects and conserving them. The more you put vulnerable objects on display or lend them to other museums, the less you can conserve. Digitizing the objects is a good complement, but it is just an interface.

There is tension between the two ideals, where the 'exposing' paradigm is contrasted with the 'conserving' paradigm. The argument about displaying the objects versus conserving them is also mirrored in internal conflicting interests and professional boundaries between different personnel categories, managers engaged in communication and pedagogical work, curators in exhibitions, and experts in conserving the objects. There also seems to be a conflict of interest between traditional museum professional profiles and the newer managerial profiles. Several respondents were genuinely worried about the lack of interest in preservation and handling of objects, and what we perceive as our heritage today versus the heritage of generations to come.

Accountability

As heads of state agencies, the interviewed museum directors are accountable to the Ministry of Culture. The relationship with the ministry is formally standardized through documents and dialogue. One of the suggestions that resulted from a government inquiry (SOU, 2009) was to strengthen the coordination of museums with an additional level in the hierarchy. This did not meet with approval at the museum level. The national museums suggested a stronger lateral collaboration, which eventually was accepted. The pronounced control from the government and the Ministry of Culture is visible when the museum directors spoke about to whom they are accountable. The predominant view seems to be that they are accountable only upwards, to the ministry and hence only indirectly to the public. Other potential stakeholders seem therefore to be neglected, which one of the museum directors illustrated in Fig. 1.

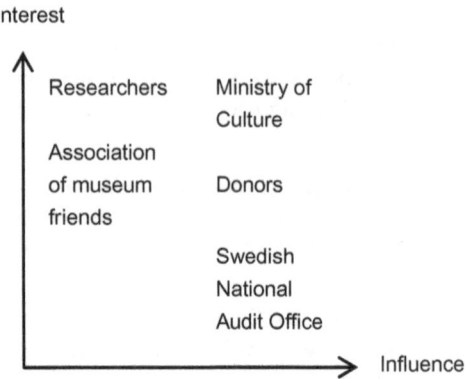

Fig. 1. Swedish National Museum Stakeholders.

The model shows the perceived interest and influence of the principal, the ministry, as well as the influence but lack of interest on the part of the auditors. In contrast, the researchers have an interest but lack influence. The museums cooperate with schools, the tourist industry, local communities and others, but do not talk about them as stakeholders. The donors in the above figure represent foundations, which contribute with donations.

The national museums are audited by the Swedish National Audit Office on a mandate from the parliament. Since audit reports are public documents, adverse remarks are of interest to the media. Several respondents expressed strong feelings about the auditors, their lack of understanding of the conditions and fundamental values of museums and the focus and relevance of auditable results. One example follows:

> They don't have many who know about museums really, and their parameters don't give the right picture. There is a lack of dialogue – you just get reactive, negative. Within the National Audit Office they just recruit economists, auditors, accountants … More diversity in competence is needed, why not humanists, anthropologists or even a few museologists?

Another respondent noted that they spend more time every year presenting results, that much of the audit discussions feel absurd as the auditors try to put price tags on all museum activities. On the other hand, some respondents thought that the auditors did a good job and are not to blame. The problem is that rules and regulations are not updated and difficult to interpret owing to the complexity of the governance model.

Performance

There has been a shift of focus in Swedish museums towards visitors and new activities to promote this shift. Different measurements are applied, both in monetary terms and also by including more qualitative aspects. This is in line with NPM, which emphasizes that high levels of autonomy must be counterbalanced by high levels of results control (Verhoest et al., 2010), and a Swedish Museum Coordinator Inquiry that states:

> It is in everyone's interest to examine how allocated resources can yield optimal outcomes. (SOU, 2009, p. 245)

In addition to a more customer-oriented approach, other initiatives have also been implemented. For example, much effort is made to conduct surveys for the collection of data including age, gender, interests and level of satisfaction on present and potential visitors:

> We make visitor surveys and we talk about how to reach those who don't visit us to investigate why and find new ways of reaching out for instance on social media.

The framework for national museums as state agencies includes performance goals and feedback requirements, volume and efficiency:

> They assume that a lot of visitors is a good thing, and if diminishing ask: why? Maybe the reason is a well thought-out high quality exhibition. Museums strive to get qualitative parameters into the dialogue, but it lacks flesh and blood. It is too much about costs and being cost-efficient.

According to another respondent, there is great interest in measuring access to the museums, but much less interest in measuring the degree of conservation. Still, the number of objects in conservation care is a number of great importance for sustainability. It appears from the interviews that quantitative data and economic metrics are also increasingly a mainstream issue in internal control, for example, in balanced scorecards or performance follow-ups. Within the museums a contemporary focus on, for example, visitors, strategic orientation and goals, different professional groups and organization and performance (measures) seems to be a core element for museums and their management.

Quantitative performance measures are relevant for certain activities, for example, digitization and the number of objects in conservation care. The urge to launch large and special exhibitions is linked not only to strengthening the brand, but also to increasing the number of visitors, a performance indicator of great importance to the ministry and national audit. Qualitative measures must be given more attention. Lesser focus on performance metrics and more on their contribution to society is hoped for. Several respondents emphasized the notion of trust. To be 'a trustworthy source of objective information' is important in relation to the public, but difficult to measure; so are other aspects in relation to the public suggested by respondents, such as being a meeting place, a place where people go voluntarily to be stimulated and a place of learning.

Whether quantitative (primarily financial) measures and follow-up systems or more qualitative measures and systems are highlighted could be related to ideas about what museums are and how they contribute. Some interviewees argued that focus is limited to measurable indicators such as costs and volume. The reason is that performance and contribution to society are considerably more difficult to measure. The 'soft policy area' of culture is described as follows:

> The policy area of culture is one of the smallest in the state budget, no room to man-oeuvre. The focus is on costs, they don't see the potential.

One interviewee claimed that the potential benefit of cultural tourism is not recognized by the government. An example is the renovation of one of the museums, the National Art Museum, which is considered to be a public cost and not an investment – a cultural resource with the potential to attract citizens and tourists to Stockholm.

CONCEPTIONS OF MUSEUM MANAGEMENT IN SWEDISH NATIONAL MUSEUMS

Swedish national museums, just like their Canadian counterparts, must now cope with a number of NPM instruments such as business plans, management accounting and various regulations. Concomitantly, museums are coping with the ongoing global museum transition from being predominantly custodial institutions (Gilmore & Rentschler, 2002) with a focus on collecting, documentation, conservation and storage, to, according to the statutes of the International Council of Museums (ICOM, 2007), being institutions in the service of society with education, study and enjoyment as their primary focus. Thus, it seems that there are various conceptions of museum management at play, which, based on our interviews, are also illustrated in the table below (Table 2).

Table 2. Conceptions of Museum Management in Swedish National Museums.

	Accessibility		Conservation
Strategic Orientation	Customer orientation	Stakeholder orientation	Collection care
	Service delivery, customer satisfaction, edutainment	Contribution to society, disseminating knowledge	Preservation of heritage for generations to come
Accountability	Upward toward the government	Upward toward the government	Upward toward the government
	Downward toward citizens as customers	Outward toward stakeholders, including, for example, researchers, sponsors and society	Forward toward society (future generations)
	Disengaged: economic/price tag audit	Engaged: stakeholder relation	Disengaged: future societies
Performance	Output • Quantity ○ Volume ○ Cost-efficiency ○ Standardization • Quality ○ Customer satisfaction	Outcome • Quantity ○ Volume ○ Funding • Quality ○ An invigorating place ○ A meeting place ○ A learning place	Output, outcome • Quantity ○ Degree of digitalization and conservation • Quality ○ Contribution to society: a trustworthy source of objective information

The results of our study show that there exist at least three conceptions of museum management that are based on two different strategic orientations, that is, accessibility and conservation, which also point to different conceptions of value. Accessibility can be understood as opening museums to new audiences, which, according to our analysis of the interviewees' statements, can be conceptualized in two ways. First is the strategic turn toward customer orientation that follows the path laid out by NPM. The task of museum managers becomes, as one interviewee put it, to introduce 'customer thinking' and align the activities of museums accordingly. This strategic orientation is also tied to a type of accountability that reduces museum activity to economical performance by, as another interviewee described it, putting 'price tags' on museum activities. Museum performance relates then primarily to output in terms of the quantity of customers that they are able to attract and how efficient they become at planning and executing exhibitions that attract as many customers as possible. In other words, performance measurement is limited to the number of customers that the museum is able to attract. Customer satisfaction is measured via visitor surveys.

Second is the opening up of museums to collaboration with stakeholders. This is an approach to museum management that emphasizes the contribution to citizenry as a whole, not as a sum of individual citizens. It involves contact with the public but not solely for the purposes of enjoyment but also to provide a meeting place and a place of learning for citizens. Accountability in this case is toward stakeholders other than the government and the citizenry, for example, toward the local community, tourist organizations, sponsors and researchers. Performance is focused on outcome and becomes both a quantitative and a qualitative issue, dealing with collaboration transactions as well as providing a meeting place and a place of learning for citizens.

This orientation towards customers, which might at first sight appear to be a positive feature because by attending to the wants of customers museums will probably increase their availability to the citizens, is not, however, necessarily positive. In effect, museum management activities can be divided into what museums do for their customers' convenience (e.g. providing longer open hours, restaurants and museum shops) and measures such as planning exhibitions that will attract customers. The first opens museums up to citizens while the second could ostensibly involve producing what the customer wants irrespective of whether or not the results coincide with an educative perspective, that is, to entertain rather than to provide knowledge. Not that there is anything wrong with entertainment, but arguably there are organizations better focused on entertainment than public museums. What seems to be at first sight a measure − customer orientation − to foster democratic values might then also be understood as a measure that in the long run can, although not necessarily so, deprive citizens of the democratization of history, art, etc., because it might not be entertaining enough. Indeed, repositioning museum management towards entertainment can lead to short-term decisions based on a perceived need and willingness to attract customers and sponsors who may or may not be interested in art, history, etc., but focus instead on entertainment.

Having placed customer − and stakeholder − orientations under a common strategic orientation of accessibility, the second strategic orientation that was identified in the empirical study is of conservation, which maintains the traditional view of collection care as the paramount activity of museums. Accountability is thus geared toward society in general and not toward individual visitors, whether they are citizens or customers. Accountability is thus also disengaged insofar as its discharge is displaced to the future. If collections are to be displayed to the public, digitization, when possible, or placing and administrating limitations on its accessibility, become the most important activities for museums in order to preserve cultural heritage in its original form. Digitization in this sense allows for efficient collection management and enables displays to be made available to the public on, for example, the Internet. Performance then becomes a question of the effectiveness of museums in conserving collections and restoring items to be conserved together with the rest of the collection for future generations to enjoy.

THE DEPENDENCY OF DIFFERENT CONCEPTIONS OF MUSEUM MANAGEMENT

Reform measures that are in accordance with NPM such as stress on private sector styles (Christensen & Laegreid, 2011; Lapsley, 2008), emphasis on control, performance management and measurement (Boston, 2011; Hood, 1995; Osborne, 2011) are being implemented in Swedish national museums and the move toward customer-oriented museum management is not only imminent but also integral to present museum management practice. As in Canada (Oakes et al., 1998), strategic and business plans have been introduced into Sweden, and performance indicators focused on costs and the recruitment of new professions, such as marketing, communications and accounting managers, bear witness to this ongoing process. It is also clear, however, that other aspects of museum management are also present, and these can be said to be partly aligned with the global museum transition from traditional custodial institutions to institutions in the service of society (Legget, 2009; Scott, 2010). Such conception might not be the primary, but they bring forth different ideals that can help to put actual museum practices into perspective.

In effect, with regard to public value, NPM appears to support a short-sighted approach that opens up museums to the public but fails to take into account that what is publicly valuable must be judged against the expectations of citizens in regards to justice, fairness, efficiency and effectiveness (Stoker, 2006). Swedish national museums are public, not private, organizations, and as such, they should focus primarily on the creation of

public value. Integrating NPM notions such as markets, customers and customer satisfaction might risk setting aside the very character of Swedish
national museums as public organizations in favour of an unsustainable
perspective that bypasses the ideas of public value and cultural heritage
when they do not coincide with the value that is determined by the market.

From a public value perspective, the challenge ahead is to engage in
dialogue with stakeholders in order to determine what is public value and
subsequently how to produce it efficiently and in a way that opens
museums up to citizens and stakeholders to claim their rights and assume
responsibility (Benington & Moore, 2011; Stoker, 2006). In order to do so,
however, the concept of museum management as conservation comes into
play insofar as public value not only concerns present but also future
generations. In effect, to keep displaying museum collections they must
also be conserved and preserved.

Although the different concepts of museum management presented
above are separated for analytical purposes, in practice they are not. As
Moore (1995) writes, although public value is a result of collective decision-
making it must still be assessed in terms of cost-effectiveness and performance. In other words, both output and outcome are needed to ensure
relevant museum management from a public value perspective. This is also
the case with regard to the accessibility and conservation concepts of
museum management. In order to be viable and meaningful, conservation
as a strategic orientation must rely on at least some degree of accessibility.
Similarly, the feasibility of accessibility as a strategic orientation must rely
on some degree of conservation and preservation.

Fig. 2.   The Interdependency of Museum Management Concepts.

Based on this study of Swedish national museums, museum management can be seen as the management of tensions between conservation and accessibility and between customer orientation and stakeholder orientation towards the creation of museum value. In other words, museum management must determine not only what value is but also for whom it is valuable, taking into account both present and future generations.

CONCLUSION

Empirical findings indicate that NPM-oriented values as presented by, among others, Hood (1991, 1995), Boston (2011) and Osborne (2011) and in a 'virtually uncountable number of empirical studies' (Diefenbach, 2009) have become part of the strategic orientation of the museum sector. Visitors have become customers or consumers and surveys are commonly used to assure that they are satisfied. Focus is on the citizen as a customer and mechanisms for public service delivery. The 'public' consists of aggregated individual customer or consumer interests. Surveys measure customer satisfaction among current citizens, and the perception of value for the taxpayers' money rests heavily on efficiency and cost-effectiveness. NPM offers an accountability structure, which is compatible with the traditional, hierarchical organization of the private sector as well as the public sector. Accountability is focused on compliance with expectations from principal and citizens. Performance, based on private sector management devices, is monitored towards set goals and targets, which are measured and evaluated in audit.

A public value-oriented approach as presented by, among others, Moore (1995), Stoker (2006), O'Flynn (2007) and Benington and Moore (2011), can to some extent be traced in the stakeholder orientation. However, such an orientation is not very dominant insofar as the only stakeholders perceived to have influence and interest in museum operations are the ministry and the visitors, as customers. Other interested parties such as researchers, associations of museum friends, etc., do not exert any formal or substantial influence on museums, and are therefore not defined as stakeholders to whom museums are accountable. Sponsors, however, seem to be a special case of stakeholder in that they, according to our interviewees, exert influence as investors, that is, they are interested in successful exhibitions. The positive effects of collaboration with other museums as well as potentially closer cooperation with stakeholders, seem to open up accessibility on a less individual basis than customer orientation, from the individual citizen as a customer to a collective citizenry. Such findings are in line with Scott's (2010) Australian study, which indicates the need for a more holistic approach and a joint effort on the part of museums, the public and stakeholders to develop a set of shared indicators.

The upward accountability towards government is dominant and was often spoken about in terms of the mandate given in instruction and governing documents, coupled with the funding from the state budget. The local community, researchers, the ICOM, the business world and organizations promoting tourism are looked upon as interested parties, in some cases as possible collaborators. Performance and operations are still much aligned to the focus and accountability of NPM, but respondents question the applicability of private sector management methods and do not wish to conform to a standardized conception of performance in line with the one-size-fits-all criterion (Hooper et al., 2005). Instead they point to the need to include, as argued by Benington and Moore (2011), outward and forward accountability, as a starting point for the creation of performance measures.

To conclude, the present study of museums as an example of a 'softer' public policy area questions the relevance of NPM because it seems to be incomplete and unable to encompass the plurality of and dependencies between concepts of museum management and conceptions of public value. Focusing on customers might be an important part of museum management development, but it may need to be complemented by an orientation towards stakeholders, where the public is one of the stakeholders, and by a conservation orientation that acknowledges that in order to be exhibited collections need to be taken care of and preserved. Indeed, focusing on customer orientation as well as accountability and performance management aligned to NPM may not serve museums well, insofar as they may promote short-termism and do not express their cultural contribution to society and citizenry, which in turn would endanger the sustainability of cultural heritage for future generations.

Further research is called for to capture a plural and shared vision of public value and public value creation, one that introduces a framing of public value in a managerial context in order to change the way in which government and stakeholders, including citizens, and the museums relate to each other.

REFERENCES

Benington, J. (2009). Creating the public in order to create public value? *International Journal of Public Administration, 32*(3–4), 232–249.

Benington, J., & Moore, M. H. (2011). *Public value: Theory and practice*. Basingstoke: Palgrave Macmillan.

Boston, J. (2011). Basic NPM ideas and their development. In T. Christensen & P. Laegreid (Eds.), *The Ashgate research companion to new public management* (pp. 17–32). Farnham: Ashgate Publishing Limited.

Broadbent, J., & Laughlin, R. (2003). Control and legitimation in government accountability processes: The private finance initiative in the UK. *Critical Perspectives on Accounting, 14*(1–2), 23–48.

Carnegie, G. D., & Wolnizer, P. W. (1996). Enabling accountability in museums. *Accounting, Auditing and Accountability Journal, 9*(5), 84–99.

Christensen, T., & Laegreid, P. (2011). *The Ashgate research companion to new public management*. Farnham: Ashgate Publishing Limited.

Cooper, D. J., & Hopper, T. (2007). Critical theorising in management accounting research. In C. S. Chapman, A. G. Hopwood, & M. D. Shields (Eds.), *Handbook of management accounting research* (Vol. 1, pp. 207–246). Oxford: Elsevier Limited.

Diefenbach, T. (2009). New public management in public sector organizations: The dark sides of managerialistic 'Enlightenment'. *Public Administration, 87*(4), 892–909.

Foley, M., & McPherson, G. (2000). Museums as leisure. *International Journal of Heritage Studies, 6*(2), 161–174.

Fountain, J. E. (2001). Paradoxes of public sector customer service. *Governance: An International Journal of Policy and Administration, 14*(1), 55–73.

Gilmore, A., & Rentschler, R. (2002). Changes in museum management: A custodial or marketing emphasis? *Journal of Management Development, 21*(10), 745–760.

Griffin, D., & Abraham, M. (2001). The effective management of museums: Cohesive leadership and visitor-focused public programming. *Museum Management and Curatorship, 18*(4), 335–368.

Hood, C. (1991). A public management for all seasons? *Public Administration, 69*(1), 3–19.

Hood, C. (1995). The 'new public management' in the 1980s: Variations on a theme. *Accounting, Organizations and Society, 20*(2–3), 93–109.

Hooper, K., Kearins, K., & Green, R. (2005). Knowing 'the price of everything and the value of nothing': Accounting for heritage assets. *Accounting, Auditing and Accountability Journal, 18*(3), 410–433.

Horner, L., & Hutton, W. (2011). Public value, deliberative democracy and the role of public managers. In J. Benington & M. H. Moore (Eds.), *Public value. Theory & practice* (pp. 112–126). New York, NY: Palgrave Macmillan.

ICOM. (2007). *Statutes*. Retrieved from http://icom.museum/fileadmin/user_upload/pdf/Statuts/statutes_eng.pdf. Accessed on June 22, 2014.

Joergensen, T. B., & Bozeman, B. (2007). Public values: An inventory. *Administration and Society, 39*(3), 354–381.

Kesner, L. (2006). The role of cognitive competence in the art museum experience. *Museum Management and Curatorship, 21*(1), 4–19.

Kotler, N., & Kotler, P. (2000). Can museums be all things to all people? Missions, goals, and marketing's role. *Museum Management and Curatorship, 18*(3), 271–287.

Lapsley, I. (2008). The NPM agenda: Back to the future. *Financial Accountability and Management, 24*(1), 77–96.

Legget, J. (2009). Measuring what we treasure or treasuring what we measure? Investigating where community stakeholders locate the value in their museums. *Museum Management and Curatorship, 24*(3), 213–232.

Meynhardt, T. (2009). Public value inside: What is public value creation? *International Journal of Public Administration, 32*(3–4), 192–219.

Moore, M. H. (1995). *Creating public value: Strategic management in government.* Harvard: Harvard University Press.

Oakes, L. S., Townley, B., & Cooper, D. J. (1998). Business planning as pedagogy: Language and control in a changing institutional field. *Administrative Science Quarterly, 43*(June), 257–292.

O'Flynn, J. (2007). From new public management to public value: Paradigmatic change and managerial implications. *The Australian Journal of Public Administration, 66*(3), 353–366.

Osborne, S. P. (2011). Public governance and public services: A 'brave new world' or new wine in old bottles? In T. Christensen, & P. Laegreid (Eds.), *The Ashgate research companion to new public management* (pp. 417–430). Farnham: Ashgate Publishing Limited.

Painter, M. (2011). Managerialism and models of management. In T. Christensen & P. Laegreid (Eds.), *The Ashgate research companion to new public management* (pp. 237–249). Farnham: Ashgate Publishing Limited.

Pollitt, C., & Bouckaert, G. (2000). *Public management reform: A comparative analysis.* Oxford: Oxford University Press.

Rentschler, R., & Potter, B. (1996). Accountability versus artistic development: The case for nonprofit museums and performing arts organizations. *Accounting, Auditing and Accountability Journal, 9*(5), 100–113.

Rhodes, R. A. W., & Wanna, J. (2007). The limits to public value, or rescuing responsible government from the platonic guardians. *Australian Journal of Public Administration, 66*(4), 406–421.

Saint-Martin, D. (2000). *Building the new managerialist state.* London: Oxford University Press.

Saz-Carranza, A. (2012). The quest for public value. *Public Administration Review, 72*(1), 152–153.

Scott, C. (2010). Searching for the 'public' in public value: Arts and cultural heritage in Australia. *Cultural Trends, 19*(4), 273–289.

SOU. (2009). *Kraftsamling — museisamverkan ger resultat (Official reports of the Swedish Government).* Stockholm: Swedish Government.

Stoker, G. (2006). Public value management: A new narrative for networked governance? *American Review of Public Administration, 36*(1), 41–57.

Talbot, C. (2009). Public value – The next 'big thing' in public management? *International Journal of Public Administration, 32*(3–4), 167–170.

Thompson, G. D. (2001). The impact of New Zealand's public sector accounting reforms on performance control in museums. *Financial Accountability and Management, 17*(1), 5–21.

Verhoest, K., Roness, P., Verschuere, B., Rubecksen, K., & MacCarthaigh, M. (2010). *Autonomy and control of state agencies: Comparing states and agencies.* Basingstoke: Palgrave MacMillan.

Zan, L., Bonini, B. S., & Gordon, C. (2007). Cultural heritage between centralization and decentralisation. *International Journal of Cultural Policy, 13*(2), 49–70.

PERFORMANCE MANAGEMENT SYSTEMS AND PUBLIC VALUE STRATEGY: A CASE STUDY

Enrico Bracci, Enrico Deidda Gagliardo and Michele Bigoni

ABSTRACT

Purpose — *This article aims to analyze the role of performance management systems (PMS) in supporting public value strategies.*

Design/methodology/approach — *This article draws on the public value dynamic model by Horner and Hutton (2010). It presents the results of a case study of implementation of a PMS model, the 'Value Pyramid' (VP).*

Findings — *The results stress the need for an improved conceptualization of PMS within public value strategy. Through experimentation using the VP, the case site was able to measure and visualize what it considered public value and reflect on the internal/external causes of both creation and destruction of public value.*

Research limitations/implication — *This article is limited to just one case study, although in-depth and longitudinal.*

Public Value Management, Measurement and Reporting
Studies in Public and Non-Profit Governance, Volume 3, 129–157
Copyright © 2014 by Emerald Group Publishing Limited
All rights of reproduction in any form reserved
ISSN: 2051-6630/doi:10.1108/S2051-663020140000003006

Originality/value — *This article is one of the first attempting to under-stand the role of PMS within the public value strategy framework, answering the call of Benington and Moore (2010) to consider public value from an accounting perspective.*

Keywords: Public value; performance management system; theatre; action research

INTRODUCTION

Since the seminal work by Moore (1994, 1995), the public value paradigm has attracted considerable interest from practitioners and academics alike (Alford, 2008; Alford & O'Flynn, 2009; Bovaird, 2007; Hefetz & Walner, 2004; Jørgensen & Bozeman, 2002; Smith, 2004; Stoker, 2006), but also critics (Rhodes & Wanna, 2007, 2009).

According to O'Flynn (2007), public value represents a way of thinking beyond the narrow market versus government failure approaches that dominated the NPM paradigm (Hefetz & Walner, 2004). Despite increasing interest in the public value concept, a clear definition remains elusive. Indeed, public value is multidimensional and its meaning can slightly change according to context (e.g. what is value for public organizations, cli-ents, individual citizens or society as a whole). As a consequence, public value should be conceptualized and then measured as a set of inter-related dimensions and indicators.

There have been calls for more empirical studies (see, e.g. Alford & Hughes, 2008; Williams & Shearer, 2011). Managing and creating public value involves a clarity of organizational mission and strategic plans, towards which politicians and public managers motivate the allocation of resources towards specific outcomes (Horner, Lekhi, & Blaug, 2006). As suggested by Spano (2009), to consider political, societal and organiza-tional dimensions, a comprehensive model to support public organizations to understand how public value is created is required, one that is capable of linking public value with management control systems. As stressed by Moore (2000) and others (e.g. Alford & O'Flynn, 2009; Kelly, Mulgan, & Muers, 2002; Williams & Shearer, 2011), the measurement of performance is not only an important issue to support public managers in evaluating the efficacy of their decisions, but also to report internally and externally (Kelly et al., 2002; O'Flynn, 2007). This is complicated by the emergence of more complex governance systems in the delivery of public services

(Benington & Moore, 2010; Broadbent & Guthrie, 2008; Stoker, 2006). Speckbacher (2006) called for more research on the role of performance management systems (PMS) in not-for-profit (NFP) organizations in pursuing value creation strategy, while Benington and Moore (2010) stressed the interest in studying public value from different disciplinary perspectives and countries as well as policy arenas.

This article aims to fill this gap in the literature, by analyzing the role of PMS in supporting public value strategies. Drawing from the public value literature, and in particular the public value dynamic model (Horner & Hutton, 2010), this article presents the results of a case study of implementation of a PMS model named 'Value Pyramid' (VP) (Deidda Gagliardo, 2002; Deidda Gagliardo & Poddighe, 2011). The study was conducted in a public-owned theatre from 2007 to 2012, through an action-research experimental approach (Argyris, Putnam, & McLain Smith, 1985; Susman & Evered, 1978).

PUBLIC VALUE: LITERATURE REVIEW

The concept of public value has several definitions, and has been equated with many elements, including outcomes (Meier, O'Toole, Boyne, & Walker, 2006); a mix of outcomes and outputs (Norman, 2011); management practice (Stoker, 2006); a contribution to storytelling (Smith, 2004) and a tool to make operational improvements (Rhodes & Wanna, 2009).

The concept of public value is central in the delivery of public services (Moore, 1994). As stressed by Moore (2000), when talking about public value the focus should be put not on the single client but on society as a whole. Value needs to be considered in terms of both benefits and costs generated by a programme, a service or a policy (Moore, 1995).

The measurement, reporting and management of public value creation represent important aspects of public value strategy (Alford & Hughes, 2008), and a way to show whether a strategy has been successful. Horner and Hutton (2010) proposed a re-interpretation of Moore's (1995) strategic triangle, stressing the importance of measuring and managing public value. In particular, the public value dynamic is created by three inter-related operations (Horner & Hutton, 2010, p. 120): authorize, create and measure (see Fig. 1).

Designing and implementing a strategy requires managers to seek to bring about alignment among the three elements, leaving open the issue of

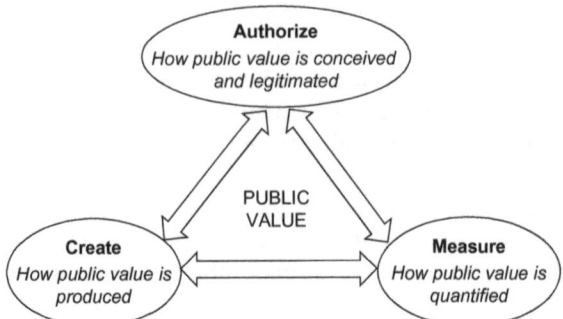

Fig. 1. The Public Value Dynamic: The Constitutive Elements. Source: Adapted from Horner and Hutton (2010, p. 120).

how to measure and evaluate the achievement of public value (Horner & Hutton, 2010). Indeed, the creation of public value is not a linear process but a multidimensional and dynamic one (Speckbacher, 2006). *Authorize* refers to what is considered as valuable by the constituencies and stakeholders in general. Moore (2000, p. 198) suggested a focus on the question of where legitimation comes from, and who provide the financial support and the necessary authorization for the activity. *Create* relates to the operations through which public value is created, and needs to be managed efficiently and effectively in order to satisfy stakeholder expectations. This refers also to the level of capability at the base of the value creating operations (Moore, 2000). With *measure* Horner and Hutton (2010) made a clear reference to the need to set up a performance measurement framework. Different ways are suggested to measure and evaluate public value: from pursuing political mandates efficiently and effectively, to benchmarking, from the use of analytical techniques (programme evaluation, cost effectiveness analysis and the like) to client/stakeholder customer analysis (Moore, 1994). The difficulty in measuring public value also stems from its multidimensional nature. Indeed, public value evaluation is related to three broad categories of services, outcomes and trust (Kelly et al., 2002).

PMS are considered important internal antecedents (Meynhardt & Metelmann, 2009) to guide managerial action towards public value creation. Indeed, the construct of management accounting systems can be used to influence and coordinate action for desired outputs and outcomes (Spano, 2009).

Based on Moore's definition of public value, public managers can 'increase the public value produced by public sector organizations in both the short and the long run' (Moore, 1995, p. 10) and they 'are obliged to hold a vision of public value, good for today and into the future' (Moore, 1995, p. 57). This implies public managers working within their organizations to implement strategies to deliver public value.

However, several authors suggest the need for further research, debate and practical application of the concept and its measurement in particular (Alford & Hughes, 2008; Williams & Shearer, 2011). We ask what is the role of PMS in supporting public value strategies and, in particular, within Honer and Hutton's public value dynamic triangle. The quest for public value measurement is considered a relevant aspect of the debate (Hills & Sullivan, 2008), even though a wider analysis on performance management seems neglected (Spano, 2009). Indeed, if public value creation represents the focus of the strategy in a public service setting, managers need tools for decision-making, managing and controlling the efficacy of their actions (Cowling, 2006; Hills & Sullivan, 2008; Moore, 1995; Spano, 2009). From Moore's work we see that the creation of performance measures against which public value must be measured represents an important managerial technology (Williams & Shearer, 2011). Public value is thus strictly linked to the performance measurement of public organizations, as well the alignment of organizational operations and resource allocation processes. Speckbacher (2006) called for more interest from researchers into the role of PMS in supporting NFP organizations in creating value for stakeholders.

MANAGING PUBLIC VALUE: A PMS CONCEPTUAL MODEL

Public value is multifaceted and its definition depends on the perspective adopted (Williams & Shearer, 2011). Public value can be considered as the joint achievement of both an economic value and a social value throughout the public administration's activity, where benefits are greater than sacrifices (Moore, 1994, 2000). However, Deidda Gagliardo (2002) argued that economic value results from the combination of both a tangible dimension (e.g. level of efficiency, productivity and overall financial performance) and an intangible dimension (e.g. human, structural, relational, empathetic, evolutionary). The social value (the value created for users/citizens) is expressed in terms of the level of quantitative/qualitative worth of services provided, the degree of user satisfaction and the medium-term to long-term impact on their well-being (Moore, 1994). As suggested by Moore (1995, 1996), public

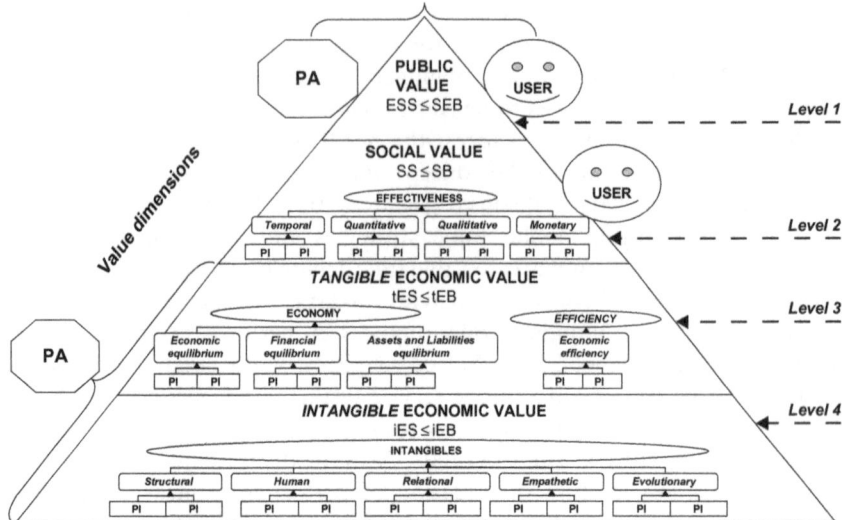

Fig. 2. The Value Pyramid Performance Management System: A Representation.
Source: Adapted from Deidda Gagliardo and Poddighe (2011).

value is the joint achievement of economic and social value through the public administration's activity, know-how, skills and competence.

The conceptual model of public value creation, structured along the above described inter-related dimensions, was adopted by Deidda Gagliardo (2002) proposing a PMS named VP (Fig. 2). The four levels are the dimensions proposed to conceptualize, measure and then manage public value.

• *Level 1: public value* (Deidda Gagliardo & Poddighe, 2011; Spano, 2009), viewed from a joint public administration—user perspective and expresses the qualities of an administrative action and the degree of overall well-being of society. In Level 1, the economic social sacrifices (ESS) and the social economic benefits (SEB) are compared (ESS ≤ SEB).

• *Level 2: social value* (Deidda Gagliardo & Poddighe, 2011; Hefetz & Walner, 2004; Mook, 2013; Spano, 2009), viewed from the sole perspective of the user and expresses the degree of satisfaction in relation to the temporal, quantitative, qualitative and monetary characteristics of the public service. The social value is derived from the prevalence of social benefits (SB) achieved by the user compared to the social sacrifices (SS), where SS should be at least equal or smaller than SB. It can be created by acting on the effectiveness sub-levels.

- *Level 3: tangible economic value* (Deidda Gagliardo & Poddighe, 2011; Spano, 2009), viewed from the sole perspective of the public administration and expresses the economic value of its tangible asset and the capacity of the public administration to increase it. The tangible economic value derives from the prevalence of tangible economic benefits (tEB) achieved by the public administration with respect to tangible economic sacrifices (tES), where the objective is to have tES equal or smaller than tEB. The instruments to increase the total economic value are the economy (based on the search of overall economic, financial, assets and liabilities equilibrium) and the efficiency.
- *Level 4: intangible economic value*, viewed from the sole perspective of the public administration and expresses the economic value of its intangible asset and the capacity of the public administration to increase it. The intangible value is the base level of the pyramid and is the vital foundation of the administration and its driving force. The intangible economic asset of the public organization derives from the prevalence of intangible economic benefits (iEB) achieved by the public body with respect to the intangible economic sacrifices (iES) borne by it, where iES should be equal to or smaller than iEB. The intangible value tools to increase the vitality of the public administration and enhance development are the functionality and harmony of its organizational structure (structural value), productivity and quality of its human resources (human value), the network of its relations with the external and internal environment (relational value) (Lev, 2001), its responsiveness to threats or opportunities (empathetic value) and its propensity for innovation (evolutionary value) (Deidda Gagliardo, 2002).

The VP looks for the stepwise accumulation of economic and social value by monitoring, and the combined action of the three lower levels. The four levels of the model should then be connected to the planning and control instruments of the public organization through Key Performance Indicators (KPIs), creating an operational alignment. To increase the value at each level of the pyramid (i.e. in tangible economic value), some combined actions must be achieved in the relevant sub-levels (i.e. on economic efficiency). To improve the performance of the sub-levels, it will be necessary to act on the specific KPIs (i.e. the operating costs of a particular service), in order to reduce the associated economic sacrifices so as to render them lower than the economic benefits obtained.

The creation of value at a lower level generates the conditions to enhance the creation of value at the upper level. In short, the intangible economic values at level 4 provide the economic stimulus for the tangible economic improvement of performance at level 3. The tangible economic value generates resources to invest in order to increase the social value at level 2; the social value generated by the overall economic health of the organization stimulates the production flow and pushes it towards the creation of economic and social value integrated at level 1. Positive or negative trends at the lower levels are the cause and explanation of the creation or destruction of public value at the higher levels. The conceptual model is based on the integrated management of various performance dimensions.

In this form, the VP is proposed as a conceptual framework for the measurement and management of the value created, and can be used as a controlling, as well as an accountability, mechanism (Deidda Gagliardo, 2002; Deidda Gagliardo & Poddighe, 2011).

METHODOLOGY

Our study adopted an action-research approach in order to investigate its main aim. Action research can be defined as a research methodology that aims 'to contribute both to the practical concerns of people in an immediate problematic situation and to the goals of social science by joint collaboration within a mutually acceptable ethical framework' (Rapoport, 1970, p. 499). Action research is considered as a 'natural' learning process where researchers 'engage with participants in a collaborative process of critical enquiry into problems of social practice' (Argyris et al., 1985, p. 237). In particular, within the action-research approach is experimental action research, where researchers and the researched actor collaborate in all phases to set up an experiment, from the taking of action and the evaluation of its consequences (Susman & Evered, 1978). Interventionist research aims at melding theory and practice, and expresses an entity of use as well as the explanation of use (Westin & Roberts, 2010). The challenge for interventionist research in accounting is experiencing practice in real terms and delivering theory from it. Learning becomes experiential, originating from two interconnected sources: the concrete experiences of practice and the abstract conceptualization.

With this approach comes challenges and limitations. In particular, Lyly-Yrjänäinen and Suomala (2012, p. vi) stressed the following: the theoretical contribution may stem not just from one intervention, but from a series of them; the researcher has to be able to recognize his/her own work and aims and not those of the internal managers; interactions between the researchers and field work may create an idiosyncratic setting, which would not have been generated without interventions. Despite these limitations, the call for accounting research to produce practically relevant theories and ideas is established (Malmi & Granlund, 2009). Field research is considered a way through which the questions of practitioners and researchers alike can be answered (Hopwood, 2002; Lukka & Mouritsen, 2002).

The research setting was a theatre owned by the Municipality of Ferrara, Italy. The longitudinal case study was conducted from 2007 to 2012. The analysis around the value creation was split into two periods: first a three-year period from 2007 to 2009 and second a two-year period from 2010 to 2011. This time frame was chosen together with the general management of the theatre because the theatre was transformed into a foundation in 2009.

The research involved an intense and continuous collaboration with the administrative director, her staff and the general manager. The initial activity concerned the discussion and sharing of practical concerns (or the problem) and the research goals. The practical concerns that emerged from the initial discussions were first, how to measure the value created or consumed in each of the five years, determining the trend of the five-year period. The second was how to extrapolate and provide theatre management with a multidimensional management framework on the causes of public value creation.

Of theoretical concern was to how to give an insight of the role of PMS within the public value dynamic triangle (Horner & Hutton, 2010), through experimentation with the VP model. In order to develop the experimentation, some preliminary activities were carried out. First, the project was presented to the president and the board of directors to receive approval, attain their commitment, and get full access to the site. Second, a project team was constituted, comprising the researchers, the administrative director, the controller and an administrative employee. The president was from time to time involved in several team meetings. Third, a training session was organized for the team members, presenting the VP methods, sharing a common language and outlining the overall aim and strategy.

In terms of research methods, the research involved direct observation and involvement of the researchers in the experiment. The notes taken during the meetings and activity were then discussed among the researchers and with the administrative director and her staff in order to share lines of activities and decisions about how to proceed and overcome the problems encountered. The results of the experimentation of the measurement framework were continuously discussed in order to evaluate their relevance, limits and overall usefulness for decision-making.

The methods included semi-structured interviews (see appendix) with the administrative director, her staff and the president to discuss the meaning of public value, assess the level of perceived usefulness of the model for decision-making and to identify problems. A total of 15 interviews were conducted, plus several other informal talks and meetings during which notes were taken.

The Case Study

The Municipal Theatre, home of Maestro Claudio Abbado's Orchestra, is a traditional Italian theatre, certified by the Italian Ministry of Cultural Heritage and Tourism. Opened in 1798, the Theatre experienced two significant legal transformations (into a municipal institution in 1994 and a private foundation with the Municipality of Ferrara as the sole shareholder in 2009).

The establishment of the foundation was intended to make the theatre less dependent on the Municipality for financing and open to other investors and/or partners. The foundation consists of the president, founding members committee, board of directors, director and council; internal audits are carried out by the board of statutory auditors. In 2012, the theatre employed 44 staff, divided between permanent, contract and seasonal employees.

With a capacity of 1,840 seats, the theatre has produced over the five years of this case study about 100 shows per year with more than 300 performances, hosting an average of 65,000 visitors per year, with over 4,000 subscribers and the participation of over 10,000 children and teenagers.

The theatre's management information system was not particularly sophisticated. Before starting the research, the theatre used traditional financial reports (budget vs. actual), integrated with some activity indicators (i.e. audience numbers, occupancy rate). In the words of the administrative director the information system was 'redundant and disorganized, generating heterogeneous and unconnected data'. The accountability relations with the Municipality were mainly driven by financial constraints and objectives, with the theatre board attempting to also demonstrate the outcomes and outputs, but with little support from management systems. These factors motivated the administrative director to experiment with the introduction of a PMS capable of measuring and supporting public value creation.

The experiment was phased along the three dimensions of the public value dynamic (Horner & Hutton, 2010). The first phase saw the team project discuss and analyze the environment and how public value could be conceptualized and then translated. The second phase concerned the measurement of public value in the five-year period implementing the VP model, and finally the project team focused on the operational factors behind the creation or destruction of public value.

PUBLIC VALUE AS A STRATEGIC CHOICE: AUTHORIZATION AND LEGITIMATION

The president and the administrative director were interested in the overall strategy and mission of the theatre as conceived by the Municipality, and the other main stakeholders. Indeed, according to Horner and Hutton (2010, p. 120) authorization is the process of defining what is considered valuable for the constituencies, and in particular for those that provide funding. The initial discussion focused on the formal authorization context, and thus the way public value is conceptualized, the political mandate, the presence of different stakeholders and the accountability processes (Horner & Hutton, 2010).

The authorization context is fundamental for any organization to achieve its own legitimacy. For the case study site, the main sources of legitimacy are considered to be the Municipality and the overall public, as the administrative director stressed: 'our strategic imperatives are to offer an attractive cultural season in the different fields of activity, to satisfy our public, and to fulfil the political mandate we receive by the Municipality'.

The different sources of legitimacy may create dilemmas for the public organization. In some situations, as in our case site, this may lead to a contrasting and confusing authorizing environment. As expressed by the administrative director:

> On one side we have a political mandate stressing both the need to break the balance, but also to guarantee a high quality services throughout the year. At the same time our customers are highly demanding and we need to increase the occupancy rate.

This view was supported by the president 'we need to improve much more than in the past in our capacity to account for the results, showing how valuable is our activity'.

Public value as a strategic imperative could also be found in the theatre's internal and external documents, including the three-year strategic plan, and in some minutes of the board of directors. This phase of the research provided content for the four levels of the VP, translating the public value strategy in the key performance areas. The quest for public value created the base for the researcher to move the discussion and action towards public value measurement.

MEASUREMENT OF PUBLIC VALUE

The VP model was then implemented in order to discuss how public value can be measured. The initial training sessions between the researchers and the team members allowed sharing of the logic and meanings of the concepts within the four VP levels. The key performance areas selected represented the base for the second phase of the experimentation. Thus, the project team was involved in the discussion to define KPIs for each level of the VP. During the meetings one question was raised: how can a comparison be made of economic values and social values expressed through different KPIs, in type and nature? The discussion was conducted freely, with the researchers not directly involved in the choice of the KPIs. This behind the scenes role of the researchers led to a general acceptance of the KPIs selected by the team. The heterogeneity of the social sacrifices and benefits compared to economic sacrifices and benefits meant comparison was difficult. To compare and measure the economic and social sacrifices and benefits a preparatory procedure was carried out for the normalization and weighting of the various performance measures. Normalization involves the attribution of values, expressed in different units of measurement, to a common measurement scale (D'Egidio, 2005). In order to do so, it was necessary to identify the extremes of the decimal scale: the highest and lowest performance possible for each sacrifice or benefit; for the sacrifices the best performance is equal to zero (no sacrifice) and the worst one is minus ten (greatest sacrifice) on the decimal scale; for the benefits the best performance is equal to ten (greatest benefit) and the worst is zero (zero benefit) on the decimal scale (Fig. 3).

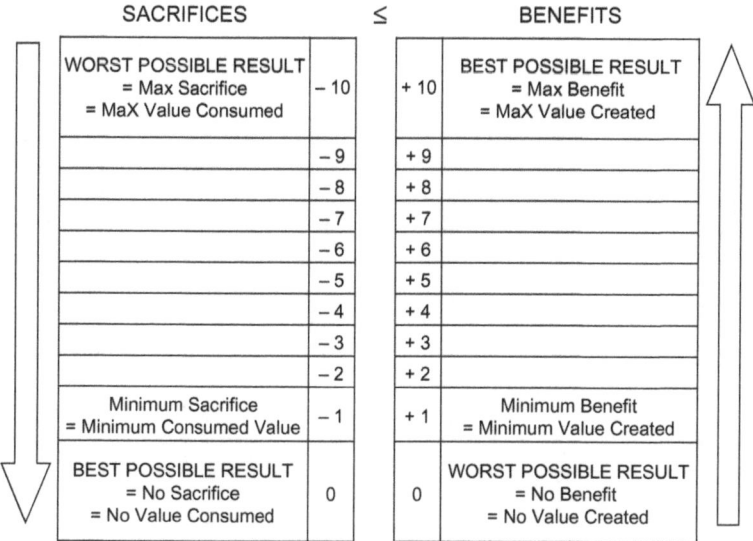

Fig. 3. The Normalization Scale Adopted.

A critical factor for the methodology of measurement lies in setting the extremes of the decimal scale. The identification of the extremes and their maintenance in different periods under investigation determines the validity of the model. For each KPI the project team discussed the type of standard to utilize as extreme. Three main criteria were followed: the use of national or local benchmarks (i.e. financial independence); the use of historical performance (i.e. seat occupancy rate) and the use of a natural number representing the target agreed with stakeholders (i.e. number of students involved in training courses). Then targets were identified among the value scale extremes and corresponded to values between the minimum and the maximum scale fluctuation.

After the choice of the KPIs and the definition of the normalization technique, two measurement tables were created (Tables 1 and 2): the first for sacrifices (decimal scale from −10 to 0), the second for benefits (scale from 0 to +10).

In both tables, for each of the three levels of the value taken from the VP, and with reference to each of the general sub-levels, the administrative director, her staff and the president identified the specific sub-levels, while paying constant attention to the sacrifice−benefit correlation between the

Table 1. Performance Measure for Value Creation: Sacrifices.

A Level	B General Sub-Levels	C Specific Sub-Levels (To Reduce Sacrifices)	D Performance Indicators (To Measure Decrease in Sacrifices)	E Worst Possible Result Max Sacrifices=10	F Best Possible Result=No Sacrifice	G1 2007	G2 2008	G3 2009	G4 2010	G5 2011	H1 2007	H2 2008	H3 2009	H4 2010	H5 2011	I Weight Sub-Levels	J1 2007	J2 2008	J3 2009	J4 2010	J5 2011	K % Level Weight	Economical and Social Sacrifices	Sacr 2007	Sacr 2008	Sacr 2009	Sacr 2010	Sacr 2011
						Neutral Sacrifices					Standardised Sacrifices						Standardised and Weighted Sacrifices											
Social value (user perspective)	Effectiveness or efficacy	Temporal efficacy (1S) Reduction of average unit waiting time at ticket office queue (for each show)	Average delay (minutes) per show (weighted according to show with and without subscription)	20	0%	5	5	4	4	4	2.50	2.50	2.00	2.00	2.00	5%	0.13	0.13	0.10	0.10	0.10	100%	Social sacrifices	4.1	4.0	3.9	4.3	4.1
		Quantitative efficacy (2S) Reduction of queues through progressive reduction of purchases at box office and correlated shows	Number of tickets purchased at box office/total number of tickets	100%	0%	85.00%	80.00%	73.75%	55.71%	48.24%	8.50	8.00	7.38	5.57	4.82	30%	2.55	2.40	2.21	1.67	1.45	40%		1.58	1.52	1.43	1.27	1.12
		Qualitative efficacy (3S) Reduction of cancelled or substituted shows	Number of cancelled or substituted shows/total	100%	0%	0.47%	0.55%	0.00%	3.85%	0.00%	0.05	0.05	0.00	0.39	0.00	40%	0.02	0.02	0.00	0.15	0.00							
		Monetary efficacy (4S) Reduction of "Club Amici del Teatro" sacrifice (gold members)	Sacrifices economic value: € average gold member (10000 +5000)/2	10000.00	5000.00	7500.00	7500.00	7500.00	7500.00	7500.00	5.00	5.00	5.00	5.00	5.00	25%	1.25	1.25	1.25	1.25	1.25							
															Social sacrifices	100%	3.9	3.8	3.6	3.2	2.8							
Tangible economic value (body perspective)	Economy	Economic equilibrium [between cost and revenues] (5S) Reduction of the percentage of operating	€ Operating costs/€ total costs	100%	0%	98.25%	99.17%	96.74%	97.40%	97.53%	9.82	9.92	9.67	9.74	9.75	25%	2.46	2.48	2.42	2.44	2.44	25%	Tangible economic sacrifices	1.33	1.43	1.22	1.69	1.68
		Financial equilibrium [between current liabilities and current assets] (6S) Reduction of the percentage of current liabilities	€ Current liabilities/ € total equity +liabilities	100%	0%	89.73%	95.24%	86.34%	82.51%	80.20%	8.97	9.52	8.63	8.25	8.02	25%	2.24	2.38	2.16	2.06	2.01							
		Assets and liabilities equilibrium (7S) Reduction of the percentage of fixed assets	€ Fixed assets/ € total assets	100%	0%	16.27%	12.93%	0.75%	0.70%	0.56%	1.63	1.29	0.08	0.07	0.06	25%	0.41	0.32	0.02	0.02	0.01							
	Efficiency	Economic efficiency (8S) Reduction of average cost of each show	€ Total/no. shows	60000.00	20000.00	23647.98	28686.95	24637.13	56218.59	56260.37	0.91	2.17	1.16	9.05	9.07	25%	0.23	0.54	0.29	2.26	2.27							
											Social sacrifices					100%	5.3	5.7	4.9	6.8	6.7		Tangible economic sacrifices					
Intangible economic value (body perspective)	Intangible values	Structural value (9S) Reduction of the percentage of fixed costs on total costs	€ Fixed costs/€ total	100%	0%	40.52%	39.41%	52.01%	53.42%	56.59%	4.05	3.94	5.20	5.34	5.66	20%	0.81	0.79	1.04	1.07	1.13	35%	Intangible economic sacrifices	1.16	1.04	1.30	1.36	1.34
		Human value (10S) Reduction of average cost per employee	€ Personnel costs/ numbers of employees	40000.00	20000.00	27503.47	26694.81	28398.38	30456.94	30972.21	3.75	3.35	4.20	5.23	5.04	25%	0.94	0.84	1.05	1.31	1.26							
		Relational value (11S) Reduction of non-formalized relationships on the total relationships	Non-formalized relationships/total relationships	100%	0%	0.00%	0.00%	0.00%	0.00%	0.00%	0.00	0.00	0.00	0.00	0.00	20%	0.00	0.00	0.00	0.00	0.00							
		Empathetic value (12S) Reduction of economic dependance on public grants and subsidies	€ Operating revenues from public subsidies and grants/€ total operating revenues	100%	0%	74.60%	59.58%	67.97%	68.51%	65.54%	7.46	5.96	6.80	6.85	6.55	15%	1.12	0.89	1.02	1.03	0.98							
		Evolutionary value (13S) Reduction of operating administrative costs on total operating costs	€ Operating administrative costs/€ total operating costs	100%	0%	22.71%	23.17%	29.83%	24.73%	23.36%	2.27	2.32	2.98	2.47	2.34	20%	0.45	0.46	0.60	0.49	0.47							
																100%	3.3	3.0	3.7	3.9	3.8							

Intangible economic sacrifices

Table 2. Performance Measure for Value Creation at the Theatre: Benefits.

A Level	B General Sub-	C Specific Sub-Levels (To Increase Benefits)	D PI – Performance Indicators – (To Measure Increase in Benefits)	E Worst Possible Result No Benefit =0	F Best Possible Result=Max	G1 2007	G2 2008	G3 2009	G4 2010	G5 2011	H1 2007	H2 2008	H3 2009	H4 2010	H5 2011	I Benefits Weight	J1 2007	J2 2008	J3 2009	J4 2010	J5 2011	K Level Weight	Economic and Social	2007	2008	2009	2010	2011
						Neutral Benefits					Standardised Benefits						Standardised and Weighted Benefits						Economic and Social	Benefits				
Social value (user perspective)	Effectiveness or efficacy	Temporal efficacy (1B)	Number of days of use of various shows/ number days in year (season extension)	0%	100%	56.44%	49.18%	45.21%	19.73%	16.99%	5.64	4.92	4.52	1.97	1.70	5%	0.28	0.25	0.23	0.10	0.08	100%	5.30 Social benefits	1.92	2.05	1.92	1.66	1.54
		Quantitative efficacy (2B)	Annual attendance number /(Annual capacity (i.e. annual potential weighted capacity numberxannual number of shows)	0%	100%	74.17%	81.00%	82.73%	62.87%	56.03%	7.42	8.10	8.27	6.29	5.60	30%	2.22	2.43	2.48	1.89	1.68							
		Qualitative efficacy (3B)	Number of shows with renowned artists/total number of shows	0%	100%	26.32%	29.67%	21.35%	23.08%	20.83%	2.63	2.97	2.13	2.31	2.08	40%	1.05	1.19	0.85	0.92	0.83	40%						
		Monetary efficacy (4B)	Benefits economic value € average gold members (10000 +5000)/2	5000.00	10000.00	7500.00	7500.00	7500.00	7500.00	7500.00	5.00	5.00	5.00	5.00	5.00	25%	1.25	1.25	1.25	1.25	1.25							
															Social benefits	100%	4.8	5.1	4.8	4.2	3.8							
Tangible economic value (body perspective)	Economy	Economic equilibrium [between cost and revenues] (5B)	€ Operating revenues/ € total revenues	0%	100%	98.18%	97.80%	99.87%	99.20%	99.15%	9.82	9.78	9.99	9.92	9.92	25%	2.45	2.45	2.50	2.48	2.48	25%	Tangible economic benefits	1.25	1.32	1.40	1.92	1.93
		Financial equilibrium [between current liabilities and current assets] (6B)	€ Current assets less inventories/€ total assets	0%	100%	83.75%	87.07%	99.23%	99.27%	99.43%	8.38	8.71	9.92	9.93	9.94	25%	2.09	2.18	2.48	2.48	2.49							
		Assets and liabilities Equilibrium (7B)	€ Equity plus long-term liabilities/equity plus long-term liabilities	0%	100%	8.12%	4.76%	13.66%	17.49%	19.80%	0.81	0.48	1.37	1.75	1.98	25%	0.20	0.12	0.34	0.44	0.50							
	Inefficiency	Economic efficiency (8B)	€ Total revenues/no. shows	20000.00	60000.00	24044.87	28877.83	24692.64	56351.95	56272.39	1.01	2.22	1.17	9.09	9.07	25%	0.25	0.55	0.29	2.27	2.27							
														Tangible economic benefits		100%	5.0	5.3	5.6	7.7	7.7							
Intangible economic value (body perspective)	Intangible value	Structural value (9B)	€ Variable costs/€ total costs	0%	100%	59.48%	60.59%	47.99%	46.58%	43.41%	5.95	6.06	4.80	4.66	4.34	20%	1.19	1.21	0.96	0.93	0.87	35%	Intangible economic benefits	2.12	2.13	1.98	1.85	1.84
		Human value (10B)	Number of shows per annum/number of employees	–	10.00	3.80	2.97	3.31	1.50	1.32	3.80	2.97	3.31	1.50	1.32	25%	0.95	0.74	0.83	0.38	0.33							
		Relational value (11B)	Formalized relationships/total relationships	0%	100%	100.00%	100.00%	100.00%	100.00%	100.00%	10.00	10.00	10.00	10.00	10.00	20%	2.00	2.00	2.00	2.00	2.00							
		Empathetic value (12B)	€ Operating revenues from tickets, subscriptions and sponsorships/ € total operating revenues	0%	100%	25.40%	40.42%	32.03%	31.49%	34.46%	2.54	4.04	3.20	3.15	3.45	15%	0.38	0.61	0.48	0.47	0.52							
		Evolutionary value (13B)	€ Operating artistic costs/ € total operating costs	0%	100%	77.29%	76.83%	70.17%	75.27%	76.64%	7.73	7.68	7.02	7.53	7.66	20%	1.55	1.54	1.40	1.51	1.53							
														Tangible economic benefits		100%	6.1	6.1	5.7	5.3	5.2							

two tables. All the KPIs inserted in the table were chosen by the administrative director and were then discussed between the researchers and her colleagues, as well as the president and the board of directors. The choice was made before the actual measurement of the indicators, to avoid biased choice towards the best performing indicators. The setting of the extremes (worst and best possible result) of the decimal scales of the sacrifices and benefits for each sub-level was the most delicate operation. KPIs were used in ratio form, that is, their extremes were the minimum and maximum of the ratio itself (100% and 0% for sacrifices; 0% and 100% for benefits) and in some cases the minimum and maximum from historically established performance extremes were used. For each of the five years, the sacrifices and benefits were first calculated according to the specific measurement of each indicator identified, and then the normalized sacrifices and benefits in terms of the decimal scale.

Before starting the measurement, the administrative director and her colleagues identified the priorities (based on the theatre's strategy and mission), both among the three value levels, placing a 40% weight on the social value, 25% on the tangible economic value and 35% on the intangible economic value, and among the sub-levels. From the intangible values, the administrative director considered the human value as the most important one for the Ferrara Theatre context (25%). From the tangible values, equal importance was allocated to all four; from the social values, the greatest weight was allocated to qualitative efficacy (40%) and quantitative efficacy (30%). It was agreed to keep the weights fixed during the period under investigation to be able to determine the value trend.

For each of the five years, the measurement table balanced and weighted automatically the normalized sacrifices or benefits, first on the basis of priorities among the sub-levels (according to the weights given by the administrative director), and then on the basis of priorities among the value levels (according to the weights given by the administrative director). Finally, the table computed the total sacrifices and benefits, measuring the intangible and tangible economic value, the social and public value, as the average of the three levels mentioned.

CREATING PUBLIC VALUE: OPERATIONAL ANALYSIS

Public value creation is the third dimension of the public value dynamic. According to Horner and Hutton (2010, p. 122), public managers must justify the allocation of resources and the related activity/project in terms of the achievement of specific outcomes. Overall, public managers are required to align the organization, and the interventions with the key performance area of public value creation (Moore, 2000).

On this basis, the project team, after the measurement of the public value generated or destroyed by the theatre (see Table 3), began an overall discussion of whether the resource allocation strategy was effective. In this phase of the project, the president of the theatre was also involved in the discussion of the relevance and interpretation of the results.

In Fig. 4 the results obtained along the four levels of the VP are presented in their temporal dynamic. It emerges that, from 2007 to 2011, the theatre created a low public value, revealing a low capacity to improve its overall performance. The theatre created ESV, which was low but slightly increased in the 2007−2008 period (+0.09); it then lost all this value in the 2008−2010 period (−0.13) due to the preparation (2008), implementation (2009) and adjustment (2010) of the legal, organizational and economic transformation into a foundation. Finally, it painstakingly began its ascent from 2010 to 2011 (+0.02) reaping the first small fruits of the transformation.

In the 2007−2008 period, the public value [ESV] increased (+0.09) mainly driven by the good performances of the social value [SV] (+0.18) and the intangible economic value [IEV] (+0.13), which managed to absorb the decrease in the tangible economic value [TEV] (−0.03): up to 2008 the theatre was focused on improving the quantity and quality of artistic performances, without particular attention to the economy of the artistic choices.

The increasing SV performances depended mainly on attendance improvement (2B: quantitative efficacy), in turn attracted by the increase of renowned theatrical shows (3B: qualitative efficacy) and supported by actions to counter inefficiency, such as reducing queues at the ticket office through the issuing of online tickets (2S: quantitative efficacy).

The positivity of the IEV derives from the existence of consolidated relationships with local, national and international partners (11SB: relational value), and the improvement in structural flexibility as a result of replacing fixed costs with variable costs (9SB: structural value) and, finally, by the economic repositioning of the theatre into its core business, with a shift from the prevalence of administrative costs to artistic costs (13SB: evolutionary value).

What dragged down the overall public value, calculated as the average of the specific value dimensions, was the performance up to the TEV. This

Table 3. The Public Value Results from 2007 to 2011.

		2007	2008	2009	2010	2011
Level 1 (joint user-body perspective)	Public value	0.41	0.50	0.46	0.37	0.39
	Supported economic and social	1.36	1.33	1.31	1.44	1.38
	(operator)	<	<	<	<	<
	Achieved economic and social benefits	1.77	1.83	1.77	1.81	1.77
	Supported economic and social ⟨=⟩ *Achieved economic and social benefits*					
Level 2 (user perspective)	Social value	0.35	0.53	0.50	0.39	0.42
	Supported social	1.58	1.52	1.43	1.27	1.12
	(operator)	>	>	>	>	>
	Achieved social benefits	1.92	2.05	1.92	1.66	1.54
	Supported social ⟨=⟩ *Achieved social benefits*					
Level 3 (body perspective)	Tangible economic value	−0.08	−0.11	0.18	0.22	0.25
	Supported tangible economic sacrifices	1.33	1.43	1.22	1.69	1.68
	(operator)	<	<	<	<	<
	Achieved tangible economic benefits	1.25	1.32	1.40	1.92	1.93
	Supported tangible economic sacrifices ⟨=⟩ *Achieved tangible economic benefits*					
Level 4 (body perspective)	Intangible economic value	0.96	1.09	0.69	0.49	0.49
	Supported intangible economic sacrifices	1.16	1.04	1.30	1.36	1.34
	(operator)	<	<	<	<	<
	Achieved intangible economic benefits	2.12	2.13	1.98	1.85	1.84
	Supported intangible economic sacrifices ⟨=⟩ *Achieved intangible economic benefits*					

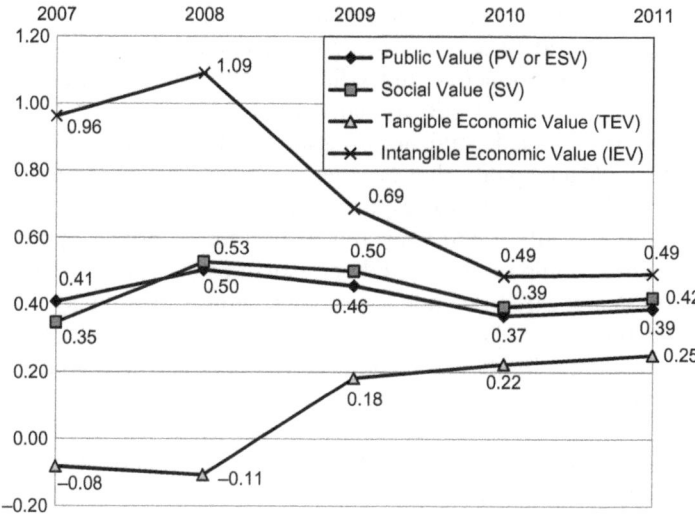

Fig. 4. Public Value Created from 2007 to 2011.

is due to three reasons: the financial distress caused by the prevalence of short-term debts compared to available liquidity (6SB: financial equilibrium), asset fragility determined by the inability to finance fixed assets with the equity and the medium/long-term liabilities (7SB: assets and liabilities equilibrium) and finally, the negativity of its operating revenues (operating loss) attributable to the failure to cover operating costs in full with core revenues (5SB: economic equilibrium).

In the 2008–2010 period, ESV was created on a decreasing scale (−0.13). ESV was dragged down by the poor performances of the IEV (−0.60) and SV (−0.14), which outpaced the economic rationalization effects connected to the transformation, which are quantifiable in an improvement in VET (+0.31 with a shift from consumption to value creation). After the preparation and implementation operations associated with becoming a foundation, the range of choices seems to have been shifted from the artistic-social to the economic, as further evidence of the inability to overcome the eternal dilemma of the marriage of the two souls of the theatre: artistic talent and economic needs. The 2008–2010 period appears burdened by the tangible and intangible start-up costs. The drastic worsening of the IEV was due to organizational operations related to the transformation: the decision to structure new organizational units and stabilize the human resources up to that period of time between the municipality and the theatre brought about a very high increase in fixed costs (9SB: structural value), increasing the average unit costs of personnel and decreasing the productive unit efficiency in relation to the number of the shows programmed (10SB: human value). Mention must be made of the increased economic dependence on grants and public subsidies (in particular from the Municipality that became the sole owner of the foundation) and the drop in the ability to respond independently to the cultural challenges of empathically identifying and exploiting economic opportunities deriving from revenue of shows and sponsorships (12SB: empathic value). The loss of SV appears to be due to strategic choices most likely influenced by the transformation. The shortening of the theatrical season for reasons including economic limits (1B: temporal efficacy) and a change in focus towards experimental theatre at the expense of traditional theatre productions, due both to artistic choice and economic needs (3B: qualitative efficacy) resulted in a decrease in audience numbers (2B: quantitative efficacy). The deterioration of social benefits reduced the positive effects of the improved efficiency of operations (2S: shortening of queues at the box office, 1S: containment of delays in starting shows, 3S: elimination of cancellations or replacement of shows programmed). Maintaining the same forms of promotion/loyalty [*Friends of the Theatre card*] did not favour a strengthening of the capacity to attract audience and sponsors (4SB: monetary efficacy).

The 2008−2010 period saw the return of the creation of increasing TEV that offset the negative impacts described above of the worsening of IEV and SV. Rationalization related to the transformation, although affected by the tightening of the above-mentioned structure costs, began to benefit from the first management results. There was a rebalancing of financial solvency due to the reduction of short-term debt in the face of increasing liquidity linked to organizational savings (6SB: financial equilibrium); asset solidity improved by virtue of the new-found ability to finance fixed investment with equity and medium/long-term liabilities (7SB: assets and liabilities equilibrium); operating profitability improved, albeit to a limited extent, through the reduction of operating costs out of total costs and the increase in operating revenues out of total revenues (including financial and extraordinary revenues) (5SB: general economic equilibrium). The profitability of the shows was positive, but very narrow (8SB: economic efficiency), due also to the above-mentioned increased stable staff cost allocation.

In the last period of analysis from 2010 to 2011, the ESV grew back slightly (+0.02), supported by the continuation of economic/financial rebalances crystallized by the TEV (+0.03), the resumption of the artistic vocation inherent in SV (+0.03) and not affected by the stabilization of the IEV (=0.00). In 2011 the first small fruits from the transformation began to appear. The growth of TEV was still limited as it was largely reinvested in the re-launch of the SV.

The limited increase of the TEV continued to benefit from rebalances but remained anchored by the weight of direct and indirect transformation costs. Strengthening the economic results of artistic performances is still a priority. The full artistic re-launch of the theatre (SV) is burdened by the constraints of artistic aspirations resulting from economic rationalization and is still manifested in the choice of shortening the season, the concentration on experimental theatre, with the net effect of loss of audience members: the incentive of reducing inefficiencies, which were already at a minimum, was not able to compensate for the loss of attractiveness resulting in the failure to renew marketing strategies.

The stabilization of the IEV continued to benefit from established relationships with many partners, and drew strength from its strategic repositioning on core business, that is, on the fine-tuning of the income statement from administrative costs to theatrical costs.

The above descriptions of the contextual and operational factors behind the creation/destruction of public value came from a discussion among the team members. In particular the administrative director found the data useful for decision-making and to implement changes: 'I had the feelings about some problem, but with the data that came out from the VP I had confirmation, and I could support my decision in the eye of the board of directors'. The PMS implemented appeared to fulfil its intended aims of not just measuring public value performances, but also managing the organization coherently.

DISCUSSION

The theatre created a low economic and social value during the period of the study, which slightly decreased throughout the five years. The birth of the foundation is the event that characterized the five-year period. The dichotomy between artistic ambitions and economic needs led to three different scenarios: before the transformation (2007–2008) there was a successful search for artistic achievement at the expense of economic sustainability and financial independence of the theatre. During the preparatory work phase and immediately after the transformation (2008–2010), there was a need to shift priorities to economic rationalization, resulting in the reduction of artistic performances. During the last period of analysis (2010–2011), the theatre's management pursued both social and economic objectives in a coordinated way, resulting in an increase in the public value created. The authorization context raised contrasting conceptions of public value, creating a dialogue between the political mandate and the managerial imperatives (Horner & Hutton, 2010).

Moore (2000) stressed the importance of placing public value at the centre of the strategy of non-profit and government organizations. That goes towards the search for an increased legitimation and support from the range of stakeholders, and society at large. In the case study, all actors interviewed and involved during the phases stressed the need for an outward strategy focused on the management of different stakeholders. This was exacerbated by its transformation to a foundation, when the search for external funding increased. As a consequence 'the possibility to measure and communicate' (administrative director) the public value created was, and still is, a priority for the theatre. However, public value has multiple objectives (outputs, customer satisfaction, outcomes, trust and legitimacy), as well as multiple accountability relations (Kelly et al., 2002).

The administrative director commented on the need to involve the existing partners and potential stakeholders to a greater extent, but at the same time to have some accountability to show the value created and the strategy the theatre pursues: 'if we want to increase the involvement of existing partners and potential stakeholders, we need to support decision-making with measurement and reporting systems able to measure the actual value produced'. The administrative director expressed the concern that measuring and reporting public value were fundamental for decision-making and overall for the relationships with external stakeholders and shareholders.

Another relevant and emerging issue was the relativity of the public value concept. Public value is indeed a very difficult concept to define and to measure as well, since public value for and to whom is always questioned (Talbot, 2006). The VP model appeared to provide a useful framework. The administrative director commented on the importance of 'the correlation between the various aspects of management and between the relevant performance measures in a multidimensional structure'. Indeed, the VP is not a prescriptive PMS model on how to measure public value, and this generated a continuous debate among the actors during the internal development of the measurement model. The selection of the indicators to measure the value created was the main difficulty, both technically and organizationally. As

Hills and Sullivan (2008) argued 'answering the question of how public value can be measured draws attention not only to the kind of measures that are needed, but also to the processes by which the measures are developed and used' (p. 14). As the case shows, the process of choosing, discussing and agreeing on the KPIs had both conceptual and technical issues. For instance, from a technical point of view, the data availability and the automation of the information systems were a constraint, meaning extra work for the administration, or limits on the choice of KPIs. Of course, this meant there was need to 'simplify and customize the language according to the different information recipients' (administrative director) and to allow readability of the data. This is important if reporting for accountability and transparency to stakeholders is to be effective.

On the other hand, it appears that practical concerns over public value measurement were also triggered by an internal driver. As stressed by the administrative director, the only accountability tool was represented by the financial report, which was considered limited in showing the value of the theatre's activity. The administrative director commented: 'we are aware of the difficult financial conditions, but it is our primary focus to show in which way we can create value to the society'. The quest for multidimensional KPIs was aimed at legitimizing the theatre's role and activity. At the same time, the administrative director stressed the importance of a PMS to link the measurement of performance, to the management of the operational drivers, to the overall public value strategy:

> If you just measure and report, it would not be enough. The rest of the organizational processes needs to be aligned to the theatre strategy, and the skills, capabilities and know how have to be developed consistently. I believe the value pyramid can support us in doing so.

Those concerns involved also the political arena, where public value appeared to become a field of discussion and confrontation. What emerged from the interviews is consistent with Moore's (2000) view that the public value framework 'makes political management as important to public managers as organizational management' (p. 199). The relationship with the political arena, represented by the Municipality, can be traced in the following comment by the administrative director: 'the VP model should be put in place at the different institutional and organizational levels of the Municipality, we need to have a common tool and language between politicians and managers'. The reason for this was to increase the capacity of the public value model to support the governance of the activities investigated to then extend beyond the organization's boundaries.

In respect to the theoretical aspect, the evidence raised showed a multi-faceted role for the PMS within the public dynamic framework of Horner and Hutton (2010). Indeed, PMS can be placed within the 'measure' element of the framework, but goes beyond it. The PMS with which we experimented in action meant also understanding of the way public value can be created and destroyed. In this sense, a PMS serves also as a framework to align public value measures with the key operations, capability and know-how that form the base of public value (Moore, 2003, 2000).

As shown in Fig. 5, we stress the need to give a wider role to PMS, as an integrating means between the two separate elements of 'create' and 'measure'. The dotted lines highlight the fact that PMS derives from, and gives content to, the elements, facilitating the alignment between the way public value is produced and how it is measured. The case study supports this idea, and that through a PMS the organization can develop a learning process of understanding what public value is, how it can be measured and created, informing a dialogue with stakeholders and searching for legitimation and success.

In the public value literature, the measurement issue and the management of services are often considered two separate, although inter-related, dimensions (Horner & Hutton, 2010; Moore, 1995). We argue for the need to consider and study the two as inextricably linked, requiring a PMS in order to create a strategic alignment towards public value creation. PMS can support the move from a static view of public value measurement to a dynamic management of all the factors that make operations and activity

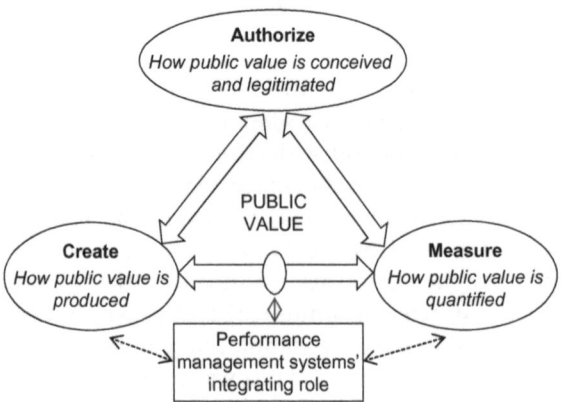

Fig. 5. The Public Value Dynamic and PMS: A Refinement.

valuable to stakeholders. As the private sector relies on the concept value-based management (Claes, 2006), in the context of public services, we may refer to a public value-based management. Speckbacher (2006) argues that in NFP organizations it could be fruitful to introduce a value-based strategic management system in order to manage, assess and account for the public value generated and/or distributed to the different stakeholders. A public value-based management can be thus considered as a managerial approach to strategically managing an organization by focusing on the key public value drivers and, in doing so, to create public value according to the authorizing context. On this line, we support the idea of the need to integrate public value measurement, with decision-making and MCS and linked to all other operations (Claes, 2006; Spano, 2009; Speckbacher, 2006), towards a strategic PMS.

CONCLUSION

We have analyzed the role of PMS in pursuing public value strategy, using an experimental action-research approach. As a consequence, this article contributes to the calls made in the literature for more applied studies in public value (Alford & Hughes, 2008; Alford & O'Flynn, 2009; Williams & Shearer, 2011) and management accounting (Lukka & Suomala, 2014; Malmi & Granlund, 2009). In addition, we have attempted to offer a theoretical contribution to the public value literature.

The integrated performance management of public value (as in the case of the VP model) would allow the design, implementation and monitoring of strategic objectives, and of each specific management implementation programme. In so doing, PMS supports the process of putting public value at the centre of strategy for the delivery of public services (Moore, 1994, 2003). However, we propose a refinement of the public value literature, and in particular of the public value dynamic proposed by Horner and Hutton (2010). We call for PMS, as a strategic managerial tool, to integrate the 'measure' and 'create' dimensions. At the same time, public value measures can be communicated, improving the accountability and transparency to multiple stakeholders (O'Flynn, 2007).

This article contributes to calls for research highlighted by Benington and Moore (2010, pp. 20–21), discussing public value from an accounting perspective, applying the public value concept to particular policy arenas (cultural services) with an attempt to assess, measure and manage public value. While we support the conceptual utility of the public value dynamic (Horner & Hutton, 2010), there are theoretical and practical concerns to consider in the development of conceptual frameworks to measure, manage and account for public value in an integrated and dynamic way. While public value concepts may be hard to grasp, its measurement and management are achievable and support public managers to go beyond mere financial performance and short-term objectives. In this sense, the PMS can play an integrative role towards the diffusion of public value-based management logics (Speckbacher, 2006), supporting public managers in focusing the allocation of resources, and improving public services.

As shown in the case of the theatre, public value was applied as a comprehensive approach and a management framework to ascertain what is valuable or not, where to allocate resources and towards continuous improvement in public services (Constable, Passmore, & Coats, 2008; Moore, 1995; Williams & Shearer, 2011). At the same time, the process of measuring public value needs to be integrated within a PMS, in order to steer and influence behaviour, as well as resource allocation and the performance assessment of the public managers and employees (Claes, 2006; Spano, 2009; Speckbacher, 2006). Overall, we support the idea that public service management needs to place a strategic orientation on the decision-making and policy-making processes, that in turn shapes constraints on performance (Boyne & Walker, 2010; Broadbent & Guthrie, 2008; Stoker, 2006). Consequently, if public value is the strategy (Moore, 1994), public service organizations are called to measure, manage and account for the public value created in an integrated way.

REFERENCES

Alford, J. (2008). The limits to traditional public administration, or rescuing public value from misrepresentation. *Australian Journal of Public Administration, 67*(3), 357–366.

Alford, J., & Hughes, O. (2008). Public value pragmatism as the next phase of public management. *The American Review of Public Administration, 38*(2), 130–148.

Alford, J., & O'Flynn, J. (2009). Making sense of public value: Concepts, critiques and emergent meanings. *International Journal of Public Administration, 32*(3–4), 171–191.

Argyris, C., Putnam, R., & McLain Smith, D. (1985). *Action science − Concepts, methods and skills for research and intervention*. San Francisco, CA: Jossey-Bass.

Benington, J., & Moore, M. H. (2010). Public value in complex and changing times. In J. Benington & M. H. Moore (Eds), *Public value: Theory and practice* (pp. 1–30). Basingstoke: Palgrave Macmillan.

Bovaird, T. (2007). Beyond engagement and participation: User and community coproduction of public services. *Public Administration Review, 67* (September–October), 846–860.

Boyne, G. A., & Walker, R. M. (2010). Strategic management and public service performance: The way ahead. *Public Administration Review, 70* (December), S185–S192.

Broadbent, J., & Guthrie, J. (2008). Public sector to public services: 20 years of alternative accounting research. *Accounting, Auditing and Accountability Journal, 21*(2), 129–169.

Claes, P. C. M. (2006). Management control and value-based management. In M. J. Epstein & J. F. Manzoni (Eds), *Performance measurement and management control: Improving organizations and society* (pp. 269–301). Oxford: JAI Press.

Constable, S., Passmore, E., & Coats, D. (2008). *Public value and local accountability in the NHS*. London: Work Foundation.

Cowling, M. (2006). *Measuring public value: The economic theory*. London: The Work Foundation.

D'Egidio, F. (2005). *Il bilancio dell'intangibile*. Milano: FrancoAngeli.

Deidda Gagliardo, E. (2002). *La creazione del valore nell'ente local*. Torino: Giuffrè Editore.

Deidda Gagliardo, E., & Poddighe, F. (2011). The system of creation and measuring of the public local value. Empirical evidence and support for the governance of the territory. In R. Mussari & E. Borgonovi (Eds), *Collaborating and competing for a responsible and fair market. Government, non-profit organizations, foundations, cooperatives, social enterprises*. Bologna: Il Mulino.

Hefetz, A., & Walner, M. (2004). Privatization and its reverse: Explaining the dynamics of the government contracting process. *Journal of Public Administration Research and Theory, 14*(2), 171–190.

Hills, D., & Sullivan, F. (2008). *Measuring public value 2: Practical approaches*. London: The Work Foundation.

Hopwood, A. (2002). 'If only there were simple solutions, but there aren't': Some reflections on Zimmerman's critique of empirical management accounting research. *European Accounting Review, 11*(4), 777–785.

Horner, L., & Hutton, W. (2010). Public value deliberative democracy and the role of public managers. In J. Benington & M. H. Moore (Eds), *Public value: Theory and practice* (pp. 112–126). Basingstoke: Palgrave Macmillan.

Horner, L., Lekhi, R., & Blaug, R. (2006). *Deliberative democracy and the role of public managers*. London: The Work Foundation.

Jørgensen, T. B., & Bozeman, B. (2002). Public Values lost? Comparing cases on contracting out from Denmark and the United States. *Public Management Review, 4*(1), 63–81.

Kelly, G., Mulgan, G., & Muers, S. (2002). *Creating public value: An analytical framework for public service reform*. London: Cabinet Office Strategy Unit.

Lev, B. (2001). *Intangibles: Management, measurement, and reporting*. Washington, DC: Brookings Inst Pr.

Lukka, K., & Mouritsen, J. (2002). Homogeneity or heterogeneity of research in management accounting? *European Accounting Review, 11*(4), 805–811.

Lukka, K., & Suomala, P. (2014). Relevant interventionist research: Balancing three intellectual virtues. *Accounting and Business Research, 44*(2), 1–17.

Lyly-Yrjänäinen, J., & Suomala, P. (2012). *Management accounting research in practice*. New York, NY: Routledge.

Malmi, T., & Granlund, M. (2009). In search of management accounting theory. *European Accounting Review, 18*(3), 597–620.

Meier, K. J., O'Toole, L. J., Boyne, G. A., & Walker, R. M. (2006). Strategic management and the performance of public organizations: Testing venerable ideas against recent theories. *Journal of Public Administration Research and Theory, 17*(3), 357–377.

Meynhardt, T., & Metelmann, J. (2009). Pushing the envelope: Creating public value in the labor market: An empirical study on the role of middle managers. *International Journal of Public Administration, 32,* 274–312.

Mook, L. (2013). *Accounting for social value.* Toronto: University of Toronto Press.

Moore, M. H. (1994). Public value as the focus of strategy. *Australian Accounting Review, 53*(3), 296–303.

Moore, M. H. (1995). *Creating public value: Strategic management in government.* Harvard: Harvard University Press.

Moore, M. H. (2000). Managing for value: Organizational strategy in for-profit, nonprofit, and governmental organizations. *Nonprofit and Voluntary Sector Quarterly, 29*(1), 183–204.

Moore, M. H. (2003). *The public value scorecard* (p. 27). Working Paper No. 18. The Hauser Center for Nonprofit Organizations.

Norman, R. (2011). Redefining 'public value' in New Zealand's performance management system: Managing for outcomes while accounting for outputs. In J. Benington & M. H. Moore (Eds), *Public value: Theory and practice* (pp. 202–2011). Basingstone: Palgrave Macmillan.

O'Flynn, J. (2007). From new public management to public value: Paradigmatic change and managerial implications. *Australian Journal of Public Administration, 66*(3), 353–366.

Rapoport, R. N. (1970). Three dilemmas in action research: With special reference to the Tavistock experience. *Human Relations, 23*(6), 499–513.

Rhodes, R. A. W., & Wanna, J. (2007). The limits to public value, or rescuing responsible government from the platonic guardians. *Australian Journal of Public Administration, 66*(4), 406–421.

Rhodes, R. A. W., & Wanna, J. (2009). Bringing the politics back in: Public value in Westminster Parliamentary Government. *Public Administration, 87*(2), 161–183.

Smith, R. F. I. (2004). Focusing on public value: Something new and something old. *Australian Journal of Public Administration, 63*(December), 68–79.

Spano, A. (2009). Public value creation and management control systems. *International Journal of Public Administration, 32*(3–4), 328–348.

Speckbacher, G. (2006). Strategic performance management in for-profit and not-for-profit organizations: What's the difference and what can they learn from each other? In M. J. Epstein & J.-F. Manzoni (Eds), *Performance measurement and management control: Improving organizations and society* (pp. 459–478). Oxford: JAI Press.

Stoker, G. (2006). Public value management: A new narrative for networked governance? *The American Review of Public Administration, 36*(1), 41–57.

Susman, G. I., & Evered, R. D. (1978). An assessment of the scientific merits of action research. *Administrative Science Quarterly, 23*(4), 582–603.

Talbot, C. (2006). *Measuring public value. A competing values approach.* London: The Work Foundation.

Westin, O., & Roberts, H. (2010). Interventionist research – the puberty years: An introduction to the special issue. *Qualitative Research in Accounting and Management, 7*(1), 5–12.

Williams, I., & Shearer, H. (2011). Appraising public value: Past, present and futures. *Public Administration, 89*(4), 1367–1384.

APPENDIX: THE SEMI-STRUCTURED QUESTIONNAIRE: OUTLINE

Public value as strategy	How do you define your strategy? How do you conceive public value? How can public value legitimize your organization in the eyes of stakeholders? Who are your stakeholders?
Measurement	How do you measure the performance of your organization? How can you conceptualize public value measure?
Usefulness for decision-making purposes	Do you think that the public value model provided you with useful information for better governance of the activity of which you are in charge?
Strengths	In your opinion what are the main strengths of the VP model?
Problems	In your opinion what are the main problems of the VP model?

STRATEGIC PRACTICES OF CREATING PUBLIC VALUE: HOW MANAGERS OF HOUSING ASSOCIATIONS CREATE PUBLIC VALUE

Kim van Eijck and Berit Lindemann

ABSTRACT

Purpose — *The creation of public value is a topical debate for Dutch civil society organizations. Over the years, moving from government to governance, they supposedly have gained responsibility and space in meeting public needs. However, meeting the priority public needs and demonstrating actual public value creation has proved difficult. This has led to many discussions on how and if these organizations are creating public value. This study therefore investigated three practical cases to explore and explain how managers of housing associations create public value.*

Method — *A case study method was employed.*

Findings — *Based on the different cases we can conclude that despite high ambitions, deviating normative views and the will to change*

Public Value Management, Measurement and Reporting
Studies in Public and Non-Profit Governance, Volume 3, 159–187
Copyright © 2014 by Emerald Group Publishing Limited
ISSN: 2051-6630/doi:10.1108/S2051-663020140000003007

displayed by the managers in the cases we investigated, we did not encounter situations where managers actually managed spaces for the creation of public value. The involved managers are still led by formal agendas and policies, rather than engaging in dialogues with their relevant stakeholders. They remain segmented in their approach and offering of services. Managers' environment and stakeholders are not yet naturally seen as a place for sharing information and reframing boundaries for creating public value.

Originality/value — The opportunity in the investigated cases and for these managers lies in mobilizing and utilizing network relationships. This article provides a public value praxis model that focuses on involving stakeholders in investigating priority needs, collectively (re)designing services that meet these.

Keywords: Public value; practice; case study; network relationships

INTRODUCTION

Governments have argued that civil society organizations are better able to solve complex social problems (Pollit & Bouckaert, 2004), and therefore power has devolved to civil society organizations, stimulating broader social responsibility. In particular, decentralization and deregulation mean that civil society organizations are taking responsibility in the areas of education, welfare, healthcare, employment, culture and housing (Minderman, 2008). The subsequent new roles and responsibilities of organizations such as housing associations are ambiguous. There is a learning process for the managers (and professionals) of these associations to give substance to, and account for, their new roles and responsibilities in solving complex social problems. The public value of their practices is questioned and debated, as the supervision and control of these associations has not prevented the occurrence of scandals and incidents that have caused a national decline of trust in, for example, the public housing sector.

As a result of these developments, a group of managers from Dutch housing associations wanted to explore how they can create (and possibly demonstrate) the public value of their practices. In this article, we present a selection of preliminary data and findings from a longitudinal study on their practices of public value (see also, van Eijck & Lindemann, 2012; van Eijck, Lindemann, & Mindermann, 2013). We first describe the current status of public value theories and its assumptions, and highlight the relative absence of empirical data. This is followed by an outline of the contextual, societal and governance trends that have confronted Dutch housing associations and their managers are described as well as their practical implications. Next we present the method for the research as well as three separate cases that have been studied. These cases and findings are described using the so-called *praxis of public value* framework. This analytical framework was developed through extensive and longitudinal research on public value creation in societal sectors (see Lindemann, van Eijck, & Minderman, 2013; van Eijck & Lindemann, 2012). Following is the analysis and comparison of the cases using the same theoretical model. Based on the findings, the final section provides conclusions and implications for both practitioners as well as academia.

CORE ASSUMPTIONS AND PROBLEMS OF PUBLIC VALUE CREATION

According to Moore's (1995) theory about public value creation, the challenge for public managers is to adapt to changes in their environments and identify new purposes through innovative and experimental actions. He argues that managers should focus their attention on orchestrating existing forces and pressures to help them achieve their purposes, instead of being dominated by 'old' steering mechanisms (such as bureaucracy or output measurement systems). Nearly two decades later, this concept continues to spark considerable interest among practitioners and academics. At the present time, the concept of 'creating public value' has evolved into a discourse that touches on a broad spectrum of disciplines, such as public administration, business administration, political science, economics, psychology and organizational science. Talbot (2009, p. 167) has stated that 'creating public value' might become the 'the next "Big Thing" in public management', as it better corresponds with 'current tumultuous events' (Talbot, 2009, p. 167). This section discusses some of the fundamental assumptions on which public value theory is built and explains which problems recent theory still fails to address.

Three Coherent Assumptions

Recent literature in the field of public management has been concerned, among other things, with shifts in society, the role of non-governmental actors and the evolving roles and practices of managers in the public sector. In our article we are especially concerned with three assumptions, about these shifts, roles and practices.

The first assumption is that of a transition, known as the 'movement from government towards governance'. The underlying axiom in the academic debate is that the movement towards governance creates space for non-governmental actors to identify and meet complex public service needs by using alternative steering mechanisms (Ebbers, 2005; Hauser, 1998; Inglehart, 1997; Pierre & Peters, 2000). Indeed, the movement towards governance suggests that mechanisms from traditional public administration (TPA) are becoming less dominant, as it fails to respond to complex social needs. An alternative mechanism, which scholars refer to as 'governance', focuses more on society's ability to steer itself via mechanisms of individual choice (new public management (NPM)) or dialogue and collaboration (public network management), rather than relying on centralized governmental power. Recently, the paradigm of public network management – also referred to as network governance – has gained popularity in the literature, with some even arguing that this has replaced the NPM approach for public sector reform (Benington, 2011). Various scholars link this steering mechanism to the concept or discourse of public value (management), which is seen as a reaction or alternative to the political predominance of neo-liberal and NPM approaches in recent decades (Benington, 2005). The term 'space' generally refers to the latitude that non-governmental actors – especially in civil society – supposedly gain as government devolves power and influence to other layers in society (Hauser, 1998) by means of public reforms. This space can be divided into two dimensions, of which the first is the overarching and prolonged space that arises between the 'central' and the 'local' as government withdraws its reach through, for example, decentralization and deregulation (Alford & Hughes, 2008; Rhodes & Wanna, 2007). The other dimension is the increasing liability of non-governmental actors in the market and civil society. As these actors gain liability, it is assumed that *they are inclined to respond to local 'windows of opportunity' that arise from events, developments and problems occurring in their daily practice* (Wei-Skillern, Austin, Leonard, & Stevenson, 2007).

The second assumption suggests that civil society actors should utilize this space, as they have gained the latitude to create public value. Scholars emphasize local deliberation and engagement as important means to identify needs and create public value (e.g. Alford & Hughes, 2008; Benington, 2012; Hartley, 2005; Sørensen & Torfing, 2007; Stoker, 2006). Governance supposedly creates the capacity and opportunities for citizens to engage in enlightened local debate (Hauser, 1998). Deliberative spaces and processes can be developed that bring a public into consciousness and action (Benington, 2012) and enable them to (re) discover which needs and values are important. The abovementioned scholars identify civil society actors as the vehicles for developing and co-constructing these local deliberations. The space produced by governance supposedly strengthens and enhances the latitude of these actors to recognize, respond and contribute to the local opportunities arising from their daily practice. This implies that civil society's responsibilities stretch beyond determining how policy goals are to be reached, as according to this second assumption, they also are free, or perhaps empowered, *to identify public goals and the needs under-lying them.*

The third assumption is that the practice of civil society managers expands to managing spaces for public value creation. Moore (1995), O'Toole, Meir, and Nicholson-Crotty (2005), O'Flynn (2005), Hartley (2005), Stoker (2006) and Benington (2011, 2012) are concerned with the evolving roles and practices of public managers in the movement towards governance and suggest that the nature of public sector managers' work, especially in civil society, is becoming increasingly political as they become social entrepreneurial agents who are exploring the question of which needs matter and which value should be created. Initially, Moore (1995) suggested that public managers should expand their practices to imagine the value they wished to create, subsequently capture this value in a proposition and convince stakeholders to authorize and realize it. This suggestion has been criticized for its somewhat heroic view of the manager as an agent capable of interpreting and determining what the public needs before seeking support among stakeholders (Rhodes & Wanna, 2007). More recently, scholars such as Benington (2012) and Meynhardt (2012) have moved away from these initial ideas by suggesting that managers should not focus their attention on determining what the public needs or value the most, but rather concentrate on 'bringing the public into existence', and thereby allowing the public to identify and understand their needs and co-create public value. Public value discourse thus seems to be shifting away from the idea that managers can intention-ally imagine and determine public value, thereby pushing the boundaries in order to gain support and realize a proposal (content strategy), and *towards the idea that managers, while subject to their environments, can deliberately influence the processes through which the content of strategies are determined.*

The Problem and Question

The intriguing problem that we encountered was that the theories on which these assumptions are built leave a behavioural and an institutional problem unanswered. From a behavioural perspective, we learned that little is known about what managers — as they develop into social entrepreneurs — do when managing spaces for public value, and it is unclear what explains this expanded practice. From an institutional perspective, we learned that the influence of institutional pressures on the extended practice of managing space for public value is not being sufficiently taken into account. After all, it is not obvious that civil society managers are able to break free from and alter the existing institutions that shape their everyday practice. We therefore set out to explore and explain how these practices work and why they differ. It is likely that the failure to address these problems to date is partly due to the lack of empirical investigations. Authors in the field of public value tend to write normative propositions, contribute to theoretical development or design analytical frames (Williams & Shearer, 2011). In short, we set ourselves the task of answering the following central question: *how do public managers (attempt to) manage public value creation?* In order to answer this question, we first had to determine the conceptual focus of our study. In the following section, we present an analytical framework that has been built in order to explore and understand the way managers manage public value creation.

PRAXIS OF PUBLIC VALUE CREATION

This section presents an analytical framework recently developed by van Eijck and Lindemann[1] that is used in order to get a better understanding of the praxis of creating public value and the strategic practice of civil society managers. This theoretical framework was developed on the basis of two longitudinal studies on public value creation in Dutch social housing and education. This research reveals that managers are involved in different activities when public value creation is achieved or interrupted, whether initiated by themselves or others. In this article, we will use this framework in order to illustrate how civil society managers frequently fail to expand their practice to manage public value creation.

Managers assess and prioritize a mix of factors, relations and information in specific circumstances when agendas emerge, and make trade-offs

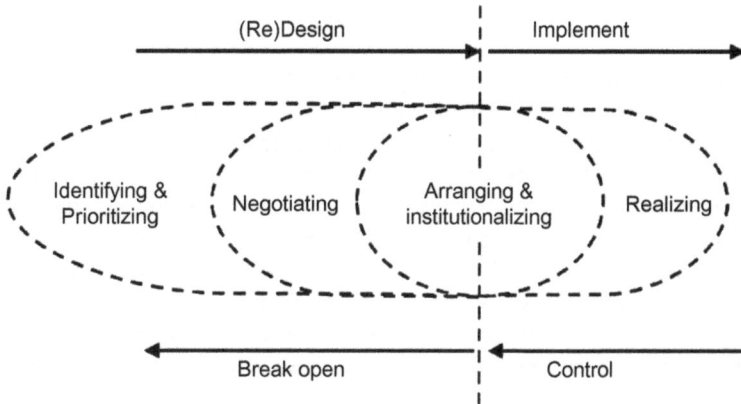

Fig. 1. Praxis of Public Value Creation.

on the basis of networks. In order to consider the range of factors used in decision-making, different work activities are organized, which can be divided into a set of four activities that form a praxis (flow of activities). We argue that creating public value roughly consists of four inter-related stages during which deliberation, collaboration and accountability take place. These stages have diverse objectives, varying from identifying relevant social issues, devising and realizing possible solutions to negotiations concerning capacities and 'ownership'. These are illustrated in Fig. 1 and explained in detail in the following paragraphs.

THE FOUR STATES OF PUBLIC VALUE CREATION

Identifying and Prioritizing

Some work activities involve deliberations in meetings, during which parties identify, assess and prioritize public needs. Such meetings vary in composition and are organized by different initiating parties. During these activities managers may stimulate deliberation with internal and external stakeholders concerning public needs and mutual responsibilities. In this process managers take part in various networks in which they share interests, exchange information, analyze problems and eventually prioritize the needs that are of importance in the local environment.

Negotiating

This work activity involves translating prioritized needs into services. This implies negotiations between network actors, during which decisions are made about ownership and service design. During this activity, individual actors' work definitions evolve as actors assess and prioritize environmental developments. In some cases, a solution may be embedded in the current services provided by an organization. However, in other cases, the outcome may be that services are delivered collectively in order to meet certain needs that spill beyond individual organizations' capacities and responsibilities. During this process individual and collective services are thus developed or transformed, as actors negotiate about allocation of resources and division of responsibilities and tasks.

Arranging and Institutionalizing

This activity concerns the process of capturing identified needs and the solutions devised to meet these in an institutional arrangement. In meetings, networks develop customs, norms and rules concerning coordination, responsibility and accountability. This may involve formalized plans in, for example, social contracts, codes or covenants, and the setting up of steering committees or similar structures, which supervise the transition. These arrangements form the basis of the implementation and control of a solution by monitoring and adjusting collective agreements.

Operationalizing and Realizing

This work activity involves the implementation and realization of agenda items (and future agenda items). During this activity, project teams translate agenda items and the devised solutions into specific plans, schemes actions and services, with rationalized and identifiable goals and solutions, initiated in order to manage the realization of collective and/or individual goals. These activities are, in contrast to the open and exploratory nature of the previous three stages, characterized as a more closed type of operational collaboration meant to rationalize and realize services. In addition, this phase also concerns the evaluation of the projects, which involves measurement of the relevance, effectiveness and efficiency of actual service delivery.

Normative Framework

If 'new' steering mechanisms were actually prevailing over 'old' steering mechanisms, this would imply that civil society actors have gained latitude to investigate local problems, identify and prioritize the public needs underlying them and formulate the interventions and objectives that might meet them. Although not made explicit in existing theory, this suggests that an alternative agenda-type – one that will capture local public needs – will emerge or is emerging in civil society and that the actors within this sector are being empowered to determine which solutions would meet these needs. This would imply that the locus of the political agenda, policy formulation and decision-making has shifted to another space and to other players. According to the third assumption discussed in the previous section, managers in civil society should, or already, manage local spaces in which these agendas, solutions and decisions emerge through deliberative and collaborative activities among civil society actors. If we place the praxis of public value creation within the normative frame of these core assumptions, it would imply that civil society managers manage public value creation by being involved in the praxis of value creation in dialogue and collaboration with their local stakeholders and by building interdependent relationships in which they push and pull information in order to authorize local public needs and values. This is done by either collectively building and setting an agenda or by gaining support for a public value proposal. They also create public value by perceiving their environment as a place where they receive and share relevant information with their stakeholders and reframe the boundaries, nature and reach of their work.

THE CASES

Method and Techniques

Case studies as a research strategy are preferred when 'how' and 'why' types of question are posed (Yin, 1995). Furthermore, the case study is appropriate when social relations between actors within a system or society are studied (see, e.g. Flyvbjerg, 2006, 2011; Swanborn, 2000). As we want to study how managers of housing associations create public value within their local contexts and practices, a multiple case study was seen as the most suitable option. Three different local projects of housing associations were selected for studying how managers of these associations create public value.

Within these three cases various research techniques have been applied. First, documents and media coverage related to these cases were studied in order to gather relevant information on activities within these projects and multiple interpretations of public value creation. This information, for example, concerned internal documents displaying the focus of decisions made by managers, the justification for their decisions and the involvement of other stakeholders. Media coverage concerned, for example, newspaper articles reporting on dissatisfied tenants who felt excluded by the housing association, or TV items publicly criticizing the project. Such information provided a view on the praxis of public value creation from different stakeholder perspectives. Second, interviews with managers of public housing associations were conducted. The selected cases on public value creation were discussed during in-depth interviews with the relevant managers. Questions were related to the praxis of public value framework. In the interviews we discussed the different steps of the framework and how the managers acted within these steps. They provided information on how they identified the public needs they wanted to serve, the services they provided and how they demonstrate and legitimize their public value creation. Furthermore, if and how different stakeholders were involved in these different steps.

Third, each case was discussed and studied during focus group sessions, in which 10−15 internal and external stakeholders related to these projects participated. Internal stakeholders were, for example, internal managers, strategic advisors, communications employees and financial managers. External stakeholders were, for example, tenants, managers of other public organizations, local entrepreneurs and policy officers from local municipalities. The different praxis of public value creation (see Fig. 1) were jointly made visible and discussed. Leading questions during these focus groups were, for example, the following: how are public needs inventoried in this case? What considerations are made in the (joint) development of services? What arrangements are made? And how are these services realized? For each of these questions, it was also noted if and how different stakeholders were involved and how they valued their involvement. Furthermore, there was discussion of whether it is both plausible and demonstrable that public value is created within the case. Through these different techniques a thorough and in-depth insight into how managers of Dutch housing associations create public value is provided.

Context of Dutch Housing Associations

Contemporary Dutch housing associations can best be characterized as private, not-for-profit organizations that provide 'social housing' for people with low incomes and groups with special needs, such as the elderly or disabled. Over 40% of the Dutch housing market comprises rented housing, of which approximately 80% is social housing (Brandsen, Farnell, & Cardoso Ribeiro, 2006). These organizations conduct activities such as 'building, managing, allocating and selling housing, supplying services to tenants and maintaining the neighbourhood in terms of its quality of life and investing in care homes'.[2] Although highly autonomous, these organizations are still influenced by European Union (EU) and state regulations. Housing associations make little or no use of subsidies; rather, income is generated from rents and sale, as well as private market funding for new construction. Moreover, most loans are provided with guarantees from the Guarantee Fund for social housing (Brandsen et al., 2006).

As a result of further privatization in the mid-1990s, a major transition occurred in the social housing sector. Following an amendment to the Decree on Social Housing Management, the tasks of housing associations were extending to preserving the 'livability'[3] of communities, in addition to their traditional responsibilities concerning the construction, management and rental of affordable housing. By investing in livability, it was assumed that the association would address a broader set of social challenges and needs. However, the core task on 'livability' is ambiguous: it is a diffuse and multidimensional concept that is not clearly defined by government or by the sector itself. Or, as van Dorst (2005) writes: 'This could apply to different scales, the livability of a rabbit hutch, the livability of the world. A livable neighbourhood seems to have a similar quality as an edible dinner or a readable book'. It has thus become unclear how far an association could, would or should go in defining and realizing its social responsibility. Furthermore, associations contribute to the presence of adequate facilities such as schools, youth centres, shops, parking facilities, street lighting, flora and fauna and public transport (Lindemann et al., 2013; Minderman, van Eijck, Lindemann, & van der Klooster, 2010).

Although it seems contrary to the developments described above, there is also a current tendency towards centralization and a strong social demand for greater control over the social housing sector. This tendency has been partially fuelled by incidents and scandals in the sector, such as fraud, excessively high salaries for board members and risky investments. In addition, this trend is related to the ongoing debate about the effect and value of social investments. It seems to be difficult to determine the value, effects and financial return of livability projects. In this discussion, many have been guided by the results of the social cost benefit analysis (SCBA) analyzes that have been conducted in the sector. Although it is plausible that housing associations' social investments have had a considerable impact on society and have also benefited (including financially) other societal organizations and local government bodies, both practitioners and academics remain broadly sceptical about attempts to rationalize these effects in measurable outputs (Minderman et al., 2010). In the following paragraphs we describe the three cases that were studied.

Case: The Dirtiest Apartment Building in the Netherlands

Hans is a manager and adviser for a housing association in a mid-sized city in the province of Twente. His work consists of developing policy on livability issues in the area and advising the board on so-called livability projects. He is also the chairman of a committee that assesses potential investments in the area where the association rents out dwellings. Hans was recently involved in a controversial case involving one of the apartment blocks that the association manages, the South Flat.

> Human faces in the elevator, urine and vomit on the stairs and a wave of burglaries. Residents of the South Flat in 'East Town' are fed up! The housing association has being letting the apartment building deteriorate for years. Several hemp plantations have been discovered and there are apartments where dealers and prostitutes provide their 'services'. The residents are fed up with the sociopathic visitors and fellow residents in and around the building. They are demanding that the housing association take measures.

The South Flat has attracted a lot of attention in the Dutch media in the past two years, as the above excerpt from a national newspaper shows. The building is located in the centre of East Town. The residents have been complaining about the physical condition of the building for more than 10 years. It started with complaints about the heating and insulation of the building, which did not meet current energy standards. However, over time there were also 'social' complaints about noise, subletting, security issues and dirt in and around the building. The complaints and problems began to pile up. The residents then involved the national media, with the result that the building was even voted 'The filthiest building in the Netherlands' on a primetime television show.

The housing association had recently designed and established a new arrangement called the PSU, a team that deals with the association's social investments. This team is responsible for decision-making on projects and activities relating to social investments, and subsequently coordinates and monitors these projects. Hans chairs the team, and his colleagues are other housing association managers with different areas of expertise, such as area development, neighbourhood management, property management and communication.

Right from the start, the members of the PSU team realized that they would have to act quickly in order to limit the reputational damage to the South Flat. At that time, they were mainly interested in addressing the tenants' increasing complaints about maintenance shortcomings. The PSU team believed that the problems in and around the South Flat were due to poor maintenance: 10 years beforehand the apartments in the building had been moderately insulated and the heating boilers were due for replacement. In the meantime, additional social problems had arisen in the surroundings of the building, such as increasing crime and violence, nuisance, pollution and drug abuse. Other parties, such as the municipality, the neighbourhood council, tenants, the police, care institutions, the media and local businesses obviously also had an interest in the issues affecting the South Flat. However, the PSU team decided not to involve these parties when dealing with the issue; rather, they took a solo approach, limiting external contact to consultation with the municipality and providing information on the proposed plans to the district council. Their main argument was that the South Flat was part of the association's real estate and the housing association was thus the logical 'owner' of this problem. Therefore, they did not involve stakeholders in the inventory of needs (including social needs), nor did they negotiate with external stakeholders about the mutual interests and responsibilities involved in the case.

The PSU team eventually decided to demolish the building and construct a new apartment complex in its place. In its analysis of the situation, the PSU team used a standard format that covered social, physical and financial aspects. On the basis of this format, considerations were made about the type of intervention that had to be made. Eventually four alternatives, mainly relating to property development, were identified: 'do nothing, renovation, demolition or sale'. They eventually opted for demolition and a new construction, because this would contribute 'to public housing (...) and our portfolio (new type of housing in a higher segment) and it is the most financially attractive decision'. With the new construction, capacity would decrease from 100 to 70 homes, including 70% social housing and 30%

high rent or sales. The social housing would be of higher quality and more expensive, which implied that all of the current residents would have to leave. In order to ensure a secure transfer to another apartment building, a social plan was drawn up for these residents. Although this was their formal decision, there was still a lack of consensus between the participants in the interactive session about the value of the decision. Table 1 shows a first analysis of the case using the praxis of public value framework.

The process of discussing, defining and prioritizing public needs was limited to members of the PSU team. The members opted for a solo approach in which they gathered relevant information for their standardized analysis and provided information about their future plans. External needs were analyzed using a standardized tool based on the association's current services and expertise. Having discussed and analyzed the situation in and around the South Flat, and considered the options, the PSU team subsequently designated a project leader to realize the demolition and the construction of a new complex. The managers tended to focus on solving the problem at hand by setting an individual agenda within a relatively small group of colleagues, before proceeding to implementation and realization. Other parties did not have a direct say in defining the problem or realizing or evaluating the proposed intervention. Furthermore, the managers involved did not explore the possibility of collaborating with external stakeholders, negotiating about shared responsibilities and sharing the investment.

Table 1. Analysis Dirtiest Apartment Building.

Activity	Description	Implication
1. *Needs identification and prioritization*	A closed deliberation between internal stakeholders, based on available expertise and current services	A limited and unilateral analyzes and prioritization of public needs
2. *Negotiating*	Internal negotiation based on a standardized and unitarily tool	Chosen intervention focuses solely on a limited number of symptoms, instead of dealing with the problem as a whole
3. *Arranging and institutionalizing*	An internal arrangement consisting of representatives of different expertise and discipline	Limited view of needs and lack of legitimization
4. *Realizing*	Interventions within the scope of the individual organization	Focus on organizational interests, instead of public needs

Case: Business Centre for Local Entrepreneurs

Eric is a unit director of a housing association in the third largest city in the Netherlands. He is responsible for managing and maintaining the housing association's property in the Marry district. This particular housing association provides approximately 30,000 units of social housing in and around the city. The core mission of the association is to provide affordable housing for people on low or medium incomes, starters, elderly people and/ or vulnerable people, such as ex-offenders, the homeless, teenage mothers and people who require long-term care. In addition, the association is concerned with maintaining and improving its current housing stock and stimulating the sustainable use of resources and improving livability in the areas where its current and future tenants live. The association has the more general philosophy and ambition of helping to create a society in which citizens enjoy equal opportunities to prosper. This implies that Eric's work also entails maintaining and improving livability in the immediate vicinity of the social housing that he manages.

Over the past two to three years, Eric has invested time and money in setting up a business centre for local entrepreneurs within the Marry district. This project arose from a covenant that was signed in 2007 by the municipality and the three housing associations within the city — including the association for which Eric works — concerning the development of social housing, the housing market and the viability of the city's neighbourhoods. This covenant was based on a proposed policy programme formulated by policymakers and senior officials within the municipality. This programme was presented, discussed and fine-tuned during a meeting with the board members of the city's three housing associations. Part of this covenant implied that the parties involved would stimulate economic prosperity in the Marry district. This point had been brought to the table during the deliberations, as it had reached the city council's political agenda. After all, improving economic growth and prosperity was an important political priority for the alderman responsible for housing, who was also responsible for policy and plans concerning the future of the Marry district. His political ambitions included stimulating economic growth and prosperity in the Marry district.

In 2008 Eric was approached by a policy advisor from the municipality who aspired to develop a specific project in order to boost economic prosperity within the district. On the basis of a survey, the policy adviser had learned that while around 400 freelance entrepreneurs lived within the district, they were not playing a visible role in the district's economic development. On the basis of this information and an exploratory meeting between

Eric, the municipal policy advisor and representatives of the other housing associations involved, the idea arose to invest in a so-called business centre where local entrepreneurs could work and meet other local entrepreneurs. A business plan was developed whereby the parties involved each agreed to invest approximately €70,000 to set up the business centre (a relatively small investment, according to Eric), with the precondition that the business centre would be self-supporting within three years. The plan was eventually accepted by the steering committee that was responsible for the overall covenant.

Subsequently, an external party was hired in 2008 to manage the property and organize the marketing of the business centre. In 2009 the business centre became a reality; however, the occupancy of the workspaces and the use of the meeting spaces turned out to be disappointing. By that time, the economic crisis had kicked in, it had become apparent that most of the freelance entrepreneurs did not work within the district, and it turned out that other market players were already supplying similar services and facilities in various places throughout the country. In retrospect, Eric and the other people involved, including the policy advisor, concluded that the project had minimal public value, as local entrepreneurs were making insufficient use of the facilities and the opportunity to meet and collaborate with other local entrepreneurs. They concluded that they had succumbed to political pressure; an attitude had arisen that something 'had to be done' in order to meet the expectations formulated in the city council's political agenda. Moreover, decisions were made without having first investigated thoroughly what the local needs were. Or, according to Eric, the project had been led by the section on the 'district economy in the covenant, rather than by the needs of the citizens in the Marry district'.

In Table 2 we provide a first analysis of the case using the praxis of the public value framework.

In this particular case, Eric and the other district managers were involved in a dependent relationship in which they played a subordinate or compliant role vis-à-vis the municipality and its existing formal agenda and institutional arrangement. These actors were 'pushed' by the municipality to translate the alderman's formal agenda into concrete actions, through existing policy programmes, budgets and covenants. Eric became involved after arrangements had been formalized in the covenant signed by the board members of the city's three largest housing associations. The main concern of Eric, the other district directors and the policy advisor was to realize a political agenda that had already been set in their absence. The case also clearly shows that Eric and his colleagues did not receive relevant

Table 2. Analysis Business Centre.

Activity	Description	Implications
Identifying and prioritizing	The manager is not involved in the activities of identifying and prioritizing needs	A limited and unilateral analyzes and prioritization of public needs
Negotiating	Others determine the work definition. The manager does not consider it his task to define work or determine work boundaries	External forces and interests are responsible for the modification, expansion or reduction of the manager's primary and transcending tasks
Arranging and institutionalizing	External arrangement is developed in the absence of the manager. The manager comes into play when outcomes of these arrangements are translated into new policies and investment schemes	Limited view of needs and a lack of local legitimization
Realizing	Manager implements and realizes the set agenda and complies with the institutional arrangements	Focus on political interests, instead of public needs

information concerning the potential users of the business centre; in the end, it proved that local entrepreneurs did not need such a service.

Case: The Heart of the Nail

The Urban and Peaceful Living housing association builds and rents social housing in one of the largest cities in the Netherlands. The association owns approximately 32,000 dwellings in the region, intended for low-cost social housing. The association believes that everyone is entitled to good, affordable and sustainable housing. The association's mission is thus to offer well-maintained housing in pleasant and safe environments to people with low- or middle-incomes, vulnerable groups, starters and the elderly. Consequently, the association states that it is responsible for issues such as sustainability, quality of life, safety, the economy and amenities in the districts in which it provides social housing, in addition to traditional responsibilities such as expanding, constructing and maintaining the housing stock.

Until late 2008, the association's headquarters were located in the so-called 'Nail district' in the eastern part of the city. Over the years the association had expanded its real estate throughout the city, and the board eventually concluded that the time had come to move its headquarters to a more strategic location. The headquarters eventually moved in late 2008 to a more central location nearby the central station. However, the association was saddled with a property with no clear purpose in the Nail district. The property could not be rented out, due to deferred maintenance and a limited rental period. As the building had no clear purpose, the former headquarters stood empty for more than 18 months. At that point the management concluded that the building did not have any commercial value: the required investment in maintenance was disproportionate to the expected rental revenue. The board therefore decided to demolish the building in late 2010 or early 2011.

In spite of the initial decision to demolish the building, however, the association took a different path in late 2010, when a district manager called Jane convinced the board that the building could serve a different purpose. Jane saw the empty building as an opportunity to tackle some of the issues she had encountered as district manager of the Nail district. She had a unique perspective on the situation, having worked in the district for several years, during which she had spoken with various residents and gathered data about the development of the district. In her view, the district is characterized by high unemployment, crime and safety issues, decay in public space and housing and loneliness and a general lack of pride among its residents. She had also identified a lack of business premises and venues for the district's 1,300 independent entrepreneurs and small businesses. She wondered how the association might exploit and solve the practical problem of the vacancy by meeting some of these needs. She came up with the idea of the 'Heart of the Nail', a multifunctional facility in which local residents could meet and local entrepreneurs, small businesses and social service providers could establish their services in close proximity to their clients.

Jane presented her alternative plan to the board of the association. Her core argument was twofold. First, she argued that the Heart of the Nail would add visible value to the neighbourhood, the district and its users. Her second argument was that her plan would be a cost-effective temporary solution to the problem of the empty building. Jane was given three months to develop a business plan for the Heart of the Nail, supported by a small team. She finally convinced the board to postpone their plans to demolish the building for 7–10 years and start the alternative project, with the precondition that the association would eventually withdraw from the project.

Jane wanted to make sure that the project would achieve rapid results, in order to enthuse residents and other local service suppliers. In addition, she also felt under pressure to convince the board of the association that they had made the right decision. She developed the concept for the building within three months. Its basic philosophy was: the Heart of the Nail belongs to, and is meant to improve, the district. In the autumn of 2011 the building was officially given a new purpose under the name, 'Heart of the Nail'. It opened with three organizations establishing their services in the building.

The association currently facilitates the Heart of the Nail and determines which parties may be accommodated there. All businesses and services are welcome to establish their services for a relatively low rent, provided that they meet one simple requirement: the service must contribute to the welfare and livability of the Nail district. Whether an organization meets this requirement is determined by Jane and her director, working on gut instinct. Currently the Heart of the Nail houses a neighbourhood meeting room, a restaurant, a hairdresser, a second-hand shop, counselling services, youth welfare services and language courses. Jane sees that local residents are making frequent use of these services, as shown by the fact that the restaurant is often fully booked. Other parties, such as the municipal council and other housing associations, are also showing interest in the project.

Jane and her director are confident that shared responsibility and collaborations will emerge between the established entrepreneurs and social services in the course of daily practice. This is currently happening on a small scale. The hairdresser, for example, offers a special rate to mothers who are on benefits. Jane had hoped that the established organizations would feel jointly responsible for the Heart of the Nail, but that is not yet the case. Jane is thus unsure as to how she will meet the challenge of withdrawing from the project (Table 3).

The case of the Heart of the Nail illustrates how Jane initially built and set a small-scale individual agenda, based on her individual views and experience. Jane linked the problems that she had encountered in the district with the opportunity of the vacancy, and then designed a concept and developed a plan within the organization. After she was given permission by the board to execute the project, she eventually stepped outside the association and attracted interested parties to establish their services within the building. The 'Heart of the Nail' is thus a relatively small project that connects with the housing association's mission and clearly goes beyond its primary work. Still, due to the scale of the project, it does not have any

Table 3. Analysis the Heart of the Nail.

Activity	Description	Implications
Identifying and prioritizing	There is little room for talk, the manager does *not* activate or engage in deliberations concerning needs. The agenda is built and set single-handedly	Needs are identified, considered and prioritized on the basis of personal views and experiences
Negotiating	The manager temporarily modifies and expands the boundaries of the work domain with a small-scale project	The manager attracts or 'pulls' an audience with specific needs
Arranging and institutionalizing	Needs and solutions are *not* translated in institutional arrangements	Lack of legitimization
Realizing	An innovative small-scale project that spills beyond the primary work of an individual organization.	A 'quick win' focused on local public needs

far-reaching consequences for Peaceful Living's work domain. Jane and her team had certain ideas about the needs that the project might meet, but there was no prioritized agenda at the basis of the project. Her personal urge to do things differently in order to solve the problems that she encountered in the past obviously played an important role. Relations are instrumental as the information received is used to determine single-handedly which intervention is appropriate. Jane believed that it would become apparent which needs would be met during realization, as more organizations and neighbourhood residents made use of the facilities and eventually took responsibly for steering and organizing the project. From her perspective, the project thus may function as a spin-off for a broader embedded agenda and policy solution.

CROSS-CASE ANALYSIS

This section examines the approaches chosen in the cases that have been presented in the previous paragraphs and analyzes these approaches in terms of public value creation. The cases illustrate the versatile and complex needs that managers within housing associations are confronted with in their daily practice. It shows how identifying these needs, considering and prioritizing them and eventually meeting them can be a challenging task as these needs often spill beyond organizational capacities and work boundaries.

In the South Flat case the approach of the housing associations for solving the problem at hand and meeting needs was to demolish the building, despite tenants' objections. In the case of the business centre the housing association followed the municipality in setting up the centre for local entrepreneurs. Nevertheless, it was unclear if local entrepreneurs actually wanted such a centre or that this could even be seen as a priority need in the Marry district. In the Heart of the Nail case the manager set up a multifunctional facility focused on stimulating local entrepreneurs and supporting local residents. Her approach was based on her identification of needs during everyday work over recent years.

How well considered are these decisions and did the associations create public value with these decisions and approaches? Following the different stages we now provide a cross-case analysis of the approaches of three cases (see Tables 4 and 5).

In contrast with the assumptions and normative framework addressed in previous sections, the cross-case analysis of the approaches reveals that:

- the manager in the case of the business centre only is involved in the realization of already set agendas and formulated policies;
- the managers in the cases of the South Flat and Heart of the Nail are involved in the praxis of value creation without involving local stakeholders. Agendas, solutions and decisions are rather formulated with internal stakeholders (South Flat) or single-handedly (Heart of the Nail);
- the manager in the case of the business centre has a dependent relationship with municipality. In this case the manager becomes an instrument of a dominant actor that determines and controls the agenda and policy goals;
- the managers in the cases of the South Flat and Heart of the Nail have an independent relationship with their local stakeholders, as agendas and policy solutions are managed single-handedly, without giving other network partners any say in the content of the agenda or the policies;
- the manager in the case of the business centre is seen by the outside world as an instrument to realize an already set agenda and formulated policy goals;
- the managers in the South Flat and Heart of the Nail perceive the outside world as an instrument to improve the relevance and quality of their work.

Table 4. Analysis of Approaches.

Activity/Approach	South Flat	Business Centre	Heart of the Nail
Identifying and prioritizing	A closed deliberation between internal stakeholders, based on available expertise and current services	The manager is not involved in the activities of identifying and prioritizing needs	There is little room for talk, the manager does *not* activate or engage in deliberations concerning needs. The agenda is built and set single-handedly
Negotiating	Internal negotiation based on a standardized and unitarily tool	Others determine the work definition. The manager does not consider it his task to define work domain or determine work boundaries	The manager temporarily modifies and expands the boundaries of the work domain with a small-scale project
Arranging and institutionalizing	An internal arrangement consisting of representatives of different expertise and discipline	External arrangement is developed in the absence of the manager. The manager comes into play when outcomes of these arrangements are translated into new policies and investment schemes	Needs and solutions are *not* translated in institutional arrangements
Realizing	Interventions within the scope of the individual organization	Manager implements and realizes the set agenda and complies with the institutional arrangements	An innovative small-scale project that spills beyond the primary work of an individual organization

Table 5. Analysis of Consequences.

Activity/ Consequences	South Flat	Business Centre	Heart of the Nail
Identifying and prioritizing	A limited and unilateral analysis and prioritization of the social problems	A limited and unilateral analysis and prioritization of public needs	Needs are identified, considered and prioritized on the basis of personal views and experiences
Negotiating	Chosen intervention focuses solely on a limited number of symptoms, instead of dealing with the problem as a whole	External forces and interests are responsible for the modification, expansion or reduction of the manager's primary and transcending tasks	The manager attracts or 'pulls' an audience with specific needs
Arranging and institutionalizing	Limited view of needs and lack of legitimization	Limited view of needs and a lack of local legitimization	Lack of legitimization
Realizing	Focus on organizational interests, instead of public needs	Focus on political interests, instead of public needs.	A 'quick win' focused on local public needs

Despite the high ambitions, deviating normative views and a will to change displayed by the managers we investigated, we did not encounter situations in these cases in which managers managed spaces for the creation of public value. Rather, the cases revealed that involved managers are led by a formal agenda and policies, an approach that consists of issues and solutions that are considered in a relatively small group of decision-makers, traditionally within legislative bodies. This was the case with the business centre for social entrepreneurs, for example. Eric and the other district directors were persuaded to follow the alderman's political agenda, which had been translated into a policy programme and formalized in an over-arching covenant. We also encountered practices embedded in an individual agenda and policies, an approach in which solutions are considered and perceived to be important by an individual or an individual organization. This was the case with the Heart of the Nail and the South Flat.

The cases show that identifying and addressing these underlying needs requires deliberation and collaboration among relevant partners. However, this is only possible if network partners interact, have a transparent agenda and open attitude towards each other's interests and eventually achieve a collective approach that meets social needs. The cases also illustrate that the strategic practice of the associations have far-reaching consequences for the capacity to create public value. The associations related to the South Flat and business centre would probably have come to a different approach if they had involved the authorizing environment during the process of identifying and prioritizing needs. The opportunity in the investigated cases is thus mobilizing and utilizing network relationships.

DISCUSSION

This section reflects on the three coherent assumptions that were addressed above. We feel that it is important to reflect on these assumptions as this article gives a more nuanced and contradictory view of what is happening in the daily practice of civil society managers and professionals.

- *The movement towards governance creates space. Civil society actors can and should utilize this space, as they have gained the latitude to create public value (assumptions 1 and 2).*

The second assumption would imply that civil society's responsibilities stretch beyond determining how policy goals are to be reached, as they also are free to identify public goals and the needs underlying them (e.g. Alford & Hughes, 2008; Benington, 2012; Hartley, 2005; Sørensen & Torfing, 2007; Stoker, 2006). However, this article revealed that the latitude enjoyed by professional civil society organizations is not self-evident, as they are being obstructed or constrained by existing institutional pressures within and beyond their organizations. Utilizing this latitude to co-create public value requires institutional change initiated by civil society. As the cases above demonstrated, this would require hard and persistent work as existing pressures continuously persuade civil society actors to fall back into 'old' roles and patterns of behaviour. This indicates that TPA mechanisms — the steering mechanisms that have apparently been left behind in the movement towards governance — continue to dictate the daily work of civil society managers and professionals. Steering mechanisms thus coexist and exert conflicting or contradictory pressures on society.

The movement towards governance may have created space as government has withdrawn its reach, but the cases illustrate that this space is not as vacant, unconstrained and obvious as the scholars discussed above suggest. The literature in the field of (new) public governance tends to portray the overarching transition towards governance as a linear and progressive movement that has been shaped by various public reforms. The literature divides this process into logical and manageable pieces, by highlighting the steps that have been taken or will be taken in the future. It helps us to understand the general phases of this overarching transition and the direction in which governance is assumed to be moving. However, the patterns of public governance that we have encountered in this study are emergent and unpredictable, meaning that the latitude enjoyed by civil society actors is by no means self-evident.

- *The practice of civil society managers expands to managing spaces for public value creation (assumption 3).*

The literature discussed above is based on the underlying assumption that civil society managers should expand their practice to 'doing politics' and, more specifically, to managing spaces in which the creation of public value takes place (e.g. Benington, 2011, 2012; Hartley, 2005; O'Flynn, 2005; O'Toole et al., 2005; Stoker, 2006). This article has given substance to this assumption by investigating what managers actually do in their daily work and by revealing the micro-dynamics that come into play when they attempt to create public value. Interestingly, the managers in the investigated cases did not set the stage for deliberation among their stakeholders. Rather, these managers were led by formal agendas and policies formulated and determined within a legislative body (business centre). On the other hand we encountered managers who built individual agendas and came up with solutions perceived to be important by an individual or an individual team within an organization (the dirtiest flat and the Heart of the Nail). The latter can be categorized as being 'undemocratic' (Rhodes & Wanna, 2008) as managers single-handedly imagine what the public needs and which value should be created, on the basis of a limited and unilateral analysis and prioritization of public needs. Although managers have the ambition to co-create public value with their stakeholders, there is thus a risk that civil society managers determine the content of their strategy within sufficiently attracting and arranging their authorizing environment.

However, it is important to emphasize that the managers in these particular cases were not able to arrange deliberative activities among stakeholders and enable them to discover (or rediscover) which needs and values are important. The managers were thus not 'bringing the public into existence', a practice that according to scholars such as Benington and Moore (2011) and Meynhardt (2012) is vital in creating public value. We would recommend further investigating which strategies, tools and techniques a civil society manager can use in order to facilitate local (democratic) deliberations among network partners.

CONCLUSIONS

The central question of this article is how do managers of housing associations (attempt to) manage public value creation? We started this article by describing the devolution of public responsibilities towards different civil society organizations, such as housing associations, to better serve social needs. It was assumed that, through this movement from government to governance, new steering mechanisms prevail over the traditional and that the practices of public managers have expanded in creating public value.

However, if 'new' steering mechanisms actually prevail over 'old' steering mechanisms, this would imply that civil society actors have gained latitude to investigate local problems, identify and prioritize the public needs underlying them and formulate the interventions and objectives that might meet them. We stated that this suggests an alternative agenda-type — one that will capture local public needs — will emerge or is emerging in civil society and that the actors, such as managers of housing associations, are being empowered to determine which solutions would meet these needs. Subsequently, these managers should be or are involved in a practice in which they manage local spaces in which these agendas, solutions and decisions emerge through deliberative and collaborative activities among civil society actors. We have placed the praxis of public value creation (needs identification and prioritization, negotiating, arranging and institutionalizing and realization) within the normative frame of these core assumptions and have posed that civil society managers manage public value creation by first, being involved in the praxis of value creation in dialogue and collaboration with their local stakeholders, second by building interdependent relationships in which they push and pull information in order to authorize local public needs and values. This is done by collectively building and setting an agenda, by gaining support for a public value proposal, or by perceiving their environment as a place where they receive and share relevant information with their stakeholders and reframe the boundaries, nature and reach of their work.

Based on the different cases we can draw several conclusions on how managers of housing associations (attempt to) manage the creation of public value. Despite high ambitions, deviating normative views and the will to change displayed by the managers in the cases we investigated, we did not encounter situations where managers actually managed spaces for the creation of public value. The involved managers are led by formal agendas and policies, rather than engaging in dialogues with their relevant stakeholders whose needs are to be met. Furthermore, by following formal agendas they limit the opportunity for interaction between network partners for creating a transparent agenda, finding a synergy in each other's interests and for achieving a collective approach that meets social needs. They remain segmented in their approach and offering of services. The relationships they build and manage are characterized by dependency (towards government) and independency (acting alone, internal oriented) rather than building interdependent relationships for authorizing and meeting public needs. Subsequently, such relations do not contribute to the collective designing and setting up of agendas. Managers' environment and stakeholders are not yet naturally seen as a place for sharing information and reframing boundaries for creating public value. It can also be concluded that the strategic practices of the associations have far-reaching consequences for the capacity to create public value. How managers involve their authorizing environment and manage relationships during their praxis of public value creation affects their approach and (perceived) public value creation. The opportunity in the investigated cases lies in mobilizing and utilizing network relationships.

An important follow up is to explore *why* these managers and associations, in managing public value creation, make certain decisions and show particular behaviour in relation to the earlier described normative view. This is currently being explored in our longitudinal study, in both housing and education, where we focus on the institutional pressures and the specific behaviour and decision-making of these managers in creating public value.

NOTES

1. See van Eijck et al. (2013); Lindemann et al. (2013).
2. www.aedes.nl

3. *Leefbaarheid*: the corporations are faced with social issues that often go beyond the issue of simply providing public housing, which has led to an additional core task concerning 'liveability'.

REFERENCES

Alford, J., & Hughes, O. E. (2008). Public value pragmatism as the next phase of public management. *American Review of Public Administration 38*, 130–148.

Benington, J. (2005). From private choice to public value, review. *The Newsletter of the Public Management and Policy Association, May*, 6–10.

Benington, J. (2011). From private choice to public value. In J. Benington & M. Moore (Eds.), *Public value, theory and practice*. Basingstoke: Palgrave.

Benington, J. (2012). Public value a contested democratic practice. Paper presented at the Creating Public Value in a Multi-Sector, Shared Power World Conference, Minneapolis, MN, September 2012.

Benington, J., & Moore, M. (2011). *Public value, theory and practice*. Basingstoke: Palgrave Macmillan.

Brandsen, T., Farnell, R., & Cardoso Ribeiro, T. (2006). *Housing association diversification in Europe profiles, portfolios and strategies*. Whitley: The Rex Group.

Ebbers, H. (2005). *Economische bedrijfsomgeving*. Amsterdam: Pearson Education.

Flyvbjerg, B. (2006). Five misunderstandings about case-study research. *Qualitative Inquiry, 12*(2), 219–245.

Flyvbjerg, B. (2011). Case study. In N. K. Denzin & Y. S. Lincoln (Eds.), *The Sage handbook of qualitative research* (4th ed.). Thousand Oaks, CA: Sage.

Hartley, J. (2005). Innovation in governance and public services. In A. Gray & J. Broadbent (Eds.), *Public money and management: Integrating theory and practice in public management*. London: Routledge.

Hauser, G. (1998). Vernacular dialogue and the rhetorically of public opinion. *Communication Monographs, 65*(2), 83–107.

Inglehart, R. (1997). *Modernization and postmodernization*. Princeton, NJ: Princeton University Press.

Lindemann, B. L., van Eijck, K. H., & Minderman, G. D. (2013). *De school in transitie. Maatschappelijke meerwaardecreatie door bundelen van krachten en onderhandelen*. Amsterdam: Zijlstra Reeks.

Meynhardt, T. (2012). Public value – turning a conceptual framework into a scorecard. Paper presented at the International Conference on Creating Public Value in a Multi-Sector, Shared Power World, Minneapolis, MN, September 2012.

Minderman, G. D. (2008). *Legitimatie and verankering: Uitdaging voor de maatschappelijke ondernemer*. Amsterdam: Vrije Universiteit.

Minderman, G., van Eijck, K., Lindemann, B., & van der Klooster, C. (2010). Van Klein naar groter: Notitie 1e fase van het onderzoek naar de maatschappelijke meerwaarde van maatschappelijke investeringen van corporaties.

Moore, M. H. (1995). *Creating public value: Strategic management in government*. Harvard: Harvard University Press.

O'Flynn, J. (2005). From new public management to public value: Paradigmatic change and managerial implications. *Australian Journal of Public Administration, 66*(3), 353–366.

O'Toole, L., Meir, K., & Nicholson-Crotty, S. (2005). Managing upward, downward, and outward: Networks, hierarchical relationships and performance. *Public Management Review, 7*(1), 45–68.

Pierre, J., & Peters, G. B. (2000). *Political analysis, governance, politics and the state.* London: Palgrave Macmillan.

Pollit, C., & Bouckaert, G. (2004). *Public management reform. A comparative analysis* (2nd ed.). Oxford: Oxford University Press.

Rhodes, R. A. W., & Wanna, J. (2007). The limits to public value, or rescuing responsible governments from the platonic guardians. *Australian Journal of Public Administration, 66*(4), 406–421.

Rhodes, R. A. W., & Wanna, J. (2008). Stairways to heaven: A reply to Alford. *Australian Journal of Public Administration, 67*(3), 367–370.

Sørensen, E., & Torfing, J. (2007). *Theories of democratic network governance.* New York, NY: Palgrave Macmillan.

Stoker, G. (2006). *Public value management and network governance: A new resolution of the democracy/efficiency tradeoff.* Working paper, Manchester.

Swanborn, P. G. (2000). *Case-study's: Wat, wanneer en hoe?* Amsterdam: Boom.

Talbot, C. (2009). Public value – The next big thing in public management? *International Journal of Public Administration, 32*(3), 167–170.

van Dorst, M. (2005). *Een duurzaam leefbare woonomgeving.* Delft: Eburon.

van Eijck, K. H., & Lindemann, B. L. (2012). Creating public value in educational practice. Paper presented at the Creating Public Value in a Multi-Sector, Shared Power World Conference, Minneapolis, MN, September 2012.

van Eijck, K. H., Lindemann, B. L., & Mindermann, G. D. (2013). *De corporatie in transitie. Maatschappelijke meerwaarde en ruimte creëren in tijden van krapte.* Enschede: Gildeprint.

Wei-Skillern, J. C., Austin, J. E., Leonard, H. B., & Stevenson, H. H. (2007). *Entrepreneurship in the social sector.* Thousand Oaks, CA: Sage Publications.

Williams, E., & Shearer, H. (2011). Appraising public value: Past, present and futures. *Public Administration, 89*(4), 1367–1384.

Yin, R. K. (1995). *Case study research. Design and methods.* Thousand Oaks, CA: Sage.

CONCEPTUAL FRAMEWORK AND EMPIRICAL EVIDENCE OF PUBLIC VALUE: THE CASE OF THE ITALIAN HIGHER EDUCATION SECTOR

Guido Modugno, Giulio Curiel and Giulia Ventin

ABSTRACT

Purpose — *To understand whether the public value approach will improve the performance and legitimacy of Italian universities.*

Design/methodology/approach — *The public value approach is used to identify the factors limiting the improvement of the performance of Italian universities over the period 2007–2009. Four cases are analyzed in order to reveal how universities measure and communicate the public value delivered. The evolution of the whole system is analysed in the light of the three paradigms on public administration: traditional public administration, new public management and public value management.*

Findings — *Recent reforms introduced by the Italian government do not facilitate the overcoming of political and organizational constraints, with*

Public Value Management, Measurement and Reporting
Studies in Public and Non-Profit Governance, Volume 3, 189–224
Copyright © 2014 by Emerald Group Publishing Limited
ISSN: 2051-6630/doi:10.1108/S2051-663020140000003008

the exception of a few noteworthy elements. The dominant role of the Ministry of Education in the definition of universities' strategic goals combined with the great autonomy traditionally granted to the departments and to single academics leave little room for manoeuvre.

Social implications − *The case of the Italian higher education system highlights the importance of the rules of governance for public value production. The analysis shows that the actual governance of the higher education institutions does not favour the construction of a public value proposition by the universities' managers. This aspect raises the more general question of identifying the necessary conditions for realizing the public value proposition and determining its presence in all public administrations.*

Originality/value − *This article contributes to the understanding of mechanisms that hinder the capability of public institutions' to develop their own public value proposition.*

Keywords: University; Italy; paradigm comparison; funding; TPM; NPM

INTRODUCTION

In recent years, the Italian Higher Education System (IHES) has faced a crisis of legitimacy and social acceptance: citizens clamour for more transparent methods to enlist academics and for increased productivity. Cases of pre-arranged public selections of academics have put a heavy burden on the entire system's credibility. This situation has also produced a migratory phenomenon involving several Italian researchers.

The low productivity of the entire IHES emerges from several indicators. The first is the high dropout rate: in 2005, less than 45% of enrolled students completed their courses. The second is the unsatisfactory international ranking of Italian universities: only 18.2% were included in the top 500 Higher Education Institutions (HEIs) list compiled in 2005 by Times Higher Education and Quacquarelli Symonds (Regini, 2009). This latter critical aspect of the IHES is also confirmed by data in the 2010 Quacquarelli Symonds SAFE ranking: Italy occupied the 10th position in the overall ranking and was only 27th in the 'flagship' ranking, which measures the performances of the leading universities in a given country.

Italian HEIs now have to demonstrate that they deliver measurable and tangible social outcomes: 'universities strive to align measures of effectiveness with coherent measures of efficiency and with their mission' (Cugini, Michelon, & Pilonato, 2011, p. 2) and citizens claim 'rights to services that have been authorised and funded through some democratic process' (Coats & Passmore, 2008, p. 4).

Moreover, the national funding for HEIs is steady if not declining: the Fund for the Ordinary Functions (FFO, i.e. the main source of funds from the central government) has been reduced in the last three years from €7,087 to €6,565 million. The FFO for 2014 amounts to €7.025 million only because of special additional funding with strictly pre-defined destinations. Consequently, universities find themselves trying to attract funds from competitive research grants and the private sector (Bronzetti, Mazzotta, & Nardo, 2011). In order to successfully face these challenges, Italian HEIs must include the management and reporting of public value. The public value approach emphasizes the link between legitimacy and the capability to improve financial and political support for public organizations. Hence, it could be the ideal perspective for redesigning processes and organizations, since it not only values outcomes but also 'processes which may generate trust or fairness' (O'Flynn, 2007, p. 358).

However, the IHES suffers from several structural limitations that may be an obstacle to a strategic approach to public value creation. First, dependence on government funds limits the autonomy of universities in the development of their own value proposition, which is based on the distinctive competencies that often reflect the peculiarities of the local community. Strategic goals are defined by the Ministero dell'Istruzione, dell'Università e della Ricerca Scientifica (Ministry of Education, University and Research (MIUR), Ministry for short), which stimulates competition among universities through a performance-based funding system. Second, the possibility for universities' managers (i.e. the rector and his/her deputies) to develop and realize a specific strategy is also hindered by the large autonomy reserved for the academic body and the organizational units (departments, faculties etc.). In other words, the internal governance of the institutions influences the capability to produce public value for the whole university. As observed by Moore (1995, p. 63), 'Taken together, these political and organizational constraints often leave relatively little room for maneuver'.

The purpose of this article is to understand whether the public value approach will improve universities and help their legitimacy. This article also aims to establish whether the reforms introduced by the Italian government in recent years are proceeding in this direction. Three aspects are taken into account:

1. the way universities conceive the delivery of public value and how they communicate it;
2. the relationships between the universities and their stakeholders, including policymakers and
3. the internal governance of HEIs and how this aspect influences managers' capability to implement each university's strategy using its localized competencies.

THEORETICAL FRAMEWORK

The delivery of public value is a central issue for Italian universities, given their need to enhance their legitimacy and increase their financial and political support. In recent times, two actions have been implemented. First, on their own initiative, some universities have begun to measure and communicate their performance; institutions increasingly emphasize performance management and try to defend their legitimacy by more effectively communicating what they actually do. Second, the Italian central government has put in place several reforms to change the internal governance of the institutions, as well as that of the whole IHES.

We now explore briefly the three paradigms on public administration discussed in the literature: TPA, NPM and PVM (e.g. Denhardt & Denhardt, 2000; Ferris & Graddy, 1998; Gruening, 2001; Hood, 1991; Kelly & Muers, 2002; O'Flynn, 2007; Stoker, 2003, 2006). The main aspects of the three paradigms can be summarized as follows. First, in TPA, efficiency and efficacy are pursued through a rigid programming scheme, the specialization of tightly assigned tasks, generally with a hierarchical approach. Compliance with tight procedures is the central element of this paradigm. Second, NPM is based on managers' empowerment and responsibility, a strong focus on measuring specific results, efficiency/efficacy as a strong driving factor, and market-driven reward schemes, both internally and towards external actors. This last factor causes public institutions to step back in favour of private actors. Third, PVM is based on users' needs and preferences, citizens' participation, the quest for consensus and legitimacy of the implemented strategy and attention to resource consumption.

The scheme elaborated by O'Flynn (2007), which compares the characteristic aspects of NPM and PVM, leads us to qualify each aspect with regard to the predominance of a TPA, NPM or PVM approach. The results are summarized in appendix.

Andersen, Jørgensen, Kjeldsen, Pedersen, and Vrangbæk (2012) highlight the connections between these paradigms and the forms of governance; moreover, these are strictly related to the value creation proposition, since the form of governance is chosen in accordance with the specific values that have to be addressed and the related needs that have to be fulfilled. The theoretical forms of governance are hierarchy, clan, network and market form (see also Ouchi, 1991). The hierarchical form can be ascribed to the TPA, in which strict adherence to the limits set by the immediate supervisor, and ultimately by elected bodies, ensures respect for the values that the mechanism of democratic representation conveys to the institutions themselves. The clan form is based on the rules agreed within a closed group of persons, who usually share a set of specific skills. This 'self-regulating profession' can also be attributed to the TPA paradigm. The network governance recalls the PVM approach, which aims to involve all stakeholders in the key decision-making processes. All stakeholders, even those in the minority, share the same right to express their needs and aspirations. Balancing these different requirements through a process of political mediation is in itself typical of this approach. In turn, this process implies the quest for legitimacy and support. The market form is clearly reflected in the NPM paradigm; the founding values are efficiency, customer satisfaction and results measurement. Competition is the driving force behind the selection process that rewards the most capable subjects in ensuring the achievement of the assigned targets.

However, these forms often hybridize into one another (Andersen et al., 2012). Italian public administration is still characterized by the predominance of a bureaucratic culture with hierarchical organizations and/or professional clans that prioritize compliance with laws and procedures, rather than the delivery of value to citizens. The IHES is no exception.

Andersen et al. (2012) assimilate universities into the second form of governance; the highly specific sets of skills and knowledge, together with a peculiar working method, suggest that the academic community can be perceived as a 'clan' governed by its own rules. Adhering to these rules is per se a value that must be respected by the clan members. The academic community tends to adhere to well-defined – even if not written – rules, in the realms of both teaching and research. This group's members consider it necessary to respect these rules in order to preserve its identity. However, building public value through a clan-based form of governance results in risky behaviour; the risk is to become self-referential, losing focus on the public value that resides outside the clan. Furthermore, a self-referential clan is at risk of losing the stimuli needed to produce value whenever the mere adherence to rules prevails over accountability for results. The smaller the clan, the higher the risk; few subjects legitimating one another tend to lose their ability to produce value. With reference to universities' members, Adam Smith (1776, p. 450) observes:

> If the authority to which he is subject resides in the body corporate, the college, or university, of which he himself is a member, and in which the greater part of the other members are, like himself, persons who either are, or ought to be teachers, they are likely to make a common cause, to be all very indulgent to one another, and every man to consent that his neighbour may neglect his duty, provided he himself is allowed to neglect his own.

Subsequent tides of reform over the last 20 years have largely modified this approach, showing signs of the quest to balance bureaucracy and democracy (Miller, 2000).

An analysis of the renewed higher education (HE) governance allows a better understanding of what might be the provision of value to users and citizens in this specific sector, as well as the future developments that could lead to an improvement in the HEIs' results. According to Eurydice (2008, p. 25), universities:

> are now also held accountable for their behaviour in new ways: they must show that they are responding appropriately to the needs of society; they must demonstrate that the public funds they receive are being used responsibly; and they must maintain standards of excellence in teaching and research, the primary missions of educational organisations. Increased autonomy and the accompanying accountability have brought about many changes, which mark a shift away from traditional modes of academic self-government in a closed community of scholars. There are new models of governance that redistribute responsibility, accountability, and decision-making power among the respective external and internal stakeholders.

In Italy, the survival of a self-referential system was ensured in past years by a continuous supply of public resources without a parallel control over results. Governance and funding systems reforms were introduced in order to disrupt this mechanism; in later sections of this article, we analyze these reforms in light of the above-mentioned paradigms.

RESEARCH METHOD

In our article, we are interested in analyzing the public value concept developed by each university, via several questions. Who are the stakeholders taken into account? What results do these institutions measure, and what strategic themes do they emphasize more? How do they communicate their results to the public? Are the stakeholders involved in the process of value definition? Does the measurement of performance reveal the existence of a value proposition, a strategy aimed at realizing the mission of the single institution?

These aspects are investigated through analysis of the social disclosures (SDs) prepared by some Italian universities. In this article, SD is considered as the result of a reporting activity that takes into account the effects produced by an institution on social resources, extending in this way the traditional object of the reports on organizational efficiency. We decided not to use the term 'Sustainability Report', which is widely cited in the literature and which has also been adopted by the Global Reporting Initiative (GRI, 2010, 2013), because of the lack of environmental issues in most of the disclosures considered here. The literature on social reporting in public administration is relatively recent; studies have been conducted on the content of disclosures (del Sordo, Farneti, Pazzi, & Siboni, 2010), and on the motivations that led to their publication (Farneti & Guthrie, 2009). Our focus is on the measurement of results; we examine the indicators used in the SDs to describe outputs, outcomes, customer satisfaction and impacts. The purpose is to deduce what aspects of achievements are measured by universities and which classes of stakeholder they mainly consider and prioritize in formulating their value propositions.

We examine how four Italian universities measure and describe the public value delivered to stakeholders. The four universities − Trieste, Bari, Ferrara and Macerata − were chosen because of the availability of two documents containing goals and performance measures: the strategic plan (SP) and the SDs for 2007−2009. The SP is a mandatory document requested by the Ministry; it describes the strategic objectives of the institution within a three-year planning period and the actions programmed for their achievement. A mission statement sometimes precedes the description of the strategic goals and actions. With the exception of Macerata, the other three universities provide the performance indicators (PIs) for the measurement of the goals within the SP. The PIs used in the SP represent the public value that each university intends to deliver; these indicators also infer the importance assigned to different classes of stakeholder. These factors describe the public value proposition shared within the institution.

The coherence between the PIs of the SP and the ones used in the SD to communicate results confirm that institutions inform stakeholders about their capability to realize the planned strategy. This is the first sign of the stakeholders' involvement in the process of defining the public value. However, the inconsistency of the PIs in the SP with those represented in the SD would suggest that the latter is used primarily for legitimacy reasons; stakeholders are informed about the results that the institution considers convenient to communicate.

From 2007 to 2009, the Ministry adopted a more flexible, performance-based funding approach. With decree no. 362/2007, flexibility was reflected in the fact that universities could weigh 21 ministerial indicators against five strategic themes. By indicating their priorities, universities declared their strategies to the Ministry and decided on which basis they wanted to be assessed. The weights assigned by each university to the ministerial indicators allow a segmentation of the institutions over an axis, with 'research-oriented universities' at one end and 'teaching and student support-oriented universities' at the other. This allows the possibility of testing the coherence of the PIs in the SP with the declared strategy; moreover, it allows the description of the value proposition made for the Ministry to be checked against that provided to the other stakeholders in the SD, ensuring consistency.

All PIs of the universities' SPs and SDs are classified by destination and by nature. The destination pertains either to the typologies of stakeholders or to the strategic themes; indicators can refer to activities (research, teaching, internationalization etc.) or to classes of subjects (local community, students, human resources etc.). The classification of indicators by strategic theme was provided by the universities themselves, either in the SD or in the SP. Sometimes it is questionable; for instance, data referring to PhD programmes are classified as 'research' by the University of Bari, while Ferrara considers them part of 'teaching'. We have not changed the classifications assigned by the universities. The two kinds of destinations, by stakeholder and by strategic theme, are interconnected; for different classes of stakeholders, various activities are performed for the delivery of value. This can be represented in a simple matrix showing what activities are performed for what stakeholders, as illustrated in Table 1.

The competitive system is formed by other universities (national and international), non-academic organizations and other partners that have cooperative relationships with the given HEI. Financial backers can be

Table 1. Areas of Interest per Stakeholder Typology.

		Stakeholders					
		Students	Human Resources	Public Administration	Competitive System	Vendors	Financial Backers	Citizenry and Territory
Activities for the provision of public value	Teaching and services for students	X	X	X	X			X
	Research and knowledge transfer		X	X	X			X
	Internationalization	X	X	X	X			
	Sanitary assistance		X	X				
	Cultural heritage	X	X					X
	Environment and safety	X	X					
	Infrastructures and technology networks	X	X			X		

divided into banks and other financial institutions that provide the necessary financial support in the form of loans, and private sponsors that financially support the HEIs' activities on a voluntary basis. Citizenry and territory may be divided into subcategories: schools, enterprises, the public health system and, more generally, the local economy that benefits from the existence of the university.

The nature of indicators refers to the object of measurement: input, output, outcome, customer satisfaction and so on. The criteria used to classify PIs by nature are described in Table 2.

Only indicators of output, outcome, impact and customer satisfaction are considered here as measures of the value delivered to stakeholders. Input, process and efficiency indicators are excluded from the analysis since they

Table 2. Classification of Performance Indicators.

Measure	Object of Measurement	Examples
1. Input	How many or what kinds of resources (human, financial, tangible and intangible) were or will be used?	Average age of academics, resources allocated to new facilities, number of cooperation agreements with other HEIs
2. Process	How are processes carried out? Do they reflect standard/desired conditions?	% of students who attended an internship during the course of study, % of students registered over the normal number of years
3. Efficiency	What is the value/volume of resources used per unit of service delivered?	Average number of teaching hours per lecturer, students/lecturers
4. Output	How many or what kinds of services have been provided? What is their monetary value? How many users does the institution have?	Number of research projects financed by the EU, number of lesson hours delivered in a year, number of students
5. Customer satisfaction[a]	How much of what the institution does and the way it is done satisfies the clients/stakeholders?	% of students who rank the library service 5/5
6. Outcome	What effects were produced for the clients and stakeholders?	Number of patents per year, % of graduates employed within one year from graduation
7. Effectiveness	What is the level of the goals' achievement?	Number of financed research projects over number of applications for research funds
8. Impact[a]	What is the university's reputation concerning its activities? Is the university attractive/legitimated?	Number of PhD scholarships financed by private entities, % of foreign students

[a]While indicators of class 5 measure the satisfaction of customers who used the service, impact indicators (class 8) measure different aspects of a university's reputation.

refer to resources used and not to service provision. Although public value is a net concept resulting both from benefits created and resources used in generating those benefits (Alford & Hughes, 2008), our focus is not on resources. Rather, we investigate the public value proposition of each university: how it is programmed, demonstrated and illustrated to stakeholders.

According to Eurydice's (2008, p. 12) documents on HE:

> governance focuses on the rules and mechanisms by which various stakeholders influence decisions .... In other words, governance encompasses the framework in which an institution pursues its goals, objectives and policies in a coherent and co-ordinated manner to answer the questions: Who is in charge, and what are the sources of legitimacy for executive decision-making by different actors?

We consider governance structures and funding policies, since these are 'crucial elements in HE reform agendas and are directly linked to the key imperative of efficient use of resources' (Eurydice, 2008, p. 13). The analysis is made by interpreting the development of system rules and the internal governance model of Italian universities, in the light of the three paradigms mentioned in the section 'Theoretical Framework'.

THE CASE OF FOUR ITALIAN UNIVERSITIES

The IHES is characterized by a performance-based funding system; a portion of government funds is distributed, depending on the results achieved by the universities, to meet the Ministry's centrally defined goals. This scheme was partially modified between 2007 and 2009: universities were allowed to prioritize goals by assigning different weights to 21 indicators distributed among five areas (i.e. teaching, research and technology transfer, auxiliary services to students, internationalization and human resources). For the first time in the republic's history, Italian universities had the potential to develop their own strategies and therefore their own version of public value.

The weights assigned by the single HEIs to the Ministry's indicators made possible a system-level analysis on the strategic propositions of all Italian universities. The assumption underlying this analysis was that the priorities assigned to the different goals revealed how each university wanted to be perceived and evaluated by its main financial backer, the Ministry. By doing this, the universities communicated to the Ministry which goals had priority in their specific strategies and what significance the Ministry should have assigned to those goals in the evaluation of the universities' performances. It can be said that a higher weight attributed to a specific goal should result in greater efforts – in terms of resources used – to accomplish it. The priority attributed to a specific goal reflected its importance in providing public value, which was conceived as an improvement over previous achievements and not as a balance between outcomes and resources used in a specific period. The Ministry decided to reward universities for their capability to advance in specific aspects of their activities (research, teaching etc.). Universities that declared an orientation to research (or, respectively, teaching) are considered likely to have more leeway for improvements in the specific area. According to this approach, public value production does not necessarily imply that citizens and clients consider the services received more valuable than the resources used, which is difficult to prove. Rather, public value creation passes through continuous improvements in performance; public value is an improvement path, not a balance.

The weighting of the performance measures provided by the Ministry is used here to divide the different HEIs according to their strategic orientations. Since 19 of the 21 indicators grouped in the five cited areas pertain to activities connected either to 'teaching and student services' or to 'research', it is possible to place all Italian HEIs in a graph where teaching-oriented institutions are separated from research-oriented ones. The two axes of Fig. 1 intersect at the point where the asserted strategic orientation is neutral.

Fig. 1 summarizes the strategic objectives chosen by the HEIs and ultimately, the public value proposition communicated to the Ministry in order to ensure the necessary financial support. Thus, research-oriented universities were supposed to put their efforts mainly into improving research activities, while the others were to focus on teaching and services to students.

We can use SPs and SDs to check the coherence of the planned strategy (from the SP) and of the realized strategy (from the SD) with this orientation.

The Ministry does not oblige the universities to provide a social report; with reference to the IHES, only 12 of the 89 universities (61 public and 28 private universities) published at least one SD over the 2004–2009 period (del Sordo, Siboni, & Pazzi, 2011).

Two official guidelines have been issued to support this practice in HE. The first was issued by the Italian Ministry of Public Affairs and indicates the principles, structure and contents for the SDs of public entities. The second guideline, the 'Document on the Social Reporting in Universities' issued by the National Study Group on Social Reporting (GBS, 2013), specifically addresses support for voluntary social reporting practices in universities (del Sordo et al., 2011).

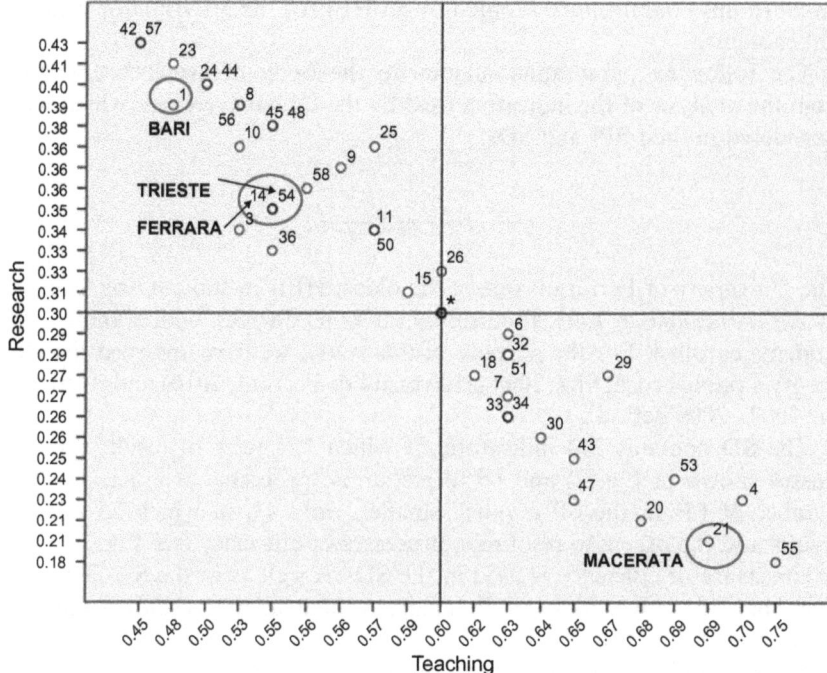

Fig. 1. Orientation to Teaching and Support Services or to Research in Italian Universities. *Note:* The symbol * corresponds to a group of 18 universities that declared a 'neutral' orientation.

It must be noted that, whereas over the past years there has been an understanding that some social feedback must be provided to the public (Cassone & Zaccarella, 2009), the central government authorities have not issued any mandatory format for this document. The lack of a standardized model suggests that there might be a parallel absence of social vision on the HEIs' role in public value creation (Cantele, Martini, & Campedelli, 2012). In the end, each HEI develops its own SD format.

We suggest that SDs can be selected as a primary source of the data needed to determine what public value is produced. This report is not only pivotal in determining the results in terms of public value creation, it can also help identify the 'realized strategy' of an institution (Gabrovec, 1999). The SP is another important source of measures for public value. This document is updated yearly and shows the 'intended strategy' for the next three years. The analysis of the intended strategy and the realized one can reveal (if any) the formula adopted by an HEI for the provision of value to stakeholders.

The following paragraphs summarize the body of evidence emerging from the analysis of the indicators used by the four universities, which were considered in their SPs and SDs.

University of Ferrara

The University of Ferrara is one of the oldest HEIs in Italy; it was founded by Alberto d'Este in 1391. It currently offers 60 degrees, with about 17,000 students enrolled. For the purpose of this study, we have analyzed the university's published SD for 2008 (Università di Ferrara, 2010) and its SP for the 2007–2009 period.

The SD contains 214 indicators, of which 129 refer to results (i.e. the classes shown in Fig. 2) and 85 to resources, processes or efficiency. The number of PIs in the SP is much smaller, only 43, of which 25 refer to results and the others to resources, processes or efficiency (see Fig. 3). Only one measure of efficiency is used in the SD, as well as in the SP. This suggests that this university carefully analyzes the available resources but fails to connect the latter to its goals.

Several other considerations can be made on the basis of our data. First, Ferrara University places more emphasis on the measurement of public

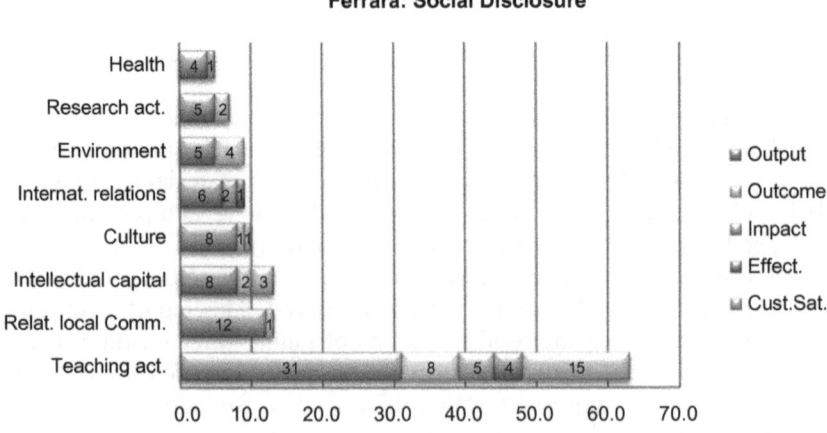

Fig. 2. University of Ferrara: Measures of Results in the SD, 2008.

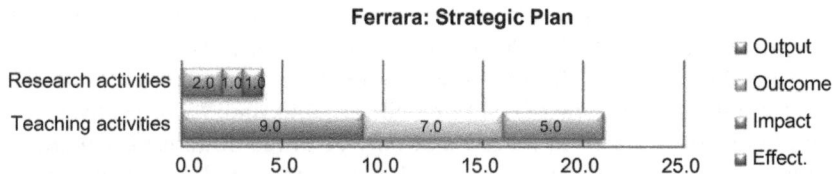

Fig. 3. University of Ferrara: Indicators of Expected Results in the SP, 2007–2009.

value delivered through teaching activities, in both the planning and the reporting phases. Although this is a research-oriented university, the focus is mainly on students, according to its strategic goals declared to the Ministry. The SP describes actions and policies aimed at improving the outcomes of research activities, but the expected results are not measured; neither target measures nor PIs to be used for programming are defined. Second, the performance measures are classified by strategic themes instead of by stakeholders; the university prefers to measure the public value created in different areas of activities, rather than the public value delivered to different classes of subjects. However, the SP's strategic themes do not coincide with those in the SD, demonstrating no clearly defined strategy in terms of public value creation. Third, measures of output are the most frequent, which may be because they are easier to obtain. Volume of services delivered refer to what the institution does for the clients, but they do not indicate the quality of the services and their effects on the stakeholders; therefore, outputs are incomplete indicators (Simons, 1995) of public value. Fourth, there is a lack of effectiveness measures; results are not compared with goals or with the performances of other universities. Moreover, only 18.6% of the PIs used in the SP are also considered in the SD; this divergence between the planned public value and the results communicated to stakeholders suggests that the latter are scarcely involved in the definition of the public value proposition. On the contrary, measures of previous periods are often used as benchmarks, confirming that improvements are considered important signals of public value creation.

Bari University

The University of Bari was established in 1925; currently, it has 15 faculties and 143 bachelor degree programmes. With its 58,000 students, it ranks as

Italy's ninth university in terms of enrolment size. The SD taken into consideration was published in 2009 (Università di Bari, 2009).

According to Fig. 1, Bari has the most obvious research orientation. The total numbers of PIs in the SD and SP are 140 and 75 respectively; the result indicators are 77 in the SD and only 21 in the SP (see Figs. 4 and 5). Only six efficiency indicators are found in the considered documents; again, the link between resources and results is not evident.

The SP and the SD reveal that Bari gives equal emphasis to 'teaching and student services' and 'research'. This becomes evident by summing up the number of indicators used to measure 'student services' and those used for 'teaching'. However, while research activities are mainly analyzed through

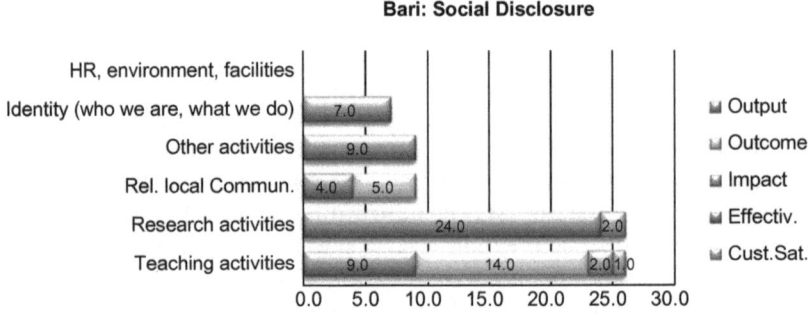

Fig. 4. Bari University: Measures of Results in the SD, 2009.

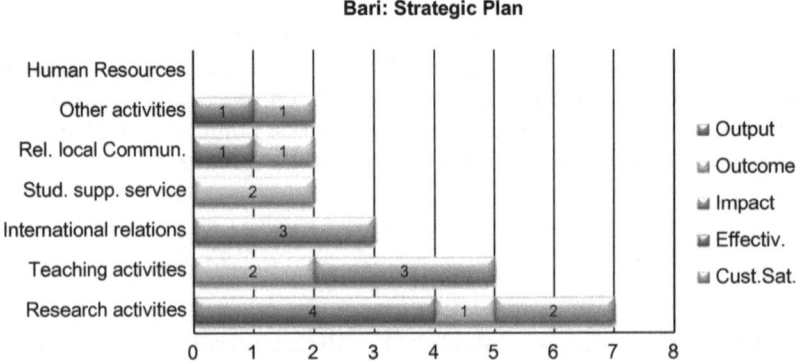

Fig. 5. Bari University: Indicators of Expected Results in the SP, 2007–2009.

output indicators, outcome measures are predominant in 'teaching and services to students'. Although some impact indicators are used for the measurement of research activities (i.e. the assessment made by a commission for the evaluation of research and the number of research grants financed by private entities), the impact factor of studies conducted by researchers is not considered.

The ordinate also shows some strategic themes (environment and development of facilities) and a typology of stakeholders (human resources), for which no result indicators are used. Only input or process indicators are delivered for these themes.

Two elements deserve further consideration: first, the lack of consistency between the strategic themes used in the SP and those in the SD, and second, the absence of effectiveness indicators. These elements reveal that reporting to stakeholders is unrelated to strategic planning. This is confirmed by the fact that only 28% of the total number of PIs (including input, process and efficiency measures) used in the SP are also considered in the SD. This could not have occurred if stakeholders were involved in the definition of strategic goals and in the end, of the public value proposition. The public value description provided to the stakeholders does not truly reveal the original project but tells, at least partially, a different story. Following Behn's (2003) considerations, it might be said that the use of dissimilar PIs in these two documents suggests different underlying rationales. The SP contains fewer indicators than those of the SD. The SP is supposed to be used in order to steer behaviours within the institution, specifying what really matters, whereas the larger number of indicators used in the SD suggests that this disclosure was published with the purpose of more accurately describing the results and celebrating success, in other words, gaining legitimacy. Nevertheless, it is questionable whether a large number of indicators actually contributes to the achievement of this goal.

University of Macerata

The University of Macerata dates back to the 16th century and offers degrees at all levels, with about 15,000 students enrolled. In this study, we consider the SDs for 2008 (Università di Macerata, 2008) and 2009 (Università di Macerata, 2009) (Fig. 6).

The case of the University of Macerata has several issues. First, Macerata does not use PIs in its SP. Its document outlines the strategic actions but does not give any guidance on how objectives are to be

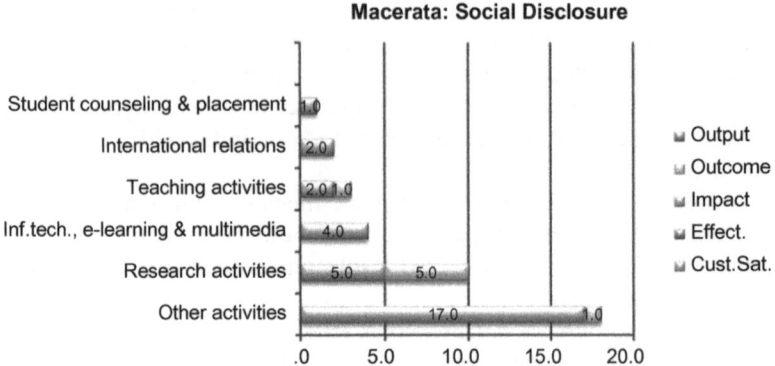

Fig. 6. University of Macerata: Measures of Results in the SD, 2008–2009.

measured. Not only are the target measures not explained, but there is also no choice indicated about the PIs to be used in order to describe the institution's goals. The SP is a typical instrument of 'management by objectives'. It reflects the typical NPM setting, which focuses on the measurement of results for clients and citizens. However, the absence of performance measures in Macerata University's SP indicates the preparation of the plan to comply with a norm, rather than as a managerial tool, demonstrating a bureaucratic approach adopted within an NPM framework.

A second issue regarding this case involves the SD's relatively small number of PIs at 102, of which only 38 refer to results. However, a specific set of indicators is used to show the achievements of each research department (i.e. the responsibility centre for research) and each faculty (i.e. the responsibility centre for teaching). This description of public value does not consider the entire institution but regards the organizational units separately. This approach seems more coherent with the purpose of evaluating the results of the responsibility centres within the institution, rather than with the objective of communicating the global public value delivered to stakeholders.

Also in this case, the SD contains only one indicator of efficiency; again, the relation between resources and results is not sufficiently investigated. With reference to the classification of indicators by destination, Macerata University demonstrates greater attention to teaching and services to students than to research activities, consistent with its strong orientation to students, as indicated in Fig. 1

University of Trieste

The University of Trieste, with a staff of 691 lecturers and professors, offers degrees at all levels to about 21,000 students. In this study, we have considered the SD for 2008 (Università di Trieste, 2008).

The SD of the University of Trieste is not immediately comparable with its SP. The PIs are classified by stakeholders in the SD and by areas of activity in the SP (Figs. 7 and 8). As specified in its introduction, this depends on the purpose assigned to the SD, which is to provide stakeholders with data on the public value delivered by the institution. From this perspective, it prioritizes the description of the results achieved for each stakeholder category; each section of the disclosure is dedicated to a specific class of stakeholders and completed with an internal analysis referring to different services delivered to them.

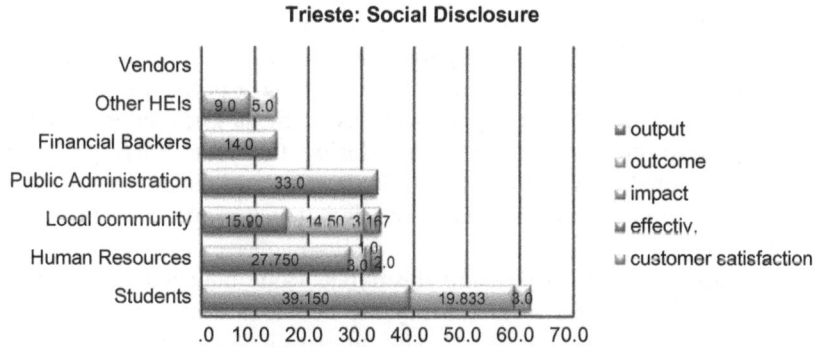

Fig. 7. University of Trieste: Measures of Results in the SD, 2008.

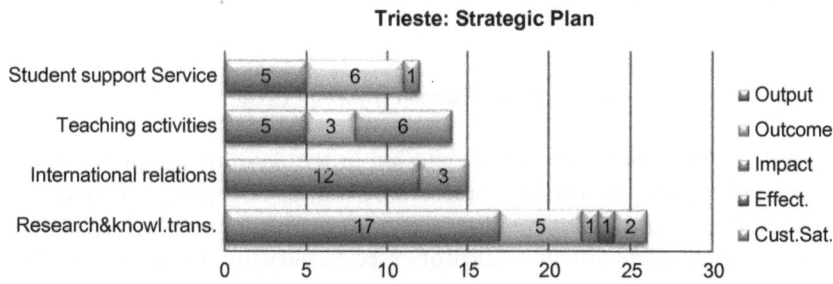

Fig. 8. University of Trieste: Indicators of Expected Results in the SP, 2007–2009.

Similar to the other HEIs considered here, the University of Trieste also makes little use of effectiveness indicators. Moreover, only 25.7% of the indicators in the SP are also considered in the SD. Both factors suggest that the emerging strategy for the public value production described in the SD does not correspond to the intended strategy stated in the SP.

In its SD, the University of Trieste provides more measures than those of the other three HEIs, totalling 486, 190 of which refer to results and the others to resources used. Specific sections are also reserved for the special issues of 'diversity' and 'intellectual capital'. Students are by far the most important stakeholders with regard to the number of measures in this document; considering the high number of indicators in this section of the SD, it can be said that the results achieved for students are measured with more accuracy.

The same level of attention is reserved for 'local community', other 'institutions of public administration' and 'human resources'. The University of Trieste aims to improve its legitimacy with external subjects, as well as the commitment and motivation of its employees, and the latter are also considered addressees of public value. The PIs concerning the local community examine, among others, the following aspects (partially over-lapping with the contents of other sections, such as knowledge transfer): university spin-offs; patents registered during the year; participation in local and national competitions for business ideas and technology transfer; employment conditions of graduates and activities performed by the career service.

These are attempts to measure the public value delivered to the local community; the method is to identify the activities that are expected to have an impact on the territory. This approach does not consider the expectations and needs of citizens, firms and institutions. The analysis does not move from a stakeholders' perspective; it rather develops the university's own viewpoints.

General Conclusions from the Cases

Several common elements can be detected in the descriptions of the public value made by the universities considered. First, there is a lack of coherence between the SP and the SD; neither the strategic themes to which the public value creation refers nor the indicators used to measure it match in the two documents. Depending on the phase of the control cycle, the public value measurement changes, whether it pertains to planning or final reporting.

This indicates the universities' failure to think and act strategically in the considered periods, which hinders the creation of a strong reputation, the latter being an intangible asset that is unlikely to be built in the absence of a shared and clear strategy.

Second, the incongruence between SP and SD also testifies that varying ideas of public value are described to different stakeholders; while the SP is an official document prepared for the Ministry, the SD is made primarily for the public, that is, enterprises, the local community members and partners. This approach could be justified, considering that each category of stakeholders is interested in specific aspects of the university's performance; nevertheless, both documents aim at illustrating the overall performance of the institution in its various dimensions.

Third, efficiency indicators are almost not used at all, suggesting the universities' inability to connect resources to objectives. It also means that resources are likely to be used without any clear idea about the final goal; the absence of a clear link between resources and institutional goals again shows an incapability to implement the strategy and to communicate it within the organization. Moreover, this leads stakeholders' to question the use of public money in this sector. This certainly imposes a limit in the perspective of value creation.

Fourth, the universities have not tried to demonstrate public value creation through comparisons between resources used and results obtained; they have rather used comparisons with previous years' performances. In this sense, public value creation is intended as a continuous process of improvement.

As specified above, during the 2007−2009 period, universities had for the first time the possibility to develop their own value propositions, although this had to be done within a general framework designed by the Ministry. Our analysis shows that this opportunity was not fully taken up; universities still had to gain awareness about the necessity to develop their own strategies and implement them. A possible explanation is that universities had limited financial and decisional autonomy; the funding approach and the governance of the system are important factors that can encourage or limit the possibility for an institution to develop its own value proposition. The internal governance of the institution may also represent a restriction in the perspective of value creation; as observed by Moore (1995), organizational constraints can also leave little latitude for managers to implement their strategies. These aspects will be considered in the next sections with reference to the Italian case.

SYSTEM-LEVEL GOVERNANCE MODEL OF THE IHES AND ITS FUNDING RULES

In this section, we analyze how the IHES is organized, considering on which legal and regulatory bases in relies, which institutions provide guidance to it and how the funds are allocated to the individual HEIs.

According to Article 33 of the Italian Constitution, universities are entities that exercise their autonomy within the limits stated by national laws. The governance of the HE system is regulated by the law, which also defines some aspects of institutional governance. We refer to governance as the set of 'rules and mechanisms by which various stakeholders influence decisions, how they are held accountable, and to whom' (Eurydice, 2008, p. 12). According to Eurydice, the main aspects of system governance are the following:

1. national and international bodies involved in the system;
2. external regulations on information sharing and transparency;
3. external regulations on institutional strategic planning; and
4. external regulations on the structure of institutional governance.

In recent years, in all European countries, important reforms were introduced that brought about many changes, which marked a shift away from traditional modes of academic self-government in a closed community of scholars. Two norms, one in 2005 and the other in 2010, promoted this shift towards a new form of governance in Italy. The first three aspects mentioned above are analyzed in the following subsections. The institutional governance requires a more in-depth focus and is analyzed in the following section.

National and International Bodies Involved in the System

The main actor in the governance of the IHES is the Ministry. It provides guidance to the entire IHES, ensures the enforcement of the relevant laws, guides system-level objectives and strategic planning, oversees the allocation of national funds to universities and determines the criteria for this allocation.

From 1993 to 2010, four different bodies had been instructed to organize the assessment of the quality of universities: the Observatory for the

Evaluation of the University System, the National Commission for the Evaluation of the University System (CNVSU), the Committee for the Evaluation of Research (Comitato di Indirizzo per la Valutazione della Ricerca or CIVR) and the National Agency for the Evaluation of Universities and Research (ANVUR). No official text explains why the previous bodie failed in their objectives. The ANVUR, which is the present committee, is an autonomous agency supervised by the Minister of the MIUR. Among its duties are the assessments of the following: the quality of the products of research; the effectiveness of educational activities (including auxiliary services to students); the ability to attract external funding and establish collaborations and exchanges among researchers; and the adequacy of public communication relating to training opportunities. In short, the ANVUR provides a peculiar form of auditing of the universities' activities. The emphasis on the audit culture is a peculiar character of NPM; the assignment of measurable goals and the evaluation of achievements, with particular attention to outcomes, is a central aspect of this paradigm (Diefenbach, 2009; Hood, 1995).

The Conferenza dei Rettori delle Università Italiane (CRUI) is the association of public and private Italian universities. Established in 1963 as a private association of rectors, the CRUI has acquired a recognized institutional role and currently represents organizations capable of influencing the development of the university system. The CRUI can be seen as an interface between the local universities and the Ministry.

The European Union funds single educational initiatives within the European Social Fund (ESF), research projects and Interreg projects. Other than this financial support, the pan-European institutions do not provide any active guidance on the Italian HE policies. At an international level, regional bodies such as international rectors' conferences have an influence on cooperative research activities and internationalization programmes for the mobility of students.

The subsequent reforms that occurred in Italy over the past decade did not change the main mission and activities of the actors cited above. However, the reforms placed an increasing emphasis on results, both in the teaching and research fields. This meant a growing accountability of all the actors in the system, depicting a scenario typical of NPM where objectives, results and rewards are tightly related and prominently in focus. Since then, the ANVUR's activities have become increasingly important, resulting in its substantial weight within the governance of the system.

External Regulations on Institutional Strategic Planning

With the 2005 reform, the national legislation introduced a mandatory strategic planning phase for the HEIs. Law 43/2005 provided thorough guidance on the planning process, including the following:

- general guidelines on the objectives of the entire system;
- the adoption by each university of a three-year SP;
- periodic monitoring and post-evaluation of the teaching programmes of individual universities, on the basis of 'parameters and criteria' (quantitative indicators) identified by the Ministry itself in accordance with CNSVU recommendations;
- the use of indicators for the allocation of resources; and
- the Ministry's presentation of regular reports to Parliament on the previous point.

This kind of planning, whilst rigid in structure, left ample leeway for individual HEIs' autonomous definition of their strategies and strategic goals in the direction of decentralized and flexible objectives, which is typical of a PVM approach. A subsequent, different orientation took place in 2009; the SP was left to individual HEIs, but they were no longer allowed to define their strategic guidelines and had to comply with the provisions for strategic guidelines provided by the Ministry, steering them back in the direction of a NPM behaviour.

External Regulations on Information Sharing and Transparency

As previously discussed, there is still no obligation for the Italian HEIs to develop and publish any form of SD or social report, nor is there a standard or recommended form for institutions that plan to release their SDs on a voluntary basis.

The previous cash accounting system has been substituted by an accrual accounting system with the reform issued in 2010 (law 240/2010); universities are supposed to implement the new accounting system in 2014. The preference for accrual accounting is also typical of reforms inspired by the NPM paradigm; the importance given to the 'bottom line' reflects the focus on the efficient use of resources. Moreover, the recent reforms introduced managerial accounting as part of a more complex management control system, which also pertains to the NPM-type reforms.

Another essential aspect refers to the financial autonomy of organizational units; under the cash accounting system, each department of each university had an autonomous budget. However, as of 2013, there is now a single budget for an entire HEI. This is another shift towards the definitive overcoming of internal self-referential clans (i.e. an overhaul of the TPA paradigm in favour of a global vision of the university as a whole), fostering an approach in which the HEI can steer its actions to comply with the stakeholders' requirements and expectations.

These changes in the accounting structure lead to more emphasis on financial management. This is a move in favour of an increased transparency on the use of resources, which is a common element of the NPM and PVM approaches.

The Funding Model at System-Level Governance

The institutions indicated in the subsection 'National and International Bodies Involved in the System' provide the most funding to individual HEIs for all their activities. According to the CNVSU (2011), the Ministry alone granted 63.2% of the Italian HEIs' total income in 2009. According to the same document, the tuition fees paid by students and their families covered 12.7% of the total income. Whilst this report does not distinguish between private funds and funds from public entities other than the Ministry, it can be observed that only a minor share of funds comes from private sponsors and that they play a limited role in the governance model.

Public funding is organized as follows.

- The European Union funds single educational initiatives within the ESF, research projects and Interreg projects.
- The Italian central government (mainly represented by the Ministry) is the primary financial supporter of the HEIs; the FFO of universities alone accounted for 56% of the total income of the HEIs as of 2009 (CNVSU, 2011), and thus, it supports most of their operating expenses. As previously described, the FFO share assigned to a single HEI is partly related to its performance, and through this means, the government authorities also provide a strong form of guidance on its activities. Other forms of financial support from the Ministry are bound to specific purposes (7.2% of total income in 2009) (CNVSU, 2011).
- Regional and local governments support HEIs' activities with subsidies that usually have specific destinations.

Table 3 provides an insight into the weights of the different funding sources of HEIs.

Table 3.   Italian Public HEIs: Percentage of Funding by Different Sources
for 2009 (MIUR).

Source of Funding	%
Tuition fees	12.7
Public funding	
Central government	63.6
Local governments	2.3
EU and other international public subjects	0.9
Private sponsors	1.3
Contracts (public and private)	
MIUR	0.4
Other public subjects	3.8
EU and other international public subjects	1.1
Private subjects	1.8
Other incomes	12.1
Total funding	*100*

Source: Adapted by the authors based on information contained in CNVSU (2011).

Given this evidence, the FFO is the main source of funding for the Italian HEIs. The criteria used to assign such funding can also be regarded as instruments that influence the HEIs' strategic choices. In other words, the FFO is in itself an instrument of policymaking.

The approach adopted by the Ministry for the distribution of funds has been evolving without interruptions since 1995. This evolution has been stimulated by the increasing accountability of all public agencies, as a consequence of citizens' requests for better public services at lower costs. From the first phase, when the so-called 'balancing fund' (a component of the FFO) was transferred on a cost basis, through the second stage, where the number of students and their learning results were introduced as competitive factors, the funding system has evolved into the third phase, where the number of students has lost most of its significance in favour of research productivity. Table 4 summarizes the distribution criteria applied from 1995 to 2009.

During the 2007–2009 period, each university was asked to assign a different weight to specific goals set by the Ministry. This was requested for the distribution of other funds adjunctive to the FFO; each of the five strategic areas identified by the central government had to be weighed within the 10–30% range, resulting in a higher level of institutional autonomy for the development of individual strategies. This scheme reflected a cooperation between the main financial backer and each institution in the definition

Table 4. Distribution Criteria of the Balancing Amount from 1995 through 2009.

1995–1997	1998–2003	2004–2007	2007 Onwards
• 100% based on the standard cost per student	• 70% based on the demand for higher education • 30% based on the results of higher education	• 30% based on the demand for higher education • 30% based on the results of teaching • 30% according to measures related to research activities • 10% based on specific goals defined by the Ministry	• 17% based on the demand for higher education • 17% based on the results of teaching • 66% according to measures related to research activities

of the public value proposition; institutions could decide which role they wanted to play in public value production. The scheme also manifested a competitive model in which each HEI pursued its own competitive strategies and goals, other IHEIs being its natural competitors.

After 2009, this was no longer possible, and a shift back to central decision making was decided; the Ministry now defines the goals and the measure of performance-rewarding funds. This reflects a quasi-market situation that forces universities to compete with one another on common goals in accessing public funds. This crucial aspect shows typical characterizations of the NPM management paradigm. Actually, the system-level governance is characterized by a strong predominance of a single financial backer, that is, the Ministry; HEIs tend to comply with its indications instead of balancing different inputs from different stakeholders.

INSTITUTIONAL GOVERNANCE

This section analyzes the institutional governance of the IHES. An understanding of the system-level mechanics is needed to assess the capability of individual HEIs to produce public value.

In fact, the possibility of implementing an individual strategy for public value creation is limited by the centralized mechanism of goal setting; on the other hand, the substantial autonomy that is traditionally attributed to academics and organizational units within the institutions hinders the possibility of developing a shared vision. This autonomy results in a structure where smaller clans develop within the institution; the coordination of these groups that often have conflicting goals will likely reduce the efficiency and effectiveness of the institution as a whole.

The reform introduced in 2010 by Minister Gelmini (law 240/2010) redesigned two main aspects of internal governance. These are outlined below.

The Power and Responsibilities of Institutional Bodies

The most important actors remain the rector and his/her deputies, the board of governors and the academic senate. The general director is in charge of the administrative functions, while the board of auditors and the Commission for the Assessment of Performances control the financial health and performance in research and teaching activities respectively. The law delineates their respective duties and responsibilities. The regulation is then supplemented by specific rules in the institutions' statutes, which also provide for the procedure of election. The rector is the university's legal representative, who directs and coordinates scientific and educational activities and is responsible for the achievement of the objectives according to quality criteria and the principles of efficiency, effectiveness, transparency and promotion of merit. Moreover, the rector proposes the SP. Prior to the reform, the rector could be re-elected for more than two mandates, but now, he/she cannot lead the institution for more than one mandate, which lasts for six years. This imposes a clear limit to the institutions' autonomy; on the one hand, this could facilitate the interruption of clan-based mechanisms; on the other hand, it could also impede the formation of strong leadership, which is a necessary condition for public value creation.

The rector chairs the board of governors, which is an elective body. After receiving the senate's opinion, the board approves the SP, the annual and three-year budgets, and human resource planning. The reform has changed the board's composition; besides elected academics and students' representatives, other qualified subjects recognized for their merits in culture and management also sit on the board now. This change stimulates external stakeholders' involvement in the definition of strategic goals.

The academic senate comprises the department deans, student representatives and other elected academics; this body now primarily plays a counselling role, while the board of governors make the most important decisions. The rector's actions remain strongly conditioned by the academic senate, but less so than in the past. The rector and the board of governors now have more responsibilities and decision-making power. The rector still has to negotiate the allocation of resources; this results in the need for him/ her to legitimate the value proposition within the institution.

The Functions, Autonomy and Dimension of the Organizational Units

The most important changes have been introduced at this level. Before the reform, faculties had the responsibility for teaching activities and departments for the researching ones. Academics were therefore coordinated by the faculty dean with regard to teaching and by the department director with regard to research. With the reform, departments have also absorbed the teaching activities; the faculties have been eliminated. The minimum number of academics in a department has been increased; as a result, the number of departments has sharply decreased in all universities. This has impeded the survival of small and inefficient structures. The internal governance resulting from the recent reform is represented in Fig. 9.

The operational level had considerable autonomy in the institutional activities (research and teaching) and in the administrative functions as well; however, the reform reduced this autonomy. Until recent years, each department even had an autonomous budget, but since 2013, according to the 2010 reform, a single budget is prepared for the entire HEI. The same situation happens for financial statements. This augments the possibilities

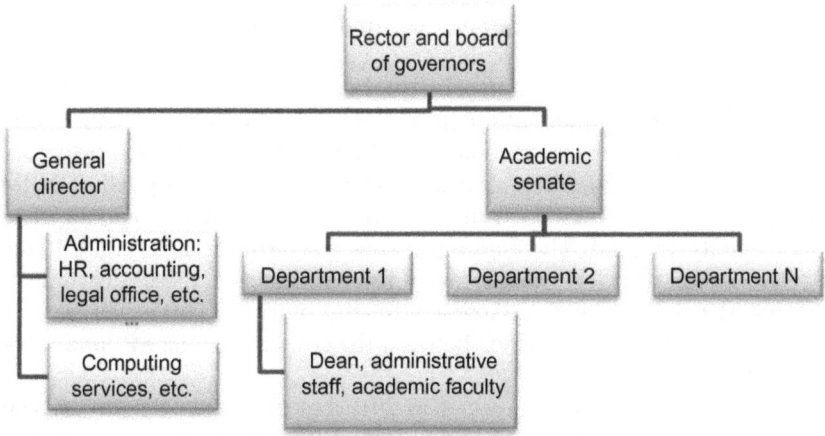

Fig. 9. Organizational Scheme of a Typical Italian HEI.

of implementing a well-defined, value creation strategy shared by the whole institution.

Similar to what is observed at the system level, the 2010 reform has also introduced some typical factors of NPM at the institutional level – the obligation to develop a managerial control system and the introduction of an internally administered fund for rewarding individual results.

CONCLUSIONS

Our analysis focused on the representation of public value provided by four Italian universities over the 2007–2009 period. It gave evidence of these institutions' difficulty in developing their own value propositions, that is, their own strategies for value creation. In the second part of the study, we analyzed the external governance and institutional structure to determine whether these factors hinder universities in the development of their own visions. The evolution of the whole system has been analyzed in the light of the three paradigms on public administration: TPA, NPM and PVM.

Our analysis confirms that 'when we enter the messy world of more specific governance elements, we find examples where classification within one overall governance form can be ambiguous'; in other words, hybrid forms of governance exist, 'also suggesting that value conflicts are part of the everyday life of administration' (Andersen et al., 2012). Even today, the IHES favours a bureaucratic approach, similar to that of the entire public administration sector; it is perhaps an unavoidable legacy of the past. Nevertheless, from the beginning of the 1990s, many reforms in different sectors of public administration have been introduced in an attempt to make the whole system more modern and efficient; the IHES has also been the subject of reforms in this direction. These reforms mainly reflect NPM principles. However, new instruments introduced by regulations are often only formally adopted. Their adoption does not result in more efficient and effective processes; the main reason for introducing these instruments remains the institutions' adherence to the norms. This emerges, for instance, from the incongruence between the contents of the SPs and those of the SDs.

The most recent reforms, issued in 2010 but executed in many aspects only since 2013, introduced the first element of participatory governance: each university's obligation to have stakeholder representatives on the board of governors. This should guarantee that these subjects' needs are also considered in the definition of the institution's public value proposition. This choice was strongly opposed by the 'public university' advocates, most of whom were academics who feared that opening to private entities and reducing public funding constituted a prelude to the adoption of the logic of profit.

The current funding system of the IHES is largely dependent on resources provided by the Ministry. This performance-based funding pays almost no attention to the needs expressed by the local communities and the private sector. The consequence is that these subjects are hardly involved in the planning phase. Their participation in the board is too recent; therefore, the effects of this new element of internal governance are not yet recognizable. The fact that the intended strategy does not result from a participatory process appears from a clear analysis of the discrepancies between the SP and the SD; far from giving a coherent image of the public value proposition, the two documents share only a relatively small number of PIs. The law states that the SP must be approved in accordance with the Ministry directives; consequently, the planning phase is directed to the Ministry, thus suggesting a quasi-market approach (results vs. funding), which is typical of NPM. On the contrary, the social reporting phase is mostly addressed to the public, the private sector and local government from a perspective that resembles the search for legitimacy and support that characterizes the PVM paradigm. While this approach is perfectly understandable, given the governance and funding model of the IHES, it prevents HEIs from thinking about the entrepreneurial local community that they insist on as a potential financial backer of primary importance. This situation might preserve the typical self-referential character of the academic community.

The bureaucratic approach typical of the TPA emerges in turn from the observation that one of the four SPs taken into account had no PIs, while the others missed representing most of their target values. Consequently, effectiveness indicators are scarcely used. Whilst comparing goals and actual performances is typical of the NPM paradigm, developing an SP without targets suggests a bureaucratic approach in fulfilling norms, regardless of their rationale and the expected results. The resulting management paradigm is a deeply fragmented one, where conflicting aspects prevent the entire system from being led by an organic logic.

The lack of a coherent description of the public value proposition in the planning and reporting phases also suggests that the HEIs have no precise idea of how they really intend to create public value. This can be ascribed to two main reasons. First, the HEIs were not used to developing their own SPs before 2007. Second, the Ministry's strong influence on the HEIs' goals, in conjunction with the broad autonomy of operational structures (the departments), hinders the possibility for the rector to strongly promote his/her own public value proposition.

The case of the IHES highlights the importance of the rules of governance for public value production. Our analysis shows that the actual governance of the HEIs does not favour the construction of a public value proposition by the universities' managers. This aspect raises the more general question of identifying the necessary conditions for realizing the public value proposition and determining its presence in all public administrations.

REFERENCES

Alford, J., & Hughes, O. (2008). Public value pragmatism as the next phase of public management. *The American Review of Public Administration, 38*(2), 130−148.

Andersen, L. B., Jørgensen, T. B., Kjeldsen, A. M., Pedersen, L. H., & Vrangbæk, K. (2012). Public value dimensions: Developing and testing a multi-dimensional classification. *International Journal of Public Administration, 35*(11), 715−728.

Behn, R. D. (2003). Why measure performance? Different purposes require different measures. *Public Administration Review, 63*(5), 586−606.

Bronzetti, G., Mazzotta, M., & Nardo, M. T. (2011). Le dimensioni della pianificazione strategica nelle università [Dimensions in the strategic planning for universities]. *Economia Aziendale Online, 2*(2), 141−155.

Cantele, S., Martini, M., & Campedelli, B. (2012). Gli atenei italiani e gli strumenti di pianificazione e controllo: A che punto siamo? [Italian universities and planning and control tools: Where do we stand?] *Management Control, 1*, 55.

Cassone, A., & Zaccarella, P. (2009). *Il bilancio sociale delle università: inventario dei problemi e analisi comparata delle esperienze italiane.* [*The social disclosure of universities: Inventory of the problems and comparative analysis of the Italian experience*]. Working Paper No. 130, POLIS Working Papers, Università del Piemonte Orientale, Alessandria.

CNVSU. (2011). *Undicesimo rapporto sullo stato del sistema universitario.* [*Eleventh report on the state of the university system*]. Retrieved from http://www.cnvsu.it/_library/down loadfile.asp?id=11778. Accessed on March 31, 2014.

Coats, D., & Passmore, E. (2008). *Public value: The next steps in public service reform.* Retrieved from http://www.theworkfoundation.com/assets/docs/publications/201_pv_ public_service_reform_final.pdf. Accessed on March 31, 2014.

Cugini, A., Michelon, G., & Pilonato, S. (2011). Performance measurement in academic departments: The strategy map approach. *Public Money and Management, 31*(4), 271−278.

del Sordo, C., Farneti, F., Pazzi, S., & Siboni, B. (2010). Voluntary reporting in Italian state universities: What is the contents of the social reports? Paper presented at the Fourth New Eland Management Accounting Conference, 18–19 November, University of Waikato, Hamilton, New Zealand.

del Sordo, C., Siboni, B., & Pazzi, S. (2011). *Pioneering practices of social reporting in universities: The Italian case.* Working Paper in INTED 2011 Proceedings, Valencia, Spain, 4180–4190. Retrieved from http://www.researchgate.net/publication/234000783_Pioneering_Practices_of_Social_Report_in_Universities_the%20Italian_Case

Denhardt, R. B., & Denhardt, J. V. (2000). The new public service: Serving rather than steering. *Public Administration Review, 60*(6), 549–559.

Diefenbach, T. (2009). New public management in public sector organizations: The dark sides of managerialistic "enlightment". *Public Administration, 87*(4), 892–909.

Eurydice. (2008). *Higher education governance in Europe – policies, structures, funding and academic staff.* Retrieved from http://eacea.ec.europa.eu/education/eurydice/documents/thematic_reports/091EN.pdf. Accessed on April 3, 2014.

Farneti, F., & Guthrie, J. (2009). Sustainability reporting by Australian public sector organisations: Why they report. *Accounting Forum, 33*(2), 89–98.

Ferris, J. M., & Graddy, E. A. (1998). A contractual framework for new public management theory. *International Public Management Journal, 1*(2), 225–240.

Gabrovec, M. O. (1999). Social and environmental responsibility – accountability and reporting in the EU. Paper presented at the III International Conference: Economic System of the European Union and Adjustment of the Republic of Croatia, 22–23 April, Lovran, Croatia.

GBS. (2013). *Standard GBS 2013 – principi di redazione del bilancio sociale.* [*Principles of social reporting*]. Retrieved from http://www.gruppobilanciosociale.org/wp-content/uploads/2014/02/Standard-GBS-2013-Principi-di-redazione-del-Bilancio-Sociale.pdf. Accessed on April 4, 2014.

GRI. (2010). *Reporting in government agencies.* Retrieved from https://www.globalreporting.org/resourcelibrary/GRI-Reporting-in-Government-Agencies.pdf. Accessed on April 3, 2014).

GRI. (2013). *G4 sustainability reporting guidelines.* Retrieved from https://www.globalreporting.org/reporting/g4/Pages/default.aspx. Accessed on April 3, 2014.

Gruening, G. (2001). Origin and theoretical basis of new public management. *International Public Management Journal, 1*, 1–25.

Hood, C. (1991). A public management for all seasons? *Public Administration, 69*(1), 3–19

Hood, C. (1995). The "new public management" in the 1980s: Variations on a theme. *Accounting, Organizations and Society, 20*(2–3), 93–109.

Kelly, G., & Muers, S. (2002). Creating public value – an analytical framework for public service reform. Paper presented at the Strategic Thinkers Seminar – Strategic Futures, 24 September, London. Retrieved from http://webarchive.nationalarchives.gov.uk/20100416132449/http://www.cabinetoffice.gov.uk/media/cabinetoffice/strategy/assets/public_value2.pdf. Accessed on March 31, 2014.

Miller, G. (2000). Above politics: Credible commitment and efficiency in the design of public agencies. *Journal of Public Administration Research and Theory, 10*(2), 289–328.

Moore, M. H. (1995). *Creating public value: Strategic management in government.* Harvard: Harvard University Press.

O'Flynn, J. (2007). From new public management to public value: Paradigmatic change and managerial implications. *Australian Journal of Public Administration*, 66(3), 353–366.

Ouchi, W. G. (1991). Markets, bureaucracies and clans. In G. Thompson, J. Frances, R. Levacic, & J. Mitchell (Eds.), *Markets, hierarchies and networks: The coordination of social life* (pp. 246–255). London: Sage.

Regini, M. (2009). *Malata e denigrata: L'università italiana a confronto con l'Europa. [Sick and denigrated: The Italian university in comparison with Europe]*. Rome: Donzelli.

Simons, R. (1995). *Levers of control: How managers use innovative control systems to drive strategic renewal*. Boston: Harvard Business Review Press.

Smith, A. (1776). *An inquiry into the nature and causes of the wealth of nations*. London: W. Strahan and T. Cadell.

Stoker, G. (2003). *Public value management (PVM): A new resolution of the democracy/efficiency tradeoff*. Working Paper, Institute for Political and Economic Governance (IPEG), University of Manchester, Manchester, UK.

Stoker, G. (2006). Public value management: A new narrative for networked governance? *The American Review of Public Administration*, 36(1), 41–57.

Università di Bari. (2009). *Bilancio sociale 2009*. Retrieved from http://www.uniba.it/ateneo/area-gestione-delle-attivita-di-comunicazione/settore-editoriale-e-redazionale/pubblicazioni/fuori-collana/bilanciosociale.pdf. Accessed on May 9, 2014.

Università di Ferrara. (2010). *Bilancio sociale 2008*. Retrieved from http://www.unife.it/ateneo/bilanciosociale/BILANCIO%20SOCIALE%202008. Accessed on May 9, 2014.

Università di Macerata. (2008). *Bilancio sociale 2008*. Retrieved from http://www.unimc.it/ateneo/Strutture-Amministrative/ufficio-innovazione-qualita/bilancio-sociale/normativa-e-documentazione/bilancio_sociale08_completo.pdf. Accessed on May 9, 2014.

Università di Macerata. (2009). *Bilancio sociale 2009*. Retrieved from http://www2.unimc.it/ateneo/Strutture-Amministrative/ateneo/universita-di-macerata/bilancio-sociale/bilancio-sociale09-VersioneIntegrale.pdf. Accessed on May 9, 2014.

Università di Trieste. (2008). *Bilancio sociale 2008*. Retrieved from http://www.units.it/ateneo/bilanci-sociali/. Accessed on May 9, 2014.

APPENDIX: PARADIGMS OF PUBLIC MANAGEMENT: WHICH IS MOST SUITABLE FOR THE IHES?

	NPM	Public Value	Italian HEIs	Prevalent Paradigm
Characterization	Post-bureaucratic, competitive government	Post-competitive	Competitive towards other HEIs, but still bureaucratic for the central role of procedures and rules of internal governance	TPA/NPM
Dominant focus	Results	Relationships	Results: efficiency and effectiveness	NPM
Managerial goals	Achieve agreed performance targets	Multiple goals, including responding to citizen/user preferences, renewing mandate and trust through quality services and steering network	Objectives stated by the Ministry and international ranks deeply influence HEIs' strategic goals; stakeholders' preferences are considered only through elective representatives of governing bodies and/or specific agreements	NPM
Definition of the public interest	Individual preferences are aggregated	Collective preferences are expressed	The definition of public interest is explicated first by the goals stated by the Ministry. The Conference of Italian Chancellors can submit proposals to the Ministry, but the system remains hierarchical	NPM
Performance objective	Management of inputs and outputs to ensure economy and responsiveness to consumers	Multiple objectives are pursued, including service outputs, satisfaction, outcomes, trust and legitimacy	Management of inputs and outputs to ensure satisfaction of funding stakeholders (mainly the Ministry); often, performance objectives are not measured and communicated within the institution, where the focus is on compliance to norms and internal rules	NPM, TPA

Appendix. (*Continued*)

	NPM	Public Value	Italian HEIs	Prevalent Paradigm
Dominant model of accountability	Upward accountability via performance contracts; outwards to customers via market mechanisms	Multiple accountability systems, including citizens as overseers of government, customers as users and taxpayers as funders	Upward accountability (Ministry) via agreed performance indicators; outwards to other stakeholders via voluntary social disclosure	NPM
Preferred system of delivery	Private sector or tightly defined arm's-length public agency	Menu of alternatives selected pragmatically	Public universities and 'private' institutions coexist, although the former are much more numerous	TPA

Source: Adapted from O'Flynn (2007, p. 361, Table 1).

POLITICS AND PUBLIC SERVICES: LOOKING BEYOND ECONOMIC RATIONALITY AND PUBLIC VALUE

Patrizio Monfardini and Pasquale Ruggiero

ABSTRACT

Purpose — *To understand whether new public management and public value theory are sufficient to guide the strategic behaviours adopted by public sector organizations for their service delivery companies.*

Design/methodology/approach — *This article uses a longitudinal case study of a joint stock company running an airport service in Tuscany.*

Findings — *Public value theory should be further developed to guide managerial behaviours in a very complex decision-making environment.*

Research limitations — *Only one case study is used so results cannot be generalized in a proper statistical way.*

Practical implications — *Public managers could learn the usefulness of managerial theories for their decision-making.*

Public Value Management, Measurement and Reporting
Studies in Public and Non-Profit Governance, Volume 3, 225–241
Copyright © 2014 by Emerald Group Publishing Limited
All rights of reproduction in any form reserved
ISSN: 2051-6630/doi:10.1108/S2051-663020140000003009

Social implications — *Theories aimed at providing managers with insights into decisions made in complex situations should be tested in the real world before being accepted or refused.*

Originality/value — *This article analyzes a case study operating under and applying the concepts proposed by new public management and public value theory. It therefore offers insights on their applicability, shortcomings and usefulness for decision-making.*

Keywords: New public management; public value theory; participation; financial results; strategy

INTRODUCTION

Scholars have developed several different theories to describe public sector functioning and to reframe public managers' and politicians' roles and responsibilities in public sector organizations (Alford & O'Flynn, 2009). In the last decades, new public management (NPM) has been widely implemented among developed countries (O'Flynn, 2007). More recently, public value theory (PVT) has offered a different interpretive scheme and rationale for the public sector (Moore, 1995).

This article attempts to understand whether these two theoretical approaches (NPM and PVT) can offer sufficient guidance for strategic decisions made in public sector organizations. The article shows that NPM provides decision-makers with an indication about what to do, while the adoption of PVT appears to be more problematic for decision-makers. The two theoretical approaches are briefly described below, and then the method and the case study are examined. The final section offers a discussion and some closing remarks.

NEW PUBLIC MANAGEMENT AND PUBLIC VALUE THEORY

The relationship between politics and administration is a topic that has been debated among scholars since the end of the nineteenth century. The 'traditional supremacy' of politics over administration, NPM proposed a kind of rebalance between the two, creating a wider space for managerial tools. As part of NPM, the 'reinventing government' movement meant the adoption of private-sector managerial tools in public sector organizations and the adoption of business values (DeLeon & Denhardt, 2000, p. 90).

Under NPM, economic rationality is considered to be dominant, meaning that it supports decisions and actions undertaken by public organizations, making them similar to private ones (Christensen & Laegreid, 2002). Scholars supporting NPM have suggested that the market is the best way to produce what can satisfy collective and social needs, rather than the production and provision by public sector organizations. According to Bozeman (2007, p. 69), 'to a large extent, the term New Public Management has become a brand, one signifying market-oriented governance'. According to the NPM doctrine, public sector organizations should become more similar to private ones and should pursue results with less attention given to processes and procedures (Hood, 1995).

NPM has been implemented in a number of countries and several patterns have been observed (Bevir, Rhodes, & Weller, 2003; Bozeman, 2007; Christensen & Laegreid, 1998; Pollitt & Bouckaert, 2000): first, factors triggering the reforms and second, managerial solutions (see, e.g. Bevir et al., 2003).

First, it was common to adopt the private-sector model to produce and provide public services, that is, fragmenting public sector organizations into a net of corporations in charge of delivering public services to citizens (Dunleavy & Hood, 1994). Second, the assumption that the market would select efficient corporations (i.e. those with lower costs and better standards) and eliminate non-efficient ones was quite wide (Hood, 1991). Third, the adoption in the public sector of well-known managerial practices coming from the private sector shows a 'stress on private-sector styles of management practices' (Hood, 1995, p. 96). As a consequence, there was also increasing attention to the bottom-line figures of the corporations, to their profitability, and 'a greater discipline and parsimony in resource use' (Hood, 1991, pp. 4–5). Competition among service providers was welcomed as a way to choose the most efficient and effective ways of producing and providing services, allowing the 'invisible hand' of the market to remove those organizations not able to compete. From this perspective, citizens are considered to be the main customers of the services and it is therefore important that they are satisfied by the services provided (Christensen & Laegreid, 2002; Osborne & Gaebler, 1992). Aggregate individual citizen/customer self-interest expressed through preferences can be considered a good proxy of the public interest (DeLeon & Denhardt, 2000;

Smith, 2004). Therefore, according to NPM, public administration should provide services using separate and independent legal entities in order to have better control over costs and results and a more direct link to the particular needs they are specifically called to satisfy (O'Flynn, 2007).

NPM and its economic rationale have been criticized (e.g. Alford & Hughes, 2008; Lapsley, 2008; Spano, 2009). Some scholars were concerned with the capacity of NPM to achieve the results it promises because the problems at stake are not eliminable (Dunleavy & Hood, 1994). Others argued against the philosophy behind NPM, which pursues individuals' preferences instead of the public good, and thus disrupts accountability and erodes traditional public sector ethics and accountability (Maesschalck, 2004).

An alternative to NPM is PVT (see Williams & Shearer, 2011 for a recent review). The PVT perspective and the policy consequences for public managers under PVT are different from NPM (Benington & Moore, 2011). Moore (1995, p. 20) redefines the role of public managers as 'explorers who, with others, seek to discover, define, and produce public value'. That is, 'the task of a public manager is to create public value' (Moore, 1994, p. 296). PVT has been considered a normative theory, prescribing to public managers what they should do (Barzelay, 2007; Moore, 1994).

Expectations of the potentiality of PVT are quite high (Davis & West, 2009); it is considered to be able to reconcile efficiency and democracy, pursuing the former but keeping politics at the centre of the public arena (Stoker, 2006). In this way it overcomes the excessive attention paid by NPM to efficiency and cost-cutting (Spano, 2009). Moreover, it fits the networked society in which public sector has been transformed through the years and is characterized by a different concept of 'publicness' (Moulton, 2009), a new form of public governance that asks for coproduction and collaboration among public, private and non-profit organizations, emphasizing relationships more than results (O'Flynn, 2007). Public value can retain the connotation of public not because it is produced by public organizations, but because it is consumed collectively (Alford & Hughes, 2008). Finally, it helps public managers understand how best to satisfy citizens' needs (Spano, 2009), conceiving a new pragmatism in which there is not a one best way (as in NPM) and, therefore, what is valuable in a certain situation is not decided ex-ante (Alford & Hughes, 2008).

Moore (1995) uses the idea of the 'strategic triangle', which consists of three components: public value outcomes, operational capacity and the authorizing environment. In developing a strategy for a public sector organization, management must ensure that what they are going to do is valued by stakeholders, is able to attract legitimacy from the environment (which means resources) and that it is feasible in technical terms (Moore, 1995). The characteristics of this triangle are interesting. Moore did not define the contents of the public value outcomes but left their definition to the community and its representatives. He simply recognizes that a common definition of value can be represented by the achievement of the public managers of the objectives they have been delegated to pursue in an efficient and effective way and to achieve customer satisfaction; he also focuses attention on the authorizing environment, suggesting that public managers should look for the necessary support through the creation of a coalition of stakeholders (Benington & Moore, 2011). The search for consensus and legitimacy toward the achievement of the desired outcomes is the task of public managers through the involvement of whoever (private-sector organizations, public organizations, non-profit) can support the mission (Monfardini, Barretta, & Ruggiero, 2013). This is consistent with the current socio-economic context in which the network is gradually becoming the most widespread service production structure. Even more explicit is the thought of Benington, which clearly connects public value with a network-based society:

> I will also argue that this reformulation of public value (as part of a deliberative process, embedded within a democratic public sphere within which competing interest and contested values can be debated and negotiated) provides a strong conceptual framework to guide the newly emerging paradigm of networked community governance, similar to the ways in which theories of public goods provide the rationale for traditional public administration (TPA), and public (rational) choice theories provides the conceptual framework for new public management (NPM). (Benington, 2009, 2011, pp. 31–32)

From these definitions it emerges that the role of public management is to facilitate the creation of public value through participation and co-production. On this particular topic, some scholars have deeply criticized the PVT. The main criticism is that they do not agree with the definition of public managers used by Moore or with the legitimacy of their role, especially in Westminster societies. According to Rhodes and Wanna (2007, p. 406), managers as defined by Moore have too much discretionary power and they look like 'Platonic Guardians deciding the public interest' without having any mandate from the citizens. Which person is in charge of taking the decisions is not an irrelevant profile, especially considering that the same concept of public value includes participation and the co-production of services. Moreover, public administrations also have binding powers; whenever the public value production requires the imposition of sanctions or limitation of access to services, it is necessary to know which person is in charge of the binding decision and who are those eligible to participate in decision-making (Wensley & Moore, 2011). In Westminster societies some of these decisions belong to politicians and cannot be attributed to public managers. Involvement and co-production requires public managers to have the ability to coordinate stakeholders with different individual and conflicting objectives (Ruggiero, Monfardini, & Mussari, 2012). In these cases, public managers should pursue sufficient, even if not complete, consensus for the decision to take (Benington & Moore, 2011). As the case study will show, stable consensus is not so easy to achieve.

The quest for involvement is the main difference between PVT and NPM, while they have in common the importance given to efficiency and effectiveness and the attention to customer satisfaction (Moore, 1994). To summarize, PVT asks public administrations to produce services efficiently and effectively, satisfying citizens' expectations and allowing participation and the co-production of services by all those who can provide support. Such participation is even more important when the public administrations are using collective resources or have to apply sanctions.

METHOD

In this article we use a longitudinal case study. The selected case is critical for the aim of the research for several reasons (Yin, 2003). First, the selected corporation has had shareholders belonging to the public and private sectors, so it represents individual and collective interests. Second, the availability of the data allows us to extend the analysis from the early 1990s to the present time, so we can examine the period in which NPM has had the maximum diffusion and in which the PVT has been proposed and developed. Finally, the corporation has survived despite its prolonged negative financial performance and low level of activity.

The case is analyzed using official documents produced by the same organization (minutes of the general assemblies and financial statements for the period 1993–2010) and by other institutions such as the Enac (the national agency for flight security); the two business plans for the development of the corporation produced by two different companies, respectively Systematica in 2005 and Galaxy Investment Fund (GIF) in 2007, have also been considered to fully describe the story of the Aeroporto di Siena s.p.a.

The selection of the information used to carry out the analysis has to be justified. Since NPM calls for efficient and profitable corporations, financial statements will be analyzed together with statistical data provided by the Enac to understand whether the survival of Aeroporto di Siena s.p.a. can be justified by its financial performance or commercial rationality. According to PVT, public value is created through the construction of consensus about expected outcomes and using participative procedures to involve stakeholders. A legitimizing environment is necessary to secure this support. Minutes of the shareholders' assemblies have also been taken into consideration in order to understand the different shareholders' opinions on the management of the corporation and to verify the existence of the legitimizing environment.

THE CASE STUDY: A BRIEF HISTORY OF THE AMPUGNANO S.P.A

The firm Aeroporto di Siena was established during the 1970s with the juridical status of a consortium. Initially the consortium partners were the main institutions located in the Siena area, namely the Municipalities of Siena and Sinalunga, the Province of Siena, the Ente Provinciale del Turismo of Siena (a public organization responsible for the development of tourism in the Siena area) two public-owned banks, Monte dei Paschi di Siena and Banca Toscana, as well as the organization representing the entreprencurs of the area (Associazione degli Industriali) and the Camera di Commercio di Siena (Chamber of Commerce or CCIAA). The new consortium began by managing the airport area and infrastructures in the locality called Ampugnano, a very small military airport operating in military lands. The military lands were converted into State lands in order to be used for non-military purposes, and the new consortium was asked to use the infrastructures and the land in order to start a civilian air transportation activity. In fact, in the beginning, the consortium's mission was to develop the airport structures in order to start operating as a civilian airport.

The main problem at that time was the inadequacy of the infrastructure, particularly the runaway length and the lack of the necessary technological instruments for allowing flights to land and to take off both during the day and the night. Only at the beginning of the 1980s, and after the acquisition of the infrastructure needed to comply with the sector's specific law and regulation, was the airport assigned the commercial traffic qualification with a limitation of executive flights.

In 1991, the consortium was converted by the partners into a joint stock company named Aeroporto di Siena s.p.a. This shift of legal status was not imposed by the law or by any sectorial regulation and took place as an autonomous decision of the partners in order to gain the advantages of commercial legal status.

Over time, the corporate governance of Siena Airport has changed many times, partly because of the introduction of new partners and partly because of the change in the legal status of some of the original founders (in 1993 Monte dei Paschi was a public bank, but in 1995 it became a joint stock company; Banca Toscana was merged into Monte dei Paschi in 2009).

When the consortium became a joint stock company the equity was distributed to the same founders of the consortium, namely the CCIAA of Siena (15%), the Province of Siena (15%), the Municipality of Siena (15%), the Municipality of Sovicille (6%), the Monte dei Paschi di Siena (20%), the Banca Toscana (20%) and the Associazione Industriali (9%).

In 2005, new shareholders became involved in the joint stock company: two associations, the CNA and the Confcommercio, the former representing the craftsmen in small and medium enterprises and the latter representing merchants; the Industrie Riunite del Panforte, a joint stock company incorporating the firms that produce Siena cake; the Aeroporto di Firenze, the joint stock company managing Florence international airport and Calp, at that time, the Italian leader in the production of handmade crystal. All these partners are located in Siena province, and they were and still are the biggest economic entities in the area. In 2005, the Foundation Monte dei Paschi, a public-owned Foundation operating in the Siena area, commissioned a specialized consulting firm (Systematica) to produce a study on the possible future development of the airport over 20 years, with the aim of understanding whether it would have been worth continuing to invest in the Aeroporto di Siena s.p.a. According to this plan, the consulting firm projected the airport's increased activity over the next 20 years, which would be achieved by setting up regular daily flight connections with the airports in Rome, Milan and other big Italian and European cities. The plan forecasted the capacity of the Aeroporto di Siena s.p.a. to produce profits from the eighth year, reaching €1 million from the end of the period of reference of the plan. Carriers would have reached breakeven from the fifth year. To reach these objectives, the plan highlighted the necessity of investing new financial resources (more than €4 million) for several reasons: first, to raise the standard of the existing infrastructure to the requirement provided by the regulation in order to be certified as an operating airport and second, to make possible the landing and taking-off of bigger planes (around €10 million). The forecast estimated the necessity of an investment of around €12 million over the next five years.

In 2007, after many discussions during assembly meetings about the need to increase equity in order to be able to invest in the infrastructure necessary to operate, the Aeroporto di Siena s.p.a began procedures prescribed by law to privatize the joint stock company, that is, to put the majority of the equity into the hands of a private-sector corporation. Since all the public administrations contributing to the equity were not able to recapitalize the company (even the two banks were not able to invest additional financial resources), the entrance of a new shareholder was considered to be necessary in order to develop the airport according to the consulting firm's suggestions. The search for new financial resources was carried out through a tender aimed at selecting an investor available to make the necessary investment. The selected investor was the GIF, a private equity fund owned by the Italian and French Cassa Depositi e Prestiti (public-owned joint stock companies in charge of managing postal deposits) and by the KfW, a German promotional bank devoted to investment in Germany and abroad with the aim of sustaining economic development. Just prior to the entrance of the GIF, 49.1% of the Aeroporto di Siena's equity was owned by the CCIAA of Siena, 6.2% by the local governments in the area, 20.3% by the Monte dei Paschi Bank and the rest by the Acroporto di Firenze s.p.a. The entrance of the GIF resulted in all the other shareholders making the decision to increase the equity to €20 million, of which €12 million was provided by the GIF, thus giving them majority ownership (56.38%). Of the remaining shares, currently the CCIAA owns 19.66% of the equity, the Province and the Municipality of Siena own 1.06% each, the Municipality of Sovicille owns 0.6%, the Aeroporto di Firenze owns 0.11% and the Monte dei Paschi owns the remaining 21.38%. In order to be selected as a private partner, the GIF realized a business plan for the development of the airport. The business plan covered the period 2008–2020. During this period, the airport was expected to increase by up to half a million passengers with around 27,000 flights. In 2009, more than €50 million was forecasted as necessary to be invested in order to build the infrastructure required to reach the aforementioned objectives. In the same year, many citizens living near the airport formed an association (Associazione Ampugnano per la Salvaguardia del Territorio) to protest against the enlargement of the airport. They lobbied the municipalities to inform the people of the province about the pollution that would be caused by a big airport, contesting the feasibility and sustainability of the project. The association is still active and against the enlargement. It has also been joined by important environmental national organizations, including the WWF and Italia Nostra.

In 2009, the Ministry of Economy stopped the operation, arguing that the selection of the private partner was not compliant with the existing regulation (art. 5 Ministerial Decree n. 521/1997). In response, the Aeroporto di Siena s.p.a. took the decision to Court. In 2010, the Court decided to confiscate the shares owned by the GIF. As a consequence the GIF abandoned the Aeroporto di Siena s.p.a. project.

Financial Performance and Activity

Throughout the history of Aeroporto di Siena s.p.a., its financial performance has not been sustainable. Since it was founded, the organization has never produced profits, with the exception of the years 1999 and 2000, in which the profits were created with extraordinary transfers from the bank Monte dei Paschi.[1]

Article 8 of the Statute allows the shareholders to transfer around €150,000 every year to the corporation; such transfers have to be approved by at least the 80% of the shareholders. Financial resources have been transferred every year from 1993 to 2005. After 2006, the contribution was reduced to €25,000 per year. Fig. 1 shows the trend of the financial result.

It is interesting to note that the loss in 2004 would have made the equity negative. In other years (1995, 1998, 2001−2007) the annual loss was bigger than one third of the equity. In both cases, according to Italian commercial law, this unsustainable situation should lead to the compulsory winding-up

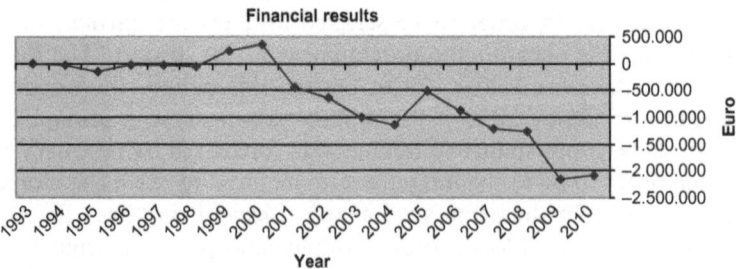

Fig. 1. Aeroporto di Siena Financial Results. *Source*: Official financial statements 1993−2010.

of the company, and indeed, this could only be avoided through the provision of new financial resources by the shareholders. The 2004 deficit has been covered through a €1.5 million recapitalization issued by the partners. The increase in equity has been achieved with no effective cash provision by the partners, but by using existing reserves, which are not included in the equity. Some of these reserves have been created using specific contributions from the Enac. In 2003, the company asked for recapitalization, but not one of the partners has subscribed. As explained above, the 2005 recapitalization was necessary to ensure the company's survival, since it was showing a negative equity. Despite such results, shareholders stated they would continue to finance the corporation. The minutes of the assembly held in June 2003 show the explicit declarations of the Province, the Municipalities of Siena and Sovicille, the CCIAA and the Associazione degli Industriali regarding their interests in the airport and in its development. Also, the Municipality of Siena recorded in the minutes of the assemblies held in 1995 and 1999 its strong interest in the development of the airport. The Municipality of Sovicille did the same in the assembly held in 1997. Also, in the minutes shareholders rarely criticized the negative financial results; they were accustomed to losses and resigned to the need to recapitalize the company, and they appeared worried only in 2003 when Monte dei Paschi refused to contribute new resources to the corporations.

The annual losses have mainly been caused by operating costs. Personnel costs, for example, have always been higher than sales revenues and often higher than total revenues. The depreciation of assets and costs for services has been increasing (i.e. maintenance costs, insurance costs and compensation for external experts). The constant low revenues have always been due to the airport's extremely low activity level. In terms of air traffic and number of passengers, the official data show very scarce numbers, listing the company as one of Italy's smallest airports. Figs. 2 and 3 show such information, which has been gathered from official statistics prepared by the Enac.

The low number of flights is due to the complete absence of flight connections in some years, and by the provision of only seasonal connections in other periods between the Aeroporto di Siena s.p.a. and other destinations. Therefore, quite often the flights using the airport have been limited to emergency and executive flights. The general assembly's minutes show the effort made by the corporation over time to find carriers available for setting up connections between Siena and other destinations in Italy and in Europe. But, the settlement in the airport would have had quite a long payoff period, often not sustainable for small carriers. In addition, the length

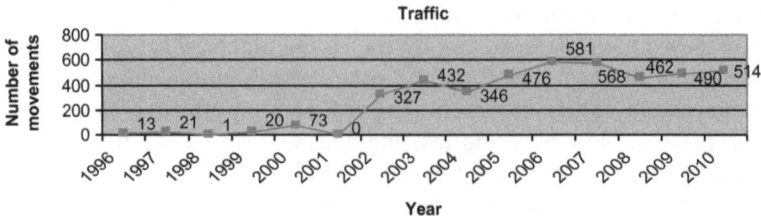

Fig. 2. Aeroporto de Siena Traffic – Number of Flights. *Source*: Enac annual statistics 1996–2010.

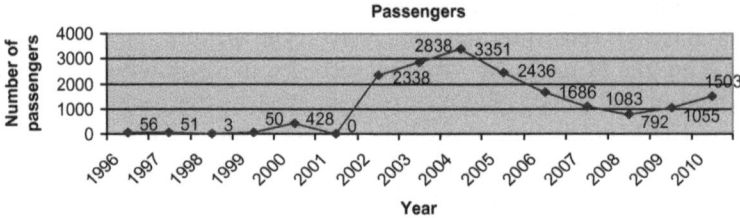

Fig. 3. Aeroporto di Siena – Number of Passengers. *Source*: Enac annual statistics 1996–2010.

of the runway has never been sufficient to allow big planes to land and take off, preventing low cost carriers to consider Siena as an option for their businesses. Both business plans mentioned in the previous paragraph specified investments for making the runway longer and fit for bigger planes.

DISCUSSION AND FINAL REMARKS

The purpose of this article was to understand whether NPM and PVT can provide indications about what strategy should be adopted to deal with a financially unsustainable public service organization. A managerial approach to public administration such as NPM provides criteria for supporting decision-makers on whether or not to allow a corporation to survive. The case of Aeroporto di Siena s.p.a. shows a poor financial performance; despite efforts, the activity of the airport has remained too small to be able to generate profits. The absence of interest in the airport by carriers can be interpreted as a lack of profitability in the business probably caused by a weak demand for air services raised by local citizens. It is therefore difficult to argue that NPM could support the decision taken by the shareholders to keep the corporation alive and continue to invest in it. The managerial approach would suggest winding up the corporation because it is not efficient, and there is not enough interest in its services. Because of this contrast between theory and practice, the actual survival of the corporation means that other criteria other than that suggested by NPM have been adopted in the strategic decision-making process.

Is PVT more promising in explaining and justifying the survival of the Aeroporto di Siena s.p.a.? Some of the elements of the strategic triangle suggested by Moore are relevant. First, according to the shareholders, the survival and development of the airport is the outcome that should represent public value. The operational capacity to keep the airport running has been achieved through the involvement of different stakeholders (suppliers, Enac etc.). The airport is indeed working, take-offs and landings are possible for some types of planes and the airport has always been used for emergency and executive flights. This means that the network in charge of providing the service has been built and the airport's required technical capacity has been reached. Moreover, many stakeholders (even if not all of them) have supported and still invest resources in the Aeroporto di Siena s.p.a.; this means that the survival of the corporation is considered valuable at least by those supporting the initiative. Unfortunately, the legitimizing environment is only apparently strong. The shareholders of the corporation are not only resource providers, but they are also representatives of other subjects with strong and sometimes contrasting interests: the community is represented by the Municipalities and by the Province, while the main economic players in the area have been and still are represented by the different collective organizations including the Cna, Associazione degli Industriali and the banks. The development plans have not yet been implemented, despite many attempts, and there has been an increasing opposition to their implementation. The formation of the association against the enlargement of the airport emphasizes that the initiative does not create public value for all stakeholders. The association includes citizens living near the airport whose interests should be represented by the municipalities that are shareholders of the airport company. So in the case of Aeroporto di Siena s.p.a. the same citizens are represented by two different institutions (the Municipality and the association) providing opposite opinions about the enlargement of the airport.

In such a case it is difficult for PVT to show whether public value has been created or not by keeping the airport running, or to provide directions regarding what to do in the immediate future, or to identify the policy makers. It is possible to argue that the development of the airport creates public value because there is support from the public administrations representing the citizens, and the airport is working, since the technical network has been created, so the lack of resources is the only obstacle to the airport's development. In addition, the two business plans drafted in 2005 and 2007 by different consultants point out that the enlargement of the airport would create many benefits for the community: economic growth (profits) and new employment, among others.

However, it is also possible to argue that the airport's survival is not creating public value, but destroying it, because the initiative is strongly criticized by citizens grouped in the association so its legitimacy is weak. The operational capacity seems limited because the length of the runway impedes the landing and taking-off of big planes and therefore profit cannot be realized. In fact, the corporation has never produced profits, or achieved satisfactory levels of activity; every year shareholders have had to add resources and cover losses. Public administrations are using public resources collected through taxation, but apparently just a few taxpayers have benefited from the airport.

In the process of evaluating the actual production (if any) of public value, what part of the strategic triangle takes priority? Listening to the relevant stakeholders to gain their support, or achieving operational capacity? And when can operational capacity be considered to have been properly achieved? In our case study, voices against the initiative were only raised when the enlargement of the project was proposed. So the small infrastructure means the airport is not fully operational, but the enlargement causes the loss of legitimacy. In such a complex scenario, a compromise is probably necessary. The reduced operational capacity could be explained as a way to minimize complaints, and therefore reduce the loss of legitimacy, but keeping both present. In the end, without clear prioritization, it may become hard to decide what to do.

To summarize, our case study shows that PVT is a possible policy maker in the decision regarding whether Aeroporto di Siena s.p.a. should be expanded or wound up: there are valid reasons to take either of these paths. And who is the policy maker in this case study? The strategic decision probably has to be made jointly by the company shareholders, and in a joint stock company, corporate governance mechanisms need to be consistent with the political responsibility for the provision of the service.

The differing interests of the stakeholders makes the legitimizing environment highly unstable, and the outcome uncertain. It is interesting to note that the association claims it is defending the public interest and accuses the shareholders (among which there are the Municipalities) of pursuing just (individual) economic benefits, while the shareholders claim the opposite. That is, they are working for the wider public interest, while the Association represents only the interests of those living in the area.

PVT calls for inclusive procedures and for coproduction in the provision of public services, so it is not possible to make a selection among those who are legitimized to participate excluding the others. PVT supports the idea of the existence of collective (public) interests created through negotiation and participation, and in this way it is different from NPM, which considers the public interest as the sum of individual preferences (Bozeman, 2007). The present case study suggests that NPM is focused on the managerial perspective, which can be subordinated by other rationales, while PVT is conceptually broad enough to include managerial and other rationales. Unfortunately, this broadness tends to result in a lack of focus when conflicting political and social interests are at stake. If value(s) are influenced by contingencies, stability is almost impossible to achieve, so managers are faced with a difficult task (West & Davis, 2011). In this sense, from a managerial perspective, the measurement of value achieved will probably require further theoretical and practical developments (Spano, 2009).

NOTE

1. Full information on financial statements' results can be provided by the authors on request.

REFERENCES

Alford, J., & Hughes, O. (2008). Public value pragmatism as the next phase of public management. *The American Review of Public Administration, 38*(2), 130−148.

Alford, J., & O'Flynn, J. (2009). Making sense of public value: Concepts, critiques and emergent meanings. *International Journal of Public Administration, 32,* 171−191.

Barzelay, M. (2007). Learning from second-hand experience: Methodology for extrapolation-oriented case research. *Governance, 20*(3), 521−543.

Benington, J. (2009). Creating the public in order to create public value? *International Journal of Public Administration, 32*(3−4), 232−249.

Benington, J. (2011). From private choice to public value? In J. Benington & M. H. Moore (Eds.), *Public value: Theory and practice* (pp. 31−51). New York, NY: Palgrave Macmillan.

Benington, J., & Moore, M. H. (2011). *Public value: Theory and practice.* New York, NY: Palgrave Macmillan.

Bevir, M., Rhodes, R. A. W., & Weller, P. (2003). Traditions of governance: Interpreting the changing role of the public sector. *Public Administration, 81*(1), 1–17.

Bozeman, B. (2007). *Public values and public interest. counterbalancing economic individualism.* Washington, DC: Georgetown University Press.

Christensen, T., & Laegreid, P. (1998). Administrative reform policies: The case of Norway. *International Review of Administrative Science, 64*(2), 457–475.

Christensen, T., & Laegreid, P. (2002). New public management: Puzzles of democracy and the influence of citizens. *The Journal of Political Philosophy, 10*(3), 267–295.

Davis, P., & West, K. (2009). What do public values mean for public action? Putting public values in their plural place. *The American Review of Public Administration, 39*(6), 602–618.

DeLeon, L., & Denhardt, R. B. (2000). The political theory of reinvention. *Public Administration, 60*(2), 89–97.

Dunleavy, P., & Hood, C. (1994). From old public administration to new public management. *Public Money and Management, 14*(3), 9–16.

Hood, C. (1991). A public management for all seasons? *Public Administration, 69*(1), 3–19.

Hood, C. (1995). The "new public management" in the 1980s: Variations on a theme. *Accounting, Organizations and Society, 20*(2–3), 93–109.

Lapsley, I. (2008). The NPM agenda: Back to the future. *Financial Accountability and Management, 24*(1), 77–96.

Maesschalck, J. (2004). The impact of the new public management reform on public servant's ethic: Towards a theory. *Public Administration, 82*(2), 465–481.

Monfardini, P., Barretta, A. D., & Ruggiero, P. (2013). Seeking legitimacy: Social reporting in healthcare sector. *Accounting Forum, 37*(1), 54–66.

Moore, M. H. (1994). Public value as the focus of strategy. *Australian Journal of Public Administration, 53*(3), 296–303.

Moore, M. H. (1995). *Creating public value: Strategic management in government.* Harvard, MA: Harvard University Press.

Moulton, S. (2009). Putting together the publicness puzzle: A framework for realized publicness. *Public Administration Review, 69*(5), 889–900.

O'Flynn, J. (2007). From new public management to public value: Paradigmatic change and managerial implications. *The Australian Journal of Public Administration, 66*(3), 353–366.

Osborne, D., & Gaebler, T. (1992). *Reinventing government: How the entrepreneurial spirit is transforming the public sector.* Reading, MA: Addison-Wesley.

Pollitt, C., & Bouckaert, G. (2000). *Public management reform: A comparative analysis.* Oxford: Oxford University Press.

Rhodes, R. A. W., & Wanna, J. (2007). The limits to public value, or rescuing responsible government from the platonic guardians. *Australian Journal of Public Administration, 66*(4), 406–421.

Ruggiero, P., Monfardini, P., & Mussari, R. (2012). Territorial boundaries as limits: A foucaldian analysis of the agglomeration of municipalities. *International Journal of Public Administration, 35*(7), 492–506.

Smith, R. F. I. (2004). Focusing on public value: Something new and something old. *Australian Journal of Public Administration, 63*(4), 68–79.

Spano, A. (2009). Public value creation and management control systems. *International Journal of Public Administration, 32*, 328−348.

Stoker, G. (2006). Public value management: A new narrative for networked governance? *American Review of Public Administration, 36*(1), 41−57.

Wensley, R., & Moore, M. H. (2011). Choice and marketing in public management: The creation of public value? In J. Benington & M. H. Moore (Eds.), *Public value: Theory and practice* (pp. 127−143). New York, NY: Palgrave Macmillan.

West, K., & Davis, P. (2011). What is the public value of government action? Toward a (new) pragmatic approach to values questions in public endeavours. *Public Administration, 89*(2), 226−241.

Williams, I., & Shearer, H. (2011). Appraising public value: Past, present and future. *Public Administration, 89*(4), 1367−1384.

Yin, R. K. (2003). *Case study research: Design and methods* (3rd ed.). London: Sage.

HARMONY IN HIERARCHY? HOW POLITICIANS AND PUBLIC MANAGERS PRIORITIZE CRUCIAL PUBLIC VALUES

Zeger van der Wal

ABSTRACT

Purpose — *This qualitative interview study compares public value prioritizations of ministers, members of parliament and senior public managers in the Netherlands. This article aims to answer the following central research question: how do Dutch political elites and administrative elites differ in their interpretation and prioritization of public values?*

Design/methodology/approach — *Based on coding and categorization of 65 interviews this article shows how government elites in advanced western democracies interpret and assess four crucial public values: responsiveness, expertise, lawfulness and transparency.*

Findings — *Political elites and administrative elites in the Netherlands are more similar than different in their prioritization and perceptions of public values. Differences are strongly related to role conceptions and*

Public Value Management, Measurement and Reporting
Studies in Public and Non-Profit Governance, Volume 3, 243–268
Copyright © 2014 by Emerald Group Publishing Limited
All rights of reproduction in any form reserved
ISSN: 2051-6630/doi:10.1108/S2051-663020140000003010

institutional responsibilities, which are more traditional than most recent literature on politico-administrative dynamics would suggest.

Research limitations/implications — *Our qualitative findings are hard to generalize to larger populations of politicians and public managers in the Netherlands, let alone beyond the Netherlands. However, the testable research hypotheses we derive from our explorative study merit future testing among larger populations of respondents in different countries through survey research.*

Practical implications — *Experienced values differences between both groups are smaller than their mutual perceptions would suggest.*

Originality/value — *Most research on public values is quantitative in nature and focuses exclusively on public managers. By adding the politician to the equation we improve our understanding of how public values are enacted in real life and set the tone for a more inclusive research agenda on public values.*

Keywords: Public values; government elites; public management; political—administrative relations

INTRODUCTION

Do political and administrative elites hold different views in relation to crucial values given their different roles in producing public value? If we use classical prescriptions of values in asking this question, our answer would be a clear yes. Values such as accountability, responsiveness, courage, entrepreneurialism and opportunism supposedly guide political actions and decisions, whereas values such as lawfulness, neutrality, expertise and impartiality should guide the conduct of senior bureaucrats (DeLeon, 1994; van der Wal, 2012). In short Machiavelli versus Weber. Because both groups of government elites adhere to a common set of values as 'rules of the game' they manage to govern and work together despite their different roles and drivers. The rules of the game include that politicians take expert advice from their senior administrative advisors seriously and consult them on a regular basis, while senior civil servants refrain from taking political standpoints and comply with the final decisions of their political bosses, even if they vehemently disagree (see Aberbach, Putnam, & Rockman, 1981; Svara, 2001; 't Hart & Wille, 2006).

Scholars and practitioners have propagated and validated this classical ideal type for decades. However, fundamental changes and disruptions have emerged in political–administrative relations and their dynamics during the last decade. Such changes include the transformation of the senior bureaucrat to a 'public manager' (Noordegraaf, 2004; O'Flynn, 2007) with a more pro-active and, in some cases, more 'political' stance towards decision-making (Gains, 2009). Consequently there is an increasing reliance by politicians on 'sensible' political advisors and a leaning towards populist opinions to produce electorally rewarding sound bites given today's mediatized environment (Butora, 2007; 't Hart & Wille, 2006). These developments necessitate more up-to-date knowledge on how both groups of government elites interpret and enact crucial public governance values because they give rise to pressing questions: if the traditional rules of the game have changed, have public values preferences changed accordingly? Or alternatively, if such preferences still have a rather 'traditional' character, will adherence to such values result in more adversarial relations because the ethos of collaboration has eroded, as some have suggested (Demir, 2009; 't Hart & Wille, 2006)?

Addressing such questions is important because, individually and together, political and administrative elites have the most substantial impact on 'what gets proposed for consideration by governments, what gets passed into law, and how law gets implemented' (Aberbach et al., 1981, p. 24). However, recent research on public value and public values does not enable us to do so because it has excluded politicians. In addition, studies on dynamics in political–administrative relations have ignored specific values to explain dynamics. This qualitative interview study aims to provide initial baseline data on the current public values frames of senior politicians and senior public managers in the Netherlands. Based on a coding and categorization of 65 interviews the study shows how these government elites interpret and assess four crucial public values: responsiveness, expertise, lawfulness and transparency. We theorize on our results and conclude with six research propositions for quantitative follow-up studies.

We aim to answer the following central research question: *how do Dutch political elites and administrative elites differ in their interpretation and prioritization of public values?*

HOW PUBLIC *VALUES* RELATE TO PUBLIC *VALUE*

Mark Moore (1995) and Barry Bozeman (2007) have published the most oft-cited works on public value and public values respectively. Quite often, both concepts are used intertwined while they denote different elements of governance (O'Flynn, 2007; van der Wal, Nabatchi, & de Graaf, 2013). How, then, should one exactly distinguish between 'public value' and 'public values'?

Public value is considered to be the potential of a given political and institutional setting that can be realized to create something substantively valuable for a given public (Moore, 1995). Moore (1995, p. 52) contends that managers can create public value in two ways: they can 'deploy the money and authority entrusted to them to produce things of value to particular clients and beneficiaries', and they can create public value through 'establishing and operating an institution that meets citizens' (and their representatives') desires for properly ordered and productive public institutions'. Public value focuses on (1) a wider range of value than public goods; (2) more than outputs and (3) what has meaning for people, rather than what a public sector decision-maker might presume is best for them (Alford & O'Flynn, 2009, p. 176). It follows that the main task of both the elected as well as the appointed government elite is to create public value and, by doing so, to pursue the public interest. Thus, public value is the ultimate aim and *outcome* of public governance.

What then are *public values*? These are behavioural and process-related principles ultimately aimed at producing public value. Bozeman (2007, p. 13) describes society's 'public values' as 'those providing normative consensus about (1) the rights, benefits, and prerogatives to which citizens should (and should not) be entitled; (2) the obligations of citizens to society, the state and one another (3) and the principles on which governments and policies should be based'. This study focuses predominantly on the third category of public values, as they supposedly guide the conduct and decision-making of government elites. Without engaging endlessly in a debate on how to define values as many others have done before us, we make a pragmatic choice for the following definition that has served well in earlier empirical studies: 'values are important qualities and standards that have a certain weight in the choice of action' (van der Wal, de Graaf, & Lasthuizen, 2008, p. 468). By means of providing a little more context, let us further assume with Bozeman (2007, p. 116) that a value is (1) relatively stable; (2) has strong potential to affect behaviour; (3) changes (if at all) only after deliberation and (4) helps define one's sense of oneself.

Empirical examples of the values of Bozeman's third category include, for *public managers,* accountability, incorruptibility, efficiency and lawfulness (van der Wal et al., 2008, p. 472), as well as adaptability and stability (Beck Jørgensen & Bozeman, 2007, p. 360). For *politicians* they include the common good, social cohesion, sustainability, will of the people, collective choice and citizen involvement, whereas political loyalty as specified through accountability and responsiveness is most important for the *relationship* between public administrators and politicians (p. 360). Therefore values such as lawfulness and efficiency will not always go in hand in hand in public governance; exactly how both groups of government elites prioritize and balance potentially conflicting values is what this article aims to find out.

COMPARING VALUES BETWEEN POLITICIANS AND CIVIL SERVANTS: EXISTING EVIDENCE

As said, studies that focus specifically on values of government elites are sparse. Between the late 1940s and late 1970s a few scholars engaged in empirical studies into values and attitudes of government elites (e.g. Aberbach et al., 1981; Putnam, 1976; Searing, 1969, 1978). However, since the seminal work of Aberbach et al. (1981), we have not seen any large-scale attempt. They conducted what is perhaps the most oft-cited study on the relations, differences and similarities between political and bureaucratic elites in western democracies. Although they did not focus specifically on values, their study provides numerous insights into related issues such as beliefs, and task and role conception. The authors discuss four images of the relationship as well as the difference between politicians and bureaucrats: the *policy/administration* image that aligns with the classical dichotomy of Goodnow (1900) and Wilson (1887); the *facts/interests* image, which assumes that both politicians and bureaucrats participate in making policy, but that they make distinctive contributions in that bureaucrats bring facts and politicians interests; the *energy/equilibrium* image in which politicians are passionate, partisan, even ideological, and bureaucrats are, by contrast, prudent, practical and pragmatic and the *pure hybrid,* which suggests a virtual disappearance of the Weberian distinction, producing hybrids that shift between roles, with senior bureaucrats that enter a ministerial cabinet to become politicians themselves a few years later as an increasing development (1981, pp. 14–20).

More recent comparative studies are virtually non-existent. An exception is a survey study among Dutch politicians and civil servants by van den Heuvel, Huberts, and Verberk (2002, p. 117), which showed that politicians embrace mostly values such as 'honesty', 'incorruptibility' and 'openness', while administrators prioritize 'expertise', 'lawfulness', 'dedication', 'serviceability' and 'efficiency'. However, when asked, administrators perceive politicians to be a little too fond of themselves when it comes to the importance of 'honesty' (and also 'impartiality'), whereas politicians argue that the emphasis on 'impartiality' and 'collegiality' of their counterparts should be put into perspective (p. 116). Sceptical perceptions of politician's values by administrators are further evidenced by Bowman and Williams (1997, p. 518) whose survey of US civil servants shows that they doubt that the 'ethical standards of elected and appointed officials are as high as those held by career civil servants' (55%). According to the authors, 'the respondents agree with Paul Appleby, who warned of the harm that can be done by top officials who are "amateurs" in governmental responsibility' (p. 518). In a follow-up study, Bowman and Knox (2008) reach a similar conclusion: this time, 58% of the respondents share doubts about the ethics of their political leadership. Interestingly, a core issue according to respondents is 'proliferation of political appointees and the politicization of upper-grade career managers' (2008, p. 629).

The dearth of recent comparative empirical studies necessitates that we collect baseline data on current value perceptions of political and administrative elites. We decided to interview a convenience sample of government elites in our home country, the Netherlands. Before we explain how we did this and whom we interviewed, we first discuss the changing roles and agendas of both politicians and public managers and their potential implications for the four crucial public values we study in this article.

DYNAMICS IN POLITICAL–ADMINISTRATIVE ROLE CONCEPTIONS

Hardly anyone seems to hold the position anymore that the modern senior civil servant is still the distant, politically neutral figure he used to be (Noordegraaf, 2004; Peters & Pierre, 2001). Recent governance developments (Osborne, 2009) seem to have created a new type of senior civil servant: the responsive, involved, pro-active and 'hands on' *public manager* (Noordegraaf, 2004). Public managers are more than classical bureaucrats, as 'public management scholars recognize the public manager as an active and motivating agent, rather than as an actor that passively executes the will of their political masters' (Alford & O'Flynn, 2009, p. 353). Arguably, even to a larger extent than becoming more business-like as a result of new public management (NPM) (see van der Wal, 2008), public managers seem to have become more assertive policy advisors who are getting closer to the domain of politics (van Thiel, Steijn, & Allix, 2007).[1]

In an overview of debates on public management and public values, Alford and O'Flynn (2009) show what this development 'from bureaucrats to public managers' implies in terms of public values. This shift has serious implications in terms of the study and practice of ethics, which is for public management scholars concerned with 'principles and values by which public managers may determine right from wrong as well as the character needed to sustain judgment and action' (Dobel, 2005, p. 156). It implies that a relatively passive role for public administrators as suggested by Dobel in his view on their moral obligation, 'obedience to the mandates of law and policy mediated by the elected and appointed officials of democratic regimes' (2005, p. 159), will not apply to senior civil servants anymore.

The classical neutral, almost amoral, notion of the civil servant made proponents of the anti-dichotomous argument criticize the ethical implications of the dichotomist view (Demir, 2009, p. 877) even before the public manager emerged as such. For instance, Adams and Balfour (1998), taking the seminal work of Arendt (1963), have argued that the idea of strict separation of policy formulation and implementation seemed to strip public administrators of their moral responsibilities. It follows upon this that calling senior civil servants public managers has important implications in terms of ethics and values. Again, rather than being actors that execute policies with adherence to classical Weberian values such as efficiency, lawfulness, neutrality and impartiality, they are increasingly seen as 'co-creators of public value'. One thus might propose that politicians and public managers have grown closer in embracing certain public values as a result of this; at least to those concerned with the development of public policy such as responsiveness, serviceability, collaboration and 'buzzword' accountability (Bovens & Schillemans, 2009).

The recent proliferation of scholarly publications on 'public value' and 'public values' that address this issue has emerged as a result of what O'Flynn (2007) considers to be the very recent and third generation of public administration reform. Arguably, this reform movement is again a reaction to the dysfunctions of the NPM model and it is yet emerging under a variety of labels, *(new) governance* and *public value* being the two most prominent. There is no settled model, however, there are common characteristics and practices emerging from the twin pressures of what *is* happening in government, and what some commentators are saying *should* happen (O'Flynn, 2007, p. 355).

A FOCUS ON FOUR CRUCIAL PUBLIC VALUES

This study focuses on four public values: responsiveness, expertise, lawfulness and transparency (e.g. Meijer, 2009, 2013; Piotrowski, 2010; van der Wal, 2008, 2011). These values are important for legislators and executives, as well as public managers, but we expect that each group will interpret and prioritize these values differently given their respective roles and responsibilities (Aberbach et al., 1981, p. 24; van der Wal, 2012, p. 263). In turn, critical reflection of elites on such prioritization should produce insightful shades of grey that add to our understanding of public values. We also selected these values because their importance is not as self-evident or prone to political correctness as cliché 'truisms' that dominate codes of conduct, such as honesty, integrity or excellence (van Rekom, van Riel, & Wierenga, 2006). In fact, enactment of these four values may very well produce tension and internal conflict (van der Wal, 2011).[2]

Responsiveness ('Meeting Wishes and Demands of Important Stakeholders')

Meeting demands and wishes of key stakeholders seems evident for politicians or 'vote-seekers' (Pedersen, 2013). Interestingly, earlier research from the Netherlands shows responsiveness is not a dominant value for politicians (van den Heuvel et al., 2002), but we should note a sizeable part of the sample in that study consisted of regional politicians who do not face much electoral pressure. However, because politicians legitimize their power through democratic processes, while public managers legitimize their power through expertise (Nieuwenkamp, 2001), we do expect political elites to not only view this value as more important but also to *characterize it differently*, by emphasizing external stakeholders rather than internal bureaucratic hierarchy. In a recent study from the Netherlands into value preferences of public and private managers, the former reject the notion of being too responsive to outside opinions; they ascribe this value to the political habitus (van der Wal, 2011). In addition, directly elected MPs and ministers may also perceive responsiveness differently; after all, their democratic legitimacy differs. To conclude, changing role conceptions of senior public managers and political and societal pressures to act more outwardly may lead to more congruence in perceptions, whereas rapid increase of populist politics and concomitant media attention in the Netherlands may imply larger differences because politicians nowadays are seen as 'hyper-responsive' (Bovens & Wille, 2010).

Expertise ('Making Decisions Based on Actual, State-of-the-Art Evidence')

Public managers derive much of their legitimacy from domain knowledge and experience, and policy expertise, whereas politicians lack such expertise with dependence on their administrative counterparts as a result (Aberbach et al., 1981; Nieuwenkamp, 2001; Weber, 1926). Indeed, previous studies suggest expertise is among the most appreciated value of public managers, both actually and ideally (van der Wal, 2008). In a study from the Netherlands, two thirds of the surveyed civil servants designated expertise as the most important value for their profession vis-à-vis less than a quarter of the surveyed politicians. However, we may expect a decrease in importance of expertise to public managers, or at least a shift in importance towards management skills rather than policy domain knowledge, as a consequence of the formation of the *Algemene Bestuursdienst* (ABD) or Senior Executive Service in 1995. The ABD'ss objectives were to improve quality, diversity and mobility across the entire national government. More than 15 years later, scholars and practitioners alike view ABD as a 'mobility machine', whose mandatory job rotation and emphasis on managerial skills has hollowed out the policy expertise of senior administrators, making them more vulnerable to political steering (Bekker, 2009). A minority opposite viewpoint is that the ABD has generated more of a common professional ethos among its members with a stronger position vis-à-vis politicians as a result (Den Boer & Noordegraaf, 2006).

Lawfulness ('Acting in Strict Accordance with Existing Laws, Rules and Regulations')

Even though the importance of lawfulness within the public sector appears to be self-evident, previous studies show a plethora of gradations among public managers regarding the extent to which they should abide by laws, rules and regulations, and whether the 'spirit' or the 'letter' of the law should be the guiding principle (van der Wal, 2011). Often, lawfulness is seen as a barrier to efficient and effective public governance. For politicians, lawfulness appears to be even less important than expertise; however, the same applies to civil servants in relative terms (van den Heuvel et al., 2002, p. 116).

Of course, a key difference here is the role of both groups in the legislative process itself: politicians usually initiate, adopt and execute laws and rules, whereas civil servants have a support function, at least formally (Bovens, 't Hart, Twist van, & Rosenthal, 2007). Moreover, because civil servants are subject to ministerial responsibility they may be more inclined to act according to the letter of the law. On the other hand, aforementioned studies also show considerable contrasts within the civil service between purists and those who are more lenient.

Transparency ('Acting Openly, Visibly and Controllably')

This value is supposedly of absolute importance to politicians (Piotrowski, 2010; van den Heuvel et al., 2002). Public managers admit they cannot, and perhaps should not always act with complete transparency, particularly during delicate decision-making processes (van der Wal, 2008, p. 83). Our study will have to show whether this applies equally to politicians. Increasing media attention to public management action is important here, because we may expect shifts in terms of how they perceive this value, also in light of their increasing 'political roles' (Bovens et al., 2007; 't Hart & Wille, 2006).

Research shows that almost 30% of the daily workload of civil servants is determined by the amount of questions MPs bring to the fore in parliament, often based on the daily news. Such hype-driven behaviour frustrates civil servants who work with a longer time-horizon (Algemene Bestuursdienst, 2006; Jeekel, 2005). Media also play an important role in the accountability obligations of government. Because of the public information act or *Wet Openbaarheid van Bestuur* (WOB) they have regular access to government data, which leads to preventive rather than informative conduct on the part of civil servants. Politicians, on their part, expect restraint from civil servants (van den Heuvel et al., 2002).

METHODOLOGY

In-Depth Elite Interviews

We employed qualitative methods because we wanted to know how particular values matter, and how their importance is worded. Aberbach and Rockman (2002, p. 673) state that 'Interviewing is often important if one needs to know what a set of people think, or how they interpret an event or series of events, or what they have done or are planning to do'. Moreover, 'elites especially — but other highly educated people as well — do not like being put in the straightjacket of close-ended questions' (Aberbach & Rockman, 2002, p. 674). Thus, we used *semi-structured* interviews consisting of 'a set of questions carefully worded and arranged for the purpose of taking each respondent through the same sequence, and asking each respondent the same questions with essentially the same words' (Patton, 1987, p. 112).

Elites are, by definition, less accessible and more conscious of their self-interest than less prominent respondents. This is exactly why elite interviews are relatively rare (Richards, 1996). As a consequence, the data we collected are unique but they should be handled with care as well. It would be naïve to act in an overly trusting manner towards individuals who are very well equipped to 'spin' facts and events, 'play' interviewers and dominate and take over conversations entirely. In fact, they would never have become government elites had they not developed such skills. Nevertheless, almost all conversations were open, critical and often quite intense. Not one respondent felt the need to substantially change, revise, let alone censor transcripts or view interview questions beforehand.

The interview ratio was basic. We used an interview guide, 'a listing of areas to be covered in the interview along with, for each area, a listing of topics or questions that together will suggest lines of inquiry' (Weiss, 1994, p. 48). We discussed at length the four aforementioned public values, how and why they are important, and in which cases they conflict. The in-depth conversations that followed lasted between 40 and 70 minutes, depending on time availability and progress. We interviewed 65 respondents between

May 2010 and August 2011. About 95% of the interviews were face-to-face and took place within the respondents' professional environment. Only a few were conducted at home, at railway restaurants or at the author's university.

Who We Interviewed and Why

Rather than selecting respondents randomly based on probability parameters, the selection here aimed to maximize range and depth (Weiss, 1994, 23). We recruited respondents through a combination of at-random probability sampling and convenience sampling because of the limited possibilities to gain access to elites without snowball sampling. Although convenience sampling may not be the ideal base for generalization, good reasons exist for using this technique here: (1) the respondents' own assessment of generalizability; (2) the interviewer's own identification of others worth recruiting and (3) 'the idea that a certain amount of universalism with regard to the phenomenon studied, exists among a certain group of respondents' (Weiss, 1994, p. 26). Table 1 shows who we interviewed.

Table 1. Interviewees by Type, Function and Party Affiliation if Applicable (*n* Between Brackets; Total *n* = 65).

Politicians	Public Managers
Member of Parliament (MP):	• Director of Agency/Quango (14)
	• Departmental Director (12)
• MPs Christian Democrats CDA (6)	• (Dep.) Secretary-General (6)
• MPs Socialist Party SP (3)	• Director-General (3)
• MPs Liberal Party VVD (3)	• Inspector-General (1)
• MPs Christian Union CU (1)	
• MPs Social-Democrats PvdA (1)	*Total: 36*
• MPs Freedom Party PVV (1)	
• MPs Dutch Pride TON (1)	
(Deputy) Minister:	
• One-term Minister (5)	
• Two-term Minister (4)	
• (Dep.) Prime Minister (3)	
• Four-term Minister (1)	
Total: 29	

We invited all 150 members of the Dutch parliament in May 2010, 16 of whom responded positively, representing seven out of 10 factions across the political spectrum. Such a low response rate is common for politicians at the national level (see Aberbach et al., 1981; van den Heuvel et al., 2002). In addition, we approached about 60 (former) ministers of the last nine cabinets (1982–2010), mainly through our personal networks. Thirteen responded positively, many of whom held multiple cabinet positions throughout the years, including a former Prime Minister and three so-called 'State Ministers'. Public managers were randomly selected from the online database of the ABD. We interviewed 23 'regular' members and 13 members of the top management group (TMG) that consists of the 70 most senior Dutch public managers (in total, the ABD has about 800 members).

Issue-focused Between-group Analysis

Since the primary objective of this study is to portray value perceptions of political and administrative elites, the data analysis was *issue focused* rather than case focused, and took place at the 'level of the generalized' rather than the 'level of the concrete' (Weiss, 1994, p. 152). Thus, single respondents and cases were less important than the objects of analysis. The aim of issue-focused analysis is 'to describe what has been learned from all respondents about people in their situation' (p. 153); in other words, to paint a general but at the same time contextual picture. According to Eisenhardt (1989), it allows the researcher to recognize general patterns in different settings.

We transcribed every interview, resulting in immense quantities of data (over 500 pages of text) that needed to be systematically analyzed. Coding of these literal transcriptions began after we created a monster-grid – a data matrix with the respondents on one axis and the core issues on the other, which is a more elaborate version of what Weiss (1994, p. 157) calls 'excerpt files'. The next step involved reading all responses to a particular question to derive first impressions of overall patterns that were then juxtaposed with the empirical data. This inductive process, described by Weiss (1994, p. 158) as 'local integration', is clearly not just a matter of counting. As a result, we repeated the inductive process many times before we wrote our first analysis.

However, data analysis is not simply a question of retrospective comparison (Strauss, 1987). Rather, analysis begins as soon as there is data

collection. Indeed, as Miles and Huberman (1994, p. 49) observe, 'the more
investigators have developed understandings during data collection, the
surer they can be of the adequacy of the data collection and the less daunt-
ing will be the task of fully analyzing the data'. In the same vein, we started
coding chronologically, regardless of whether the interviewee was a politician or a public manager.

Coding and Reporting

Each relevant quotation (288 in total) received an initial 'open code' that
characterized the statement's core. During a process of going back and
forth more definitive codes were established as new codes were created or
old ones adapted (Klostermann, 2003, p. 43). In the final analysis we translated our codes into motivational categories. Because qualitative data analysis is as much 'data reduction' as quantitative data analysis (King,
Keohane, & Verba, 1994; Miles & Huberman, 1994), we tried to limit the
number of categories for each value by grouping resembling statements
across groups into identical categories (in this case, in between three and
six). We coded inductively without any pre-conceived categories or theoretical assumptions in mind.

Given the nature of our analysis we categorized by counting statements
and not individual respondents. Moreover, as the number of respondents
differs quite substantially between our groups, we use percentages to indicate how our three groups of elites compare in terms of how they interpret
and weigh each value. We use some of the most characteristic quotes of
participants to illustrate our propositions.

ANALYSIS OF RESULTS

Responsiveness

We can distinguish five different perspectives with regard to the importance
and meaning of responsiveness (see Table 2). The most dominant view on
responsiveness is that of a critical evaluation of different interests and their
claims. For civil servants, this frame is *political*: they weight stakeholders'
demands on the basis of political guidelines or mandates. For politicians,
this frame means having the patience to hear out many different

Table 2. How Political and Administrative Elites View Responsiveness.

Responsiveness	Public Managers (*n* = 36)	MPs (*n* = 16)	Ministers (*n* = 13)
1. As critically weighing and balancing different interests	35%	69%	38%
'Stakeholders are important and you have to listen to them. But you should not take at face value what these stakeholders try to tell you'.			
2. As being loyal and serviceable to politics	30%	0%	0%
'You are not here to push through your own political viewpoints. So responsiveness means you have a well-developed ability to react and adapt to the policy questions of the politician'.			
3. As subordinate to lawfulness	22%	8%	13%
'So, responsiveness is an important value but it can never be decisive for the direction that is ultimately chosen. Laws and their interpretation take precedence in setting such directions'.			
4. As coupled with transparency	9%	8%	50%
'In the end we try to decide on the basis of objective criteria, as objective as possible. Different deliberations play a role. So, stakeholders are important but you can never satisfy everybody. As such, responsiveness is very much linked to transparency because taking into account stakeholders implies transparency in decision making'.			
5. As subordinate to effectiveness	4%	15%	0%
'I find organizational effectiveness much more important. It's fine with me to meet stakeholder demands but I cannot meet all demands of all stakeholders'.			
Total	100%	100%	100%

stakeholders and constituents, and having the guts to say no to their demands, as a former MP and minister illustrates:

> You ask, we provide: I am very much against that. I am in favor of good listening and not excluding certain voices and views. Despite your convictions you need to be able to adapt and fine-tune. So be responsive, but based on a clear stance and position. In most areas you have a set of norms, a framework of reference which guides your actions, and you want to include the outside world in that framework, rather than the other way around.

Half of the ministers we interviewed link responsiveness to transparency: what is important is to *clarify why* you cannot meet certain demands of certain groups. A large number of the public managers in our sample view responsiveness as being loyal and serviceable to the political leadership rather than to outside parties. In their disdain of 'pleasing' voters and stakeholders they frame this value in traditional terms. A final observation is that many respondents *juxtapose* this value *against* other important public governance values, such as lawfulness and transparency.

Overall, however, respondents' perceptions of responsiveness show many similarities: four out of five categories apply to politicians as well as public managers. Differences lie in towards whom government should be responsive.

Expertise

Government elites' views of expertise also show a number of similarities, albeit less than for responsiveness: three out of six views are shared between groups (see Table 3). Both political and administrative elites emphasize the importance of domain knowledge. Even more important is the ability *to organize sufficient expertise* when having all the necessary knowledge 'in house' seems impossible. Particularly MPs adhere to this view of expertise:

> I have to research dossiers with half a staffer a week whereas ten civil servants can debate over one single report. They say, on their turn: those MPs, they are never well prepared, they have no clue. This is true, but for both sides. I also know civil servants who don't know what they're talking about ... The art for the politician is to tap into all the expertise that is available in society nowadays, rather than having all the expertise yourself.

Logically, a view that we find only among public managers is expertise as political loyalty and serviceability: respondents with statements in this category feel a duty and responsibility to feed their political masters with sufficient factual information so they can make sound decisions. As a corollary, about one third of the ministers see expertise as a purely administrative responsibility.

Lawfulness

Safeguarding lawfulness and legality seem self-evident in public governance but the process of doing so produces many dilemmas for government elites. Even though a substantial number of respondents in all three groups view

Table 3. How Political and Administrative Elites View Expertise.

Expertise	Public Managers (*n* = 36)	MPs (*n* = 16)	Ministers (*n* = 13)
1. As combination of domain knowledge and management skills	31%	0%	8%
'*To me, striking a balance between having people with domain knowledge and people with process skills is of the utmost importance'.*			
2. As loyalty and serviceability to politicians	19%	0%	0%
'*Making sure politicians are really well informed when they make decisions. Having looked at the pros and cons of things. Technical pros and cons are even more important than political pros and cons'.*			
3. As *organizing* sufficient expertise	19%	57%	33%
'*You do not always have to possess this expertise yourself but you have to utilize it. So, when making decisions it is crucial to make sure you're well-informed. You do not have to know everything yourself but you should know how to make use of available knowledge'.*			
4. As specific domain knowledge	15%	36%	17%
'*I just don't believe managers can be managers everywhere. I see too many things go wrong. A certain state of knowledge has to be present at each level of the organization. Whether in the public or the private sector. People who do not have such expertise fall short sooner or later'.*			
5. As management skills	15%	0%	8%
'*For most functions general management qualities are what matters. Being good at telling people what to do, and what they should not do. And make clear why. This goes for almost all parts of the central government; such an approach works well there'.*			
6. As *administrative* responsibility	0%	7%	33%
'*In this, of course, you depend on your civil servants'.*			

lawfulness as *sine qua non*, as shown in Table 4, a fair share of public managers and ministers ascertain that lawfulness is subordinate to efficiency and effectiveness. Clear unlawful action is always rejected and is viewed at odds with both the letter and spirit of the law. However, to improve efficiency and effectiveness in producing public value, strict adherence to the letter of the law is seen as constraining, particularly by ministers.

Another oft-mentioned view links lawfulness to accountability; as long as one can account for non-abidance with the letter of the law, such

Table 4. How Political and Administrative Elites View Lawfulness.

Lawfulness	Public Managers ($n=36$)	MPs ($n=16$)	Ministers ($n=13$)
1. As all-important value ('letter of the law')	46%	36%	25%
'Every now and then you encounter limitations. Something is not possible. And those limitations have been established collaboratively and democratically. I'm very straightforward, you have to maintain those. Otherwise it's the end of all things'.			
2. As subordinate to efficiency and effectiveness ('spirit of the law')	31%	14%	42%
'In certain process lawfulness is a constant barrier. In my opinion, government should operate in the spirit of the law more frequently'.			
3. As subordinate to righteousness ('spirit of the law')	0%	14%	0%
'Yes, 'it's all fine we have rules but rules should be there because of people and not because of rules as such. We tend to forget that sometimes. I see a lot of rigidity when it comes to rules: 'yes, we do this because the rules say so'. Rules should follow interests and not the other way around. Righteousness, that's what it's all about'.			
4. As linked to accountability ('spirit of the law')	23%	36%	33%
'In my view, you have to be able to explain why you do things. If I cannot explain why I am doing something I am not doing it right. If there are no arguments to say: 'I do this because of that'. And if it's lawful it fits in a certain framework. And I have a good story to tell'.			

conduct is acceptable. Strikingly, political and administrative elites are rather similar in how they categorize lawfulness: three out of four perspectives occur in each group, sometimes with small relative differences. Just as for responsiveness, we see that elites often juxtapose lawfulness against other values.

Public managers, though, seem stricter in their views: almost half of them never want to tamper with the *letter of the law*. Even though they seek room to manoeuvre, it is not up to the civil servants but up to politicians to alter laws if they become burdens, as voiced by a departmental secretary:

> It is my job to make sure lawfulness occurs in relation to efficiency. Of course, that produces tensions. In some case, you have more leeway than in others, certainly when time

is of the essence. But still it's better to facilitate politicians to change laws than to act less lawful. As a government, you cannot delegate such decisions to the individual civil servant.

Transparency

As Table 5 shows, clear differences exist in how our three groups of elites view transparency. Again, we see how respondents (in this case, a majority of MPs and many civil servants) link this value with accountability. An MP of a majority faction explains:

> When you're part of a coalition, there are moments when you have to make deals and you cannot be transparent. If media ask you out, you just have to stay silent. But in those cases I just say: 'listen, these are rules of the game we've agreed on'. Rather than coming up with all sorts of excuses. Backdoor politics? What is that? Everyone knows you sometimes have to keep things inside until you can communicate a final decision.

We do not find this view among ministers. They go even one step further, and see transparency as subordinate to efficiency and effectiveness. According to them, transparency in every phase of the decision-making process is not conducive to good outcomes in terms of public value. They highly value the secrecy of weekly council meetings and European summits:

> I am against transparency in such processes. The council of ministers has to be able to debate freely and disagree vehemently. But you also know you have to present a joint

Table 5. How Political and Administrative Elites View Transparency.

Transparency	Public Managers ($n = 36$)	MPs ($n = 16$)	Ministers ($n = 13$)
As linked to accountability	45%	62%	0%
'It means of course I have to account for things and be responsible for them, just like the words say. I have to show what I've done with the resources allocated to me'.			
As subordinate to efficiency and effectiveness	45%	23%	83%
'But if you would communicate everything real-time you could bring government to a halt. There has to be a space to provide advice in all confidentiality'.			
As most important value, as sine qua non	10%	15%	17%
'The most important of all things. You cannot be transparent enough as a government'.			

solution at the end of the day. You cannot defend such a solution wholeheartedly if the
whole world has tuned in on your negotiations.

In this context, a majority of ministers expresses very negative views
on phenomena such as Wikileaks. Openness about outcomes is held in
high regard whereas openness about processes is considered not useful.
Still, a minority in all three groups sees transparency as a most important
value.

DISCUSSION AND HYPOTHESES

Our study aimed to answer the following central research question: *how do
Dutch political elites and administrative elites differ in their interpretation
and prioritization of public values?* In this section we answer this question
by discussing the main differences we found. We use our qualitative results
to formulate testable propositions for quantitative follow-up studies.

As we discussed at the beginning of this article, the traditional dichoto-
mous view of political–administrative relations pre-supposes that both
groups hold different views of public values and prioritize different values
as most important. The results of our study do not fully support this traditional view. Public managers and politicians, particularly ministers, sometimes display *very similar views* on how crucial values should play a role in
their daily operations aimed at producing public value. Such an outcome is
partly in lieu with the fourth emerging ideal type of Aberbach et al. (1981),
the pure hybrid. Many of the most senior public managers frame, for
instance, responsiveness in political terms, and enact this value by weighing
different stakeholder interest just as MPs do. This observation brings us to
our first proposition:

> **P1.** As the proximity increases of public managers to ministers, they
> increasingly frame responsiveness as weighing choices between interests
> of different external stakeholders

Still, we also find classical 'Weberian' elements in the value orientation
of public managers, mitigating full hybridity. For instance, a large share of
the public managers in our sample views responsiveness and expertise in
terms of loyalty and serviceability to politics. This group also frequently
mentions the importance of loyalty and neutrality. In addition, public

managers hold a stricter interpretation of lawfulness than MPs and ministers, which seems somewhat at odds with earlier findings by van der Wal (2011).

P2. Public managers place more value on abiding by the letter of the law than do politicians

P3. MPs place more value on abiding by the letter of the law than do ministers

Besides political sensitivity, public managers seem to assume responsibility for producing public value. They consider it their duty to point out to politicians all aspects of upcoming decisions, and to be critical, and provide opposing viewpoints. A combination of these political elements and classical Weberian values and role conceptions seems to characterize the administrative elite in the Netherlands. Previous studies have stipulated that Dutch public managers still embrace traditional civil service values (Nieuwenkamp, 2001, p. 302; 't Hart & Wille, 2006, p. 132; van der Wal, 2008). Our study sees the situation as more nuanced, drawing again upon the imagery of modern public managers as *businesslike* managers (Noordegraaf, 2004). However, our results do corroborate shifts in views and the importance of expertise, arguably as a result of the formation of the Senior Executive Service, mandatory job rotation, and the emphasis on the senior civil servant as 'public manager' (Alford & O'Flynn, 2009). This brings us to propositions four and five:

P4. An increase in the mobility of public managers results in a view of expertise with less emphasis on domain knowledge

P5. An increase in the mobility of public managers results in a view of expertise with more emphasis on management skills

Finally, our study concludes that politicians and public managers differ most when it comes to their views of transparency. Despite the recent surge in studies on transparency within the domain of public management (Meijer, 2009; Piotrowski, 2010) we know very little about whether, why and how politicians and administrators (should) view this value differently. Based on our data we formulate the following proposition for future study:

P6. Ministers place less value on transparency than do MPs and public managers

CONCLUSION

The past decade has seen a heated debate among academics and practitioners about the alleged erosion of the traditional 'social contract' between politicians and senior civil servants. It is clear that emphasizing and exaggerating mutual differences is not very conducive for fruitful collaboration between the political and administrative elite in their pursuit of public value. According to De Carufel (1994), increasing value congruence may mitigate conflicts between both groups. We are not sure if this is true. Both groups have different roles and interpret values differently. If government elites respect each other's roles, their ethos and its boundaries, they may very well be able to collaborate effectively and respectfully. What can be seen, however, is an increasing notion of distrust and lack of clarity of mutual understanding as to how roles may be shifting due to some recent developments we outlined in this article, such as external populist and media pressures on politicians and managerial pressures on public managers with entrepreneurial ambitions as a role. Our study shows at least as much congruence as it shows contrast between perception of enactment of key public values, and *mutual awareness of such congruence may mitigate tensions rather than factual congruence as such.*

According to the norm of 'primacy of politics' (Nieuwenkamp, 2001; Rhodes & Wanna, 2007) politicians should make political decisions that are to be implemented and executed by loyal and politically neutral administrators. Our study does not provide support for a decrease in loyalty and neutrality among public managers, nor a devaluation of crucial public values. However, the renewed call for the primacy of politics as a response to public value management (Rhodes & Wanna, 2007) has partly been answered by the Senior Executive Service and its core principles: through function rotation and a rebalance in the expertise disparity between political and administrative elites, public managers are restrained in their dominant influence on policy outcomes.

Moreover, our study shows public managers see it as their responsibility to point out the risks of particular decisions to their political bosses, and even their political adversaries, to provide critical 'counter-advice' while they accept at the same time that politicians bear decision-making power *and* the responsibility that comes with that power. Public managers seem to be able to align their immense influence potential with democratic responsibilities. Perhaps we worry too much about the erosion of mutual trust between government elites, and all that is needed is increased mutual understanding of each other's position towards and enactment of public values.

NOTES

1. It should be noted that this emergence of the public manager is primarily a non-US phenomenon because senior bureaucrats in the United States have always been more involved in 'direct political activities' (Aberbach et al., 1981, p. 23); in some cases they are directly politically appointed. Thirty years ago these authors stated that 'the distinction between civil servants and political appointees is much more blurred in this country than in Europe' Aberbach et al. (1981, p. 23). This development has been quite profound in our country of study, the Netherlands, as evidenced by the work of Noordegraaf (2004) and van Thiel et al. (2007) among others.

2. Each value is defined in relation to conduct, prescribing to 'act' in a certain manner. These definitions were one-on-one presented to the respondents in the interviews. These definitions proved to be useful before in empirical studies into value prioritization and interpretation of senior officials in the public and private sector (van der Wal, 2008, 2011; van der Wal et al., 2008).

ACKNOWLEDGMENTS

The author is grateful to the Netherlands Institute of Government; without its support, this study would not have been possible. In addition, the author is indebted to all of the respondents who participated in the study.

REFERENCES

Aberbach, J., Putnam, R. D., & Rockman, B. A. (1981). *Bureaucrats and politicians in Western democracies*. Cambridge, MA: Harvard University Press.

Aberbach, J. D., & Rockman, B. A. (2002). Conducting and coding elite interviews. *Political Studies, 35*(4), 673–676.

Adams, G., & Balfour, D. (1998). *Unmasking administrative evil*. London: Sage.

Alford, J., & O'Flynn, J. (2009). Making sense of public value: Concepts, critiques and emergent meanings. *International Journal of Public Administration, 32*(3–4), 171–191.

Algemene Bestuursdienst. (2006). *Bekend maakt bemind. Tweede Kamerleden en ambtenaren in gesprek*. Den Haag: Ministerie van Binnenlandse Zaken en Koninkrijksrelaties, Algemene Bestuursdienst.

Arendt, H. (1963). *Eichmann in Jerusalem: A report on the banality of evil*. Faber and Faber, London.

Beck Jørgensen, T., & Bozeman, B. (2007). Public values: An inventory. *Administration and Society, 39*(3), 354–381.

Bekker, R. (2009). *Liaisons dangereuses. Enige beschouwingen over de arbeidsverhoudingen bij de overheid, met name tussen politici en ambtenaren*. Leiden: Universiteit van Leiden.

Bovens, M. A. P., & Schillemans, T. (2009). *Handboek Publieke Verantwoording*. Den Haag: Boom Lemma.

Bovens, M. A. P., 't Hart, P., Twist van, M. J. W., & Rosenthal, U. (2007). *Openbaar bestuur. Beleid organisatie en politiek*. Alphen aan den Rijn: Kluwer.

Bovens, M. A. P., & Wille, A. C. (2010). *Diplomademocratie. Over de spanningen tussen meritocratie en democratie*. Amsterdam: Bert Bakker.

Bowman, J. S., & Knox, C. C. (2008). Ethics in government: No matter how long and dark the night. *Public Administration Review, 68*(4), 625–637.

Bowman, J. S., & Williams, R. L. (1997). Ethics in government. From a winter of despair to a spring of hope. *Public Administration Review, 57*(6), 517–526.

Bozeman, B. (2007). *Public values and public interest: Counterbalancing economic individualism.* Washington, DC: Georgetown University Press.

Butora, M. (2007). *Democracy and populism in Central Europe: The Visegrad elections and their aftermath*. Bratislava: Kubon and Sagner AOC.

De Carufel, A. (1994). Organizational culture change for public sector managers. *Optimum, 25*(2), 16–24.

DeLeon, L. (1994). The professional values of public managers, policy analysts and politicians. *Public Personnel Management, 23*(1), 135–152.

Demir, T. (2009). The complementarity view: Exploring a continuum in political-administrative relations. *Public Administration Review, 69*(5), 876–888.

Den Boer, M., & Noordegraaf, M. (2006). Verlangen naar het 'vak' van topambtenaar. Opkomst en evolutie van de Algemene Bestuursdienst. *Bestuurskunde, 15*(3), 11–22.

Dobel, J. P. (2005). *Public integrity*. Baltimore, MD: The John Hopkins University Press.

Eisenhardt, K. M. (1989). Building theories from case study research. *Academy of Management Review, 14*(4), 532–550.

Gains, F. (2009). Narratives and dilemmas of local bureaucratic elites: Whitehall at the coal face? *Public Administration, 87*(1), 50–64.

Goodnow, F. J. (1900). *Politics and administration*. New York, NY: Macmillan.

Jeekel, H. (2005). *De ontbrekende dialoog. Over nieuwe ambtenaren, nationale politici en de noodzaak tot dialog*. Den Haag: Sdu Uitgevers.

King, G., Keohane, R. O., & Verba, S. (1994). *Designing social inquiry. Scientific inference in qualitative research*. Princetown, NJ: Princetown University Press.

Klostermann, J. (2003). *The social construction of sustainability in Dutch water companies*. Rotterdam: Erasmus University.

Meijer, A. J. (2009). Understanding modern transparency. *International Review of the Administrative Sciences, 75*(2), 255–269.

Meijer, A. J. (2013). Understanding the complex dynamics of transparency. *Public Administration Review, 73*(3), 429–439.

Miles, M. B., & Huberman, A. M. (1994). *Qualitative data analysis: An expanded Sourcebook*. London: Sage.

Moore, M. (1995). *Creating public value. Strategic management for government*. Cambridge, MA: Harvard University Press.

Nieuwenkamp, R. (2001). *De prijs van het politieke primaat. Wederzijds vertrouwen enloyaliteit in de verhoudingen tussen bewindspersonen en de ambtelijke top*. Delft: Eburon.

Noordegraaf, M. (2004). *Management in het publieke domein. Issues, instituties, Instrumenten.* Bussum: Coutinho.

O'Flynn, J. (2007). From new public management to public value: Paradigmatic change and managerial implications. *Australian Journal of Public Administration, 66*(3), 353–366.

Osborne, S. (Ed.). (2009). *The new public governance?* London: Routledge.

Patton, M. Q. (1987). *How to use qualitative methods in evaluation.* London: Sage.

Pedersen, L. H. (2013). Committed to the public interest? Motivation and behavioural outcomes among local councillors. *Public Administration.* doi:10.1111/j.1467-9299.2012.02107.x

Peters, B. G., & Pierre, J. (Eds.). (2001). *Politicians, bureaucrats and administrative reform.* London: Routledge.

Piotrowski, S. J. (2010). *Governmental transparency and secrecy: Linking literature and contemporary debate.* Blue Ridge Summit: Lexington Books.

Putnam, R. D. (1976). *The comparative study of political elites.* Englewood Cliffs, NJ: Prentice-Hall.

Rhodes, R. A. W., & Wanna, J. (2007). The limits to public value, or rescuing responsible government from the Platonic guardians. *Australian Journal of Public Administration, 66*(4), 406–421.

Richards, D. (1996). Elite Interviewing: Approaches and pitfalls. *Politics, 16*(3), 199–204.

Searing, D. D. (1969). The comparative study of elite socialization. *Comparative Social Studies, 1,* 471–500.

Searing, D. D. (1978). Measuring politicians' values: Administration and assessment of a ranking technique in the British House of Commons. *The American Political Science Review, 72*(1), 65–79.

Strauss, A. (1987). *Qualitative analysis for social scientists.* Cambridge, MA: Cambridge University Press.

Svara, J. H. (2001). The myth of the dichotomy: Complementarity of politics and administration in the past and future of public administration. *Public Administration Review, 61*(2), 176–183.

't Hart, P., & Wille, A. W. (2006). Ministers and top officials in the Dutch core executive: Living together, growing apart? *Public Administration, 84*(1), 121–146.

van den Heuvel, J. H. J., Huberts, L. W. J. C., & Verberk, S. (2002). *Het morele gezicht van de overheid: Waarden, normen en beleid.* Utrecht: Lemma.

van der Wal, Z. (2008). *Value solidity. Differences, similarities and conflicts between the organizational values of government and business.* Amsterdam: VU University.

van der Wal, Z. (2011). The content and context of organizational ethics. *Public Administration, 89*(2), 644–660.

van der Wal, Z. (2012). Elite Ethiek. Hoe politici en topambtenaren invulling geven aan publieke waarden. *Beleid en Maatschappij, 39*(3), 258–279.

van der Wal, Z., de Graaf, G., & Lasthuizen, K. (2008). What's valued most? A comparative empirical study on the differences and similarities between the organizational values of the public and private sector. *Public Administration, 86*(2), 465–482.

van der Wal, Z., Nabatchi, T., & de Graaf, G. (2013). From galaxy to universe? A cross-disciplinary review and analysis of public values publications from 1969 to 2012. *American Review of Public Administration.* doi:10.1177/0275074013488822

van Rekom, J., van Riel, C. B. M., & Wierenga, B. (2006). A methodology for assessing organizational core values. *Journal of Management Studies, 43*(2), 175–202.

van Thiel, S., Steijn, B., & Allix, M. (2007). New public managers' in Europe: Changes and trends. In C. Pollitt, S. van Thiel & V. Homburg (Eds.). *New public management in Europe: Adaptation and alternatives* (pp. 90–106). Basingstoke: Palgrave MacMillan.

Weber, M. (1926). *Politik als beruf.* Berlin: Duncker and Humblot.

Weiss, R. S. (1994). *Learning from strangers. The art and method of qualitative interview studies.* New York, NY: The Free Press.

Wilson, W. (1887). The study of public administration. *Political Science Quarterly, 2*(2), 197–222.

CO-GOVERNING PUBLIC VALUE IN LOCAL AUTHORITIES

Francesco Badia, Elena Borin and Fabio Donato

ABSTRACT

Purpose – *The purpose of this article is to explore the concept of co-governance and its implications on public value, with particular reference to local authorities in the Italian context.*

Design/methodology/approach – *The research aim is pursued by means of a literature review and an empirical research. The empirical research is developed through a questionnaire, sent to the 119 municipalities of the Italian provincial capitals. The overall response rate was 41.18% (49 responses).*

Findings – *In Italian local authorities the process of increasing citizens' participation and citizens' involvement as co-producers of public value by means of co-governance and participatory governance tools is still ongoing. More than 50% of the local authorities of the research sample have introduced co-governance or participatory governance tools and activities but they are still facing problems in implementing them.*

In general, the level of citizens' participation seems not to be fully developed.

Public Value Management, Measurement and Reporting
Studies in Public and Non-Profit Governance, Volume 3, 269–289
Copyright © 2014 by Emerald Group Publishing Limited
All rights of reproduction in any form reserved
ISSN: 2051-6630/doi:10.1108/S2051-663020140000003011

Research limitations/implications — *The empirical part of the research focuses only on the application of co-governance and participatory governance tools in the Italian context, therefore the main limitation lies in the difficulties of extending their application to the international context. In addition, the questionnaire was designed only for medium- to large-sized local authorities. Thus, the research does not consider the possible implications for small municipalities.*

Practical implications — *This article considers some of the possible difficulties of implementation of co-governance and participatory governance tools.*

Social implications — *This article highlights the link between the creation of public value and the adoption of public policies based on citizens' involvement and consultation.*

Originality/value — *This article underlines the link between public value creation and co-governance. It also offers a broad empirical survey on the presence of co-governance and participatory governance tools and activities in the Italian context; this topic was not examined in prior studies.*

Keywords: Co-governance; participatory governance; public value; Italian local authorities; citizens' participation

INTRODUCTION

The ways, forms and methods for rethinking new public management (NPM; also known as new public financial management)[1] are some of the most debated themes in the public sector, both at a theoretical and practical level. Indeed, in recent years many studies have developed a critical approach to NPM aimed at repudiating its core philosophies.

From 2000, the public sector, in particular local authorities, has observed the impact of the global financial crisis on its budgets and expenditure, and therefore the consequences on the provision of public services to the community. The effects of the crisis have created a need to ascertain the sustainability of public sectors within western democracies, both in terms of public spending and the quantity and quality of service provision. Rethinking public service delivery also means analyzing the existing patterns of governance and management and evaluating the possible need (or opportunity) for change. The crisis has thus motivated some of the reflections on overcoming or rethinking NPM that were already being debated, especially at the municipality level.

Different approaches are emerging and they will be considered and evaluated in this article. In summary, strategies to overcome or rethink NPM are applied differently to the decision-making process in the public sector, to the context of public intervention and to the management of public services, especially those with a strong impact on the local community. For all of these areas, the concept of 'public value' is key. Its impact is more evident at local level, since the governance and production of local public services should be primarily shaped by the concept and significance of public value for the local community. On that basis, elements of great interest are emerging from research studies that have addressed the issue of co-governance (both in the public and private sectors).

Therefore, the main objective of this article is to analyze the use of co-governance and participatory governance tools in an Italian case study.

The achievement of the research objective has been pursued through two phases. The first is based on an analysis of the literature, the second is mainly empirical. In particular, our first research phase is related to the identification of the key elements, boundaries and possible applications of the concept of co-governance. This concept is normally applied to those situations where organizations (in particular belonging to the not-for-profit sector) co-operate, especially in the field of social services and welfare. However, the main principles of co-governance can also be applied to other functions of public administration, as well as to networks of not-for-profit organizations, private companies and the local community.

The second research phase is related to the analysis of the degree of application of co-governance tools. An empirical survey on Italian municipalities was carried out in order to develop this step. Municipalities were chosen since they represent the level of government closest to the community.

We begin with an analysis of the current context of the public sector that is also linked to the proposals for rethinking NPM, exploring the concepts of public value and co-governance, then introduce and explain the empirical investigation into Italian municipalities. Finally, we present our interpretation of the results as well as calling for future studies to be carried out on the contribution of co-governance to the creation of public value.

THE POST-NPM CONTEXT AND THE CONCEPT OF PUBLIC VALUE

There have been recent calls for further discussion of the theory and implementation of NPM (De Vries & Nemec, 2013). Two different issues are debated in the search for a new framework. The first concerns the size of the public sector (Osborne & Gaebler, 1992); the second concerns the principles, criteria and tools that should be adopted by public organizations (Hood, 1991). While this debate began before the global financial crisis, the crisis has undoubtedly accelerated it.

The debate principally relates to the re-definition of the size and role of the public sector in society. Indeed, the application of principles, criteria and tools for increasing efficiency and effectiveness within the management of public services is rarely questioned. Some critical issues may be highlighted, but the basic idea remains: managerial tools should be used to pursue institutional goals maintaining financial balance (Pollitt & Bouckaert, 2004). There is general agreement that public organizations should be more result-oriented, efficient and accountable. But different standpoints emerge surrounding the scope of public administration and the choices of outsourcing, privatization and liberalization (Drechsler, 2005; Lapsley, 2010; Levy, 2010; Osborne, Radnor, & Nasi, 2013). Some authors have called for a comprehensive re-definition of the public management system according to a 'Whole-of-Government' perspective (Christensen & Laegreid, 2008); others have proposed a re-definition of the role of public authorities in the framework of the creation of a complex system of multiple networks including public bodies, not-for-profit organizations and private companies (Kooiman, 2003; Rhodes, 1997).

The crisis has mainly concerned the most advanced countries (the so-called G7 countries), leading to a strain on public finance. Decreases in GDP, along with the rise in the unemployment rate, have forced these countries to intervene, through measures of public spending. The result has seen increased pressure on public deficits and debts. As a consequence, these advanced countries have had to undertake public spending reviews, while also considering the size and scale of the public sector.

Underlying this debate is the concept of public value. The concept of public value can provide a conceptual map to rethink NPM; public value was introduced as a substantially different concept from private business value, and public value theory is often interpreted as a reaction to NPM. Moore (1995) described it as a framework that helps public leaders and managers understand what their 'public' values are, how to connect them and what they consider valuable and requiring public resources. More specifically, the idea of public value, as represented by Moore's strategic triangle, was inserted in the framework of the re-definition of the core strategic functions of public management on the basis of a higher focus on the values for the community. The three specific processes that characterize Moore's theoretical framework are the processes of definition of public value, that is, the importance of clarifying and specifying strategic goals and public value outcomes, the process of authorization (i.e. the creation of an 'authorizing environment' that is required to sustain and achieve the planned outcomes); the process of building necessary operational capacity (i.e. the organization of operational resources to achieve planned outcomes). In this scenario, public managers play a key role, not only in public strategy definition, but also in building legitimacy, in sustaining the above-mentioned authorizing environment and in being constantly accountable for their actions. The concept of public value was further explored and related to different aspects of the public sector. Some scholars (Kelly, Mulgan, & Muers, 2002; Stoker, 2006) highlighted its potential in promoting a new approach to public governance and overcoming the weaknesses of the NPM paradigm, including the concept that individual preferences can be aggregated to reflect what the public requires from government. According to Kelly et al. (2002) and Stoker (2006), public value management provides a post-competitive approach with a dominant focus on relationships expressing collective preferences. In particular, Stoker articulated a public value management model that aimed at moving beyond the competitive framework he identified with NPM, and towards collaborative network forms of governance. In this framework, public managers' role was crucial in learning how to manage through networks, to be open to learning in different ways, and to draw on resources from a range of sources (Stoker, 2006).

Le Grand (2003) advocated rethinking the process of the creation of public value so that concepts such as goal-setting, strategy definition and regulations engage the active participation of citizens and other stakeholders, shifting away from previous 'producer-led models' of government and public service delivery to more actively engage users of public services. Public sector managers should therefore interact with communities and other stakeholders (e.g. in sectors such as education and health) to co-create public services.

According to the literature, public value should be continuously defined and redefined through the social and political interaction between politicians, public officials and communities (O'Flynn, 2007; Smith, 2004). In particular, O'Flynn (2007) focused on the paradigm shift, brought about by the adoption of a public value perspective, in the role of public managers. According to his analysis, managers within the public sphere are presented with a series of challenges related mainly to the ability to deal with the complexity of the public value perspective. Indeed, his public value perspective implies a new concept of leadership, associated with the pursuit of multiple objectives identified through engagement of public service users within the perspective of accountability towards the community.

In recent years, public value is increasingly being linked to the idea of a more co-operative environment and the co-production of value. Benington (2011) reformulates the concept of public value by linking it with the notion of public sphere, arguing that public value can be defined not only in terms of 'what does the public most value' but also in terms of 'what adds value to the public sphere' (Benington & Moore, 2011). The author argues that the conceptual framework provided by this reformulation guides the emerging paradigm of networked community governance, based on the blurring of the boundaries between different spheres and levels of government, and between producers and users of services, thus implying various forms of co-production between public service workers and their clients. Benington's public value stream, therefore, focuses on processes and outcomes and is rooted in the concept of co-production: 'public value creation can be pictured in terms of an open system in which inputs are converted, through activities and processes, into outputs and outcomes, with the active help of co-producers and partner organization' (Benington & Moore, 2011, p. 47).

As seen above, there is a range of different interpretations of the concept of public value; different concepts of public value are consistent with different forms of governance. For the purposes of this article, we decided to analyze the forms of governance based on the logic of bottom-up development processes by means of participatory practices.

CO-GOVERNANCE AS AN EVOLUTION OF GOVERNANCE IN THE PUBLIC SECTOR

The development of value co-production systems for the delivery of local public services has led scholars to consider the need to implement consistent governance models. The concept of co-governance has thus emerged in the management literature, especially that focusing on the transition from NPM to (new) public governance (Kooiman, 2003). Usually, the concept of co-governance is applied to those situations where organizations (in particular belonging to the not-for-profit sector) co-operate, especially in the field of social services and welfare (Bode, 2006; Pestoff, Osborne, & Brandsen, 2006). However, the main principles of co-governance can also be applied to other functions of public administration, as well as to networks that involve not-for-profit organizations, private companies and the local community.

Moreover, in recent years there has been increasing attention applied to systems of participatory governance where the community becomes a key part of the co-governance process, consistent with models of direct democracy (Austin, 2010; Pestoff, 2009). In this context, participation is not merely listening to the opinions of users, but rather an attempt to make co-governance effective (Ackerman, 2004).

Hence, there is a growing need for management tools able to encourage the participation of the community in the most relevant processes of public decision making that may lead to 'participatory governance' approaches with stakeholder involvement and, more generally, of all citizens (Lovan, Murray, & Shaffer, 2004; Zittel & Fuchs, 2007). Participatory budgeting can be a tool that may lead to the fulfilment of the above-mentioned principles (Cabannes, 2004). Participatory budgeting was first conceived during the experience of Porto Alegre, Brazil, at the end of the 1980s (De Sousa Santos, 1998). Recently, there has been renewed attention from scholars to this issue, not only because of debates about NPM but also due to the global financial crisis and its impact on public finance (Pinnington, Lerner, & Schugurensky, 2009; Rossmann & Shanahan, 2011; Sintomer, Herzberg, & Röcke, 2008).

However, participatory budgeting is not the only tool for the promotion of participatory governance. Indeed, in recent years, other tools have been successfully introduced for this purpose, including community maps (Clifford & King, 1996), management plans for World Heritage Sites (Badia & Donato, 2013) and local agenda 21 (Lafferty, 1998). Finally, it is possible to adopt participatory governance tools and social reporting, if they are approached via participatory methods that include the contributions of the local community.

RESEARCH METHOD

The first phase of this research was the research design, during which we contacted managers of local public authorities, in order to investigate their point of view and perspective on the meaning and implications of co-governance. We decided to focus our analysis on municipalities for the following three reasons:

1. municipalities are the public authorities with a leading role in inter-organizational relationships and involvement in local communities in provinces;
2. we assume that usually a municipality has sufficient resources for the development of co-governance and participatory governance tools;
3. the average size of most municipalities suggests a stronger interest in the implementation of the above-mentioned tools (in small municipalities, co-governance and participatory governance systems may not be needed because the same goals may also be achieved in an informal and unstructured way).

In the next step we investigated first the generic presence of co-governance and participatory governance tools, second the degree of their actual application and finally the difficulties of their implementation. Among the research methods used in public administration studies (McNabb, 2013) are questionnaires. We adopted this method and sent questionnaires to all municipalities.

The questionnaire was sent to all the 119 municipalities that are provincial capitals in Italy. The overall response rate was 41.18% (49 responses), a number that is considered enough to draw some conclusions. The questionnaire was sent by post and/or e-mail to those organizations in the period between December 2011 and May 2012. As recommended by the literature on research methodology (Blumberg, Cooper, & Schindler, 2011; Zikmund, Babin, Carr, & Griffin, 2013), the questionnaire was tested with selected municipalities in November 2011. In some cases there were interviews with the managers of the selected municipalities.

The questionnaire was divided into two main parts: co-governance (questions 1−2); and participatory governance (questions 3−6). In the questionnaire, the following definitions of co-governance and participatory governance were provided, in order to share terminology with respondents.

1. co-governance refers to the local authorities' means of planning, monitoring and controlling the external entities/companies that deliver or co-deliver public services on the basis of an agreement or a service contract. The key elements for the implementation of a co-governance system are the relationship with an external subject in the local authority (including also its own subsidiary companies) and the signing of a

formal document, aimed at formalizing the co-operation between the parties. Service contracts, Citizen's Charter[2] and the tools of corporate governance for the municipality and its subsidiaries are potential tools for implementing co-governance.

2. participatory governance relates to the local authority's methods of planning, monitoring and controlling public services provided in the territory, that are performed in close contact and/or with the involvement of the community or other stakeholders. Also in this case, we provided some examples of tools that could be considered useful for the implementation of participatory governance. These tools are participatory budgeting, community maps, world heritage site management plans, tools related to the local Agenda 21, other participatory planning tools and social reports (if arising from participatory processes).

The questionnaire can be found in Appendix. The next section discusses the results emerging from the analysis of the responses received to the questionnaire.

RESULTS

Regarding the implementation of co-governance tools and activities, 59.19% of respondents reported having co-governance tools or activities. We expected a higher number of municipalities implementing co-governance tools. The fact that more than a third of the sample has not even signed a service contract could be due to the complexity of Italian legislation with regard to public services. Table 1 shows the results for co-governance tools.

Table 2 analyzes co-governance implementation difficulties (question no. 2), presenting not only the overall results but also the figures related to difficulties experienced or those that prevented the use of co-governance tools where they have not been adopted (question 2b).

Table 1. Co-Governance Tools (Question 1a).

Co-Governance Tools/Activity	Number of Municipalities	Percentage Out of Affirmative Answers
Service contracts	18	62.07
Citizen's Charter	14	48.28
Corporate governance tools	18	62.07
Other tools	13	44.83

Table 2.   Implementation Difficulties of Co-Governance Tools
(Question 2: 2a and 2b).

Difficulties	Number of Municipalities (Total Sample)	Percentage (Total Sample)	Number of Municipalities (Question 2a)	Percentage (Question 2a)	Number of Municipalities (Question 2b)	Percentage (Question 2b)
High costs	14	29.79	5	17.24	9	50.00
Focus on other priorities	13	27.66	2	6.90	11	61.11
Poor knowledge	10	21.28	3	10.34	7	38.89
Unbalanced forces, skills and bargaining power	10	21.28	9	31.03	1	5.56
Practical problems	4	8.51	4	13.79	0	0.00
Little or no use of the tools	3	6.38	2	6.90	1	5.56
No difficulties	3	6.38	3	10.34	0	0.00
Other difficulties	2	4.26	2	6.90	0	0.00

Table 3.   Participatory Governance Tools (Question 3a).

Participatory Governance Tools/Activities	Number of Municipalities	Percentage Out of Affirmative Answers
Social reporting (with participatory elements)	12	40.00
Tools of local Agenda 21	11	34.38
Sectorial or district participatory planning	10	31.25
Strategic plans	5	15.63
Participatory budgeting	4	12.50
Negotiating tables, social forums	4	12.50
World heritage site management plans	3	9.38
Corporate governance tools	3	9.38
Other tools	8	25.00

With reference to the third question, regarding the implementation of participatory governance tools and activities, 61.22% of the sample had already implemented or were planning to implement them, while 34.69% had decided not to implement them (see Table 3). Therefore, the percentage of municipalities having participatory governance tools is slightly (but not significantly) higher than the percentage of municipalities implementing

Table 4. Implementation Difficulties of Participatory Governance Tools (Question 4: 4a and 4b).

Difficulties	Number of Municipalities (Total Sample)	Percentage (Total Sample)	Number of Municipalities (Question 4a)	Percentage (Question 4a)	Number of Municipalities (Question 4b)	Percentage (Question 4b)
Focus on other priorities	15	31.91	8	25.81	7	43.75
High costs	13	27.66	9	29.03	4	25.00
Poor knowledge	11	23.40	6	19.35	5	31.25
Practical implementation problems, among which:	11	17.02	9	29.03	2	12.50
– Involvement of relevant stakeholders	5	10.64	4	12.90	1	6.25
– Initial difficulties of implementation	3	6.38	3	9.68	0	0.00
– Difficulties in results evaluation	3	6.38	2	6.45	1	6.25
Lack of interest by the stakeholders/citizens	4	8.51	3	9.68	1	6.25
Little or no use of the tools	3	6.38	1	3.23	2	12.50
Other difficulties	2	4.26	2	6.45	0	0.00

Table 5.   Degree of Participation of Citizens (Question 6).

	Average Rating
Municipalities with participatory budgeting	6.50
Municipalities with social reporting	6.29
Municipalities with participatory governance tools	6.05
Total sample	5.66

co-governance tools and activities. However, again we expected a higher figure, given the increasing relevance of direct participation of citizens.

Table 4 highlights the difficulties related to the processes of implementation of these tools (question 4).

As shown in Table 3, social reporting was the most common participatory tool used by our sample. Therefore, the analysis of the results emerging from question 5 (regarding the presence of participatory phases in social reporting) is particularly interesting. Of the 17 municipalities using social reporting with participatory phases, 12 municipalities were already analyzed in the figures related to question 3; in the five additional cases, social reporting with participatory phases was planned before the ongoing municipality mandate but then not implemented. It emerges that the number of municipalities using social reporting with participatory phases does not change if we consider only the municipalities that are still using this tool or if we include also the municipalities that planned its introduction and later abandoned it.

Finally, the last question consisted of the assignment of a 1−10 rating scale on the level of quality perceived by the respondent on the effective participation of the community in the processes of participatory governance. All the municipalities were asked to answer this question (independently from their answers to question 3). The results are shown in Table 5.

Overall, the analysis suggested some practice of co-governance and participatory governance tools. This is mainly through the involvement of the local community. This is discussed in more depth in the next section.

DISCUSSION

This section uses profiles of critical analysis to discuss the results. With reference to the use of co-governance tools, service contracts and corporate governance tools are the most commonly adopted, but in general co-governance tools are relatively evenly distributed. Among 'corporate governance tools', technical committees for the monitoring of subsidiary companies, governance and control regulations and strategic plans are those with which municipalities experience the most difficulties. Among 'other tools', the most recurring categories are: services' delivering agreements; services' price agreements; guidelines for the management of outsourced services; special committees for users' involvement; performance assessment; inter-organizational cohesion and customer satisfaction surveys. In some cases co-governance is strongly outward-oriented, even involving service users, such as in the case of customer satisfaction surveys, users committees, committees monitoring service delivery and internal committees for the support of subsidiary companies.

With reference to the difficulties of implementation for co-governance tools and activities, the data, shown in Table 2, demonstrates that in general high implementation costs of co-governance tools are the most frequent constraint. From the analysis of the figures above in relation to question 2a, high costs remain a difficulty, however, only for 17.24% of the municipalities that implement co-governance tools or activities. In contrast, for these municipalities, the most notable limitation is that forces, skills and bargaining power are in fact not balanced, the local authority often being the weakest component and the service company the strongest. In terms of the figures relating to question 2b, with reference to the municipalities that do not implement co-governance, high costs are a significant problem for 50% of the sample. The main factor influencing the decision not to implement co-governance tools is that they had to focus on other priorities: this could be due to their distrust of the effective contribution of co-governance tools and activities on the management of their public authority.

Table 3 demonstrates that there is a much wider variety of participatory governance tools than of co-governance tools. The most widespread are social reporting (where citizens are involved in direct participation), tools of local Agenda 21 – although in some cases their adoption seems a little outdated – and sector or district participatory planning. This last form of planning differs from participatory budgeting, since it is usually aimed at involving specific groups of citizens (e.g. the inhabitants of a defined area where the municipality is planning to take specific action, where citizens could be directly impacted by local, territorial and environmental policies or by choices relating to general social, environmental and educational services). Moreover, participatory budgets must also be integrated with final reports, while the other participatory planning tools usually include citizens' direct participation only in the initial phase (e.g. through consultation or dialogue on a specific issue).

Participatory budgeting may be the best tool for effective participatory governance, but its use is not widespread with only 12.5% of the municipalities implementing it. Given the theoretical studies outlined in this article, this result is below our expectations, demonstrating that the importance of participatory tools in fostering and promoting citizens' engagement is probably underestimated by public servants and managers.

As for strategic planning, municipalities' main aim is to set the long-term goals of the public authority rather than to involve citizens; however, some participatory phases, such as consultation with stakeholders, are often included.

The following participatory governance tools are used in a relevant yet limited number of the analyzed municipalities:

- negotiating tables or social forums that often precede the implementation of the participatory plans discussed in the previous paragraph;
- World Heritage Site plans, that can be implemented only in the municipalities belonging to the UNESCO List of World Heritage Sites, and are therefore limited;
- corporate governance tools, in which participation is mostly interpreted (possibly in an incorrect manner) as accountability towards the community itself.

The category 'other tools' includes budgeting and quality control and/or customer satisfaction surveys, which only appear twice.

For participatory governance, of the answers linked to the difficulties of implementation, 'focus on other priorities' is the most commonly reported difficulty, followed by 'high costs', 'poor knowledge' of the tools and, finally, 'practical problems', as shown in Table 4. This latter category comprises three main types of difficulties: those related to the involvement of relevant stakeholders, those linked to the initial phase of the implementation of the participatory tools and those associated with the complexity of results evaluation. These categories emerged from the analysis of the open-ended questions.

The comparison between these figures and those referring to co-governance tools shows that the focus on other priorities is the main obstacle preventing municipalities from introducing both co-governance tools and participatory governance tools (questions 2b and 4b). This difficulty, however, is also more relevant for those municipalities implementing participatory tools than for those introducing co-governance tools.

In short, the most relevant difficulty for the implementation of participatory tools is the focus on other priorities whilst the leading problems for the implementation of co-governance tools are high costs. The relevance of the difficulties in relation to high costs and practical problems is higher in the municipalities with participatory tools and activities (both 29.03%) than in those introducing co-governance tools (respectively 17.24% and 13.79%). This shows that the implementation of participatory tools, although potentially fruitful in terms of citizens' involvement and consensus-building, requires significant economic and organizational efforts.

Concerning Table 5, the general level of trust in participatory governance tools falls just below sufficient (5.66). However, more qualified samples (such as those including municipalities only implementing participatory budgeting or social reporting) demonstrate an increased level of trust. The sample of municipalities with participatory budgeting had the highest average rating (6.50). Those municipalities with social reporting have a rating above the average; interestingly the municipalities with participatory governance tools express an evaluation that exceeds the average rating.

CONCLUSIONS

The importance of involving citizens and creating an authorizing environment — one of the key points of Moore's strategic triangle — around measures, such as spending cuts and spending reviews, necessarily implies greater consultation between citizens and public authorities, where public value is created not only in the short term but also in the longer term (Benington, 2011).

Our research has attempted to assess the development of this rethinking process in Italian local authorities; the presence and implementation of co-governance and participatory governance tools and activities could be considered a strong indicator of the level of participation of the citizens as well as the public authorities' increased attention towards citizens as co-producers of value. The results have shown that more than 50% of the sample introduced co-governance or participatory governance tools and activities but that they still face problems in implementing co-governance and participatory tools, especially in relation to cost, institutional focus on other priorities and lack of the necessary knowledge for implementing these tools and activities. In general, local authorities consider citizens' participation in these co-governance and participatory governance processes insufficient.

However, the results show that the local authorities who have already implemented these tools perceive a higher citizen participation level.

Co-governance means a stronger relationship and engagement of citizens in the choices and policies of the public sector. In its practical application this means the participation of small selected groups of citizens. However, co-governance in a broad sense can also be interpreted as the overall participation of citizens in the administration of their community, in particular by means of participatory budgets. Based on our findings, participatory budgeting seems an appropriate means of fully involving citizens in the management and administration of the local community and of stimulating their active contribution as co-producers of public value.

On the basis of our results, the introduction of participatory tools could demonstrate public authorities' increasing attention to citizens and, in turn, increase citizen participation and engagement in decision-making processes.

In periods of financial crisis it is important to close legitimacy gaps by developing new processes of consultation (Benington & Moore, 2011) in order to close the gap between citizens and governments, otherwise there is potential for an imbalance to become entrenched between the efforts of government and the benefits received by citizens.

There are many aspects of co-governance and participatory tools that can be further investigated in terms of creation of public value. Further research in this field could include the analysis of whether the implementation of participatory tools is a pull process (i.e. a process generated by citizens) or a push process (i.e. a process instigated by political authorities). Further research could investigate different aspects related to the implementation of these tools and activities, for example, assessment of the degree of effectiveness of participatory governance, or investigation of whether participation is continuous and leads to a different evaluation of the public sector. Another interesting research topic could be the role of politicians and public sector managers in the implementation of co-governance tools, and if more satisfactory results are obtained by means of participatory processes generated by citizens (pull processes) or by public authorities (push processes).

NOTES

1. See Guthrie, Humphrey, Jones, and Olson (2005), which emphasize the financial dimension of the NPM reform (p. 2): 'we identified at least five different key elements or dimensions of "financial" reform, including changes to financial reporting

systems; the development of commercially based, market-oriented management systems and structures to deal with the pricing and provision of public services; the development of a performance measurement approach; the devolution of, or delegation of, budgets; changes to internal and external public sector audits, notably in terms of monitoring service delivery functions and providing reviews of service efficiency and effectiveness'.

2. At first, we thought it was not correct to include service charters in co-governance tools, since the implementation of this tool is often a task of the service companies and not of the local authority (as in most cases it is required when the service has been outsourced). The testing phase of the questionnaire, however, has shown that different subjects regarded the charter as a co-governance tool, as it monitors the relation with the service company by means of the control of the standards established in this document.

REFERENCES

Ackerman, J. (2004). Co-governance for accountability: Beyond exit and voice. *World Development*, *32*(3), 447−463.

Austin, E. K. (2010). The possibility of effective participatory governance: The role of place and the social bond. *Public Administration and Management*, *15*(1), 221−258.

Badia, F., & Donato, F. (2013). Performance measurement at world heritage sites: Per aspera ad astra. *International Journal of Arts Management*, *16*(1), 20−34.

Benington, J. (2011). From private choice to public value? In J. Benington & M. Moore (Eds.), *Public value: Theory and practice* (pp. 31−51). Basingstoke: Palgrave Macmillan.

Benington, J., & Moore, M. (Eds.). (2011). *Public value: Theory and practice*. Basingstoke: Palgrave Macmillan.

Blumberg, B., Cooper, D. R., & Schindler, P. S. (2011). *Business research methods* (3rd ed.). London: McGraw-Hill.

Bode, I. (2006). Co-governance within networks and the non-profit−for-profit divide. A cross-cultural perspective on the evolution of domiciliary elderly care. *Public Management Review*, *8*(4), 551−566.

Cabannes, Y. (2004). Participatory budgeting: A significant contribution to participatory democracy. *Environment and Urbanization*, *16*(1), 27−46.

Christensen, T., & Laegreid, P. (2008). NPM and beyond − Structure, culture and demography. *International Review of Administrative Sciences*, *74*(3), 7−23.

Clifford, S., & King, A. (1996). *From place to place: Maps and parish maps*. London: Common Ground.

De Sousa Santos, B. (1998). Participatory budgeting in Porto Alegre: Toward a redistributive democracy. *Politics and Society*, *26*(4), 461−510.

De Vries, M., & Nemec, J. (2013). Public sector reform: An overview of recent literature and research on NPM and alternative paths. *International Journal of Public Sector Management*, *26*(1), 4−16.

Drechsler, W. (2005). The rise and demise of the new public management. *Post-Autistic Economics Review*, *33*. Retrieved from http://www.paecon.net/PAEReview/issue33/Drechsler33.htm. Accessed on April 1, 2014.

Guthrie, J., Humphrey, C., Jones, L. R., & Olson, O. (Eds.). (2005). *International public financial management reform. Progress, contradictions and challenges.* Greenwich: Information Age Publishing.

Hood, C. (1991). A public management for all seasons? *Public Administration, 69*(1), 3–19.

Kelly, K., Mulgan, G., & Muers, S. (2002). *Creating public value. An analytical framework for public service reform.* London: Cabinet Office.

Kooiman, J. (2003). *Governing as governance.* London: Sage.

Lafferty, W. M. (1998). *From the earth summit to local Agenda 21. Working towards sustainable development.* London: Earthscan.

Lapsley, I. (2010). New public management in the global financial crisis – Dead, alive or born again? Paper presented at IRSPM conference, April 6–9, Berne, Switzerland. Retrieved from http://www.rcpar.org/mediaupload/publications/2010/20100413_Lapsley_New_public_management_in_the_global_financial_crisis.pdf. Accessed on April 1, 2014.

Le Grand, J. (2003). *Motivation, agency and public theory.* Oxford: Oxford University Press.

Levy, R. (2010). New public management: End of an era? *Public Policy and Administration, 25*(2), 234–240.

Lovan, W. R., Murray, M., & Shaffer, R. (2004). *Participatory governance. Planning, conflict mediation and public decision making in civil society.* Aldershot: Ashgate.

McNabb, D. E. (2013). *Research methods in public administration and nonprofit management: Quantitative and qualitative approaches* (3rd ed.). New York, NY: Sharpe.

Moore, M. (1995). *Creating public value: Strategic management in government.* Harvard, MA: Harvard University Press.

O'Flynn, J. (2007). From new public management to public value: Paradigmatic change and managerial implications. *Australian Journal of Public Administration, 66*(3), 353–366.

Osborne, D., & Gaebler, T. (1992). *Reinventing government. How the entrepreneurial spirit is transforming the public sector.* New York, NY: Plume.

Osborne, S. P., Radnor, Z., & Nasi, G. (2013). A new theory for public service management? Toward a (public) service-dominant approach. *The American Review of Public Administration, 43*(2), 135–158.

Pestoff, V. (2009). Towards a paradigm of democratic participation: Citizen participation and co-production of personal social services in Sweden. *Annals of Public and Cooperative Economics, 80*(2), 197–224.

Pestoff, V., Osborne, S. P., & Brandsen, T. (2006). Patterns of co-production in public services. Some concluding thoughts. *Public Management Review, 8*(4), 591–595.

Pinnington, E., Lerner, J., & Schugurensky, D. (2009). Participatory budgeting in North America: The case of Guelph, Canada. *Journal of Public Budgeting, Accounting and Financial Management, 21*(3), 455–484.

Pollitt, C., & Bouckaert, G. (2004). *Public management reform. A comparative analysis.* Oxford: Oxford University Press.

Rhodes, R. A. W. (1997). *Understanding governance. Policy networks, governance, reflexivity and accountability.* Maidenhead: Open University Press.

Rossmann, D., & Shanahan, E. A. (2011). Defining and achieving normative democratic values in participatory budgeting processes. *Public Administration Review, 72*(1), 56–66.

Sintomer, Y., Herzberg, C., & Röcke, A. (2008). Participatory budgeting in Europe: Potentials and challenges. *International Journal of Urban and Regional Research, 32*(1), 164–178.

Smith, R. F. I. (2004). Focusing on public value: Something new and something old. *Australian Journal of Public Administration, 63*(4), 68–79.

Stoker, G. (2006). Public value management: A new narrative for networked governance? *American Review of Public Administration, 36*(1), 41–57.

Zikmund, W. G., Babin, B. J., Carr, J. C., & Griffin, M. (2013). *Business research methods* (9th ed.). Mason, OH: South Western.

Zittel, T., & Fuchs, D. (Eds.). (2007). *Democracy and political participation. Can participatory engineering bring citizens back in?* New York, NY: Routledge.

APPENDIX

The questionnaire included the following questions:

1. *has the Municipality implemented or is preparing co-governance tools or activities? If so, please specify (1a) the specific co-governance tools or activities.The second question consisted of a choice between two sub-questions dependent on the answer given to question 1:*
2. *(2a) if so, please describe the emerging difficulties in implementing the co-governance tools;*
   (2b) if not, please specify the main obstacles in adopting co-governance tools.

The possible answers to questions 2a and 2b were the same, enabling the results to give both a general overview of the implementation difficulties along with a more detailed focus on each specific group of municipalities.

Questions 3 and 4 dealt with participatory governance tools and activities:

3. *has the Municipality implemented, or is preparing to implement participatory governance tools or activities? If so, please specify (3a) the participatory governance tools or activities.*
4. *the fourth question consisted of two sub-questions, dependent again on the response given to question three:*

   (4a) if so, please describe the emerging difficulties in implementing the participatory governance tools and activities;
   (4b) if not, please specify the main obstacles in the adoption of participatory governance tools and activities.

Similar to question 2, the possible answers to questions 4a and 4b were the same: therefore again, the results could give both a general overview of the implementation difficulties and a more in-depth focus on each specific group of municipalities.

The next two questions are aimed at investigating the possible link between social reporting practices and participatory governance activities. Question 5 of the questionnaire investigated the participatory phases of social reporting (although it is more traditionally considered as an accountability tool rather than a participatory governance tool):

5. *are there participatory phases in your institution's social report? If so, at what level (municipality, district, both)?*

   Question 6 aimed at testing the level of citizens' participation in participatory governance processes:

6. *please rate the level of participation/interest of your community in the processes of participatory governance on a scale of 0 to 10 (0 – no participation/interest; 6 – sufficient participation/interest; 10 – participation of the entire community and its representatives).*

PUBLIC (DIS)VALUE: A CASE STUDY

Paolo Esposito and Paolo Ricci

ABSTRACT

Purpose — *This article has two main aims. First, to observe the different causes of public (dis)value. Second, to explore, through a case study, an example of public value regeneration through the social reuse of assets seized from criminal organizations.*

Design/methodology/approach — *This is a theoretical article with a case study, utilizing semi-structured interviews.*

Findings — *The study analyzes the factors resulting from the regeneration of new public value within an initially compromised context. This is achieved by 'freeing' and converting properties seized from the Mafia in public goods available to the community (Plus-Value). The article finds that the different causes of public (dis)value are Mafia infiltration in public goods, corruption, tax evasion, abstaining from voting, (ab)use of power and (ab)use of law.*

Practical implications — *The study may help both scholars and practitioners to identify strategies to offset (dis)value factors, something that would be easy to imagine as having managerial implications.*

Public Value Management, Measurement and Reporting
Studies in Public and Non-Profit Governance, Volume 3, 291–300
Copyright © 2014 by Emerald Group Publishing Limited
All rights of reproduction in any form reserved
ISSN: 2051-6630/doi:10.1108/S2051-663020140000003012

Social implications — *The value regenerated with respect to properties confiscated from the Mafia and then converted to social activities for the community highlights how it is possible to transform public (dis)value to public value.*

Originality/value — *The article explores a little examined area of public value, that is the destruction of value or (dis)value.*

Keywords: Public (dis)value; social reuse; seized assets; public integrity; criminal organizations

INTRODUCTION

The theme of public value has been much discussed by the academic community but little attention has been given to issues of public (dis)value (Esposito and Ricci, forthcoming, 2015). This article has two main aims. First, to observe the different causes of public (dis)value. By public (dis) value we mean 'public value destruction'. Second, to explore, through a case study, an example of public value regeneration through the social reuse of assets seized from criminal organizations.

Among the different causes determining public (dis)value issues we can list Mafia infiltration in public goods, corruption, (ab)use of power, (ab)use of law, abstaining from voting and tax evasion (Esposito and Ricci, forthcoming, 2015). The research aims to explore the different causes of public (dis)value, highlighting the processes that lead to its regeneration. We analyze the regeneration of value by presenting a case study of social reuse of assets seized from criminal organizations. This is difficult to quantify and we also aim to understand the different dimensions within the Italian context of public (dis)value (Bozeman, 2002, 2007; van der Wal, Huberts, van den Heuvel, & Kolthoff, 2006; van der Wal, Nabatchi, & de Graaf, 2013).

Public value is a concept used in its various stages of creation, transformation and destruction to define public governance features used in assessing the sustainability of public policies (Benington, 2009; Benington & Moore, 2011; Boyne, 1999; Broadbent & Guthrie, 2008; Moore, 1995; Thompson, 1991). Public value is generated by political capital, that specific component or sub-configuration of social capital (Putnam, 1993, 1995) that is behind political action and can be seen as a complex and ever-changing combination of ideologies, skills, relations and constraints (Dahrendorf, 1994, pp. 42–193).

In order to understand the regeneration of new public value within an initially compromised context, we use a case study method to examine the social reuse of properties confiscated from the Mafia and made available to the community (Plus-Value).

In the pursuit of greater clarity and to understand different perspectives of public value, some scholars have attempted to clarify the public value concept according to different criteria (van der Wal & Huberts, 2008; van der Wal et al., 2006, 2013). Moreover, scholars have approached their research from many different conceptual angles: '... existing literature reviews, classification systems and conceptual maps are based on rather narrow assessments of the topic, so it is perhaps more accurate to say that scholars have touched upon various galaxies of rather than the entire universe' (van der Wal et al., 2013, p. 2). For example, Beck Jørgensen and Bozeman's (2007) construction of the public value universe contains 72 categories of public value. Beck Jørgensen and Bozeman's article (2007) identifies a method of creating an inventory for public value, reviewing and interpreting the relevant literature on the subject (Beck Jørgensen & Bozeman, 2007, p. 354) and suggesting some categories of public value (or constellations) within the public value universe. However, their study relies on a relatively narrow review of the literature, using only British, American and Scandinavian public administration journals from 1990 to 2003. The authors explain that considering public value out of any specific context allows for easier analysis: 'values are set free from partial understanding and from deadlocked, polarized debate, making it possible to construct new perceptions and judgments' (Beck Jørgensen & Bozeman, 2007, pp. 357–358). Beck Jørgensen and Bozeman also highlight that there are few systematic studies on the public value concept available and that the framework they provide could be used as a starting point for future investigations, including those involving case studies.

The approach followed by Beck Jørgensen and Bozeman is also the starting point to highlight several issues using the 'constellation-based' reference model, which nevertheless shows both pros and cons for public value production (Beck Jørgensen & Bozeman, 2007). The pros are represented in our study by the empirical evidence of re-acquisition of assets seized from the Mafia and by the ethical regeneration of new public value from previous forms of (dis)value. The cons are clearly represented by public value conceptual inversion: the (dis)value. This study differs from that of Beck Jørgensen and Bozeman, as well as from other previous studies, in its focus on public (dis)value (a new dimension of the public value concept) in order to examine when public value is destroyed and regenerated. The study may help both scholars and practitioners to identify strategies to offset (dis)value factors, which are likely to have managerial implications.

The study addresses the following research question: is it possible to regenerate public value through the social reuse of assets seized from criminal organizations? Our study is a first step towards understanding public (dis)value, filling a gap in the current literature on public value.

METHODOLOGY

The research uses a case study method, which can help to understand the complexities of 'the negative corruption effect', also characterized by forms of capital rationing that affect both current and future communities. In general, the case study method (Yin, 1995) has the dual aim of detailing the main characteristics of a phenomena and understanding the dynamics of a given process. From a methodological point of view, the development of a case study represents a 'strategy of research that is concentrated on the comprehension of the dynamics that characterizes specific contexts' (Eisenhardt, 1989, p. 532). Qualitative approaches and forms of research in action (Fayolle, 2004) allow the researcher to describe, explain and understand situations in context. The case study method is a valuable tool to 'capture' different dimensions of public (dis)value, and to suggest criteria for further action (Craig, 2003).

UNDERSTANDING PUBLIC (DIS)VALUE

The research was motivated by the debate that began in 1995 with Moore, and which has developed into a model representing an alternative to new public management, known as public value management (Alford & O'Flynn, 2009; O'Flynn, 2007; Stoker, 2006). The rationale behind our research lies therefore in the acknowledgement that the notion of public value has many facets, and that this has several consequences on public governance. Through social action, value is either created or destroyed and this value is not exclusively financial, but may also be:

1. hybrid in nature, as it can be studied for different aims and from different points of view;

2. constantly changing and able to be measured, albeit in a complex way.

Public value is created and destroyed whenever activities are undertaken in relation to a public service (Denhardt & Denhardt, 2003; Kelly, Mulgan, & Meurs, 2002). These activities produce disvalue when their actual target becomes different from that originally planned.

Corruption within the Italian public administration distorts public policies, taking funds away from meeting collective needs, and creating public (dis)value. Scarce political capital resources invested in different representative and democratic processes cause destruction of value or (dis)value that prevents a sustainable and transparent development of public policies and is marked by persistent decision-making discretion, arbitrariness and abuse of political power. All this contributes to the erosion not only of public value, but also of the connecting fabric existing between the ethical infrastructures of a community and the sense of belonging manifested by its citizens (Benington & Moore, 2011; Moore, 1995; Stoker, 2006). The mismanagement of public affairs prepares the ground for corruption (Della Porta & Vannucci, 2012), which 'is a malignant tumor that surrounds the most vital and active ganglia in the country and does not seem to go away' (Court of Auditors, 2011).

Instability in the political-institutional system allows for the growth of groups, lobbies and special interests, either lawful or unlawful. Examples of this are healthcare mismanagement, illegitimate appointments, a frequent use of negotiated procedures, an opaque system of public procurement, EU fraud schemes and scams related to local tax collection and appointments related to the performance and delivery of local public services, which have been perhaps the most striking case of 'cost of democracy' since the 1970s (Esposito, 2012).

It is possible to represent these possible causes of corruption in the delivery of a public service as cases of public (dis)value where the robust pressure exerted by political parties on the regulatory process is a characteristic. Fig. 1 shows that political parties heavily affect decisions made by civil servants, suppliers and politicians in order to determine the private destination of public resources (Esposito, 2012). Their management is therefore not always transparent, particularly when it is aimed at satisfying private rather than collective interests. In particular the causes highlighted in Fig. 1, also examined by the Italian accounting judiciary (Court of Auditors, 2011), are examples of low public and political responsibility, or of social irresponsibility (Ricci, 2011). It also shows that the growing importance of political parties, caused by (ab)use of power and (ab)use of

law, has produced public (dis)value in the form of corruption in public procurement procedures and public service management (Esposito & Ricci,
forthcoming, 2015; Shah, 2007).

SOCIAL REUSE OF ASSETS SEIZED FROM CRIMINAL ORGANIZATIONS

According to data released by the State Property Agency, of 6,556 assets
seized from the Mafia from 1983 to 2005, only 2,962 were later restored.
Prevention measures were undertaken (L. 31 May 1965 n. 575 and subsequent amendments and additions) aimed to ensure not only the seizure of
assets from organized crime, but also their return to lawful economic use,
entrusting an organization (State Property Agency) with the management
of those assets in view of their subsequent use. Between 2007 and 2008,
84% of confiscated property was located in Sicily, Calabria, Campania and
Puglia. In 2009, the European Commission argued that criminal revenues

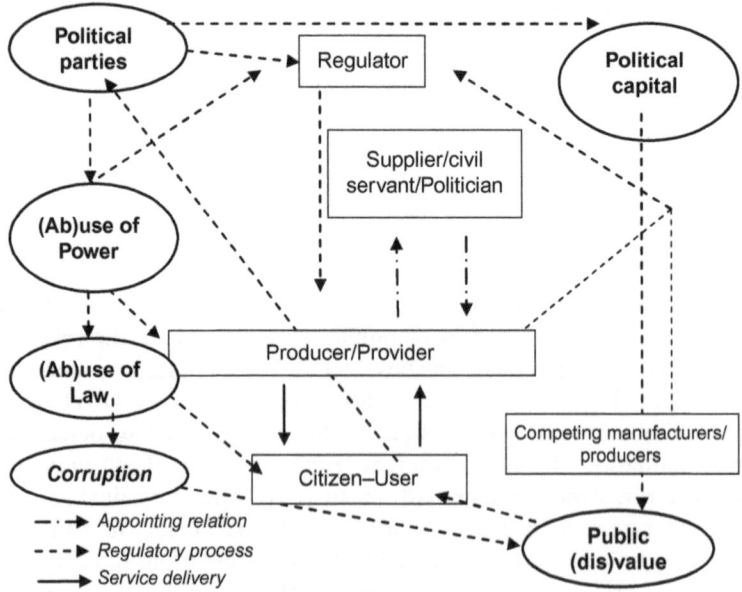

Fig. 1.   Possible Causes of Corruption in the Delivery of Public Services: A 'Map'
of Public Disvalue.

accounted for an estimated 3.6% of global GDP, or USD \$2.1 trillion. Most of the 'dirty money' was laundered and reinvested in the legal economy, with less than 1% of criminal revenues being confiscated. Despite the simplification of administrative procedures and the expectation of shorter times for the allocation of goods, problems related to the application of complex administrative procedures led to the appointment of a Government Special Commissioner for confiscated property.

The State Property Agency's (the Agency) report showed that there were initiatives aimed at streamlining procedures and monitoring seized goods. In many cases the non-use of the goods in question was due to technicalities pertaining to the judicial phase, or to difficulties in managing the assets (because of the existence, e.g. of third-party rights on the assets themselves), or simply because properties have not been physically delivered.

PUBLIC VALUE REGENERATION: A CASE STUDY

It is difficult to quantify the public value assets seized from the Mafia and managed by the Agency. According to the National Agency of Confiscated Goods, the supposed value corresponds to a financial budget of about 30 billion euros, including properties, real estates and businesses, of which 10% is in cash and securities.

The case study organization is Placido Rizzotto. Since the early 1990s, Libera Terra's social cooperatives – including Placido Rizzotto Social Cooperative – have been inspired by principles of legality and solidarity. They have managed to promote and support the employment of disadvantaged people in the production and distribution of natural organic products, on the land seized and confiscated from the Mafia. Placido Rizzotto Cooperative, created in 2001, obtained 384 acres of free loan land confiscated from the Mafia.

The Cooperative's young members have so far had to face several difficulties. First, the Cooperative often lacks funds and equipment. It could not access the bank credit system as it does not have any collateral guarantee funds to offer to its lenders. Every confiscated property is assigned to the Cooperative under a free loan agreement. This means that the property cannot be considered an asset for banks wishing to lend money. Second, the Cooperative's members had to face a difficult relationship with the local community. Many attacks and intimidations have taken place. Despite this, the Cooperative currently employs 11 members (one third of which come from a disadvantaged background), and 23 workers for seasonal work (harvesting, pruning, olive harvest, harvests).

CONCLUSIONS

The study analyzes the factors resulting from the regeneration of new public value within an initially compromised context. This is achieved by converting properties seized from the Mafia to public goods available to the community (Plus-Value). It may help both scholars and practitioners to identify strategies to offset (dis)value factors, something that would be easy to imagine as having managerial implications. This article shows that Mafia infiltration in the public sector, corruption, tax evasion, abstaining from voting, (ab)use of power, (ab)use of law are all causes of public (dis) value. Corruption, triggered by criminal alliances and joint ventures, increases the costs necessary to buy, renovate, maintain and re-convert properties.

To simplify the relevant procedures, local councils have argued that they should not only take part in technical workshops to determine guidelines and goals for the whole process, but also make sure that all critical issues are not transferred to local authorities, which often have to face abnormal problems and challenges, well beyond ordinary local government standards.

Italian local authorities acting as carers of the properties seized do not usually have the economic resources necessary to restore them, and therefore try to assign them in the same condition in which they received them. Economically disadvantaged community members who are given use of the goods are often not able to access them, as they might not have enough resources to invest in properties they do not fully own. The value regenerated with respect to properties confiscated from the Mafia and then converted to social activities for the community highlights how it is possible to transform public (dis)value to public value.

Confiscation, as well as creating public value regeneration in economic and financial terms, is also a re-creation of 'reputation' value for the public sector, boosting public confidence and trust in institutions. This regeneration of reputational value, linked to 'non-financial information', requires, however, appropriate tools suitable for non-financial assessment and evaluation.

REFERENCES

Alford, J., & O'Flynn, J. (2009). Making sense of public value: Concepts, critiques and emergent meanings. *International Journal of Public Administration, 32*, 171–191.

Beck Jørgensen, T., & Bozeman, B. (2007). Public values. An inventory. *Administration and Society, 39*(3), 354–381.

Benington, J. (2009). Creating the public in order to create public value? *International Journal of Public Administration, 32*(3–4), 232–249.

Benington, J., & Moore, M. (Eds.). (2011). *Public value: Theory and practice.* Basingstoke: Palgrave Macmillan.

Boyne, G. A. (1999). Processes, performance and best value in local government. *Local Government Studies, 25*(2), 1–15.

Bozeman, B. (2002). Public value failure: When efficient markets may not do. *Public Administration Review, 62*(2), 145–161.

Bozeman, B. (2007). *Public values and public interest: Counterbalancing economic individualism.* Washington, DC: Georgetown University Press.

Broadbent, J., & Guthrie, J. (2008). Public sector to public services: 20 years of contextual accounting research. *Accounting, Auditing and Accountability Journal, 21*(2), 129–169.

Court of Auditors. (2011). *Misure e stime della corruzione: Una sfida (im)possibile.* Italy: SSPA.

Craig, S. N. (2003). Corporate social responsibility: Whether or how. *California Management Review, 45*(4), 52–76.

Dahrendorf, R. (1994). *The condition of citizenship.* London: Sage.

Della Porta, D., & Vannucci, A. (2012). *The hidden order of corruption: An institutional approach.* Burlington, VT: Ashgate.

Denhardt, J., & Denhardt, R. (2003). *The new public service − Serving not steering.* New York, NY: M.E. Sharp.

Eisenhardt, K. (1989). Building theories from case study research. *Academy of Management Review, 14*(4), 532–550.

Esposito, P. (2012). Integrity distortions and public policies in the local P.A.s. Theoretical lines, emerging practices, contradictions: A first path of conceptualization. *Rirea,* 7/8.

Esposito, P., & Ricci, P. (forthcoming, January, 2015). How to turn public (dis)value into new public value? Evidence from Italy. *Public Money and Management, 35*(1).

Fayolle, A. (2004). À la recherché du coeur de l'entrepreneuriat: Vers une nouvelle vision du domaine. *Revue Internationale P. M. E., 17*(1), 101–121.

Kelly, G., Mulgan, G., & Meurs, S. (2002). *Creating public value: An analytical framework for public service reform.* Discussion paper prepared by the Cabinet Office Strategy Unit, UK.

Moore, M. (1995). *Creating public value.* Harvard, MA: Harvard University Press.

O'Flynn, J. (2007). From new public management to public value: Paradigmatic change and managerial implications. *Australian Journal of Public Administration, 66*(3), 353–366.

Putnam, R. (1993). *Making democracy work: Civic traditions in modern Italy.* Princeton, NJ: Princeton University Press.

Putnam, R. (1995). Bowling alone: America's declining social capital. *Journal of Democracy, 6*, 65–78.

Ricci, P. (2011, July). Article 41 of the Italian constitution and the Italian model of corporate social responsibility. *Review of International Comparative Management, 12*(3), 497–506.

Shah, A. (2007). *Performance accountability and combating corruption*. Washington, DC: The World Bank.

State Property Agency. (2010). Report on the management of assets confiscated from organized crime. Retrieved from http://www.agenziademanio.it

Stoker, G. (2006). Public value management. A new narrative for networked governance? *American Review of Public Administration, 36*(1), 41–57.

Thompson, F. (1991). Management control and the Pentagon: The organizational strategy-structure mismatch. *Public Administration Review, 51*(1), 52–66.

van der Wal, Z., & Huberts, L. W. J. C. (2008). Value solidity in government and business. Results of an empirical study on public and private sector organizational values. *American Review of Public Administration, 38*(3), 264–285.

van der Wal, Z., Huberts, L. W. J. C., van den Heuvel, J. H. J., & Kolthoff, E. W. (2006). Central values of government and business: Differences, similarities, and conflicts. *Public Administration Quarterly, 30*(3), 314–364.

van der Wal, Z., Nabatchi, T., & de Graaf, G. (2013). From galaxy to universe. A crossdisciplinary review and analysis of public values publications from 1969 to 2012. *The American Review of Public Administration*.

Yin, R. K. (1995). *Case study research. Design and methods*. Thousand Oaks, CA: Sage.

MEASURING PUBLIC VALUE IN BUREAUCRATIC SETTINGS: OPPORTUNITIES AND CONSTRAINTS

Enrico Guarini

ABSTRACT

Purpose — *In recent years, public management research has been focused at the public value paradigm. However, many discussions on this topic are motivated at least as much by theory as by evidence. We do not yet have a comprehensive empirical understanding of what happens when the public value paradigm is translated into practice within organizations. An important theoretical question is how to match the public value approach and measurement to specific contexts. Understanding barriers to effective implementation and identifying what might be done to overcome obstacles are interesting issues for advancing theory and practice.*

Design/methodology/approach — *By deploying and testing the same approach and method of measuring public value in two local governments, this article aims to shed light on barriers to implementing the public value paradigm in practice.*

Public Value Management, Measurement and Reporting
Studies in Public and Non-Profit Governance, Volume 3, 301–319
Copyright © 2014 by Emerald Group Publishing Limited
All rights of reproduction in any form reserved
ISSN: 2051-6630/doi:10.1108/S2051-663020140000003013

Findings — *The study's findings show little evidence to support claims for a paradigmatic shift towards the public value paradigm in the Italian case.*

Practical implications — *Managerial implications of public value measurement are also taken into consideration.*

Originality/value — *We know little about what conditions drive individual governments towards the adoption of a public value approach and measurement. Undoubtedly, this issue has huge practical relevance when introducing public value discourses in bureaucratic governmental settings.*

Keywords: Public value; performance measurement; local government; bureaucratic setting

INTRODUCTION

In recent years, public management research has been focused at the public value paradigm (Stoker, 2006; van der Wal, Nabatchi, & de Graaf, 2013; Williams & Shearer, 2011). Evidence of this is the rising number of publications on the topic, as well as a growing number of sessions and papers at academic conferences.

However, many discussions on its relevance are motivated at least as much by theory as by evidence. We do not yet have a comprehensive empirical understanding of what happens when the public value paradigm is operationalized into management practice within organizations. Performance measurement and reporting systems play an important role in achieving this goal. But comparatively little analysis of success and failure has been undertaken, and the issue of suitability of different approaches is often ignored. Hence, an interesting theoretical question is how to match approaches and methods of measuring public values to specific contexts.

Although some scholars (Benington & Moore, 2011; Moore, 1995, 2003) have focused on strategic performance measurement and public value creation, there have been relatively few attempts to design performance measurement and reporting in order to provide information in a form that will readily assist public managers and elected politicians in understanding and evaluating their role in creating public value (Stoker, 2006). Only recently, Moore's (2013) work has attempted to answer the question of how a public manager can recognize and count (also in an accounting sense) when public value has been created. Moore proposes a public value account and a public value scorecard as devices to help the public manager to identify a specific value, to focus on the actions necessary to build legitimacy for this value and to improve government operational capacity. The public value account is basically a two-column outline listing desired results on the right and associated costs on the left. This is an interesting perspective in order to fill the measurement gap but it seems to ignore the inter-organizational issues of public value creation and measurement in complex networks. Moreover, the approach proposed by Moore is rooted in the government structures and managerial values of the Anglo-Saxon tradition and this gives rise to the question of whether it can be applied by public managers acting in different public administration contexts. Similar managerial tools may have different meanings and different prospects for success when applied in countries with distinct national administrative traditions (Loughlin, 1994; Ongaro, 2009; Pollitt & Bouckaert, 2000).

From this perspective, implementing the public value paradigm and tools in different countries will be 'path dependent', that is, final outcomes will largely depend upon initial conditions. Since context matters in public administration (Pollitt, 2013), the issue of how to embed the public value perspective in government decision making cannot be considered in isolation from administrative traditions and culture. What are the effects of the various approaches and methods in different country contexts? In what kinds of situations is the public value paradigm most beneficial for public managers and elected officials?

The main assumption here is that the values and understandings embedded within government structures and institutions will be among the principal influences shaping how, if any, the public value paradigm is adopted into government routine. Starting from the perspective of public management, this study aims to shed light on contextual opportunities and constraints for implementing a public value approach in governments.

This article discusses the results of two case studies in local government in Italy experiencing public value measurement and reporting. The goal of the research was to explain the extent to which the development of public value measurement is relevant for public managers and political leaders in bureaucratic contexts. This article is organized as follows. The next section details key concepts used to structure the analysis. This leads to a discussion of the research method used, a description of the empirical context and a summary of key outcomes in the two cases. As a conclusion, some managerial implications are discussed and recommendations for further research are outlined.

PREVIOUS STUDIES

The concept of 'public value' has been framed differently depending on the approach adopted by scholars and the emerging theories. Some scholars have emphasized the 'organizational' issues of public value creation — networks, cross-sector collaborations, leadership and governance (Agranoff, 2006; Bryson, Crosby, & Stone, 2006; Goldsmith & Eggers, 2004; Gray, 1989; Kickert, Klijn, & Termeer, 1995; Klijn & Koppenjan, 2000; OECD, 1997; Osborne, 2010; O'Toole, 1997; Stoker, 2006). Others have worked from the perspective of the 'value for the society' — what the public values (Bozeman, 2007; Frederickson, 1991; Jørgensen, 2007; Jørgensen & Bozeman, 2007; Julnes, 2012) — or the social responsibility of business (Porter & Kramer, 2011; Schwab, 2008). As clearly emphasized by the corporate social responsibility paradigm, the public interest can also be pursued through the private sector: socially responsible actions contribute to the creation of public value since they provide some public services and benefits (Porter & Kramer, 2011). Regardless of which theoretical approach is taken, in recent years it has been generally recognized that the complexity of social needs requires the cooperation of several organizations, public agencies, not-for-profit organizations and for-profit organizations (Cleveland, 2002; Crosby & Bryson, 2005). This approach is especially suitable in policy making and implementation since public and private institutions are interrelated and interdependent in public value creation. As pointed out by Stoker (2006), this new multi-actor context begs the question: what is an appropriate management response?

Networked governance requires public managers to work across boundaries and develop a new culture and leadership skills to fit better with a multi-actor frame. More fundamentally, it requires an ability to select which governance structure or sector (public, private or not-for-profit) is most appropriate in what conditions (O'Flynn, 2007). Government structures and tools are often inadequate in the task of enabling public officials to carry out their responsibilities in complex policy networks (Osborne, 2010).

In managerial-driven performance measurement systems, public managers determine what measures to collect and how to report and distribute the information to internal and external audiences. The internal focus of such systems is an important tool for programme and service delivery management, but there is no guarantee that what is measured is relevant in order to guide the organization towards public value.

Although scholars have focused on public value, there have been relatively few attempts to redesign performance measurement and reporting in light of new cross-sector environments. In particular, the 'how' and 'why' of public value measurement is still little understood.

RESEARCH METHODS

This research is based on descriptive case studies of two large regional governments in Italy that have deployed a 'public value' approach in their own performance measurement system. The first regional government (case A) is a case of a performance measurement system designed to comply with the new legislation requiring strategic control for government agencies. This government was among the first to comply with the new law. The second regional government (case B) is a case of voluntary performance measurement for external reporting and accountability purposes. This government has been recognized as an early innovator and best practice in public value reporting.

Both organizations underwent material changes in their performance measurement system following the expressed will of elected politicians to adopt the public value paradigm in measuring government performance. The analysis in this study is the result of an action research project undertaken over a 12-month period by the author in the two regional governments.

Information in this study comes from personal memos gathered during the 12-month process, data gathered from internal documents and conversational interviews (Werner & Schoepfe, 1987). An Appendix lists the range of meetings attended and the types of individuals in managerial positions who led the change and with whom the researcher had conversations.

Direct observation of meetings and interviews with all levels of the regional government management have been useful to understand the critical issues identified by the different actors involved in the process and the agreement with the new public value performance measurement and reporting system. Also, they have been helpful in order to understand the actual use of the new tool, that is, its managerial impact. While the choice of two single organizations limits the statistical generalizability (Yin, 1989) of the study, it was appropriate for the research aim to develop an understanding of how public managers perceive the design and operation of public value measurement in context.

Italian public bureaucracy offers an interesting setting to investigate the contextual suitability of the public value paradigm because of its strong Napoleonic administrative tradition (Ongaro, 2009; Pollitt & Bouckaert, 2000). Within this tradition, public institutions are inspired by bureaucratic values, and legislation plays a fundamental role in shaping government behaviours.

In this perspective, the regional government constitutes an interesting unit of analysis. First, regional governments in Italy have similar legal and service responsibilities but are allowed to set their own policy and service delivery in their jurisdiction on a large number of topics, the most important being health care. Second, regional governments act mainly as re-distributors of resources and, as a result, they are more likely to be sensitive to public value creation and cross-sector collaborations since their performance is related to the effective collaboration of other local public authorities and private local actors. Two main steps were considered in both cases.

First, a common logic of measuring and reporting government performance was developed to help public managers assess public value in the context of a multi-actor policy network. Second, the logic was applied to regional policy fields and programmes by collecting financial and performance data. Continuous interaction and discussion of results with key actors was in place during the whole project.

CONTEXT OF THE CASES

Government Structures

The Italian government is split into four levels, the central (parliament and the cabinet), the regional (20 regions), the provincial (110 provinces) and the municipal government (8,092 municipalities). Each level is multi-functional in that it has jurisdiction over several issues and activities. Regions play a limited role in the production of services and they act mainly as regulatory actors and re-distributors of resources.

Municipalities are allowed to raise local taxes and charge tariffs for the services they provide: about 60% on average is still represented by transfers from higher levels of government. Provinces have a similar system, although their taxing authority is much more limited. Each region has a president, a cabinet, a regional council and a professional bureaucracy. The president is the head of the executive, is elected directly by the citizens and appoints the members of the cabinet. The regional council is also elected directly by the citizens. Regions are allowed to raise autonomous taxes but a large percentage of their inflows (30% on average in 2011) is still represented by transfers from central government.

Under Italian legislation, public managers of different levels of government have full autonomy in bureaucratic decisions (i.e. procurement, administrative rules, process management, etc.) but most strategic decision making about programme implementation (partnerships, funding, etc.) or user charges must be formally approved by the cabinet or the council members of the agency.

Organizational Settings

Regional government A is among the biggest and most populated regions in the south of Italy (5.8 million citizens) and regional government B (4.8 million citizens) is located in the north and is among the wealthiest and most industrialized regions of the country. The reputation of the two governments is quite different at the national level. Regional government A has been the subject of attention in the media for its poor service performance, sluggish bureaucracy and financial mismanagement. By contrast, regional government B is well-known for its high efficiency, performance and innovative approach.

Before starting with the new public value approach, both regional governments A and B relied on bureaucratic forms of measurement and reporting schemes required by legislation. A large amount of financial and non-financial data were collected about government activities in the two organizations, but the measurement process lacked a managerial control perspective. As this is very common in Italian public administration, the pervasive requirements of legislation had accustomed the two organizations to collect performance data mainly for compliance goals rather than for strategic control and accountability.

The very relevant management tool in this context was the budgetary accounting system since it provided the basis for budgetary control over spending and taxation. This situation began to change when legislation required local government to develop performance measurement systems. 'Public value' language has become familiar in Italian public administration in the wake of new public management reforms over the last decades. The public value paradigm spread across government levels also as a result of the growing number of executive education programmes on the topic

attended by public officials. This was also the case with regional governments A and B.

In both organizations, the implementation of such measurement tools
was a priority in the political agenda and was patronized by the alderman in charge of financial issues. In particular, in case A, the development of a strategic performance measurement system was considered an
opportunity to comply with legal requirements and at the same time a
way to convey a paradigmatic shift towards creating public value. In case
B, the new measurement tool was developed voluntarily as an opportunity for communicating government performance and engaging with stakeholders. Here, the political commitment and sponsorship of the elected
president was also crucial for the launch of the initiative. In both cases, a
project management structure was arranged for the design and implementation of the new tool.

CORE ASPECTS AND OVERALL LOGIC OF THE NEW PERFORMANCE MEASUREMENT SYSTEM

Moving from the political will to measure and disclose the 'public value'
created by each organization, the first issue the organizations confronted
was that of developing a logic of public value identification, measurement
and assessment within organizational routine. Since in Italy elected politicians are legally responsible for the adoption of organizational innovations
required by law, it was immediately clear that the proclaimed new tool
should be a priority for the management team.

Department managers were much more interested in the integration of
this approach with existing tools and procedures rather than adding a new
'bureaucratic' one. Indeed, during initial conversations about public value
and public values, it emerged that regional managers considered public programmes the relevant unit of analysis to start measuring public value. They
looked at goals, results and final recipients of programmes as important
dimensions connected to public value. They were especially interested in
how much money government spent for each programme. They also recognized that public value creation at the local level may be embedded in a
larger stream of dimensions involving other organizations (Agranoff &
McGuire, 2003; Rhodes, 1997; Stoker, 2006).

In fact, most public programmes are delivered through a number of public and private actors that receive money from the regional government or

are contracted to provide public services to recipients, as illustrated in Fig. 1.

In order to include this holistic perspective, the logic of the new system was that of measuring public value within the networked patterns of programme implementation at the local level. The conceptual framework for this logic draws from the 'value chain' model developed by Porter (1985) and public policy studies (Hall & O'Toole, 2004; Kisby, 2007).

Measuring public value within this approach required primarily reclassification of programme data split by the final recipients and actors involved, as well as collecting performance data from other local organizations within the cross-sector delivery system. Expenditure data were extracted from the accounting system by allocating expenses by 'recipient' and 'categories'. This kind of information was derived from legislation that outlines details about the required content of public decisions.

The recipients of funds were firstly specified according to the actor involved in the implementation (i.e. non-profits, firms and other public agencies). This information was systematically recorded by the accounting system but until then it had never been reported or used for decision making. Following this stage, expenditures by 'actor' were re-allocated to final recipients as well as data on programme performance. An example of data coming out of this logic is shown in Table 1. The data, reported by regional government B, show that 77% of the regional spending (i.e. the 'financial

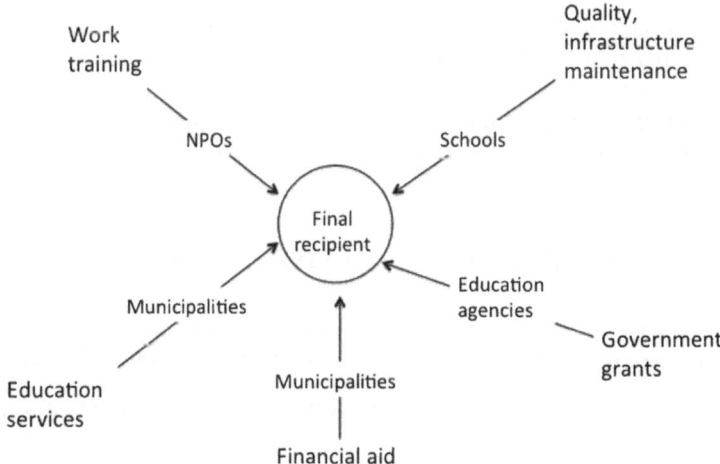

Fig. 1. Public Programmes and the Service Provision Network.

Table 1. Public Value Shaped by Regional Government Expenditure.

Actors	Programmes			... (%)	Total (%)
	Education (%)	Welfare (%)	Research (%)		
Business	6	15	90	...	53
Non-profits	48	63	8	...	24
Local government	33	17	–	...	17
Direct value	13	5	2		6
Total	100	100	100	100	100

value') is distributed to final recipients through firms (53%) and non-profits (24%), 17% is delivered through local governments and regional agencies. Only 6% is related to direct value towards recipients.

This kind of measurement allows public officials to recognize the 'financial' weight of non-governmental actors and facilitates a collective view of the 'financial' value created by an organization or programme in the service delivery network.

Also, this logic implies that the government preference for more (less) spending, being a proxy of public value, should include both the regional government itself as well as the policy network as a whole. Of course, shifts in government support for more spending might primarily reflect shifts in policy, but the preferred level of spending in each programme may remain largely limited while the policy network's spending itself changes over time.

It should be noted that within this kind of bureaucratic context without a 'financial' perspective the public value discourse may not find acceptance among decision makers. Driving management attention on this type of 'public value' information contained in bureaucratic regulations or in the accounting system is a good opportunity to embed the new logic into routine.

THE IMPLEMENTATION PROCESS

Following an initial two-month period of discussion and analysis of existing data, department managers in the two governments were asked to:

1. map the implementation structures explicitly required or encouraged by legislation itself;
2. collect network data (financial and non-financial data);
3. arrange reports for internal use.

The full set of laws passed by the regional council was reviewed and all the policy fields were phased into the analysis.

To measure programme performance it was first necessary to draw the attention of public managers to some information connected to public value creation, such as (i) the type and the level of services provided compared with service demand, (ii) the criteria for programme prioritization, (iii) the form of programme delivery (i.e. in-house, contracted-out, partnership, market) and (iv) the form of programme financing (i.e. user charges, grants, etc.). Accounting for such items, public managers were required to retrace expected results for each programme, to consider what was stated in official strategic plans and to measure effective results.

Case A

The implementation of the new measurement tool was not easy in case A because most of the information required was not included in strategic documents and scattered in functional organizational units developed like silos. In the context of the Italian public administration, it should be noted that since strategic goals are set by elected politicians, most expected results appear too vague and not measurable in quantitative terms, or sometimes too ambitious. On this issue, cabinet members pointed out that vagueness of goals was connected to the political debate and the need to embed several constituents' interests in external strategic plans. Moreover, with regard to the lack of disclosure on programme prioritization, public managers and elected politicians noted that service levels resulted in a 'bottom-up' way, just following the demand of current users. At the same time, they pointed out that understanding potential user needs, and also why public services are not requested, would be relevant information for the assessment of public value creation.

Drafts were shared by top managers and cabinet members before reporting during internal meetings. Public managers and politicians appeared to be more interested in financial data rather than programme performance.

Based on insights gained from document analysis and face-to-face interviews, a round of meetings was launched in order to reinforce the process and discuss with top executives and cabinet members the potential benefit of public value measurement and reporting. Public managers and cabinet members found this information helpful to recognize what public value means for the government and other network actors.

Although at the first stage of the work there was team consensus to report on these measures, the disclosure was strongly conditioned by the lack of data. The presentation of information reflected the limits of existing measurement and reporting arrangements and sometimes it was not possible to have comparable data and benchmarks, especially with regard to non-financial indicators. In many cases, output data was collected by intermediate recipients of regional funds and it was not consolidated into the regional government's information system.

On this issue, public managers were aware that they exclusively focused attention on transfer of money to intermediate actors and legislation compliance rather than asking accountability on results.

Similar difficulties were raised by outcome measurements. These included statistical data on GDP growth, economy, welfare and so on. However, while the reporting process was ostensibly recognized to be helpful for developing awareness on public value by both top executives and political leaders, its practice was let fall. The reason was that cabinet members were worried about poor results and so they did not feel outcome indicators to be helpful for explaining government performance. This political scepticism is illustrated in the words of one cabinet member:

> I feel outcome (or impact) is biased by a lot of external variables and the performance of the regional economy (i.e. the GDP) is not a good proxy of our government performance. That is why no specific outcome target was settled in our public strategic plan.

It should be noted that because of the harsh political environment in this context, cabinet members were probably much more sensitive to media comment on failures in public value creation than they were interested in information to support internal strategic decision making.

Hence, although the initiative was initially patronized by the financial alderman, in the end it seemed that the real political interest was just to be compliant with the law. The lack of real interest from elected politicians in measuring outcomes resulted also in the low commitment of the management team in the adoption of the public value paradigm.

Public managers were much more aware of following the right bureaucratic procedures required by the legislation rather than developing organizational awareness towards creation of public value. Two of the top executives affirmed they were not much interested in measuring public value since 'bureaucratic procedures and rules in government protect public values and allow the organization to move towards public value creation'. Other executives used evidence from the reclassification of accounting data to underline the importance of bureaucratic rules and legislation to shape patterns of strategic programme implementation. They felt that 'financial data in end-year reports were in some way an adequate tool of public value measurement'. Anyway, the implementation of the strategic control system − as required by legislation − took place without embedding a real 'public value' paradigm and it was merely developed as a performance-related pay tool to monitor progress of operations connected to political priorities. This kind of control system is still in place. As the controller pointed out, this is because elected politicians felt 'This system was most suitable to keeping public managers accountable than a public value management system'.

Case B

The same approach to measurement was tested in the context of the northern regional government. In this case, the measurement and reporting framework was effectively translated into a quantitative scheme. The political commitment of an elected member of the cabinet and the passionate leadership of the chief budget officer were crucial for the implementation of the public value measurement and reporting. Public managers tracked financial and performance data by involving local stakeholders. A set of significant outcome measurements was validated through community engagement. Multi-stakeholder forums were also organized by the cabinet with 150 representatives of business, civil society and local governments involved in the implementation process of public programmes.

The community leaders were involved in two informal meetings, in which a preliminary set of indicators set out by the regional government was proposed for discussion. From this list, each institutional partner was required to determine which items were likely to be of sufficient significance to its operations to be worth measuring in a systematic way by the regional government and also to advance outcome indicators to be collected within the network.

This type of reporting was identified by different members of the forum to be a crucial issue and one that they could not easily ignore. The examination of the expenditure data (see Table 1) reinforced the output obtained from the analysis of programme implementation networks. All participating actors were very surprised about figures showing the 'financial' weight of different kinds of actors in the implementation process. The relevant weight of business and non-profits was not known before, and none of the representatives expected it to be so high. These data were also reported and discussed by local newspapers.

Further, public value 'channels' shaped by the expenditure process tended to call for even more ambitious social responsibility of private sector organizations than do the formal design of programmes explained by regional acts. Stakeholders recognized that this kind of disclosure could result in a marked improvement of interaction with the regional government. But this discussion was much more focused on government responsibility rather than corporate social responsibility. For example, some business representatives called for more regional governance in trade incentives and a larger quantity of government funding was believed to be a preliminary condition for shared responsible business partnerships.

A key conclusion of both public managers and politicians was that citizens and final recipients had a more clear understanding of paths along which public value is created (or destroyed). Such a measurement and reporting system was in place for six years, but fell into disuse after a political turnover, since the newly elected politicians were not much interested in public accountability issues and community engagement.

DISCUSSION

The performance measurement tools that have been used in 'traditional' public administration have often been found to be ineffective for guidance towards public value creation (Osborne, 2010; Stoker, 2006). The approach advanced here shows that in a bureaucratic setting the public manager is in the best position and has a responsibility to measure and to report the public value that the organization is to achieve. The conditions for effective implementation of public value measurement in this kind of setting include the following points.

First, the focus of the process should be on managers' ability to identify those critical cross-boundary measurements that they need to achieve in a networked setting and to interact with the network's actors. Because of government fragmentation, most services are developed incrementally as silos, often through categorical programmes with eligibility rules that did not align with other organizations' efforts.

Discerning multi-actor implementation arrays sketched through public policy may be helpful for a public manager to visualize tracks along which the value created by each network's actor — business, civil society, government – should be counted and recognized. To this aim, using routine financial data and formal products of rule-making processes may be helpful in order to find acceptance among public managers and elected politicians. Evidence provided by case B reinforces conclusions drawn from previous studies (Hall & O'Toole, 2004).

Second, the level of accountability is relevant. Managers concentrate only on critical information and poor accountability results in a lack of public manager commitment, as shown in case A. Compliance with a set of legislative norms seems to be the prevailing motivation of Italian public managers, as well as of elected officials, as confirmed by both cases. But case B is an excellent illustration of success in the application of the public value approach. The importance of this dual evidence is embedded in the realities of the public sector. This recognizes the public manager as an entrepreneur who has the ability – and also the responsibility – to drive the organization toward public value (Moore, 1995, 2013). But also, it confirms that political leadership and commitment is crucial to support acceptance of the public value paradigm, especially in those bureaucratic settings – such as the Italian case – where politicians strongly influence managerial decisions. In case B, it is not unrealistic to suppose that, in the words of the chief budget officer, 'without political support, the public value measurement would have been a purely "academic" exercise'. The evidence that the public value reporting was abandoned by the newly elected officials when the political leader left office supports this hypothesis. Hence, improving real managerial autonomy in a bureaucratic setting is a fundamental prerequisite for governments who wish to create and measure public value.

While it seems that public value measurement is most beneficial for elected politicians interested in communicating government performance (case B), both cases illustrate that the public value paradigm does not serve a particularly important role in the planning and control system, but rather existing bureaucratic processes – as framed by legislation and internal procedures – are perceived by public officials as the important devices for achieving or realizing in practice more specific public values. This perspective differs from much of the prior research that has focused on factors that influence managers' orientation towards public value (Benington & Moore, 2011; Moore, 1995), and further research might be helpful to explore this issue further.

Third, strong relationships with key political and professional constituencies within the organization and within the network – as developed in case B – are crucial in order to develop mutual trust and commitment towards the measurement and assessment of public value. Where trust has not been built or fostered (case A), the consequences are managerial–political detachment and bureaucratic routines.

Finally, traditional financial data, normally used by governments for budget authorization, may be effective tools for helping public managers and political leaders to recognize the organization's public value creation, especially in legislation-driven administrative traditions. However, financial information still needs to pull out non-financial measures that are necessary for assessing public value. Setting up a cross-sector measurement system consistent with the public manager's routine and understanding is the key to the successful implementation of the public value framework, as confirmed by evidence in case B.

CONCLUSION

The development of managerial tools in governments faced with the public value paradigm is at a very early stage. The cases discussed in this article contribute to the public value literature by exploring the dynamics of public value measurement and the factors that influence its design in bureaucratic settings.

The proposed approach argues that local public managers and elected politicians can effectively identify, measure and assess public value and public values jointly with both businesses and non-profit organizations. Reporting data and performance in both directions is an essential prerequisite for cross-sector collaboration. Ultimately, the effectiveness of public value management is seen to rest on its ability to point to a measurement and reporting system (Moore, 2013). But changing the culture and competences of public managers working in bureaucratic settings, supported by political leadership, this study suggests, is the most important key to public value measurement.

These two Italian cases also question the continued dominance of the public value paradigm in the public management literature and illustrate how the institutional environment − political and managerial culture, leadership and the legislative setting − matters for public value measurement. In particular, the legislation might be an important facilitator or inhibitor of public managers' motivation towards public value. Politicians' interest in public value measurement may be also a relevant driver and it represents an under-investigated topic. Hence, future research is necessary to specify more clearly the relations among technical and political environments of governments and public value management.

REFERENCES

Agranoff, R. (2006). Inside collaborative networks: Ten lessons for public managers. *Public Administration Review*, 66(1), 56−65.

Agranoff, R., & McGuire, M. (2003). Inside the matrix: Integrating the paradigms of intergovernmental and network management. *International Journal of Public Administration*, 26(12), 1401−1422.

Benington, J., & Moore, M. H. (Eds.). (2011). *Public value theory and practice*. Basingstoke: Palgrave Macmillan.

Bozeman, B. (2007). *Public values and public interest: Counterbalancing economic individualism*. Washington, DC: Georgetown University Press.

Bryson, J. M., Crosby, B. C., & Stone, M. M. (2006). The design and implementation of cross-sector collaborations: Propositions from the literature. *Public Administration Review*, 66(1), 44−55.

Cleveland, H. (2002). *Nobody in charge: Essays on the future of leadership*. New York, NY: John Wiley.

Crosby, B. C., & Bryson, J. M. (2005). *Leadership for the common good: Tackling public problems in a shared-power world* (2nd ed.). San Francisco, CA: Jossey-Bass.

Frederickson, H. G. (1991). Toward a theory of the public for public-administration. *Administration & Society*, 22(4), 365−398.

Goldsmith, S., & Eggers, W. D. (2004). *Governing by network: The new shape of the public sector*. Washington, DC: Brookings Institution.

Gray, B. (1989). *Collaborating: Finding common ground for multiparty problems*. San Francisco, CA: Jossey-Bass.

Hall, T. E., & O'Toole, L. J. (2004). Shaping formal networks through the regulatory process. *Administration & Society*, 36(2), 186−207.

Jørgensen, T. (2007). Public values, their nature, stability and change. The case of Denmark. *Public Administration Quarterly*, 30(4), 365−398.

Jørgensen, T., & Bozeman, B. (2007). Public values: An inventory. *Administration & Society*, 39(3), 354−381.

Julnes, G. (2012). Developing policies to support valuing in the public interest. *New Directions for Evaluation*, 133, 109−129.

Kickert, W. J. M., Klijn, E. H., & Termeer, C. A. M. (1995). Managing networks in the public sector. *Public Administration*, 73(3), 437−454.

Kisby, B. (2007). Analysing policy networks. Towards an ideational approach. *Policy Studies*, 28(1), 71−101.

Klijn, E. H., & Koppenjan, J. F. M. (2000). Public management and policy networks. *Public Management: An International Journal of Research and Theory*, 2(2), 135−158.

Loughlin, J. (1994). Nation, state and region in Western Europe. In L. Beckemans (Ed.), *Culture: The building-stone of Europe*. Brussels: Presses Interuniversitaires.

Moore, M. H. (1995). *Creating public value: Strategic management in government*. Harvard, MA: Harvard University Press.

Moore, M. H. (2003). *The public value scorecard: A rejoinder and an alternative to strategic performance measurement and management in non-profit organizations by Robert Kaplan.* Working paper no. 18, Hauser Center for Non-profit Organizations, John F. Kennedy School of Government. Cambridge, MA: Harvard University Press.

Moore, M. H. (2013). *Recognizing public value.* Cambridge, MA: Harvard University Press.

OECD. (1997). *Managing across levels of government.* Paris: OECD.

O'Flynn, J. (2007). From new public management to public value: Paradigmatic change and managerial implications. *The Australian Journal of Public Administration, 66*(3), 353–366.

Ongaro, E. (2009). *Public management reform and modernization: Trajectories of administrative change in Italy, France, Greece, Portugal and Spain.* Cheltenham: Edward Elgar Publishing.

Osborne, S. P. (2010). *The new public governance? New perspectives on the theory and practice of public governance.* London: Routledge.

O'Toole, L. J. (1997). Treating networks seriously: Practical and research-based agendas in public administration. *Public Administration Review, 57*(1), 45–52.

Pollitt, C. (2013). *Context in public policy and management: The missing link.* Cheltenham: Edward Elgar Publishing.

Pollitt, C., & Bouckaert, G. (2000). *Public management reform. A comparative analysis.* Oxford: Oxford University Press.

Porter, M., & Kramer, M. (2011). Creating shared value. *Harvard Business Review, 89*(1–2), 62–77.

Porter, M. E. (1985). *Competitive advantage. Creating and sustaining superior performance.* New York, NY: The Free Press.

Rhodes, R. A. (1997). *Understanding governance: Policy networks, governance, reflexivity and accountability.* Milton Keynes: Open University Press.

Schwab, K. (2008). Global corporate citizenship: Working with government and civil society. *Foreign Affairs, 87*(1), 107–118.

Stoker, G. (2006). Public value management. A new narrative for networked governance? *American Review of Public Administration, 36*(1), 41–57.

Van der Wal, Z., Nabatchi, T., & De Graaf, G. (2013). From galaxies to universe: A cross-disciplinary review and analysis of public values publications from 1969 to 2012. *The American Review of Public Administration.* Advance Online Publication. doi: 10.1177/0275074013488822.

Werner, O., & Schoepfe, G. M. (1987). *Systematic fieldwork: Foundations of ethnography and interviewing* (Vol. 1). Newbury Park, CA: Sage.

Williams, I., & Shearer, H. (2011). Appraising public value: Past, present and futures. *Public Administration, 89*, 1367–1384.

Yin, R. K. (1989). *Case study research: Design and methods.* Newbury Park, CA: Sage.

APPENDIX

Table A1. Types of Meetings and Key Informants.

Case	Type of Meetings	Key Informants	Leading Actor
Case one – Regional government A	*Ad hoc attendance:* Divisional meetings (3) Management meetings (5) *Regular attendance:* Monthly workgroup meetings	Chief budget officer (1) Controller (1) Chief information officer (1) Top managers (20) Middle managers (50) Cabinet members (2)	Controller
Case two – Regional government B	*Ad hoc attendance:* Management meetings (10) Cabinet meetings (1) Stakeholders' forums (3) Community meetings (4) *Regular attendance:* Monthly workgroup meetings	Chief budget officer (1) Director of statistics (1) Top managers (10) Middle managers (30) Cabinet members (6)	Elected cabinet member Chief budget officer

Note: Numbers in parentheses denote the number of meetings attended and the number of individuals with whom the researcher had conversations.

PART III
FROM THEORY TO PRACTICE

PUBLIC VALUE THEORY IN THE CONTEXT OF PUBLIC SECTOR MODERNIZATION

Giuseppe Marcon

ABSTRACT

Purpose – *This conceptual article aims primarily to illustrate the impact of public value thinking on the process of public sector modernisation. Public value management (PVM) is analysed from two perspectives. First, the principles and features of PVM approaches are detailed, including a comparison of the literature on the other approaches characterizing the modernisation process, that is, traditional public administration (TPA), new public management (NPM) and new public governance (NPG). Then PVM is contrasted with NPM and TPA. Subsequently, the elements connecting PVM with NPG are explored. Second, the theoretical and methodological frameworks within which public value has been operationalized are investigated. One of the core topics is the measurement of public value, which is illustrated focusing on the link between public value (in the singular) and public values (in the plural). The impact that the adoption of public value thinking exerts on the multiple performance objectives for public sector organisations is also investigated. Ultimately, the article aims to highlight the potential*

Public Value Management, Measurement and Reporting
Studies in Public and Non-Profit Governance, Volume 3, 323–351
Copyright © 2014 by Emerald Group Publishing Limited
All rights of reproduction in any form reserved
ISSN: 2051-6630/doi:10.1108/S2051-663020140000003014

of the public value view – considered in conjunction with performance measurement and performance management systems – without neglecting the challenging and problematic aspects of this wave of reform. The comparison with other waves of reform is intended to provide a clearer picture of the way forward for PVM.

Design/methodology/approach — *Theoretical and methodological investigation, elaborating on the relevant literature on the process of public sector modernisation, is carried out.*

Findings — *The approaches that have emerged during the last two decades (PVM, NPG) are other than alternative solutions. But also less recent waves of change have left, or are expected to leave, their own legacy for public administration over time. This could be the case for NPM, although, according to many scholars, it is in trouble and has lost its driving force, while others see it as simply 'dead' and doomed to give way to the 'digital-era governance'. Several core elements of NPM are no longer in evidence either in PVM or in NPG. Different distinguishing elements have been brought into the foreground. For instance, the idea of the public as citizens characterises PVM and NPG, instead of the public as customers, qualifying NPM. What we are seeing is a progressive expansion of the public's involvement, through co-production and participation. Contemporary public officials interact with members of the public in ways that involve all of their possible roles: as citizens, customers, partners. There are two salient aspects under which public value thinking can contribute. First, a focus on public value can – better than other approaches – represent a 'glue' capable of bringing together debates involving 'values, institutions, systems, processes, and people' (Smith, 2004, p. 18). Second, such a focus makes it possible to link insights from different analytical perspectives, fostering a broader view on the determinants of public sector change. This could be of decisive importance for the purpose of reshaping performance measurement and performance management systems, which is a crucial step in public sector reform.*

Originality/value — *Significant contributions are offered under two aspects. First, in terms of exploration of the concepts of public value (also in relation to public values) and private value. Second, in terms of analysis of the impact that PVM can exert on the logic of performance measurement and performance management.*

Keywords: Public value; new public management; traditional public administration; new public governance; theory

INTRODUCTION

The late 1970s and early 1980s have seen numerous waves of reform internationally, aimed at modernizing the public sector, known as new public management (NPM) and, later, new public governance (NPG) and public value management (PVM). While several scholars see these as 'new paradigms' of public management and administration, others consider them 'policy and implementation regimes' (see Osborne, 2010b), or, still more generically, 'approaches'.[1] In this article, the broader term approaches will be preferred.

PVM will be analyzed from two perspectives. Firstly, the principles and features of the PVM approach will be detailed, including a comparison of the literature on the other approaches. Then PVM will be contrasted with traditional public administration (TPA) and with NPM. Subsequently, the elements connecting PVM with NPG will be explored. Secondly, the theoretical and methodological frameworks within which public value has been operationalized will be investigated. The measurement of public value will be illustrated focusing on the link between public value (in the singular) and public values (in the plural). The impact that the adoption of public value thinking exerts on the multiple performance objectives for public sector organizations will also be considered. This article aims to highlight the potential of the public value view − considered in conjunction with performance measurement/management − without neglecting the challenging and problematic aspects of this wave of reform. The comparison with other waves of reform is intended to provide a clearer picture of the way forward for PVM.

The concept of public value is widely discussed (e.g. Alford & O'Flynn, 2009; Benington & Moore, 2011a; Bozeman, 2002; Cole & Parston, 2006; Kelly, Mulgan, & Muers, 2002; Moore, 1994, 1995, 2003; O'Flynn, 2007; Stoker, 2006). It originated in North America and has been associated − usually within the expression 'public value management' − with the process of public administration modernization, particularly since the late 1990s. Before delving into this, a succint recall of the genesis of PVM's antecedents is appropriate. The beginning of the NPM movement can be traced back to the late 1970s. However, its first conceptualization was developed much later by Hood (1991).[2] NPM-type initiatives have been diffused throughout the OECD countries and have impacted most of the Commonwealth nations, as well as the former Communist countries (Borins, 1998; Hood, 1991, 1995), but without uniformity of application. The modernization profiles of the various countries range from (Naschold, 1996):

- a resolute opening up to market forces and privatization (Great Britain), to a radical reengineering of private sector models (e.g. New Zealand)

and to the opening of more prudent and limited internal modernization initiatives (e.g. Norway);

• cases of rapid advancements towards managerialism to cases of coexistence with persisting links to more traditional forms of bureaucratic governance by rule (e.g. Japan, Germany, Austria).

The impact of NPM has been greater in Anglo-Saxon contexts, compared to continental western European contexts (Ferlie et al., 1996). NPM cannot be conceived of either as a monolithic construction, or as a continuous, uniform drive towards a common model of the public sector.[3]

Central to NPM are such concepts as 'novelty', 'modernity' and 'change'. The underlying idea is the overcoming of 'traditional public administration' or 'old public administration'. The TPA approach stems from the thinking of Woodrow Wilson, Frederick Winslow Taylor and Max Weber.[4] Wilson (1887) argued for a clear separation between politics and administration. Politics 'sets the tasks for administration', but 'it should not be suffered to manipulate its offices'. In addition, service should be made nonpartisan, as a premise to make it 'businesslike' (p. 210), or 'less unbusinesslike' (p. 201). Wilson advocated a science of administration committed to supporting this outcome, as a way to 'straighten the paths of government'. Taylor (1911) argued for the existence of one method, which is quicker and better than all the others to execute each task. Weber (1947) regarded bureaucracy as the most efficient organizational mechanism, thus connecting his thought to Taylor's principles of scientific management. Although working separately, these three thinkers had in common the search for ways to improve efficiency through the adoption of principles of scientific management. On the academic side, a decisive blow came from Herbert Simon, who found defects in most propositions of administrative theory of the time, demonstrating that for almost every principle there was an 'equally plausible and acceptable contradictory principle' (Simon, 1946, p. 53).

The traditional model of public administration has been regarded as 'the longest standing and most successful' theory of public sector management (Hughes, 2003, p. 17). Such approaches as NPM, NPG and PVM aim at replacing it, even though some elements of TPA still persist. The theoretical framework of TPA is now considered no longer adequate for the needs of modern, rapidly changing societies. However, transition to new approaches has happened progressively. The advent of NPM was preceded by several attempts to amend the traditional model, without subverting its overall logic. The 'neo-bureaucratic model', the 'new public administration', the 'institutional model', and the 'public choice model' are notable examples (e.g. Bourgon, 2011; Gruening, 2001).[5] In this article we refer to the core features of the overall logic of TPA, without entering the details of the specific and limited reform attempts just mentioned.

TPA, NPM AND PVM

TPA, NPM and PVM approaches rest upon different assumptions. As highlighted in the Appendix, there are ten elements that can used to indicate similarities and differences between TPA, NPM and PVM.

Characterization and Dominant Focus

TPA has a bureaucratic character, inclined towards control by rules and a clear delineation of authority and jurisdictions. TPA is based on the view that the needs and problems facing public bodies are reasonably unambiguous, and the solutions are known and understood, and that the provision of public services will be mainly ensured by public organizations (Benington & Moore, 2011b, pp. 13–14).

NPM is labelled as post-bureaucratic, since it aims at superseding the bureaucratic model in various ways. Its underlying philosophy is that of 'competitive government', relying on the market and individual in the definition and satisfaction of needs. Within this movement, recurring bywords are corporatization, privatization (in its diverse dimensions, e.g. formal, substantial, mitigated, cold) and externalization. One corollary is the dominant focus on 'results' – although the term is interpreted and adopted in a somewhat limited sense.

PVM places itself beyond TPA's bureaucratic logic and the core aspect of the NPM approach, to take a 'post-competitive government' characterization, in which relationships are a dominant focus. This approach requires 'thinking about government and public services less as machines or structures and more as "complex adaptive systems"'; it distinguishes itself by its 'capacity to analyse and understand the interconnections, interdependencies and interactions between complex issues' (Benington & Moore, 2011b, pp. 14–15).

Process of Definition of the Public Interest

Defining the public interest in terms of TPA is a role taken by politicians and experts, with little room for public input. For PVM, the definition hinges on the interaction between internal and external stakeholders and on deliberative processes – involving traditional representative channels and elected user representatives, as well as a series of filtering devices, such as the media, polling and focus groups – to delineate underlying public preferences (Kelly et al., 2002, p. 31ff.). NPM takes a middle ground – where the key actor is the customer – assuming that the public interest can be derived from the aggregation of individual preferences, and pivots on the role of senior politicians or managers, substantiated by evidence about customer choice.

Contribution to the Democratic Process and Role for Public Participation

The three approaches have significant differences in terms of the possible contribution to the democratic process and role for public participation. PVM postulates a circular and continuous process of democratic exchange as essential to the development and implementation of public value thinking. Active participation of the relevant social actors is essential – participatory budgeting is an example. Dialogue and dialogic democracy are recurring terms evoked to define the way binding collective decisions should be made at each stage of the decision-making process (i.e. problem definition, agenda setting, definition and analysis of solutions, choice and implementation).

Bohm (2003, p. 6) states that dialogue can be understood as a 'stream of meaning', flowing 'among' and 'through' people and 'between' people, with an inherent potential to generate some new understanding. The shared meaning produced by dialogue is 'the "glue" or "cement" that holds people and societies together' (Bohm, 2003, p. 6). Dialogue differs from common participation in that the actors involved play *with* each other, instead of *against* each other, portraying a so-called win-win situation.

A variant of public participation is deliberative democracy, understood as a form of democracy characterized by a '*reason-giving* requirement', in which the need is affirmed to 'justify decisions made by citizens and their representatives' (Gutmann & Thompson, 2004). In addition to the principle of reasoning between people as the leading political procedure – as opposed to 'bargaining between competing interests or the aggregation of private preferences' – deliberative democracy assumes the principle that the crucial political act is a public act – as opposed to 'the purely private act of voting' (Parkinson, 2006, p. 3).[6]

In contrast, the democratic process appears to be limited in both the TPA and the NPM contexts. In the first, it is limited to defining an essential accountability framework, centred on the competition between elected leaders. In the second, it is restricted to setting objectives and checking their outcomes, while how these outcomes are achieved is left to managers. For TPA, public participation is confined to the mechanisms of voting in elections and exerting pressure on elected representatives, while NPM focuses mainly on such instruments as customer satisfaction surveys.

Attitude towards Public Sector Ethos

Concerning the public sector ethos, TPA and NPM are poles apart. In the TPA view, public organizations have a monopoly on the service ethos, where it is assumed that there are characteristics and fundamental values peculiar to the public sector, making it significantly different from the private sector. This assumption relates to different elements, such as the ways public services are delivered, the values driving their delivery, the nature of public sector employment and how public sector workers and users create the public sector and perceive its services (Lethbridge, 2009, p. 2). NPM, on the other hand, rejects the idea of a public sector ethos, since, according to its philosophy, the public sector ethos is simply meant as a 'cover for inefficiency and empire building by bureaucrats' (Stoker, 2006, p. 46).

PVM combines aspects of TPA and NPM. The public value approach implies a *public service* ethos instead of a *public sector* ethos,[7] assuming an open-minded approach to the procurement of services, with no ideological connotations to its choice between public or private service providers and no special moral virtue attached to those working with public organizations (Stoker, 2006, p. 48). The best supplier is chosen based on expected end results, regardless of whether it belongs to the public, private or non-profit sectors. In some circumstances, direct public provision might be preferable, while in others private for-profit and non-profit organizations might be more appropriate and advantageous. Two rival positions concerning public service, categorized as myths – 'only public service can properly deliver public services' and 'there is nothing special that distinguishes public services from private services' – are rejected (House of Commons, 2002, pp. 5, 11ff.). From this, in the mixed economy of public service, it is possible for private (for-profit and non-profit) organizations to 'uphold the public service ethos'.

Moreover, PVM, consistent with its position on such dimensions as the definition of public interest, the contribution of the democratic process and the role of public participation, hinges on a relational approach to service procurement, implying that client and contractor act cooperatively, according to a partnership logic. Aldridge and Stoker (2002, p. 17ff.) propose a concept of public service ethos with five distinctive dimensions: performance culture, commitment to accountability, capacity to support universal access, responsible employment practices, and contribution to community well-being. Their proposal is rooted in a conceptual pattern in which diversity, contestability and competition in public service provision are favourably considered as capable of stimulating innovation and optimization of limited resources. Proposals for public service codes suggest similar, but significantly differentiated, components. For instance, the House of Commons (2002, p. 18ff.) suggested the following: ethical behaviour, holding providers to account, being open with the public, commitment to quality services, fairness to staff and users, and good administration, reliability and safety.

Preferred System of Delivery

The TPA model of organization and delivery of public services hinges on such principles as bureaucratic hierarchy, centralization, planning, direct control, and self-sufficiency. The NPM approach aims at the disaggregation of previously monolithic public sector bodies, unbundling U-form (i.e. unitary or functional) organizational structures into decentralized and corporatized arm's length units based on products/services, so that separable functions give rise to separate agencies. It favours private sector organizations or 'lean, flat, autonomous organizations drawn from the public and private sectors and steered by a tight central leadership corps' (Stoker, 2006, p. 46). PVM implies keeping doors open to a wide range of alternative solutions, between which to choose pragmatically. These alternatives include public sector agencies, private companies, joint venture companies, community interest companies, and community groups (Kelly et al., 2002, p. 10). The impact of the increasing role for user choice has also to be recalled here, as a means to promote the search for new alternatives and to improve their selection. Finally, also worth considering is the PVM reflexive approach to intervention mechanisms. Engaging in reflexivity means surfacing the assumptions underlying administrative practice, providing 'a means for thinking more critically about the impact of such practice', and possibly leading 'to the construction of new organizational and social realities' (Cunliffe & Jun, 2005, p. 227; see also Lethbridge, 2009). Adaptability and flexibility are decisive virtues, and in actively exerting their role in contriving to make the system work, managers need to realize that it will only work if it is adjusted on a continuous basis. All of this is meant to improve the process of achieving the outputs (and consequently the outcomes) of public sector service delivery.

Key Performance Objectives and Dominant Model of Accountability

Two of the elements listed in the Appendix, the key performance objectives and the dominant model of accountability, are closely related to the performance measurement/performance management dimensions of public management. Moving from TPA through NPM to PVM, performance objectives appear to extend their scope. The TPA approach hinges essentially on managing inputs, with the further limitation of concentrating primarily on their financial dimension. The control system focuses chiefly on expenditure rather than on the cost of production of public services. Inputs are just the first component of the process of producing and delivering public services – the other components being the outputs and outcomes. The paucity of inputs management with respect to the complexity of overall performance is self-evident. A tendency to rely on expenditure control instead of cost control adds to the risk of biasing performance consciousness.

Under the NPM approach objectives are centred on managing inputs and outputs and their relationship. Relevant performance measures are economy and efficiency, while outcomes and effectiveness tend to be overshadowed, thus 'largely reflecting the economic framing of government activity and the reconstruction of citizens as customers' (O'Flynn, 2007, p. 360). The emphasis on narrow concepts of cost-efficiency and the neglect of other dimensions of performance, such as quality and effectiveness, are a sign of a well-known risk experienced in the implementation of performance management systems. We refer to the tendency to transform into objectives only those variables or aspects that are easily measurable, while downplaying or ignoring those that cannot be measured (Kelly et al., 2002, p. 9). Under the NPM approach the practice of 'government by contract'[8] focuses on the purchase of outputs, while government's collective interest is often difficult to put in terms of outputs (Schick, 1998). There has been widespread criticism with respect to performance measurement, with a focus on the problem of selection of targets. Importing private business models into public sector organizations – without adequate adjustments – raises a number of risks, such as: (a) underestimating outputs that some investments will generate and deliver in the future; (b) overlooking the possibility that conventional output measures fail to reflect fully quality improvements and, more broadly, intangible components of outputs; (c) losing sight of possible distorted effects of targets, in the absence of appropriate incentives, and (d) overshadowing values other than efficiency, such as equity, equality of opportunity and staff loyalty (among many others, see Christensen & Lægreid, 2007; Coats, 2006; Hood, 1991; Pritchard, 2003). Furthermore, the fact that public service delivery is more about outcomes than outputs has been overshadowed (Coats, 2006).

PVM assumes the concept of public value and the process of creating and measuring it as core features. Public value pursuit and achievement is its overarching objective. This involves all public managers (elected and non-elected officials) gauging whether public interventions are achieving their expected social and economic outcomes:

> It is not enough to say that public managers create results that are valued; they must be able to show that the results obtained are worth the cost of private consumption and unrestrained liberty forgone in producing the desirable results. (Moore, 1995, p. 29)

Within the PVM approach the term 'results' is assumed in its widest sense, since it not only includes inherently all performance variables (inputs, outputs, outcomes), their features and reciprocal relationships (economy, efficiency, effectiveness, quality) and their links to *public values* (in the plural), but also assumes one indicator – public value – as a general conceptual synthesis of public service performance. While the NPM movement is focused on the enhancement of output controls, PVM shifts attention to the end results (i.e. the satisfaction of the needs of public services' users and the community). This leads to the central issue of the definition of public value. The public value perspective takes a holistic approach to public management. In fact, it looks at the whole of the impact of public bodies' actions, aiming at contributing to the improvement of policy decisions and the relationship between public administration and citizens. It is central not only to policymakers' decisions, but also – or especially – to public managers' activities. As Benington (2011, pp. 42–43) writes – within the framework of 'networked community governance' – public value has two main dimensions: 'what is the public value?' and 'what adds value to the public sphere?'. The public sphere is intended as 'a democratic space within which citizens address their collective concerns, and where individual liberties have to be protected'. In this way public value is embedded in a dialogic and/or deliberative process, meant as an arena where competing interests and contested values can be settled through debate and negotiation. Public service value management is citizen-centric. Kelly et al. (2002, p. 35) argue that the public value approach proposes 'a broader way of measuring government performance and guiding policy decisions'. However, it is not just a way of *measuring* performance: it is a broader way of *conceiving* performance.

To understand public value better, a comparison with the concept of private value is useful. Private value is created and revealed through the market exchange. Private value is the result of business actions aiming at meeting individual customer preferences – which are to be signalled by the price mechanism – by using factors of production (labour and intellectual capital, physical capital and financial capital). Privately added economic value – which is typically measured in monetary terms – turns out in an operating surplus, allowing returns to be delivered to shareholders. For the measurement and evaluation of private value, businesses resort to largely used metrics, such as profitability ratios, while a range of decisive information is collected and circulated by the stock markets. Public sector organizations are in search of analogous measures of performance. Public value is proposed as an advanced version of such measures. There are components of public value that simply lie outside private value, while others require different metrics. There is just one case in which the two concepts may happen to be not that distant, in *practical* terms, that is, when public services are delivered in a competitive context and on a purely commercial basis, strictly following market mechanisms. In this framework, the monetary value of the outputs may happen to reflect citizens' satisfaction to an acceptable degree. However, most situations are quite different from this. For instance, when public services are delivered on a commercial basis, the user/client/customer may accept the exchange conditions even though the service features are not perceived as satisfactory, simply because of the difficulty or impossibility to exert the exit option. Most importantly, the case has to be considered of one of the two types of citizens' aspirations described by Moore (1995, pp. 52–53):

- those concerning collective things that, though 'individually desired and consumed', cannot be provided and delivered via market mechanisms (since referring to indivisible goods or services);
- those concerning 'political aspirations that attach to aggregate social conditions', such as social justice and the like.

Clearly, measuring public value is more difficult than measuring private value. This is because of a series of factors, including:

- the crucial circumstance that the citizens − to whom ultimately the task pertains of defining public value[9] − are inspired by different and contested public values (in the plural), which influence the way they assess public value;
- a particular characteristic of many public services is the involvement − often unavoidable, sometimes only preferable − in processes of co-production (Alford, 2011; Moore, 1995, p. 105ff.).

One particular aspect worth noting is that public managers have responsibilities to focus on longer-term public interest and future generations of citizens (Benington, 2011, p. 49).

The NPM approach assigns centrality to the optimization of the systems of delivery of public services and to the process of production, although with special emphasis on output − a consequence of the logic of market mechanisms. On the contrary, within PVM, attention is focused on system maintenance (i.e. on the whole set of conditions − internal and external − and relationships on which the creation of public value depends).

Role of Managers

Under the TPA approach, managers are concerned primarily with ensuring that appropriate procedures are followed (according to the principle of control by rules). Within the NPM approach the focus is on determining and meeting pre-defined performance targets. The PVM approach encompasses a quite active role for managers, with a distinctive responsibility for the functioning of the networks through which participated decisions take place and services are delivered. They are assumed to be the core actors for the maintenance of the public sector organization's capacity to generate value.

PVM AND NPG

Governance is a multifaceted concept. Rhodes (1996, 1997, 2000) has repeatedly addressed the topic of the possible uses of, or approaches to, governance, proposing successive, partially divergent, taxonomies. In his latest contribution to this subject, he has pinpointed no less than seven distinct uses of governance, comprising governance as NPM. Hirst (2000) notes five versions of governance, and within each field of interest the concept may be developed and specified into a series of variants.

What is mentioned above suggests that the term governance is both rich and somewhat imprecise, due to its multiple meanings and a good deal of ambiguity surrounding its different uses. This appears even more evident when we turn our attention to the public sector. Osborne (2010b) proposes a tripartite classification of the schools of governance: corporate governance ('concerned with the internal processes that provide direction and accountability to any organization'); good governance ('concerned with the promulgation of normative models of social, political and administrative governance by supranational bodies') and public governance. Public governance, in turn, can be expanded into several distinct theoretical perspectives, including network governance.[10] Despite this multiplicity of strings, perspectives, constituent elements, meanings and nuances, the literature allows concentration on some core aspects, which can somehow be conducive to a significant, although tentative, synthesis, at least for the specific purpose of this study. The preeminent feature is the importance of networks, which have come to dominate public policy. Other relevant features include the shift in the state's role from control to influence, the blending of public and private resources and the use of alternative policy instruments, within a framework of public–private partnerships (Peters & Pierre, 1998, pp. 225–227). As Rhodes (2000, p. 59) states, networks are 'the analytical heart of the notion of governance in the study of Public Administration', hence, 'governance refers to governing with and through networks' (Rhodes, 2007, p. 1246). Networks are one of the most powerful institutional settings in which – formally and/or, most frequently, informally – public actors interact with private actors, both for-profit and non-profit. This centrality of the network dimension is so pervasive in the literature that such expressions as 'network governance' or 'networked governance' are frequently employed synecdochically for public governance.

The reasons behind the emergence of networks as decisive components of public action and management are numerous and varied. One of these is the development of the knowledge society, with the consequent need to integrate human capital into collaborative activities, such as identifying problems, strategic brokering and problem solving. Another reason is rooted in the changes involving government roles and operations, and particularly in the withdrawal of the state from direct operation, in favour of other actors, and in the decentralization of functions. A third reason is the tendency of organization structures to evolve into collaborative and hier-archically flexible forms. Overall, these drivers give rise to 'multiple over-lapping connections', within which managers are 'forced to network collaboratively' in order to successfully face the challenge of increasing complexity.

Against this backdrop, attempts have progressively emerged – especially in the mid to late 1990s – to develop a NPG theory aspiring to represent a new, distinctive approach. The expression 'new public governance' has been formulated and developed by Osborne, amongst others (2006, 2009, 2010a, 2010b).[11] As a starting point for this move, there is the recognition of the ongoing transformation of the state in a 'plural and pluralist' direc-tion (Osborne, 2010b; see also Osborne, 2006; Osborne, McLaughlin, & Chew, 2010). Thus, NPG can be understood as a logic aimed at effectively addressing the complexities inherent in these two dimensions of plurality (Osborne, 2010b, p. 7). Plurality involves multiple actors in the delivery of public services and the co-existence of multiple processes informing the policy-making system. The joint adoption of the network view and the plurality perspective entail a twofold shift: from a vertical/hierarchical dimension of public management and administration to a horizontal one, and from an intra-organizational logic to an inter-organizational one.

The core features of NPG are:

1. public sector organizations are assumed to operate in a complex and continuously changing environment, and being outward-looking, against a backdrop in which inter-organizational relations are given centrality;
2. civil society plays a pivotal role in shaping public sector organizations' strategies; this, in turn, entails a decisive role for public participation and co-production processes;
3. due to the plurality perspective, the value base appears 'dispersed and contested' (Osborne, 2010b);
4. the dominant focus is on networks and relational contracts (Osborne, 2010b), or networks, partnerships and civic leadership (Hartley, 2005); these same elements define the resource allocation mechanism;
5. network management – with its inherent components of communica-tion, involvement and negotiation – becomes the crucial ability of man-agers and administrators; closely linked to this feature is the ability to conduct decision-making processes in a participatory/collaborative manner;
6. the preferred provision system is based on collaboration between public and private actors, within networked relations.

The public value approach includes acceptance of government activity being characterized by interconnection and interdependence. Explicit theoretical attempts to link PVM with network governance mechanisms unavoidably result in warnings that public managers need to 'manage by networks', since PVM 'bases its practice in the systems of dialogue and exchange that characterize networked governance' (Stoker, 2006, p. 41). Indeed, the PVM approach is achieved by means of network governance, combining democracy and efficiency, since public value 'is defined and redefined through social and political interaction' (Smith, 2004, p. 68).

A few aspects warrant further discussion. The aim of enabling or empowering citizens, inherent in the service concept adopted, belongs to the same logic of NPG. Torfing and Triantafillou (2013, p. 14) suggest as an NPG output, new tools (compared with TPA and NPM) 'aiming to empower and engage private stakeholders in public problem-solving and service production'. This connects with co-production and participation. Osborne et al. (2012) attribute to NPM two flaws, defined as 'fatal': failing to focus on inter-organizational processes and failing to recognize that what public sector organizations produce has the nature of 'services'. The characteristics of services, as drawn from business practice and service management and service-dominant theories, suggest a 'public service-dominant' approach, which can arguably enable public sector organizations to face effectively a new public service reality where (pp. 137–138):

- the nature of service provision is inter-organizational and interactive;
- the nature of service delivery is processional and systemic.

It is argued that NPG can be a solution for both the flaws mentioned above. Another aspect is also worth noting. Within this framework, in which co-production is relevant, not only the user, but also the citizen is situated as a primary stakeholder in the processes of both *public policy* and *public service delivery*. Hartley (2005, p. 28) indicates co-production as the role of the population in networked governance. Martin (2003, p. 217) defines co-production as 'active involvement of the public in policy decisions and/or service design/delivery'. The introduction of this broadened concept of co-production leads to widening the analysis to the theme of participation.[12] Referring to the 'ladder of citizen participation' proposed by Arnstein (1971), the rungs at the upper end of the ladder involve approaches that empower the public: partnership, delegated power and citizen control. The correspondence with some key components of PVM (the process of definition of the public interest, the contribution to the democratic process and the role for public participation) does not need to be demonstrated.

PUBLIC VALUE AND PUBLIC VALUES:
SOME ISSUES

This section discusses the theoretical and methodological framework within which public value thinking can be operationalized. Adequately dealing with this issue is preliminary to defining the potential impact of PVM on the performance measurement/management system.

First, reflections are needed on organizational values and public values, which constitute the foundation on which public value construction, creation and measurement take place. When it comes to interpreting value-creating processes, the organization's values system and culture are decisive variables. In general terms, organizational theory indicates that values are fundamental components of organizational culture; as such, they are understood as 'instrumental in determining, guiding and informing behavior' (MacCarthaigh, 2008, p. 4). In the same way, public service cultures have been described as consisting of 'ideas, values, and practices that *motivate and fashion individual and collective behaviours*' (Horton, 2008, p. 22; emphasis added). Beck Jørgensen and Bozeman (2007, p. 355) reinforce that 'public values and public valuing in some respects *define* those fields of inquiry and separate them from others' (emphasis added).

Public values (in the plural) are relevant to detect, define, interpret, operationalize, weigh, rank, quantify and hence integrate into performance measurement. The literature offers a wide range of attempts to both clarify their defining qualities and dimensions, and make sense of the different analyses of what they constitute. The 'inventory' of public values elaborated by Beck Jørgensen and Bozeman (2007) exhibits something like 21 items, out of an original list of 72, which were selected through critical comparison. The authors subdivide them into a number of categories or 'constellations of the public values universe' (p. 360). The main conclusions deriving from this analysis follow.

First, public values are not ingrained exclusively in public bodies: indeed, they are ultimately a product of culture and social interactions, wherein organizations, groups and individuals have a role. Second, at least a part of public values are neither explicitly defined nor universally shared, which does not imply the mitigation of their ability to determine citizens' obligations and expectations. Third, although a number of public values are felt as prime values, frequently a 'subset of prime values that are not instrumental but are ends in themselves' (Beck Jørgensen & Bozeman, 2007, p. 375) defies identification. Fourth, the types of analysis appropriate to define public values (i.e. in these authors' view, moral reasoning and causal reasoning) often get mixed up. Finally, there are multiple interrelationships between public values, and they have to be explored and sorted out in order for public values to have an effective usefulness in guiding public action consciously. Conclusively, 'public values remain [...] an ambiguous but potentially viable set of criteria for action and accountability' (p. 377).

As Talbot (2010, p. 130) illustrates, the *possibility* can be explored to build on the so-called values-based theories in order to construct a unified model of human values applied to public bodies' performance. The reference here is to such theories as 'four cultures (or ideologies) theory' (as Talbot names it), 'cultural theory', 'competing values framework', 'relational models theory' and 'reversal theory'.

> Values lie at the core of any assessment of public sector performance, so having some framework for understanding them is essential. (p. 137)

> That we are still struggling to integrate values into other aspects of Performance suggests this is not an easy problem to solve. (p. 138)

Once the public values concept has been discussed, then the next step is turning attention to the ways in which public value can be measured. Public value can be assumed as a general conceptual synthesis of public service performance. This does not mean that it can be expressed by just one comprehensive measure. It is a multifaceted concept, which justifies using the expression 'multiple objectives', as in the Appendix. Several models have been proposed, suggesting a list of different dimensions to be integrated. For instance, Cresswell, Burke, and Pardo (2006) propose the following list of impacts on the interests of public stakeholders, which, taken together, would compose the public value:[13]

- financial (impacts on income, asset values, liabilities, entitlements);
- political (impacts on influence on public bodies' actions or policy, role in political affairs, influence in political parties, prospects for future public office);
- social (impacts on family or community relationships, social mobility, status and identity);
- strategic (impacts on economic/political advantage/opportunities, goals, resources for innovation or planning);
- ideological (impacts on beliefs, moral or ethical commitments, alignment of public actions/policies or social outcomes with beliefs/moral or ethical positions);

- stewardship (impacts on the public's view of government officials as stewards/guardians of the value of public bodies in terms of trust/integrity/legitimacy).

Each of these *components* of public value has to be linked to value-generating mechanisms, such as improvements in efficiency, effectiveness and quality, including enablement of valuable activities, fostering transparency or reducing social differences.

Benington (2011, pp. 45–46) singles out five public value dimensions:

- economic (deriving from market economic considerations);
- social and cultural (related to such factors as social capital, community well-being, cultural identity);
- political (related to democratic dialogue, citizen participation and engagement);
- ecological (essentially related to behaviours inspired by sustainable development principles).

Following a similar trajectory, the BBC (2004) indicates its contribution to public value as made up of five dimensions:

- democratic;
- cultural and creative;
- educational;
- social and community (promoting social cohesion and tolerance);
- global (contributing to provide news and information and spread English culture to a global audience).

All these dimensions contribute to shedding light on the complex social construction of public value. A closer understanding of such a construction is pursued by detailing the 'recipients' of the value generated, that is, individuals (users), citizens (the community, receiving an additional value, socially recognized as extending beyond users' individual advantage from the service), and 'the wider commercial market' (indirect impacts on its net economic value; multiplier effect).

The literature, drawing from Moore (1995), outlines the following, well-known, essential aspects of public bodies' performance:

- delivering actual services (i.e. value created by services for users);
- achieving social outcomes (exceeding users' personal benefits);
- maintaining the trust and legitimacy of the agency.

Practice offers a range of observable examples of attempts to measure public value (in the singular), in some way inspired by the views expressed above. They include, for instance, the BBC model (BBC, 2004; BBC Trust, 2012), the studies promoted by the Work Foundation (Coats, 2006; Coats & Passmore, 2008; Collins, 2007; Cowling, 2006; Hills & Sullivan, 2006; Talbot, 2008), the public ROI framework (Cresswell et al., 2006), and the Accenture Public Service Value Governance Framework (Accenture, 2008; Parston & Goodman, 2008).

The evaluation of the documentation emerging from the pioneering practice of public value measurement allows some initial analysis. First, most of the materials are 'works in progress'. This is because some of the core issues of public value thinking appear to be still unsettled. So far, the construction of values applied to public bodies' performance is still only a theoretical hypothesis. Different sets of criteria are proposed to classify those values, which, in turn, brings difficulties both in embedding the public value ethos in the public management objectives and in 'rebalancing' the traditional performance measurement/management systems. However, the problem remains of how to operationalize the adopted theoretical and methodological framework (i.e. how to make it work). Of course, this is hardly surprising, because:

a) PVM is currently considered by many scholars as a new paradigm, even though this view is subject to criticism; either way, the intended changes are far from marginal or incremental;
b) there has to be awareness of the necessity to create the conditions for change, which, in this context, takes quite a long time.

A second aspect concerning the instruments proposed to apply the principles of PVM is that the various models or frameworks appear to speak different languages. Needless to say, different languages turn into different ways of understanding and guiding the processes, and hence different behaviours and end results for the reform efforts.

A third consideration is directed to the usefulness of the systemic approach to public value thinking, involving the diverse research fields, subjects and operating contexts to which public value logic can apply. For instance, Hills and Sullivan (2006, p. 63) observe that 'there are discussions already taking place that are very relevant to the whole question of measuring public value, but as yet are not being directly linked to public value discussions'. They note that 'there has not been a great deal of discussion about the implications of the concept of public value in the evaluation community'. Nor has there been significant attention paid to the relationships between the adoption of public value thinking in the domains of public management and public policy. A unitary, systemic, vision would be appropriate.

CONCLUSIONS

Stimuli for public sector change come from multiple sources: economy, society and politics itself. Waves of reform come one after the other. Against this backdrop, reform agendas partially overlap, and the same applies to scholarly speculations about theoretical and methodological standpoints. According to many scholars, NPM is in trouble and has lost its driving force, while others see it as simply 'dead' and doomed to give way to 'digital-era governance' (Dunleavy, Margetts, Bastow, & Tinkler, 2005). Several core elements of NPM are no longer in evidence either in PVM or in NPG. Different distinguishing elements have been brought to the fore, including the idea of the public as citizens rather than customers. What we are seeing is a progressive expansion of the public's involvement, through co-production and participation. Contemporary public officials interact with members of the public in ways that involve all of their possible roles: as citizens, customers, partners (Thomas, 2012, p. 42). Osborne et al. (2012) propose their 'public service-dominant' approach within the NPG logic, but drawing from business practice and service management, which is compatible with NPM. They observe that the proposed framework 'does not replace the previous foci, but rather embeds them in a new context' (p. 136).

Two aspects under which public value thinking can contribute are discussed in this article. The first is that a focus on public value can represent a 'glue' capable of bringing together debates involving 'values, institutions, systems, processes, and people' (Smith, 2004, p. 18). The second is that such a focus makes it possible to link insights from different analytical perspectives, fostering a broader view on the determinants of public sector change. These analytical perspectives encompass economics, public policy, policy analysis, ecology, philosophy and political science, together with public administration and public management (see Benington & Moore, 2011b, p. 2; Smith, 2004, p. 18). This could be important for the purpose of reshaping performance measurement and performance management systems, which is a crucial step in public sector reform. PVM has the potential to encapsulate the multiple components of public sector performance.

As Constable, Passmore, and Coats (2008, p. 9) argue, public value is 'a comprehensive approach to thinking about management and about continuous improvement in public services'.

Brief final considerations relate, on the one hand, to an issue that PVM (and NPG alike) must face, and, on the other hand, to future perspectives. The issue to be faced concerns the co-production and participation components. These components are the cornerstone of the approaches we are investigating, yet their implementation is challenging. Indeed, involving the public and managing by networks challenges public officials, since the need emerges for new roles, characterized by increased consultation, communication and deliberation, not to mention the task of defining and measuring public value. The question ensues of whether public bodies have these capabilities, or are able of creating them (O'Flynn, 2007, pp. 361–362; Smith, 2004, pp. 69–70).

PVM is not exempt from criticism. Williams and Shearer (2011, p. 1367) criticize the 'apparent silence of public value on questions of power and heterogeneity' and the absence of empirically testable propositions. Morrell (2009, p. 11), attributing to the public value concept the limit of vagueness, indicates a lack of 'identifiable propositions or suggestions for empirical development'. However, in this article we argue that the concept is complex and multifaceted, rather than vague. Spano (2009) suggests that public value should be re-thought in a more systemic approach, 'analyzing the link between institutional, political and managerial dimensions' (p. 328). This is seen as a condition to guarantee goal congruence. In more general terms, the usefulness emerges, once more, of some integration between public value thinking and performance measurement/performance management studies.

NOTES

1. For an in-depth discussion on the paradigmatic nature of NPM, useful also for a more general evaluation, see, for example, Gow and Dufour (2000).

2. See Osborne and Gaebler (1992); Aucoin (1995); Ferlie, Ashburner, Fitzgerald, and Pettigrew (1996); Minogue, Polidano, and Hulme (1998); Barzelay (2001); Kettl (2005); McLaughlin, Osborne, and Ferlie (2005); Christensen and Lægreid (2002, 2007); Pollitt, van Thiel, and Homburg (2007); Pollitt and Bouckaert (2011) and Lægreid and Christensen (2013).

3. A clear view of how the 'general trends in administrative design' (Hood, 1995) implied by the NPM ideas can be associated with a set of differentiated solutions is given by such elaborations as Naschold's reconstruction of modernization

profiles of the OECD countries (Naschold, 1996) or Ferlie and colleagues' typology of NPM ideal types (Ferlie et al., 1996).

4. For in-depth analyses see Hughes (2003, pp. 17−43); Bourgon (2011, pp. 25−35); Gruening (2001); Pfiffner (2004) and Hartley (2005).

5. What existed before these attempts to amend the public administration model is often defined as the 'classic' model of public administration.

6. Although studies of dialogue and deliberation belong to different disciplines, developing in parallel to respond to analogous social, political and organisational challenges, there are efforts to bridge the two currents of thought, with the aim to free their respective potential for reciprocal cross-fertilisation. These efforts have been generating interesting proposals of frameworks designed to structure dialogue *and* deliberation in order to create spaces for a range of communication patterns (for a remarkable example, see Escobar, 2011, p. 40ff., and his proposed analysis of the design of public engagement processes).

7. The public service ethos can be understood as 'the sum of ideals which define an overall culture in the public service' (OECD, 1996, p. 14). For an in-depth analysis of public service ethos and public sector ethos and for a comparison between the two concepts, see Horton (2008, p. 22ff.).

8. On the contractual approach, prevailing in New Zealand NPM-style reform, contrasted with the managerial approach, prevailing in other countries, see, among others, Schick (1996).

9. See Moore (1995, p. 179ff.) on public deliberation and social learning, and Horner and Hutton (2011). '[T]he proper arbiter of public value is society as a whole' (Benington & Moore, 2011b, p. 10).

10. Socio-political governance, public policy governance, administrative governance, contract governance, and network governance.

11. See also Osborne, Radnor, and Nasi (2012).

12. For in-depth analyses and further references on co-production and citizen participation, see, among others, Bovaird and Löffler (2012); Pestoff (2011); Pestoff, Brandsen, and Verschuere (2012) and Thomas (2012).

13. The framework presented by the authors is applied specifically to the field of public administration IT; however, the approach it follows and the logical categories it uses make it suitable for reflections of general application on public value.

REFERENCES

Accenture. (2008). *Measuring people's impressions of public service value*. Retrieved from http://www.majorcities.org/generaldocuments/pdf/s_impressions_of_public_services.pdf

Aldridge, R., & Stoker, G. (2002). *Advancing a new public service ethos*. London: New Local Government Network.

Alford, J. (2011). Public value from co-production by clients. In J. Benington & M. H. Moore (Eds.), *Public value: Theory and practice* (pp. 144−157). Basingstoke: Palgrave Macmillan.

Alford, J., & O'Flynn, J. (2009). Making sense of public value: Concepts, critiques and emergent meanings. *International Journal of Public Administration, 32*(3−4), 171−191.

Arnstein, S. (1971). The ladder of citizen participation. *Journal of the Royal Town Planning Institute, 57*(1), 176–182.

Aucoin, P. (1995). *The new public management.* IRPP. Montreal, Québec: Ashgate.

Barzelay, M. (2001). *The new public management.* Berkeley, CA: University of California Press.

BBC. (2004). *Building public value: Renewing the BBC for a digital world.* Retrieved from http://downloads.bbc.co.uk/aboutthebbc/policies/pdf/bpv.pdf. Accessed on June 8, 2014.

BBC Trust. (2012). *Public value in practice. Restoring the ethos of public service.* Retrieved from http://www.bbc.co.uk/bbctrust/governance/tools_we_use/public_value_practice.html. Accessed on June 8, 2014.

Beck Jørgensen, T., & Bozeman, B. (2007). Public values: An inventory. *Administration and Society, 39*(3), 354–381.

Benington, J. (2011). From public choice to public value? In J. Benington & M. H. Moore (Eds.), *Public value: Theory and practice* (pp. 31–51). Basingstoke: Palgrave Macmillan.

Benington, J., & Moore, M. H. (Eds.). (2011a). *Public value: Theory and practice.* Basingstoke: Palgrave Macmillan.

Benington, J., & Moore, M. H. (2011b). Public value in complex and changing times. In J. Benington & M. H. Moore (Eds.), *Public value: Theory and practice* (pp. 1–30). Basingstoke: Palgrave Macmillan.

Bohm, D. (2003). *On dialogue.* London: Routledge.

Borins, S. (1998). Lessons from the new public management in Commonwealth nations. *International Public Management Journal, 1*(1), 37–58.

Bourgon, J. (2011). *A new synthesis on public administration: Serving in the 21st century.* Kingston, ONT, Canada: McGill-Queen's University Press.

Bovaird, T., & Löffler, E. (2012). From engagement to co-production. In V. Pestoff, T. Brandsen & B. Verschuere (Eds.), *New public governance, the third sector and co-production* (pp. 35–60). London: Routledge.

Bozeman, B. (2002). Public-value failure: When efficient markets may not do. *Public Administration Review, 62*(2), 145–161.

Bozeman, B. (2007). *Public values and public interest: Counterbalancing economic individualism.* Washington, DC: Georgetown University Press.

Christensen, T., & Lægreid, P. (2002). *New public management: The transformation of ideas and practice.* Aldershot: Ashgate.

Christensen, T., & Lægreid, P. (2007). Introduction – theoretical approach and research questions. In T. Christensen & P. Lægreid (Eds.), *Transcending new public management: The transformation of public sector reforms* (pp. 12–30). Aldershot: Ashgate.

Coats, D. (2006). *Reviving the public: A new governance management model for public services.* London: The Work Foundation.

Coats, D., & Passmore, E. (2008). *Public value: The next steps in public service reform.* London: The Work Foundation.

Cole, M., & Parston, G. (2006). *Unlocking public value: A new model for achieving high performance in public service organizations.* Hoboken, NJ: Wiley.

Collins, R. (2007). *Public value and the BBC.* London: The Work Foundation.

Constable, S., Passmore, E., & Coats, D. (2008). *Public value and local accountability in the NHS.* London: The Work Foundation.

Cowling, M. (2006). *Measuring public value: The economic theory.* London: The Work Foundation.

Cresswell, A. M., Burke, G. B., & Pardo, T. A. (2006). Advancing return on investment: Analysis for government IT. A public value framework. Center for Technology in Government. Retrieved from http://www.ctg.albany.edu/publications/reports/advancing_roi/advancing_roi.pdf

Cunliffe, A. L., & Jun, J. S. (2005). The need for reflexivity in public administration. *Public Administration & Society, 37*(2), 225–242.

Dunleavy, P., Margetts, H., Bastow, S., & Tinkler, J. (2005). New public management is dead – long live digital-era governance. *Journal of Public Administration Research and Theory, 16*, 467–494.

Escobar, O. (2011). *Public dialogue and deliberation. A communication perspective for public engagement practitioners.* Edinburgh: Beltane. Retrieved from https://dl.dropbox.com/u/11082373/Public%20Dialogue%20and%20Deliberation.%20Oliver%20Escobar%202011.pdf

Ferlie, E., Ashburner, L., Fitzgerald, L., & Pettigrew, A. (1996). *The new public management in action.* Oxford: Oxford University Press.

Gow, J. I., & Dufour, C. (2000). Is the new public management a paradigm? Does it matter? *International Review of Administrative Sciences, 66*, 573–597.

Gruening, G. (2001). Origin and theoretical basis of new public management. *International Public Management Journal, 4*, 1–25.

Gutmann, A., & Thompson, D. (2004). *Why deliberative democracy?* Princeton, NJ: Princeton University Press.

Hartley, J. (2005). Innovation in governance and public services: Past and present. *Public Money and Management, 25*(1), 27–34.

Hills, D., & Sullivan, F. (2006). *Measuring public value 2: Practical approaches.* London: The Work Foundation.

Hirst, P. (2000). Democracy and governance. In J. Pierre (Ed.), *Debating governance: Authority, steering and democracy* (pp. 13–35). New York, NY: Oxford University Press.

Hood, C. (1991). A public management for all seasons? *Public Administration, 69*(1), 3–19.

Hood, C. (1995). The 'new public management' in the 1980s: Variations on a theme. *Accounting, Organizations and Society, 20*(2–3), 93–109.

Horner, L., & Hutton, W. (2011). Public value, deliberative democracy and the role of public managers. In Benington, J., & Moore, M. (Eds.), *Public value: Theory and practice* (pp. 112–126). Basingstoke: Palgrave Macmillan.

Horton, S. (2008). History and persistence of an idea and an ideal. In J. L. Perry, & A. Hondeghem (Eds.). *Motivation in public management* (pp. 17–32). New York, NY: Oxford University Press.

House of Commons. (2002). *The public service ethos.* Public Administration Select Committee, Seventh Report of Session 2001–02, Volume I, Report and Proceeding of the Committee. London: The Stationery Office Limited.

Hughes, O. (2003). *Public management and administration: An introduction.* Basingstoke: Palgrave Macmillan.

Kelly, G., Mulgan, G., & Muers, S. (2002). *Creating public value: An analytical framework for public service reform.* Discussion paper prepared by the Cabinet Office Strategy Unit, United Kingdom. Retrieved from http://webarchive.nationalarchives.gov.uk/+/http://www.cabinetoffice.gov.uk/strategy/downloads/files/public_value2.pdf

Kettl, D. F. (2005). *The global public management revolution*. Washington, DC: Brookings Institution.

Lægreid, P., & Christensen, T. (Eds.). (2013). *The Ashgate research companion to new public management*. Aldershot: Ashgate.

Lethbridge, L. (2009). *Promoting public sector 'ethos'*. Paper prepared for the EGPA Conference '*The Public Service: Service Delivery in the Information Age*', 2–5 September, Saint Julian's, Malta. Retrieved from http://www.pa-education.eu/public/upload/papers/files/Lethbridge.pdf

MacCarthaigh, M. (2008). *Public service values*. Dublin: Institute of Public Administration. Retrieved from http://www.cpmr.gov.ie/Documents/Public%20Service%20Values.pdf

Martin, S. (2003). Engaging with citizens and other stakeholders. In T. Bovaird & E. Löffler (Eds.), *Public management and governance* (pp. 212–225). London: Routledge.

McLaughlin, K., Osborne, S. P., & Ferlie, E. (Eds.). (2005). *New public management: Current trends and future prospects*. London: Routledge.

Minogue, M., Polidano, C., & Hulme, D. (Eds.). (1998). *Beyond the new public management*. Cheltenham: Edward Elgar.

Moore, M. H. (1994). Public value as the focus of strategy. *Australian Journal of Public Administration, 53*(3), 296–303.

Moore, M. H. (1995). *Creating public value: Strategic management in government*. Harvard, MA: Harvard University Press.

Moore, M. H. (2003). *The public value scorecard*. Retrieved from http://www.hks.harvard.edu/hauser/PDF_XLS/workingpapers/workingpaper_18.pdf

Morrell, K. (2009). Governance and the public good. *Public Administration, 87*(3), 538–556.

Naschold, F. (1996). *New frontiers in public sector management: Trends and issues in state and local government in Europe*. Berlin: Walter de Gruyter.

OECD. (1996). *Ethics in the public service: Current issues and practice*. PUMA, Occasional Papers, 14. Paris: OECD.

O'Flynn, J. (2007). From new public management to public value: Paradigmatic change and managerial implications. *The Australian Journal of Public Administration, 66*(3), 353–366.

Osborne, D., & Gaebler, T. (1992). *Reinventing government*. Reading, MA: Addison-Wesley.

Osborne, S. P. (2006). The new public governance? *Public Management Review, 8*(30), 377–388.

Osborne, S. P. (2009). Delivering public services: Are we asking the right questions? *Public Money and Management, 29*(1), 5–7.

Osborne, S. P. (2010a). Delivering public services: Time for a new theory? *Public Management Review, 12*(1), 1–10.

Osborne, S. P. (2010b). The (new) public governance: A suitable case for treatment? In S. P. Osborne (Ed.), *The new public governance? Emerging perspectives on the theory and practice of public governance* (pp. 1–16). London: Routledge.

Osborne, S. P., McLaughlin, K., & Chew, C. (2010). Relationship marketing, relational capital and the governance of public services delivery. In S. P. Osborne (Ed.), *The new public governance? Emerging perspectives on the theory and practice of public governance* (pp. 185–199). London: Routledge.

Osborne, S. P., Radnor, Z., & Nasi, G. (2012). A new theory for public service management? Toward a (public) service-dominant approach. *The American Review of Public Administration, 43*(2), 135–158. doi:10.1177/0275074012466935.

Parkinson, J. (2006). *Deliberating in the real world: Problems of legitimacy in deliberative democracy.* New York, NY: Oxford University Press.

Parston, G., & Goodman, J. (2008). *High-performance government organizations: Principles for creating public value.* Accenture. Retrieved from http://www.accenture.com.sa/Microsites/public-transportation/Documents/pdf/Accenture-High-Performance-Government-Organizations.pdf

Pestoff, V. (2011). Co-production, new public governance and third sector social services in Europe. *Ciências Sociais Unisinos, 47*(1), 15–24.

Pestoff, V., Brandsen, T., & Verschuere, B. (2012). *New public governance, the third sector and co-production.* London: Routledge.

Peters, B. G., & Pierre, J. (1998). Governance without government? Rethinking public administration. *Journal of Public Administration Research and Theory, 8*(2), 223–243.

Pfiffner, J. P. (2004). Traditional public administration versus the new public management: Accountability versus efficiency. In A. Benz, H. Siedentopf, & K. P. Sommermann (Eds.), *Institutionenbildung in regierung und verwaltung: Festschrift fur Klaus König* (pp. 443–454). Berlin: Dunker and Humbolt.

Pollitt, C., & Bouckaert, G. (2011). *Public management reform: A comparative analysis – New public management, governance and the neo-Weberian State.* Oxford: Oxford University Press.

Pollitt, C., van Thiel, S., & Homburg, V. (Eds.). (2007). *The new public management in Europe: Adaptation and alternatives.* Basingstoke: Palgrave Macmillan.

Pritchard, A. (2003). Understanding government output and productivity. *Economic Trends, 596*(July), 27–40.

Rhodes, R. A. W. (1996). The new governance: Governing without government. *Political Studies, 44*, 652–667.

Rhodes, R. A. W. (1997). *Understanding governance: Policy networks, governance, reflexivity and accountability.* Buckingham: Open University Press.

Rhodes, R. A. W. (2000). Governance and public administration. In J. Pierre (Ed.), *Debating governance: Authority, steering and democracy* (pp. 54–90). New York, NY: Oxford University Press.

Rhodes, R. A. W. (2007). Understanding governance: Ten years on. *Organization Studies, 28*(8), 1243–1264.

Schick, A. (1996). *The spirit of reform: Managing the New Zealand state sector in a time of change.* New Zealand: State Services Commission and the Treasury.

Schick, A. (1998). Why most developing countries should not try New Zealand's reforms. *World Bank Research Observer, 13*(1), 123–131.

Simon, H. (1946). The proverbs of administration. *Public Administration Review, 6*(1), 53–67.

Smith, R. F. I. (2004). Focusing on public value: Something new and something old. *Australian Journal of Public Administration, 63*(4), 68–79.

Spano, A. (2009). Public value creation and management control systems. *International Journal of Public Administration, 32*(3–4), 328–348.

Stoker, G. (2006). Public value management: A new narrative for networked governance? *American Review of Public Administration, 36*(1), 41–57.

Talbot, C. (2008). *Measuring public value: A competing values approach.* London. The Work Foundation. Retrieved from http://www.theworkfoundation.com/Reports/202/Measuring-Public-Value-A-competing-values-approach

Talbot, C. (2010). *Theories of performance.* New York, NY: Oxford University Press.

Taylor, F. W. (1911). *The principles of scientific management.* New York, NY: Harper and Brothers.

Thomas, J. C. (2012). *Citizen, customer partner: Engaging the public in public management.* Armonk, NY: M.E. Sharpe.

Torfing, J., & Triantafillou, P. (2013). What's in a name? Grasping new public governance as a political-administrative system. *International Review of Public Administration, 18*(2), 9–25.

Weber, M. (1947). *The theory of social and economic organization* (A.M. Henderson & T. Parsons, Trans.). Glencoe, IL: The Free Press.

Williams, I., & Shearer, H. (2011). Appraising public value: Past, present and futures. *Public Administration, 89*(4), 1367–1384.

Wilson, W. (1887). The study of administration. *Political Science Quarterly, 2*(2), 197–222.

APPENDIX

Table A1. Various Approaches to Public Management.

Elements	Traditional Public Administration (TPA)	New Public Management (NPM)	Public Value Management (PVM)
1. Characterization	Bureaucratic government	Post-bureaucratic, competitive government	Post-competitive
2. Dominant focus	Strong bent for control by rules and clear delineation of authority and jurisdictions	Results	Relationships
3. Process of definition of the public interest	By politicians or experts: little in the way of public input	Aggregation of individual preferences, in practice captured by senior politicians or managers supported by evidence about customer choice	Individual and public performances produced through a complex process of interaction Deliberative reflection over inputs and opportunity costs
4. Contribution to the democratic process	Delivers accountability: competition between elected leaders provides an overarching accountability	Delivers objectives: limited to setting objectives and checking performance, leaving managers to determine the means	Delivers dialogue: integral to all that is undertaken – A rolling and continuous process of democratic exchange is essential
5. Role for public participation	Limited to voting in elections and pressure on elected representatives	Limited – apart from use of customer satisfaction surveys	Crucial – multifaceted (customers, citizens, key stakeholders)
6. Attitude towards public sector ethos	Public bodies have monopoly on service ethos	Sceptical about public sector ethos (blamed for inefficiency and empire building) – Customer care privileged	No one sector has monopoly on public service ethos, and no one ethos always appropriate – Maintaining relationships through shared values seen as essential

7. *Preferred system of delivery*	Hierarchical department or self-regulating profession	Private sector or tightly defined arm's-length public agencies	Menu of alternatives selected pragmatically A reflexive approach to intervention mechanisms to achieve outputs
8. *Key performance objectives*	Politically provided inputs; services monitored through bureaucratic oversight	Managing inputs and outputs in a way that ensures economy and responsiveness to consumers	Public value as an overarching goal – Multiple objectives, including service outputs, satisfaction, outcomes and maintaining trust/legitimacy – Greater effectiveness orientation – Stretches from service delivery to system maintenance
9. *Dominant model of accountability*	Upwards through departments to politicians and through them to Parliament	Upward accountability via performance contracts; outwards to customers via market mechanisms	Multiple accountability systems, including citizens as overseers of government, customers as users and taxpayers as funders
10. *Role of managers*	To ensure that rules and appropriate procedures are followed	To help define and meet agreed performance targets	Active in steering networks of deliberation and delivery and maintain the overall capacity of the system

Source: Adapted from Kelly et al. (2002), Stoker (2006) and O'Flynn (2007).

HOW DO WE MEASURE PUBLIC VALUE? FROM THEORY TO PRACTICE

Alessandro Spano

ABSTRACT

Purpose — *To fill the gap in the literature with regard to public value measurement (PVM) and to provide a model for measuring public value at an individual organizational level, based on managerial control systems (MCS).*

Design/methodology/approach — *This article helps review the literature on PVM and propose a model for measuring the value generated by individual organizations. Measurement challenges and potential solutions are investigated.*

Findings — *Public value generated by an individual organization can be calculated by measuring if and to what extent the organization's outcomes and objectives have been achieved. Public value production and measurement are part of a wider PVM process, which is congruent with the major elements of MCS, from planning to operations, and measurement to evaluation.*

Public Value Management, Measurement and Reporting
Studies in Public and Non-Profit Governance, Volume 3, 353–373
Copyright © 2014 by Emerald Group Publishing Limited
All rights of reproduction in any form reserved
ISSN: 2051-6630/doi:10.1108/S2051-663020140000003015

Research limitations/implications — *This article provides knowledge to support the measurement of public value produced by public sector organizations. However, the suggested use of MCS for a comprehensive measure of the public value produced by a public body does not allow for a comparison of the public values generated by different organizations, as the value is calculated against the objectives set by that specific organization. More research is needed in order to fully utilize this model in practice.*

Practical implications — *The findings may help public sector organizations, policymakers and public managers measure the public value produced by a public organization as a whole.*

Social implications — *This article may help citizens and other stakeholders understand the public value produced by a public organization.*

Originality/value — *This article is based on an original research undertaken by the author and faces the relatively neglected issue of PVM. It suggests the use of public value MCS as a model for measuring public value produced by individual organizations.*

Keywords: Public value; measurement; managerial control systems

INTRODUCTION

Following Moore's (1995) seminal work, public value began attracting interest from scholars and practitioners, but there was a period in which it was relatively neglected. Public value is now back and over the last few years it has attracted growing interest. This attention notwithstanding, there is still no unique definition of what public value is (Horner & Hazel, 2005; O'Flynn, 2007). In any case, public value is a 'useful new story' (Smith, 2004, p. 68).

How then can the value created by public sector organizations be defined and measured? Several definitions of public value have been provided, but many of them remain elusive (O'Flynn, 2007). Some definitions attempt to set clear tracks within which public value flows, to provide accurate definitions of what public value is, how it can be produced and how it impacts citizens' lives. Other studies simply point to the philosophical features that characterize a public value approach. In the work of Moore (1995) a clear definition of public value is lacking, as Moore was more interested in developing a conceptual framework to help public managers increase their strategic thinking and initiative in their daily work. In fact,

Moore devoted less attention to defining what public value was in theoretical terms, than in practical terms (Benington & Moore, 2011):

> Public managers create public value. The problem is that they cannot know for sure what that is ... It is not enough to say that public managers create results that are valued; they must be able to show that the results obtained are worth the cost of private consumption and unrestrained liberty forgone in producing the desirable results. Only then can we be sure that some public value has been created. (Moore, 1995, pp. 57–29)

This growing interest in public value has also given rise to criticism, notably from Rhodes and Wanna (2007), who found seven issues where public value is confused or wrong. However, none of them relate to measurement.

While several scholars have tried to provide a theoretical and operational definition of public value, less attention has been devoted to how public value can be measured and this is probably a consequence of the lack of clarity on what constitutes public value (Williams & Shearer, 2011).

This article aims to fill the gap in the literature regarding public value by investigating the measurement side of public value and setting up a model to measure public value at the level of individual organizations.

WHAT IS PUBLIC VALUE?

Before deciding how public value can be measured, it is necessary to ask: What is public value? Changing the meaning one attaches to public value may determine a different set of measures to gauge public value. According to Barzelay (2007, p. 526) public value is a 'normative theory'. Other scholars (Kelly, Mulgan, & Muers, 2002; O'Flynn, 2007; Stoker, 2006) consider public value to be a 'paradigm'. However, O'Flynn (2007, p. 358) also describes public value as a 'new approach'.

The first important question to ask is whether or not public value may be considered a paradigm. According to the Free Dictionary (2013), a paradigm may be defined as 'A set of assumptions, concepts, values, and practices that constitutes a way of viewing reality for the community that shares them, especially in an intellectual discipline'. The Webster's (2013) dictionary provides a similar definition, and notes that a paradigm is 'a theory providing a unifying explanation for a set of phenomena in some field, which serves to suggest methods to test the theory and develop a fuller understanding of the topic, and which is considered useful until it is replaced by a newer theory providing more accurate explanations or explanations for a wider range of phenomena'. So, is public value a paradigm?

Some scholars have posed a similar question with regard to 'New Public Management', underlying that although the 'paradigm' is widely used in the social sciences, little reflection has occurred to verify the validity of the use of this term as developed by Kuhn (1970). Gow and Dufour (2000) define it as 'universally recognized scientific achievements that, for a time, provide model problems and solutions for a community of practitioners', although Kuhn did not consider the concept of paradigm to be appropriate for the social sciences. According to Kuhn (1970), there are three levels of paradigm (Eckberg & Hill, 1979; Masterman, 1970). In the first level, *metaphysical or epistemological*, Kuhn (1970) equates paradigm with a set of beliefs (Gutting, 1980; Masterman, 1970). The second level is that of 'universally recognized scientific achievement', which Masterman calls *sociological* (Masterman, 1970, p. 65). At this level, there is not just a theory, but a set of theories, as well as beliefs, values, symbolic generalizations and the like (Gow & Dufour, 2000). According to Kuhn, proof of the existence of a new paradigm is a theory that is better than other theories. The third and last level is where 'exemplars' or 'artefacts' are found. An exemplar is a well-known usage of a theory. According to Kuhn, science alternates periods of normality with periods of dramatic change, when a revolution takes place, bringing a new paradigm. During a paradigm's life, scientists encounter puzzles, which are solved using the dominant theory, and the solutions adopted are the exemplars. Exemplars are the toolbox of a scientist, and are the 'concrete problem-solutions that students encounter from the start of their scientific education, whether in laboratories, on examinations, or at the ends of chapters in science texts' (Kuhn, 1970, p. 187).

According to Gow and Dufour (2000), the answer to the question as to whether or not NPM can be considered a paradigm is both yes and no: yes as regards the first level, the epistemological one, because NPM provides a new way of looking at public administration; but it is not a paradigm as regards the second level (because there is not a universally recognized scientific achievement); or with regard to the third one (as the exemplars used in NPM are not tied to a more general theory).

The same analysis may be applied to public value, and again the answer as to whether or not public value is a paradigm is yes and no. If public value is a paradigm, what impacts does it have on the possibility of measuring the public value produced by a public organization? If public value theory is recognized as a paradigm, scientists would agree on what specific aspects should be taken into consideration to measure it and how to measure it. If scientists have incommensurable theories, they cannot communicate, and a paradigm provides a common basis for scientists to communicate. Moreover, in Kuhn's third level, a paradigm is capable of providing artefacts, which are well-known usages of a theory; so if public value were a paradigm, it would be able to provide scientists with a tool-box to find solutions to a common problem. This could be extremely useful in making comparisons between the public value produced by different public organizations, or by the same organization over time. At present, there is no agreement on these aspects.

Horner, Lekhi, and Blaug (2006b) provide five answers to the question of what public value is:

1. an academic approach, so it is a new theory of public management based on the work of Moore;
2. a 'corrective' and alternative to NPM;
3. a rhetorical device, and a plea to public service providers to revive the public sector;
4. a distinctive kind of institutional governance, based on networks, rounded accountability and multiplicity of providers with public funding;
5. analogous to private consumer value, created in the market by private companies.

However, these answers do not help us measure public value. According to Kelly et al. (2002, p. 17), public value has three 'building blocks': services, outcomes and trust. Services are the actual vehicle that delivers public value; outcomes represent a higher achievement, such as public health. Finally, trust is critical to public value creation; in fact, even though the desired outcomes are achieved, a failure in building trust can destroy public value.

According to Benington (2011) public value is a combination of two elements: (1) what the public values; and (2) what can add value to the public sphere. These two aspects allow some light to be shed on how to measure public value. Focusing attention on what the public values helps in moving from a producer-based approach to a consumer-led model of government and public service. However, what the public values might not necessarily be what the public needs, wants or desires (Benington, 2011). As a consequence, the concept of public value is a changing one, which evolves over time, taking advantage of increased knowledge: what was of value yesterday may not be of value tomorrow. Also, public value is a concept that builds on previous ground, that is, what is valued today may be taken for granted tomorrow. Another good example is related to environmental issues; today preserving the environment is a sensitive issue and people value those policies and regulations aimed at preserving the environment for future generations. That was not the case a few decades ago, when the general sensibility towards and knowledge of these aspects were much lower than they are today. This brings us to the second aspect highlighted by Benington — what adds value to the public sphere — which considers a wider public interest. It also enlarges the time horizon, from a short-term to a long-term perspective, involving more than just one generation. Even though it leaves the question of who decides what adds value to the public sphere, unresolved public value has to deal with outcomes and impacts, not just with inputs and outputs.[1]

PUBLIC VALUE MEASUREMENT (PVM): A LITERATURE REVIEW

Most studies on public value focus on such questions as: What is public value? How can it be produced? Who is responsible for producing it? Less attention has been devoted to the issue of measurement.

Even without providing specific indications on how to measure public value, Alford and O'Flynn (2009) believe that performance measurement is an important part of the development of the public value approach. Other scholars who have investigated the measurement aspect of public value focused on the reasons why it should be measured. Hills and Sullivan (2006), for example, state that PVM is required to provide an answer to three questions.

1. What needs to be measured in relation to public value?
2. How should it be measured, in terms of some suggested guiding principles?
3. When might such measures be used?

A similar approach was followed by Moore (2007), who attempted to provide an answer to three questions in his investigation of the measurement of public value.

1. Why is public value measured?
2. Where should public value be measured along the 'value chain'?
3. Should customer satisfaction be measured?

This article intends to provide an answer to four questions: (1) Why is public value measured? (2) What aspects of public value should be measured?

(3) How should public value be measured? (4) When should public value be measured?

A tentative answer to these questions is provided in the following subsections.

Why Is Public Value Measured?

The specific value to be measured, the related measures and the time at which the measurement takes place should be determined after deciding what the purposes of measurement are. How public value measures will be used is particularly important, as it may influence the choice of the measurement system and the indicators to be used. In fact, it is reasonable to believe that different uses of public value measures may require different forms of measurement.

According to Behn (2003, p. 593) performance measures in public sector organizations have eight different functions: (1) to evaluate; (2) to control; (3) to budget; (4) to motivate; (5) to promote; (6) to celebrate; (7) to learn and (8) to improve. Each objective requires different measures.

According to Behn (2003), the last reason − improving performance − is the fundamental aim of performance measurement in public sector organizations and the seven others are just means to achieve this ultimate purpose. Taking Behn's position, PVM should help answer the following question: 'What exactly should be done differently to improve performance?' (Behn, 2003, p. 588).

Similarly, Moore (2007) argues that PVM allows a focus on improvement, because it is important to understand whether or not there has been an improvement in public services. Moreover, Moore (2007) highlights three reasons for measuring public value: (1) to meet demands for external accountability; (2) to establish a clear, significant mission and goal for the organization and (3) to foster a strong sense of internal accountability.

In particular, Moore (2007, p. 98) suggests that 'the use of performance measures forces us to be much more concrete and explicit about the nature of the public value we are trying to create on behalf of our authorisers. If we cannot make it concrete, we cannot measure it'.

What Should Be Measured?

The first question posed by Hills and Sullivan (2006) regards what should actually be measured. It relates to the different values that can be measured, and the actual choice of the values is part of the public value process. This question is quite similar to Moore's second question, which is related to where public value should be measured along the 'value chain' (Moore, 2007, p. 101). In fact, Moore suggests that public value can be measured in connection with the different steps of the value chain, that is, inputs, programmes, procedures, processes, activities, outputs or outcomes. Moore (2007, p. 103) also suggests that, even though it is important to measure both outputs and outcomes, it must be noted that 'outcome is a direct measure of the public value that we are trying to produce'.

Other scholars also suggest measuring outcomes, as outcomes are one of the main features of public value (Hills & Sullivan, 2006). If the focus on outcomes rather than on outputs is necessary to measure public value, inferring the reason for generating a specific outcome is quite difficult (Kelly et al., 2002).

Benington (2011) suggests broadening PVM to include the impact of policies and programmes, not just outcomes. He argues that once we understand that it is necessary to focus on outcomes, then we need to investigate the long-term impact of policies, in particular in those fields, for instance in education, where effects are visible after many years.

A significant problem in deciding what to measure is that public agencies have multiple tasks and, as a consequence, if one would like to measure the amount of value produced, it would be necessary to decide whether to measure and evaluate performance in relation to all tasks or to a selection of them. Assuming that, broadly speaking, they are not on their *production possibility frontier*,[2] public organizations should not make trade-offs among competing performance goals, but they should try and 'improve performance on some attributes of performance without sacrificing performance on other attributes of performance' (Moore, 2007, p. 111). This means that public value produced in relation to all tasks should be measured.

Also, in the first case (all tasks) it would be necessary to find some methods to weight the various tasks. If not, focusing on some tasks only (i.e. those that are more easily measured) will draw attention away from the others (Flamholtz, 1996), with the risk that overall performance will decrease.

How Is Public Value to Be Measured?

The third question refers to the PVM process, which needs to be investigated to verify the specific measurement tools used and whether or not the process has been designed in such a way as to provide a fair view of the public value produced. Measuring public value requires designing a process through which the measures are developed and used and this is as important as the actual measures chosen (Hills & Sullivan, 2006).

Hills and Sullivan (2006) provide a scheme to understand the relationships between what is measured and the way measurement is carried out. In particular, as regards the first aspect, measurement may concern such dimensions as effectiveness and efficiency, and the outcomes or impacts of policy and programmes.

Moore (2007) suggests two different approaches for measuring public value, the programme evaluation/cost–benefit perspective and the business management perspective. A similar approach is taken by Horner et al. (2006b). According to the first approach, public value can be measured using traditional programme evaluation techniques and cost–benefit analysis. As regards the first approach, economics, and welfare economics in particular, have elaborated some methods to measure utility (or impact or result), that is, to a certain extent a proxy for public value. Broadly speaking, there are two general models: the *Stated Preference Model* (i.e. what individuals say is valuable to them) and the *Revealed Preference Model* (i.e. what individuals actually use); both are based on the concept of utility. The first model is mainly used to calculate the value of such resources that are difficult to express in monetary terms, such as the environment or the impact of pollution; in these cases, it is difficult to calculate a market price, even though they produce utility. With the second model, individuals' preferences are calculated by asking them how much they would be willing to pay for a specific service, or how much reduction in service quality and/or quantity they would be willing to accept to get a reduction in monetary sacrifices (i.e. a tax reduction). The underlying idea is that if 'citizens would like government to produce something, but they are not willing to give anything up in return, then it is doubtful that the activity in question will genuinely create value' (Kelly et al., 2002, p. 4). These methods require that individuals be asked about their preferences, but not too much weight should be placed on the findings of polls (Collins, 2007) and surveys are to be used with caution (Cowling, 2006).

Willingness to Pay (WTP), Willingness to Accept (WTA) and Travel Cost Methods (Cowling, 2006; Spano, 2009) are commonly used and are a useful way to attach monetary value to individual preferences, but they have to be used with caution, as they are affected by some significant limits, such as the value individuals give to intangible aspects, such as fairness (Cowling, 2006; Horner et al., 2006b) or trust, which may be considered as an important value produced by public activities and policies. Another important issue that these methods are not capable of measuring and which is the basis for a public value approach is 'the responsiveness of a public organization to citizens' preferences' (Horner et al., 2006b, p. 8).

The point is: what do these calculations really tell us about public value? Not much, probably! These methods are notoriously unreliable and they miss what is actually valuable to citizens (Mulgan, 2011). Public value requires additional dimensions, such as citizens' participation and the responsiveness to citizens' preferences, or fairness, democracy and the process by which the public is engaged and consulted (Cowling, 2006).

Also, a comparison can be made between two policies that, according to some variables, can be considered to be similar. So, one can evaluate the amount of public value produced by two policies or programmes in two different organizations, provided that they can be compared. From this point of view, realist evaluation attaches a significant role to the context where the policy and/or programme are implemented (Pawson & Tilley, 1997).

As regards the business management approach, Moore argues that it is more viable in practical terms than the first approach (Moore, 2007). Hills and Sullivan (2006) state that traditional tools of measurement continue to be valid if applied to public value; they simply need to be conceptualized differently, in order to provide a measurement more in tune with public value principles. In fact, traditional performance measurement systems (PMS) in the public sector often suffered from significant problems, for example, performance measures have become too bountiful and too operationally focused (Atkinson & McCrindell, 1997), and performance measures have become overwhelming and do not always meet the needs of relevant stakeholders (Kloot & Martin, 2000).

There is also a problem with the choice of indicators used to measure performance and public value, which can determine a gap between what performance indicators say and what service users perceive, creating what is called a 'delivery paradox', which means that the apparent results measured against specific targets improved, while people perceived a decline in service quality (Horner & Hutton, 2011; Horner et al., 2006b, p. 6). This happens when meeting targets is more important than satisfying needs. A report by the House of Commons Public Administration Select Committee (2003) found some noteworthy examples of targets misuse in the United Kingdom. The report found that, to meet response time, ambulance services introduced single paramedic fast response capability or even lay first responders, with little effect in case of real emergency situations. Other studies reported some strategies or even gaming to achieve the response time target for ambulances; for example, some Health Trusts concentrated ambulances in areas with high population density, at the expense of rural areas; others corrected the response times, or classified the calls according to the probability of achieving the target (Bevan & Hamblin, 2009). Other examples show a large amount of creativity' to achieve performance targets, such as the removal of wheels from trolleys to consider them as beds or re-designating them as 'beds on wheels' and so reducing waiting times; or considering corridors and treatment rooms as 'pre-admission units' (p. 19). This is linked to what is called Goodhart's Law, which can be summarized as follows: 'When a measure becomes a target, it ceases to be a good measure'.[3] Also, there are some other possible explanations for the delivery paradox such as ineffective communication of service improvement, limited choice, unrealistic expectations by the public and limited orientation to consumer satisfaction (Blaug, Horner, & Lekhi, 2006). The paradox may be 'unintended' (due to minimal accountability requirements, elusiveness of policy objectives, difficulty in quantifying and measuring policy goals and a strong emphasis on monitoring and efficiency) or deliberate (van Thiel & Leeuw, 2002, p. 268). This paradox is, at least in part, due to the NPM philosophy, which sees the user as 'consumer' whose needs have to be satisfied (Horner et al., 2006b, p. 20).

The use of a public value performance indicator (PVPI) has been proposed in the broadcasting industry in the United Kingdom, as a tool to measure the public value produced by the BBC (Collins, 2007). The indicator is based on: (1) deliberate engagement with the public in goal setting, planning and decision making; (2) consultation to inform decision making and (3) consumer feedback via satisfaction surveys. One of the key elements of the PVM system within the BBC is customers' WTP the licence fee: BBC viewers and listeners were prepared to pay more than twice the level of the present licence fee.[4]

Cost reduction could also be considered as a way to measure public value, but only to a certain extent. In fact, this is just one side of the equation, as cost is not the same as value and one needs to measure whether or not benefits are increased as well (Jackson, 2001).

One of the common aspects often cited as a tool to measure public value is citizens' satisfaction and this implies that public value is created when citizens' needs are satisfied. This is certainly important, as needs satisfaction is paramount for the public value movement, although benefits generated have to be higher than the sacrifices required (Spano, 2009; Moore, 2007). However, several studies show that satisfaction is not reliable as a driver for responsiveness and as an indicator for service improvement, because citizens may not have an accurate understanding of how services are performing (Horner et al., 2006b).

When Is Public Value to Be Measured?

The last question refers to the moment when public value measures are actually done. Public value can be measured ex-ante (referring to the results expected from an organization as a whole, or a policy or a programme, before the activities begin); *ongoing* (during the development of the activities) and ex-post (after the end of the activities). This, for instance, is the approach used by the European Commission for the European Structural Funds (European Commission, 2007, 2014).

PUBLIC VALUE PRODUCED BY MULTIPLE OR INDIVIDUAL ORGANIZATIONS

Public value may be created through the cooperation and/or joint operation of different organizations, both public and private, acting in a network and by individual organizations (Alford & Hughes, 2008; Bouckaert & Halligan, 2008; Moore, 2007). For example, increasing the level of public health requires the joint action of different organizations such as hospitals, general practitioners, municipalities, the State, in addition to the participation of individuals. At the same time, public value can be created by a single health trust.

This is related to what Bouckaert and Halligan (2008) consider the *depth* of performance, which is one of the two dimensions of performance together with *span*. Depth is about performance that may be measured at different levels, ranging from individual organizations to policy field. Span refers to the breadth of performance, and it may range from inputs, to outputs, to outcomes and to impacts. The two levels (individual or multiple organizations) are not alternative to each other, but they co-exist and are, in a way, part of a system. However, when it comes to PVM, choosing the first or the second level has different implications.

Public Value Produced by Multiple Organizations

With regard to public value created by multiple organizations, as part of a network, in reference to a policy or a programme, the first of the two approaches suggested by Moore can be utilized, and different methods are available for measurement and evaluation, including cost−benefit analysis, policy and programme evaluation and the like (Horner et al., 2006b). Outcomes and impacts are a good proxy for public value produced by multiple organizations, despite not being easy to measure and evaluate (Fig. 1).

It seems that the business management approach is not the right one in the case of multiple organizations, as public value is linked to the outcomes and objectives set by each organization, and it would be difficult to measure all the outcomes and objectives achieved by all the organizations involved.

Public Value Produced by Individual Organizations

In the literature it is relatively easy to find examples of measurements of the value produced by a specific public organization, but they usually refer to specific aspects, such as patient satisfaction in hospitals, crime reduction, tenant satisfaction in social housing (London Borough of Camden, 2002), refuse collection, etc. In these cases, public value is measured at a policy or programme level, so attention is focused on how much public value specific policies or programmes undertaken by a specific organization have created. The above approach, which is used to measure and evaluate policies and programmes undertaken by multiple organizations, can also be used to measure public value produced by an individual organization in relation to a specific policy or programme. It is much more difficult to provide a comprehensive measure of public value produced by a public body as a whole, for instance by a municipality. And when this is done, the result is a calculation of public value produced against specific objectives and goals set by that specific organization (Horner, Fauth, & Mahdon, 2006a).

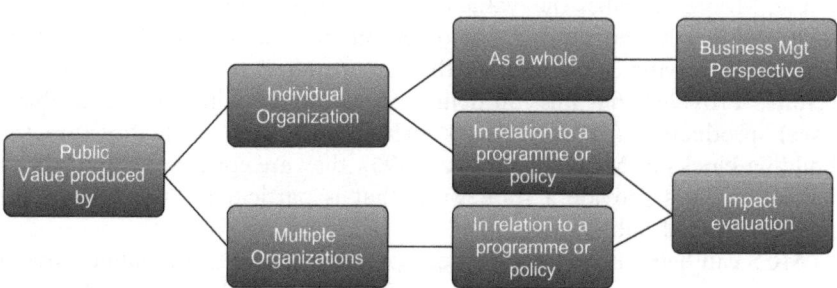

Fig. 1. Dimensions of Performance for Measuring Public Value.

The next section investigates in more depth the role of managerial control systems (MCS) for public value creation and measurement from a business management perspective.

MEASURING PUBLIC VALUE: THE ROLE OF MANAGEMENT CONTROL SYSTEMS

From a business management perspective, public value created by a single organization can be measured through the achievement of the organization's desired outcomes and impacts. This implies: (1) setting the desired outcomes in advance and, in turn, establishing a goal-setting process to link these outcomes to more specific objectives and (2) focusing on production processes (Benington, 2011; Hills & Sullivan, 2006). The first point tells us that it is important to consider planning as a fundamental aspect in the public value creation process, for both political and managerial reasons (Spano, 2009). The second tells us about the importance of focusing on internal production processes, aimed at delivering services to citizens and identifying inefficiencies. In addition, this approach, based on production processes, contributes to creating public value culture and capabilities because the process of achieving a result may be as important as the result itself. For instance, the process of co-creation helps build public trust (Martin & Cradden, 2006).

Even though he does not explicitly mention the role of MCS, Moore (2003, p. 11) makes a clear reference to some of the main elements of MCS, that is (1) the mission that defines an organization's ends (i.e. the valued results), and (2) the more specific goals and objectives that represent the 'means the organization relies upon to achieve the desired results'. In so doing, Moore describes the 'value chain' or 'logic model' 'that specifies the relationship between desired outcomes on one hand, and the resources, processes, activities, and outputs that are required to achieve the desired results'. Provided that mission definition, planning (with goals and objectives), production (or operations), measurement and evaluation are the building blocks of MCS (Flamholtz, 1996), they are coherent with Moore's indications and provide a framework that is particularly suitable for the measurement of public value.

MCS can help public organizations produce and measure public value if they are designed around the concept of public value. This means that each phase in a MCS has to be designed around the idea of public value. While

PMS traditionally implemented in public sector organizations have tended to focus more on how to achieve pre-determined performance targets, a public-value-based PMS is rather aimed at better understanding the needs of the individuals the services are meant to serve (Mager, 2007).

The main differences between traditional MCS and what can be called a 'public value MCS', can be found in the planning and measurement phases. The first phase in MCS is planning, which plays a key role in the public value production process. On creating public value, public organizations are asked to meet citizens' needs, with a level of sacrifice that is lower than the benefits produced. As a consequence, one of the key issues in public value creation is its focus on what the public values (Benington, 2011). Although this can be considered populist and subject to political games, it is an important feature of public value. For this reason, it is necessary to find adequate methods to gather 'the voice of the citizens'.[5] This does not or should not mean 'government by opinion poll' (Hills & Sullivan, 2006, p. 34), but it requires enough humility by politicians and public managers to understand that they are not solely capable of determining what the public values. Also, it is necessary to be able to interpret and fully understand what the public say it values (taking into account the fact that some people may not be sufficiently competent to have an informed opinion), go beyond stated preferences and beyond today's preferences, have a vision of the future and mediate between different positions.

This requires a need to be translated into desired outcomes, then into more specific objectives in such a way that, if achieved, they allow for the satisfaction of the selected needs (internal coherence), by producing goods and delivering services. For each outcome, objectives and specific indicators and targets need to be set, in order to measure their achievement or non-achievement. Thus, indicators and targets provide a numerical value of the *satisfying* capacity of that organization. More broadly, this means that public value is to be linked to the planning and control process, and to the MCS (Spano, 2009). In fact, the measures are to be congruent with the outcomes and the objectives an organization aims to achieve. In turn, outcomes, objectives, indicators and targets have to be consistent with citizen's expectations and needs.

As public needs are ongoing, one of the first steps in a public value-creating process is a political decision about what needs must be satisfied first, and at what level. The role of politics in the decision-making process is of particular importance in the public value approach. One of the innovative aspects of Moore's 'strategic triangle' was an in-depth analysis of the role of the political dimension; in particular, he analyzed the links between the authorizing environment, the operational (managerial) capacity and the generated outcomes (Moore, 1995). However, the link between managers and politicians was more devoted to understanding to what extent managers get support from politicians, in order to do their job, rather than considering both as key actors of a planning process, within a wider MCS (Spano, 2009). In Moore's initial framework (1995) the role of politics was present, even though it was not analyzed in depth. NPM scholars have considered politics as a mere element of the context in which public organization operate. On the contrary, public value scholars see the role of politics in a different way compared to traditional public administration and NPM (O'Flynn, 2007; Stoker, 2006), and politics is embedded in the public value production process. For example, given that public value is created when it is linked to collective rather than individual preferences, the role of politics is fundamental as it mediates collectively determined preferences (Alford, 2002; Kelly et al., 2002; Moore, 1995; O'Flynn, 2007).

After deciding on the desired outcomes, and how to specify them in more detailed objectives, the next step is the development of production processes to achieve those outcomes and objectives. The organization's measures not only concern outputs, but outcomes as well, and eventually impacts. As regards the measurement phase, there are significant differences between traditional PMS and PVM systems. The main limit of traditional performance measurement is its strong focus on indicators and targets, which can determine negative unintended consequences, such as the above-cited delivery paradox, or the prevalence of hitting the target regardless of the actual satisfaction of citizens needs. As we have seen, there are plenty of examples where this destroys value, rather than creating it. In fact, the mere use of objectives, indicators and targets does not necessarily imply a public value approach. In traditional PMS, the targets selected are more focused on internal management, audit and control issues, rather than on what is really useful for citizens (Coats & Passmore, 2008). As a consequence, 'creating a new "currency" or system of metrics – an alternative to price – to measure, for example, whether a school or hospital creates more value is both impossible and undesirable in that it would undermine democratic processes' (Horner et al., 2006b, p. 8).

In addition, traditional PMS do not allow getting hold of some intangible and fundamental components of public value (Kelly et al., 2002), such as participation or trust. In fact, public value has as its central element citizens' involvement to determine what the value one wants to measure is. Also, trust is of particular importance, as it is both an outcome of public value production processes and a prerequisite for producing public value.

CONCLUDING REMARKS

One of the main merits of public value is that it helps overcome some of the limits of previous paradigms or schools of thought in the public sector (Stoker, 2006). These include an excessive reliance on rules and laws and bureaucratic oversight, which is typical of traditional public administration, or an overwhelming tendency to focus on a market-based approach and on efficiency and a limited attention to immaterial aspects, such as citizens' participation and public trust that characterize NPM.

Studies and research on public value have increased in number and quality over the last 10 years or so, but not enough attention has been devoted to the issue of PVM. In order to measure public value, it is first necessary to establish the reasons of the measurement, and then what aspects of public value are to be measured and how this should be done. Even though multiple organizations may be involved in producing public value, the actual measurement of the public value produced may be done at an individual organization level. Public value generated by a policy or a programme can also be calculated, using as a proxy the impacts or effects achieved, and using programme evaluation techniques. In this case, however, it is possible to determine the public value produced by that single policy or programme, not the public value produced by an individual organization or by all the organizations involved. For the latter purpose, MCS can be used, and the public value generated by an individual organization is calculated by measuring if and to what extent the organization's outcomes and objectives have been achieved. Public value production and measurement are part of a wider public value management process, which is congruent with the major elements of MCS, from planning to operations, and measurement to evaluation.

PVM and public value MCS are based on traditional MCS, but they differ in the role given to outcomes and in the way objectives are set, in order to take into account the public value approach.

NOTES

1. Outcomes refer to the direct results of a public intervention whereas impacts are those effects that can be felt at the larger community or societal levels. Bouckaert and Halligan (2008, p. 21) make a distinction between 'intermediate outcomes' and 'ultimate outcomes' or impacts.

2. A production possibility frontier is 'A curve depicting all maximum output possibilities for two or more goods given a set of inputs (resources, labor, etc.). The PPF assumes that all inputs are used efficiently' (see http://www.investopedia.com/terms/p/productionpossibilityfrontier.asp, accessed 22 October 2013).

3. Charles Goodhart was a banker and Professor at the London School of Economics. He formulated what is known as Goodhart's Law: 'As soon as the government attempts to regulate any particular set of financial assets, these become unreliable as indicators of economic trends' (Goodhart, 1984). The reason for this is that investors try to anticipate the foreseen effects of the regulation in order to benefit from it. The most popular formulation of Goodhart's Law, 'When a measure becomes a target, it ceases to be a good measure', was created by British feminist anthropologist Dame Ann Marilyn Strathern.

4. The BBC implemented a public-value-based performance management system based on some dimensions such as reach, impact, quality and value for money. It seems that the BBC performance management system does not intend to achieve an overall measure of public value; rather the performance management system is designed around the main public value building blocks, such as co-production, for example. Given that the BBC is considered one of the most advanced examples in the literature of practical implementation of public value concepts, this re-enforces the idea that measuring public value per se is an almost impossible (and probably, useless) task. What is interesting in the BBC example is that the corporate performance management system has been explicitly built around public value principles.

5. The methods to measure public opinion abound, for instance: service satisfaction surveys; complaints/suggestion schemes; consultation documents; focus groups; public meetings; service user forums; citizens' panels; area/neighborhood forums; community plans/needs analysis; other opinion polls; question and answer sessions; co-option/committee work; issue forums; shared interest forums; visioning exercises; user management of services; referendums; citizens' juries (Hills & Sullivan, 2006).

REFERENCES

Alford, J. (2002). Defining the client in the public sector: A social exchange perspective. *Public Administration Review*, *62*(3), 337–346.

Alford, J., & Hughes, O. (2008). Public value pragmatism as the next phase of public management. *The American Review of Public Administration*, *38*(2), 130–148.

Alford, J., & O'Flynn, J. (2009). Making sense of public value: Concepts, critiques and emergent meanings. *International Journal of Public Administration*, *32*(3–4), 171–191.

Atkinson, A. A., & McCrindell, J. Q. (1997). Strategic performance measurement in government. *CMA Magazine*, April, 20–23.

Barzelay, M. (2007). Learning from second-hand experience: Methodology for extrapolation-oriented case research. *Governance*, *20*(3), 521–543.

Behn, R. D. (2003). Why measure performance? Different purposes require different measures. *Public Administration Review*, *63*(5), 586–606.

Benington, J. (2011). From private choice to public value? In J. Benington & M. H. Moore (Eds.), *Public value: Theory and practice* (pp. 31–51). Basingstoke: Palgrave Macmillan.

Benington, J., & Moore, M. H. (2011). *Public value: Theory and practice.* Basingstoke: Palgrave Macmillan.

Bevan, G., & Hamblin, R. (2009). Hitting and missing targets by ambulance services for emergency calls: Effects of different systems of performance measurement within the UK. *Journal of the Royal Statistical Society, 172*(1), 161–190.

Blaug, R., Horner, L., & Lekhi, R. (2006). *Public value, citizen expectations and user commitment. A literature review.* London: The Work Foundation.

Bouckaert, G., & Halligan, J. (2008). *Managing performance. International comparisons.* New York, NY: Routledge.

Coats, D., & Passmore, E. (2008). *Public value: The next steps in public service reform.* New York, NY: The Work Foundation.

Collins, R. (2007). *Public value and the BBC. A report prepared for the work foundation's public value consortium.* London: The Work Foundation.

Cowling, M. (2006). *Measuring public value: The economic theory.* London: The Work Foundation.

Eckberg, D. L., & Hill, L. H., Jr. (1979). The paradigm concept and sociology: A critical review. *American Sociological Review, 44*(6), 925–937.

European Commission. (2007). *The new programming period 2007–2013. Indicative guidelines on evaluation methods: Evaluation during the programming period* Working Document No. 5. Brussels: European Commission.

European Commission. (2014). *The programming period 2014–2020. Guidance document on monitoring and evaluation. European regional development fund and cohesion fund. Concepts and recommendations.* Brussels: European Commission.

Flamholtz, E. G. (1996). *Effective management control: Theory and practice.* Boston, MA: Kluwer Academic Publishers.

Goodhart, C. A. E. (1984). *Monetary theory and practice: The UK experience.* London: Macmillan.

Gow, J. I., & Dufour, C. (2000). Is the new public management a paradigm? Does it matter? *International Review of Administrative Sciences, 66*(4), 573–597.

Gutting, G. (1980). Introduction. In G. Gutting (Ed.), *Paradigms and revolutions. Appraisals and application of Thomas Kuhn's philosophy of science* (pp. 1–21). Notre Dame, IN: University of Notre Dame Press.

Hills, D., & Sullivan, F. (2006). *Measuring public value 2: Practical approaches.* London: The Work Foundation.

Horner, L., Fauth, R., & Mahdon, M. (2006a). *Creating public value: Case studies.* London: The Work Foundation.

Horner, L., & Hazel, L. (2005). *Adding public value.* London: The Work Foundation.

Horner, L., & Hutton, W. (2011). Public value, deliberative democracy and the role of public managers. In J. Benington & M. H. Moore (Eds.), *Public value: Theory and practice* (pp. 112–126). New York, NY: Palgrave Macmillan.

Horner, L., Lekhi, R., & Blaug, R. (2006b). *Deliberative democracy and the role of public managers.* London: The Work Foundation.

House of Commons Public Administration Select Committee. (2003). *On target? Government by measurement.* London: Stationery Office. Retrieved from http://www.publications.

parliament.uk/pa/cm200203/cmselect/cmpubadm/62/62.pdf. Accessed on January 31, 2013.

Jackson, P. M. (2001). Public sector added value: Can bureaucracy deliver? *Public Administration, 79*(1), 5–28.

Kelly, G., Mulgan, G., & Muers, S. (2002). *Creating public value: An analytical framework for public service reform.* London: Cabinet Office Strategy Unit.

Kloot, L., & Martin, J. (2000). Strategic performance management: A balanced approach to performance management issues in local government. *Management Accounting Research, 11*(2), 231–251.

Kuhn, T. (1970). *The structure of scientific revolutions.* Chicago, IL: University of Chicago Press.

London Borough of Camden. (2002). *Second interim report of the Scrutiny panel into choices about the financing of capital projects.* London: London Borough of Camden.

Mager, C. (2007). *Public value and leadership. Exploring the implications.* Centre for Excellence in Leadership. Retrieved from http://webarchive.nationalarchives.gov.uk/20130802100617/http:/lsis.org.uk/Services/Policy/legacy/Documents/PublicValueLeadership.pdf. Accessed on December 20, 2012.

Martin, B., & Cradden, C. (2006). *Partnership and productivity in the public sector. A review of the literature.* Wellington, New Zealand: Partnership Resource Centre, Department of Labour.

Masterman, M. (1970). The nature of a paradigm. In I. Lakatos & A. Musgrave (Eds.), *Criticism and the growth of knowledge* (pp. 59–89). London: Cambridge University Press.

Moore, M. H. (1995). *Creating public value: Strategic management in government.* Harvard, MA: Harvard University Press.

Moore, M. H. (2003). *The public value scorecard: A rejoinder and an alternative to 'Strategic Performance Measurement and Management in Non-Profit Organisations' by Robert Kaplan.* Hauser Center for Nonprofit Organizations, John F. Kennedy School of Government. Retrieved from http://www.innovations.harvard.edu/showdoc.html?id=5020. Accessed on December 19, 2013.

Moore, M. H. (2007). Recognising public value: The challenge of measuring performance in government. In J. Wanna (Ed.), *A passion for policy: Essays in public sector reform.* Canberra: The Australian National University Press.

Mulgan, G. (2011). Effective supply and demand and the measurement of public and social value. In J. Benington & M. H. Moore (Eds.), *Public value: Theory and practice* (pp. 212–224). Basingstoke: Palgrave Macmillan.

O'Flynn, J. (2007). From new public management to public value: Paradigmatic change and managerial implications. *The Australian Journal of Public Administration, 66*(3), 353–366.

Pawson, R., & Tilley, N. (1997). *Realistic evaluation.* London: Sage.

Rhodes, R. A. W., & Wanna, J. (2007). The limits to public value, or rescuing responsible government from the platonic guardians. *Australian Journal of Public Administration, 66*(4), 406–421.

Smith, R. F. T. (2004). Focusing on public value: Something new and something old. *Australian Journal of Public Administration, 63*(4), 68–79.

Spano, A. (2009). Public value creation and management control systems. *International Journal of Public Administration, 32*(3), 328–348.

Stoker, G. (2006). Public value management: A new narrative for networked governance? *American Review of Public Administration, 36*(1), 41–57.

The Free Dictionary. (2013). *Paradigm*. Retrieved from http://www.thefreedictionary.com/ paradigm. Accessed on January 10, 2013.

van Thiel, S., & Leeuw, F. L. (2002). The performance paradox in the public sector. *Public Performance & Management Review, 25*(3), 267–281.

Webster's. (2013). *Paradigm*. Retrieved from http://www.webster-dictionary.org/definition/ paradigm. Accessed on July 23, 2013.

Williams, I., & Shearer, H. (2011). Appraising public value: Past, present and future. *Public Administration, 89*(4), 1367–1384.

SUSTAINABLE PUBLIC VALUE INSCRIPTIONS: A CRITICAL APPROACH

Federica Farneti and John Dumay

ABSTRACT

Purpose — *This article critically reviews the latest Global Reporting Initiative (GRI) guidelines and recommended sustainability topics for public agencies, and presents normative argument by using Gray's (2006) ecological and eco-justice (EEJ) approach to produce public value inscriptions of sustainability to represent sustainable public value.*

Design/methodology/approach — *The study presents a critical analysis and discussion of the changes to the GRI G4 and sustainability topics for public agencies from a managerialistic and EEJ approach.*

Findings — *We observe that the GRI continues to evolve while paying scant attention to furthering the Sector Supplement for Public Sector Agencies as it remains in its pilot form since its inception in 2005. Changes to the GRI are somewhat enlightening because several of the changes do begin to address a more comprehensive view of how any organization, including public agencies, can contribute to an EEJ approach to sustainability.*

Public Value Management, Measurement and Reporting
Studies in Public and Non-Profit Governance, Volume 3, 375–389
Copyright © 2014 by Emerald Group Publishing Limited
All rights of reproduction in any form reserved
ISSN: 2051-6630/doi:10.1108/S2051-663020140000003016

Practical implications − *In the future it is important to be aware that, as inscriptions, the GRI guidelines have the potential power to influence how managers in public agencies approach sustainability. As Dumay, Guthrie, and Farneti (2010) previously argued, if guidelines continue to approach sustainability from a 'managerialistic' approach then there is little hope of public sector agencies adopting EEJ practices. We argue that organizations should act referring to Gray's EEJ approach.*

Keywords: Global Reporting Initiative; sustainable public value; ecological and eco-justice approach; critical analysis; public agencies

INTRODUCTION

There is negligible institutional debate about the fundamental assumptions upon which GRI is based and any dissatisfaction is framed as an immanent dissatisfaction with the TBL itself and its application in GRI − not with the failures of either TBL or GRI to address sustainability. (Milne & Gray, 2013, p. 19)

This article's purpose is to build upon what has changed since the first critical review of the Global Reporting Initiative (GRI) guidelines for public agencies by Dumay, Guthrie, and Farneti (2010). In their article, Dumay et al. (2010) defined 'sustainability value', from a public sector perspective based on their critique of the usefulness of the GRI and the pilot version Sector Supplement for Public Sector Agencies (SSPSA) (GRI, 2005). Since then the GRI has developed further with a new version of the guidelines (G4) (GRI, 2013) and to complement the SSPSA (GRI, 2005) recommendations of sustainability topics for public agency reporting under the GRI based on stakeholders' suggestions (GRI, 2014a).

This article proceeds as follows. Next we outline the concept of sustainable public value followed by a critical analysis and discussion of the changes to the GRI G4 and sustainability topics for public agencies from a managerialist and ecological and eco-justice (EEJ) approach. We then conclude the article by offering our insights into how the GRI has progressed along the EEJ approach and what this means for developing sustainable public value in the future.

SUSTAINABLE PUBLIC VALUE

To begin our article it is first necessary to define public value (Moore, 1995) in terms of sustainability. This is difficult because there is no generally accepted definition. For example, public value is the delivery of public services and other activities undertaken by public providers and thus 'refers to the value created by government through services, laws regulation and other actions' (Kelly, Mulgan, & Muers, 2002, p. 4). However, Talbot (2011, p. 28) has a more contemporary and philosophical view, arguing that 'public value is considered what the public values' and 'the combined view of the public about what they regard as valuable'. Therefore, while there are different definitions of public value these authors reinforce the idea that, in creating value, public sector agencies[1] should refer to citizens' needs, acting transparently, and by referring to value beyond financial measures (see Dumay, 2009).

As a result, we introduce the concept of sustainable public value based upon Dumay et al.'s (2010, p. 539) concept of 'sustainable value'. We argue this is necessary because society is demanding more from both private and public organizations in terms of how they contribute to sustainability. In this respect we adopt the Bruntland Report's definition of sustainability, which is to 'meet the needs of the present without compromising the ability of future generations to meet their own needs' as this is the same definition adopted by the GRI G3 (GRI, 2006). Public agencies play a pivotal role in the delivery of public value. Therefore, we consider the evolving issues related to sustainable development, which are becoming pivotal from a public value perspective as 'a way of understanding government activities, informing policy-making and constructing service delivery' (O'Flynn, 2007, p. 353) because every activity undertaken by organizations delivering public services 'shapes how people live their lives' (Birney, Clarkson, Madden, Porritt, & Tuxworth, 2010, p. 3). Thus, we need to be concerned with not only how organizations deliver public services today, but how they will continue to deliver them satisfactorily in the future.

As Dumay et al. (2010, p. 539) outline, the problem with the way public sector organizations engage with sustainability is that:

> ... while there is evidence that public and third sector organizations are beginning to consider and report on sustainability issues, there is a perceived problem in relation to what 'sustainable value' these organizations create. This is because, in public and third sector organizations, the notion of value needs to encompass much more and is separated from the notion of monetary value.

Thus, the public sector should not be concerned with creating just public value because there is 'the value of life, the value of society, the value of quality and, if one is of a religious bent, the value of creation itself' (Gray, 2006, p. 809). By successfully implementing sustainability practices public agencies are, in fact, creating sustainable public value encompassing meeting the needs of their constituents without compromising the ability to meet constituents' needs in the future.

However, there is a problem with how the public sector engages in reporting sustainable public value because the available frameworks – being the GRI (2006) guidelines and the SSPSA (GRI, 2005) – fall within a 'managerialist' approach (Gray, 2006) to sustainability as the guidelines advocate that the 'context or state of environment' are not reported (Tort, 2010, p. 5). According to Gray (2006, p. 803) this approach is counterproductive because

> there is assumed to be little or no conflict between traditional economic criteria and social or environmental desiderata or the exigencies of sustainability. With such data, no reader could make any kind of reliable estimate of the organisation's social or environmental performance.

Therefore, we argue that, as at 2010, the guidelines mainly used by the public sector did not promote creating sustainable public value.

As for the guidelines, we think about the reports created from them as inscriptions dependent upon specific settings. As Robson (1992, p. 689) outlines 'inscriptions refer to the various techniques of "marking" an object or event that is to be known – writing, recording, drawing, tabulating' and, as a consequence, inscribe knowledge about a particular setting as an outcome of developing a GRI or sustainability report. In essence, a sustainability report issued by a public agency is an artefact of a managerial process whereby the agency addresses issues of sustainability over time, and subsequently writes up reports as evidence of the process. However, if these guidelines lead public agencies to report in a specific way by advocating a managerial approach, as opposed to an 'ecologically- and eco-justice-informed (EEJ) approach to sustainability reporting' (Gray, 2006, p. 803), then there might be little hope of public sector providers ever creating sustainable public value.

In Dumay et al.'s (2010, p. 545) previous study, they explored how public agencies disclose economic, social and environmental information concluding that:

> This then leads to the opportunity for further research into the development of [sustainability reports] SRs in public and third sector organizations, examining those organizations which use either the Global Reporting Initiative (GRI) or other guidelines in developing an EEJ approach to sustainability.

Thus, their conclusion advocates the undertaking of further studies. Similarly, Gray, Adams, and Owen (2014, p. 289) reinforce this view by arguing that the topic of social and environmental and sustainability accounting is a matter for the public sector just as much as it is for the private sector to develop forms of accountability. However, there is little critical analysis of the new GRI guidelines used to create sustainability inscriptions in public agencies, thus there is the opportunity to conduct a critical review of the recent changes to the GRI and the publishing of the recommended sustainability topics for SSPSA since Dumay et al. (2010) last performed this task.

CRITICALLY EVALUATING THE GRI AND SUSTAINABILITY TOPICS FOR PUBLIC AGENCIES

Given the relevance of sustainable value, the two most recognized guidelines for public sector sustainability disclosure are the GRI (2006) and the related SSPSA (GRI, 2005). Since 2010 the GRI has developed further, releasing a new version of the guidelines (G4) (GRI, 2013). In addition, to complement the SSPSA, the GRI published recommended sustainability topics for public agencies based on stakeholders' suggestions (GRI, 2014a). The latter contains a table outlining a list of topics identified as relevant by different stakeholder groups and outlines how organizations can incorporate stakeholders' suggestions when preparing sustainability disclosures. As a result, this offers the opportunity to critically examine whether these recent developments counter criticism levelled at the guidelines that they are 'managerialistic', concentrating on creating monetary value. We examine whether they have, in some way, begun to move towards an EEJ approach to creating sustainable public value, which according to Dumay et al. (2010, p. 534):

> ... the EEJ approach to sustainability focuses on establishing whether or not organizations act as socially and environmentally sustainable members of society, with the default being that all organizations are currently unsustainable.

In developing our assessment of changes to these guidelines, we take a critical perspective requiring us to reflect on those issues with both positive and negative outcomes, encouraging rethinking through ideas and redirecting the future (Alvesson & Deetz, 2007, p. 18). The purpose of critique 'is to counteract the dominance of taken-for-granted goals, ideas, ideologies and discourses which put their imprints on management and organization phenomena'. Considering the GRI has been identified as the dominant, or taken-for-granted, sustainability guideline we agree with Dumay et al.'s (2010, p. 531) argument that if it remains so or does not change substantially from the managerialistic approach of the G3, then the GRI 'may not contribute to sustainability', remaining an exercise in rhetoric. In this regard, Milne and Gray (2013, p. 21) state:

> They [GRI] are partial in that the full range of social and environmental actions and interactions are incomplete − representing (in part) the difficulty of producing acceptable indicators and (in part) the reluctance of member organizations to sign up to indicators which were too demanding ... The GRI's representations are incoherent in the sense that there is no apparent over-arching framework − theory if you prefer − that guides the selection of indicators and ensures their relationships one to another and between the issues of concern and the entity.

The G3 can be considered as offering a representation of the social, economic and environmental that is both partial and incoherent.

The remainder of the article aims to develop a critical overview of the recent changes to the GRI and classifies the new and recommended sustainability topics for SSPSA as managerialistic or taking an EEJ approach.

GRI AND THE CHANGES FROM G3 TO G4

We first consider the changes between the G3 and G4 guidelines (GRI, 2013) because while public agencies can use the SSPSA it appears they have not been widely adopted for reporting − between 2005 and 2009 there were only 21 examples of reports issued by 12 different public agencies using the SSPSA (GRI, 2010). However, there are also few public agencies referring to the GRI. Examining the GRI database we found 54 reports for 2010, 63 reports for 2011, 73 reports for 2012 and 67 reports for 2013 (GRI, 2014b). It seems that not many public agencies embed the GRI in their reporting practices. The concern here is that the total number of public organizations reporting is relatively insignificant compared to the private sector: the 67 reports issued in 2013 are disproportionate when compared to over 3,500 reports from other organizations (GRI, 2014b), particularly considering that public agencies alone represent about 40% of all economic activity (Ball & Grubnic, 2007, p. 243).

The current analysis builds on observing the changes from the G3 (GRI, 2006) and the G4 (GRI, 2013) versions.[2] The aim of this analysis is to observe if the changes undertaken are in line with a managerialistic or EEJ approach as displayed in Table 1. We will now discuss four findings in relation to (i) general standard disclosure and disclosures on management approach, (ii) economic indicators, (iii) environmental indicators and (iv) social indicators.

Table 1. Changes from G3 to G4 with Managerial/EEJ Classification.

G3	G4	Managerialistic Approach	EEJ Approach
1.1	G4-1		X
2.3	G4-17 (moved to 'identified material aspects and boundaries' in G4)	X	
2.8	G4-9	X	
	G4-10 (former G3 indicator LA1)	X	
	G4-12	X	
2.9	G4-13	X	
3.5	G4-18	X	
	G4-19	X	
3.6–3.8	G4-20, G4-21	X	
3.12	G4-32	X	
3.13	G4-33	X	
4.1	G4-34, G4-38	X	
4.3	G4-38	X	
4.4	G4-37, G4-49, G4-53	X	
4.5	G4-51	X	
4.6	G4-41	X	
4.7	G4-40		
4.9	G4-45, G4-47	X	
4.10	G4-44	X	
	G4-35	X	
	G4-36	X	
	G4-42	X	
	G4-43	X	
	G4-46	X	
	G4-48	X	
	G4-50	X	
	G4-52	X	
	G4-54	X	
	G4-55	X	
4.17	G4-27		X
	G4-56	X	
	G4-57	X	
	G4-58	X	
	G4-DMA		X
EC2	G4-EC2		X
EC4	G4-EC4	X	
EC5	G4-EC5	X	
EC6	G4-EC9	X	
EC7	G4-EC6	X	
EN3	G4-EN3		X
EN4	G4-EN3		X
	G4-EN4		X
	G4-EN5		X
EN5	G4-EN6		X
EN6	G4-EN7		X

Table 1. (*Continued*)

G3	G4	Managerialistic Approach	EEJ Approach
EN7	G4-EN6		X
EN8	G4-EN8		X
EN9	G4-EN9		X
EN10	G4-EN10		X
EN13	G4-EN13		X
EN16	G4-EN15, G4-EN16		X
EN17	G4-EN17		X
	G4-EN18		X
EN18	G4-EN19		X
EN19	G4-EN20		X
EN20	G4-EN21		X
EN21	G4-EN22		X
EN22	G4-EN23		X
	G4-EN32		X
	G4-EN33		X
	G4-EN34		X
LA1	G4-10 (moved to 'organizational profile' in G4)	X	
LA2	G4-LA1	X	
LA3	G4-LA2	X	
	G4-LA3	X	
LA7	G4-LA6	X	
LA10	G4-LA9	X	
LA12	G4-LA11	X	
LA13	G4-LA12	X	
LA14	G4-LA13		X
	G4-LA14	X	
	G4-LA15		X
	G4-LA16	X	
HR1	G4-HR1		X
HR5	G4-HR4	X	
HR6	G4-HR5		X
HR7	G4-HR6		X
	G4-HR9		X
	G4-HR11		X
	G4-HR12		X
SO1	G4-SO1		X
	G4-SO2		X
SO2	G4-SO3		X
SO3	G4-SO4	X	
SO4	G4-SO5	X	
SO6	G4-SO6	X	
	G4-SO9	X	
	G4-SO10		X
	G4-SO11	X	

The General Standard of Disclosure and the Disclosures on Management Approach

The first finding relates to the general standard disclosure. The GRI has a new measure G4-1, which requires a statement from the most senior organizational decision maker (such as CEO, chair or equivalent senior position) about the relevance of sustainability to the organization and the organization's strategy for addressing sustainability. This strategic approach to sustainability should clearly state the relevance of sustainability in the organization and its position in creating sustainable public value. The G4-1 emphasizes that organizations must actively manage their significant economic, environmental and social impacts. We argue that this attitude is consistent with an EEJ approach. Also, the GRI (2013, p. 3) outlines what constitutes a sustainability report:

> A sustainability report conveys disclosures on an organization's impacts – be they positive or negative – on the environment, society and the economy. In doing so, sustainability reporting makes abstract issues tangible and concrete, thereby assisting in understanding and managing the effects of sustainability developments on the organization's activities and strategy.

The general standard disclosure G4-27 is an indicator requiring the reporting of key topics and concerns that stakeholders raise through engagement, as well as how the organization responds to these. The emphasis of this indicator is on stakeholder engagement. We argue that complying with G4-27 and reporting to stakeholders about key issues are consistent with the EEJ approach.

We also observe that the disclosures on management approach (G4-DMA) can generally contribute towards an EEJ approach because its intention is to give the public agency an opportunity to explain how it manages its material economic, environmental and social impacts. Also, the approach provides narrative information on how an organization identifies, analyzes and responds to its actual and potential material economic, environmental and social impacts. Specifically, G4-DMA suggests reporting the impacts that make an aspect material (GRI, 2013, p. 46).

Economic Indicators

Turning to economic indicators we observe that only G4-EC2 is consistent with an EEJ approach. This indicator refers to the implications for organizations of climate change. It requires reporting on the risks and opportunities posed by climate change that have the potential to generate substantive changes in operations, revenue or expenditure. However, rather than just focusing on the financial implications, it requires the organization to assess the risk or opportunity as physical, regulatory or other.

Environmental Indicators

The environmental indicators are the richest in terms of changes with respect to the previous G3 version. From G4-EN3 to G4-EN34 there are 23 (new or changed) indicators for measuring an organization's environmental impacts. Discussing each one in depth is not the aim of this article; rather we will give examples that add to the overall argument that several of the changes added to the G4 version encourage organizations to think about whether their behaviour is unsustainable behaviour on how to limit environmental impacts. For example, the G4-EN6 indicator is aimed at reducing energy consumption. This indicator requires the organization to highlight reductions in energy consumption achieved as a direct result of conservation and efficiency initiatives (in joules or multiples), indicating the type of energy (fuel, electricity, heating, cooling, etc.). It also requires reporting of the basis for calculating reductions in energy consumption such as base year or baseline. We argue that a public agency accounting for G4-EN6 is able to provide evidence that it rationalizes the use of energy, thus decreasing and improving its environmental impacts.

A further example is the new indicator G4-EN32. It requires indicating the percentage of new suppliers screened using environmental criteria, allowing an assessment by the organization of the sustainability practices of its potential business partners. This indicator is consistent with the EEJ approach.

Social Indicators

In relation to social indicators our analysis shows there are 12 changed or new indicators we classify as promoting an EEJ approach. To explain these, we provide some examples.

The new indicator G4-HR12 refers to the number of grievances related to human rights impacts filed, addressed and resolved through formal grievance mechanisms. It requires the organization to identify grievances, indicating how many were addressed during the reporting period and how many resolved during the same reporting period; also to report the total number of grievances about human rights impacts filed prior to the reporting period that were resolved during the reporting period. The rationale undermining this indicator is to consider grievances about human rights impacts before acting. We argue that this is consistent with the EEJ approach.

Indicator G4-SO1 focuses on the percentage of operations involving local community engagement, impact assessments and development programmes. Probably, this is one of the best examples in terms of how the new G4 addresses issues relating to the EEJ approach. In fact, this indicator encourages organizations to report on the use of social impact assessments and gender impact assessments, based on a participatory processes; it directly relates to the impacts that the organization produces, in conjunction with seeking evaluation from the local community. This indicator encompasses impact on the local community, by encouraging the seeking of feedback from the local community as a form of stakeholder engagement, and requiring organizations to respond. For example, a local government may seek stakeholder feedback on a new construction development in a previously undeveloped area. Or, a university could seek feedback from the local community in terms of proposed courses in order to understand if there is a demand in the community for these courses.

In classifying the GRI indicators, we have not analyzed those that we classify as taking a managerialistic approach. We do make the point, however, that the GRI continues to send mixed messages to public agencies about what is important: making money or creating a better world? From a public agency perspective, the G4 guidelines offer additional opportunities for presenting a story of how sustainable public value is developed. However, these are just guidelines and there is nothing specific for public agencies. Therefore, it is up to individual public agencies to choose which indicators they can use to report sustainable public value. Thus, the lack of specific guidelines and the fact that very few public sector agencies actually report using the GRI suggest that either the GRI guidelines are unsuitable for reporting for public sector agencies, or that stakeholders have yet to apply pressure to public sector agencies to report how they create sustainable public value.

ISSUES FOR PUBLIC SECTOR AGENCIES

In May 2014, the GRI released a document outlining what stakeholders think are the important issues for public agencies to report (GRI, 2014a).

This document specifically addresses public agencies from all tiers of government – including ministries, federal agencies, regional governing bodies, state agencies, city councils, departments, international organizations, whole governments and cross-agencies. The document clarifies several items already in the SSPSA without adding anything new. Among those issues, which we identify as having potential from a sustainable public value and EEJ perspective, are the issues of 'Migrant workers'. This indicator requires organizations to address aspects such as the number of migrant workers employed, countries of origin, gender of workers, positions within company, length of contracts, recruitment and so on. Arguably, by disclosing this information, a public agency is contributing to improving social justice.

Stakeholders also raised the topic 'conflict of interest'. Serving the public interest is the fundamental mission of governments and public institutions and citizens should expect public officials to perform their duties with integrity. Additionally, governments increasingly want to show that public officials do not allow their private interests and affiliations to compromise official decision making and public management. This indicator also can be considered as taking an EEJ perspective.

A third topic is that of 'public policy positions', which requires public agencies to consider plastics use and management, particularly focusing on how the use and disposal of plastics can generate significant positive or negative impacts on the economy, environment and society. The GRI advocates that public agencies should disclose how they approach managing plastics, including related governance, strategy, risks and opportunities. We argue that public agencies operating in this regard act in line with the EEJ approach.

It is interesting to note that of the 11 topics raised in the GRI stakeholder document, only three support an EEJ approach. Sufficient changes have not yet been made to consider that public agencies have shifted to an EEJ approach in their reporting.

CONCLUSION

The sustainability reports of public agencies can be considered as an inscription representing an artefact of management practice. Thus, when public sector agencies produce reports, what is inscribed in them represents how the agency wants to communicate sustainable public value. Our research suggests that public sector agencies are reluctant to communicate sustainable public value, given their relatively small number of reports registered with the GRI (Ball, Grubnic, & Birchall, 2014, p. 187). There appears to be no impetus for change in this respect since Dumay et al.'s (2010) initial critique of the GRI. It seems that the GRI is not used or useful for reporting sustainable public value, and indeed may lead to greater levels of unsustainability.

The GRI continues to evolve but does not seem to focus on the SSPSA, given that it has remained in its pilot form since its inception in 2005. While the stakeholder feedback is important, it does not inspire public agencies to develop sustainability practices and inscribe their actions into reports.

However, the outlook is not all gloomy. There is some progress towards promoting an EEJ approach by the GRI with the requirement in G4-1 of a statement from the most senior organizational decision maker (such as CEO, chair or equivalent senior position) about the relevance of sustainability to the organization and the organization's strategy for addressing sustainability. Should public agencies take up this challenge, it requires managers in public agencies to think and act in a way that promotes an EEJ approach, rather than a purely managerialistic approach, which goes some way towards creating sustainable public value. The requirement in the G4 for a greater level of stakeholder engagement is also a positive move in the direction of EEJ.

Inscriptions such as the GRI guidelines have the potential power to influence how managers in public agencies approach sustainability. We share Ball et al.'s (2014, p. 191) view that sustainability disclosures are a key mechanism for increasingly engaging people in the work of public agencies for understanding 'its contribution to sustainability' and call for the guidelines to further incorporate an EEJ approach. If they do not then 'paradoxically, they may reinforce business-as-usual and greater levels of unsustainability' (Milne & Gray, 2013, p. 13).

NOTES

1. We refer to the terms 'public agency' and 'public agencies' in this article as this is the term used by the GRI (2014a, 2014b, p. 1) encompassing 'all tiers of government — including ministries, federal agencies, regional governing bodies, state agencies, city councils, departments, etc. International organizations, whole governments and cross-agencies'.

2. The changed indicators have been published on the GRI website: https://www.globalreporting.org/resourcelibrary/GRI-G4-Overview-Tables-G3-vs-G4.pdf

ACKNOWLEDGMENTS

The authors thank Fiona Crawford from the Macquarie University and Nicola Jane Altera for their editorial assistance.

REFERENCES

Alvesson, M., & Deetz, S. (2007). *Doing critical management research*. Thousand Oaks, CA: Sage.

Ball, A., & Grubnic, S. (2007). Sustainability accounting and accountability in the public sector. In J. Unerman, J. Bebbington, & B. O'Dwyer (Eds.), *Sustainability accounting and accountability* (pp. 243–265). New York, NY: Routledge.

Ball, A., Grubnic, S., & Birchall, J. (2014). Sustainability accounting and accountability in the public sector. In J. Bebbington, J. Unerman, & B. O'Dwyer (Eds.), *Sustainability accounting and accountability* (pp. 176–195). New York, NY: Routledge.

Birney, A., Clarkson, H., Madden, P., Porritt, J., & Tuxworth, B. (2010). Stepping up: A Framework for Public Sector Leadership on Sustainability, London, Forum for the Future. Retrieved from http://www.forumforthefuture.org/sites/default/files/project/downloads/steppinguppub-sector-leadership.pdf

Dumay, J. (2009). Intellectual capital measurement: A critical approach. *Journal of Intellectual Capital, 10*(2), 190–210.

Dumay, J., Guthrie, J., & Farneti, F. (2010). GRI sustainability reporting guidelines for public and third sector organisations. *Public Management Review, 13*(4), 531–548.

Global Reporting Initiative (GRI). (2005). *Sector supplement for public sector agencies: Pilot version 1.0*. Amsterdam: Global Reporting Initiative.

Global Reporting Initiative (GRI). (2006). Sustainability reporting guidelines. Retrieved from https://www.globalreporting.org/reporting/G3andG3-1/g3-guidelines/Pages/default.aspx. Accessed on June 16, 2014.

Global Reporting Initiative (GRI). (2010). GRI reporting in government agencies? Retrieved from https://www.globalreporting.org/resourcelibrary/GRI-Reporting-in-Government-Agencies.pdf. Accessed on May 30, 2014.

Global Reporting Initiative (GRI). (2013). G4 sustainability reporting guidelines. Retrieved from https://www.globalreporting.org/reporting/g4/Pages/default.aspx. Accessed on December 1, 2013.

Global Reporting Initiative (GRI). (2014a). Sustainability topics for sectors: What do stakeholders want to know? Retrieved from https://www.globalreporting.org/resourcelibrary/52-Public-Agencies.pdf. Accessed on January 29, 2014.

Global Reporting Initiative (GRI). (2014b). Sustainability disclosure database. Retrieved from http://database.globalreporting.org/search. Accessed on January 29, 2014.

Gray, R. (2006). Social, environmental and sustainability reporting and organisational value creation? Whose value? Whose creation? *Accounting, Auditing and Accountability Journal, 19*(6), 793–819.

Gray, R., Adams, C., & Owen, D. (2014). *Accountability, social responsibility and sustainability*. London: Pearson.

Kelly, G., Mulgan, G., & Muers, S. (2002). Creating public value. An analytical framework for public service reform. Retrieved from http://www.maliye.gov.tr/IPA%20Projesi/E%C4%9Fitim%20Sunumlar%C4%B1%20ve%20E%C4%9Fitime%20%C4%B0li%C5%9Fkin%20Dok%C3%BCmanlar/5.%20Kamu%20De%C4%9Feri%20-%20Politika%20Analizi%20ve%20De%C4%9Ferlendirme/%C4%B0ngilizce%20Dok%C3%BCmanlar/Petrus%20Kautto/%C4%B0lgili%20Dok%C3%BCmanlar/Creating%20Public%20Value.pdf. Accessed on March 22, 2014

Milne, M., & Gray, R. (2013). W(h)ither ecology? The triple bottom line, the global reporting initiative and corporate sustainability reporting. *Journal of Business Ethics*, *118*(1), 13–29.

Moore, M. H. (1995). *Creating public value*. Cambridge, MA: Harvard University Press.

O'Flynn, J. (2007). From new public management to public value: Paradigmatic change and managerial implications. *The Australian Journal of Public Administration*, *66*(3), 353–366.

Robson, K. (1992). Accounting numbers as inscription: Action at a distance and the development of accounting. *Accounting, Organizations and Society*, *17*(7), 685–708.

Talbot, C. (2011). Paradoxes and prospects of public value. *Public Money & Management*, *31*(1), 27–34.

Tort, L. E. (2010). *GRI reporting in government agencies*. Amsterdam: Global Reporting Initiative.